John Alexander Steuart

In the Day of Battle

A Romance

John Alexander Steuart

In the Day of Battle
A Romance

ISBN/EAN: 9783744694131

Printed in Europe, USA, Canada, Australia, Japan

Cover: Foto ©Thomas Meinert / pixelio.de

More available books at **www.hansebooks.com**

IN THE DAY OF BATTLE

A ROMANCE

BY

JOHN A. STEUART

AUTHOR OF "KILGROOM: A STORY OF IRELAND," ETC.

Both through the lore of the muses and the higher learning have I sped, and after turning over many a maxim, many a theme, I have found that naught is mightier than Necessity.

The Alcestis of Euripides.

LONDON

SAMPSON LOW, MARSTON, AND COMPANY

LIMITED

St. Dunstan's House

FETTER LANE, FLEET STREET, E.C.

1895

CONTENTS.

CONTENTS.

IN THE DAY OF BATTLE.

CHAPTER I.

A KINSMAN AND AN ENEMY.

AFTER five and forty years, they tell me, turbulent students of the University of Edinburgh listen with envy to stories of the battles of Peter Clephane and Angus Glenrae. To one whose sun is far past its meridian, and who ought rather to be engaged with his evening prayer than his morning folly, ungracious memories of headlong, random youth can afford little matter of consolation and none of pride.

Nor will such reminiscences be revived here, save in so far as they are essential in giving clearness and coherency to the motive and events of this history. One's own good name is a jewel that needs delicate and discreet handling. Easily defaced, it is exceedingly hard to repair, and, what is worse, the utmost skill in patching is apt to leave traces of the blemish the owner would fain conceal. Moreover, he were infected by an odd malice towards himself who would gratuitously flaunt his failings in the public eye. To such a person belongs by birthright the motley coat and fool's cap, however zealously he may masquerade in the guise of a moralist.

On the other hand, the honest historian will tell the truth, the naked ungraced truth, though he turn crimson in the telling. No fear of present pain, no hankering after ulterior glory, will induce him to play the hazardous and futile game of juggling his part and trying to give delinquencies a heroic and virtuous colouring. For, not to soar into ethical regions (where indeed we might not feel at home), the open course is least likely to give occasion of repentance. That experimental philosopher who tried both ways and found honesty the best policy, settled once and for ever a troublesome question. An enlightened race now discerns that death itself is not more certain than the ultimate confusion of the hypocrite.

Let me frankly own then, it causes me no surprise to learn that the feud between Peter and myself is still a rife theme in the mouths of our successors; for if fervency of hate could ensure remembrance of strife ours might well be immortal. Jonathan and David made a covenant of love, and ardently strove to keep it; we swore vows of vengeance, and sacrificed much to taste the sweetness of performing them.

They who seek diligently find. It is astonishing how frequently we found the opportunity of catching each other on the hip and feeding fat our mutual grudge. Had we been half as assiduous in our studies as we were in planning our disreputable frays, we should have left the University with the renown of Admirable Crichtons. But so far as I have ever learned, old heads seldom adorn young shoulders. When the phenomenon becomes common the millennium may be expected to be at hand.

It is scarcely necessary to say that the ends to which we devoted our energies speedily brought us under the blackest ban of constituted authority. Never before or since can guilt have been affrighted with direr threats and predictions than fell daily to our lot. Almost as regularly as the sun appeared in the heavens, we were comforted by appalling lectures on our crimes, and harrowing prophecies of the inevitable fate of young reprobates who opened a career of insubordination, rebellion, and general wickedness by setting their preceptors at naught.

"It will be a prison crop and three yards of hemp rope before all's done," roared a red-faced professor

one day, when we had carried our quarrel into the
class-room; and it was felt that he had condensed
the prevailing opinion into a sentence. I, being the
greater transgressor (from causes which may presently be appreciated), had to endure the fiercer outbursts of wrath.

But the censors might have saved their breath. If
these warnings had any effect at all on Peter and me
it was but to stimulate and embitter our enmity; for
with the stubbornness of original sin we cherished it
the more the more it brought us into disrepute.
There are certain moods in which admonition but
fans into flame the spark of rebellion that lies in
every unregenerate human bosom. Such a mood, I
fear, was ours. Defiant, scornful, and impenitent,
we saw without compunction the appealing looks, the
mortification, the tempests of choler, resulting in
apoplectic faces and shaken nerves of the Senatus
Academicus; and were scarcely sorry when we
caused a member of that august and illustrious body
a fit that nearly put blood on our heads. For the
living devil was rampant within us, and our sins
which were as scarlet were a thing of exultation.
One of us, at least, was to suffer grievously for it;
and to learn, in bitterness of spirit and in the dust,
what it is to have the neck of his pride broken.
Looking back my wonder is that we were not ignominiously expelled; a little while longer, and that
course would doubtless have been adopted. But before the long-suffering authorities could make up
their minds to resort to extreme measures, destiny
took the matter out of their hands.

Peter and I were kinsmen, and the deadlier enemies on that account. We had come up in the same
month of the same year to pursue our studies—as
college pastimes are ironically styled—he from Dundee, I from a remote part of the Highlands; and as
we had never previously met nor even heard of each
other save by vague and casual reports, our introduction was that of strangers. For cousins, the meeting

was not cordial.   A town-bred exquisite and the sole
heir of a lawyer with a big bank account and a safe
full of mortgages, Peter had a lofty nose and proud
stomach for all unfortunates who were not of the
gilded court of mammon.

Himself one of its shining ornaments, he was naturally a stickler for prerogative.   Of what he reckoned to be his due of subserviency, he would not
abate a jot to save an empire; rather would he sacrifice an empire (were the stake possible) to gratify his
vanity.   Lusting for dominion with the unhallowed
passion of the despot, he would have bartered his
immortal soul to obtain it.   An axiom often on his
lips aptly expressed his philosophy.   "Sovereignty,"
he would say with the air of an oracle, "is to him
who resolves to play first fiddle and acts on the resolution.   Study Alexander, Cæsar, Cromwell, Napo-
leon; study the men who made themselves rulers of
their fellows, and tell me the secret of their supremacy.   The world is for him who can take it firmly by
the nose and show that he is its master."

In aiming at his own ideal he observed scarce more
nicety of method than marked the conduct of his
heroes.   Itching with ambition, aggressive, arro-
gant, hard of heart and of conscience, he had a spirit
for any feat of audacity, any piece of tyranny that
promised reward to self-love.   Glorying in his
guineas he was tremblingly jealous of the power
they conferred; yet he exercised it, on the whole,
with consummate tact.   The fact is, nature and fortune had both been uncommonly kind to him.   One
bestowed gifts, the other furnished tools and mate-
rial.   Between the man and his environment there
existed that perfect harmony which results in success as inevitably as the rising of the sun results in
light, or the spread of fire in conflagration.

Though he was often in trouble for acts of unruli-
ness and violence, he was not rash nor fiery.   No
touch of the Celtic weakness of impulsiveness or im-
petuosity marred his character.   On the contrary, a

vulpine calculation and duplicity marked all his doings. He studied his friends minutely, not for the
pleasure of knowing them, but for the purpose of
using them; and he sneered at their shallowness
while taking advantage of it. I do not believe he
ever took a living soul thoroughly into his confidence;
but an engaging manner, unrivalled ingenuity in
dropping hints, and a dissimulation so exquisite that
it wore the very face of veracity, gained him the
credit of being frank with his friends.

Resourceful and astute, he managed his dupes
with admirable and unfailing skill. Knowing the
distinguishing traits of each as if he had them in-
scribed upon tablets, he easily avoided errors of policy. The arts of the diplomatist and courtier, indeed, were natural to him, and even I could not help
admiring the perfect craft with which he suited
word and act to the needs of the moment and the
furtherance of his own designs. He could be conde-
scending, affable, familiar, generous, whimsical, tol-
erant, intolerant, conciliatory, cajoling, haughty, or
arbitrary as might be expedient. Withal, though he
employed his patronage entirely as a usurer who has
a single eye to returns, his cunning got him the repute of a benefactor. And the extent of his gratui-
ties gave him unquestioned power: for it is not in
man, even in the adolescent student stage, to be a
debtor and independent.

When a vain head and a long purse are united,
sycophancy grows rank. Quick as was his apprehension in such matters, Peter had barely time to realize the glories of his position, when he had a body of
parasites fawning upon him, licking his hands like
spaniels, scraping the earth before him like flunkies,
and contending for a place under his banner. Fed
on the grossness of their flattery, his conceit waxed
till the world outside of himself and his concerns existed on sufferance. The little tyrant of a little
clique assumed the strut and port of a universal dic-
tator; and there were times when he appeared to be

of a mind to improve on his Roman model by blotting out the sun and putting the moon in his pocket. Assuredly were modesty a deadly disease, he might live for ever.

Next to the business of receiving the adulation of his toadies, his main occupation was to prove, by the many means at his disposal, how despicable was the wretch who could not gratify spendthrift tastes or lacked the graces which a fashionable tailor alone imparts. That, too, he accomplished with his usual success.

To the charmed inner circle of his worshippers I was never for a moment admitted. Yet none of those who basked in his favours touched him so closely as I did, or yielded him so keen a pleasure. They flattered, but I served as target for his wit, an unenviable capacity that was as gratifying to him as it was galling to me. Never an opportunity of vexing me did he miss; not once during the two years we were together did he forego the slightest chance of taunting and ridiculing me. Though naturally averse to toil, he would cheerfully have laboured for half a day to coin a sentence that would sting or contrive an insult that would humiliate me.

At our first meeting, though I spoke a purer English than his own, he begged for an interpreter, as unhappily he had not the delightful Celtic dialect at his command; expressed surprise that one born to the heritage of a kilt should demean his fine legs with trousers, and these not even made of the resplendent tartan; and then, with a sarcasm that was alternately like ice and fire in the blood, he commented on the instructive and interesting antiquarian cut of breeches made in the Highlands.

"As for your coat," said he, "it is the finest specimen of the antique I have seen, and I more than half suspect you of being the lucky finder of a garment dropped from the ark during its cruise among the northern peatbogs. As an antediluvian relic there would be a fortune in the thing. Why don't you exhibit yourself?" Whereupon his satellites, laughing uproariously, called out that it wasn't fair to purloin the clothes of Noah and say never a word about it.

I left him with a crimson face, and my heart already a furnace of hate. Thenceforward we were as powder and flame to each other; we had but to come into contact to go off. Psychical experimenters hold that an idea is a force of which the natural tendency is to translate itself into action. When we were together the tendency of our ideas was generally violently that way.

In the tongue I was no match for Peter; nor, indeed, in the entire University was there his equal in the use of that diabolical weapon of offence. In three minutes he could have blackened the character of a saint beyond hope of recognition, and put a much more patient man than Job beside himself with passion. As for me, a single sentence, sometimes a single sneering little laugh or curl of the lip, was enough to bring my blood to the boiling point and create an itching in my fingers to close on his throat. One must be just even to one's enemy. He took no pains to evade the natural consequences of his provocation. He did not once afford me the gratification of calling him coward, and I was pagan enough to love him none the better for it.

When we laid aside our coats to settle differences I generally managed to pay off·scores satisfactorily; for, though he was my master with the tongue and three years my senior to boot, I, being bred a hunter and climber of hills, had the firmer muscle. Perhaps, too, I had the greater ardour in crucial moments, and if that had its effect mine was not the first instance in which the spark of naphtha-fire in the Celtic blood told in the fight.

But the fortunes of war are variable. It chanced that one day my enemy caught me with a crippled arm; he railed upon me as was his wont,—I retaliated; we fought, and the victory was with him. If he had whipped the whole British nation, instead of a maimed and insignificant unit of it, he could not have exulted more; nor if he had been of the race of rebel angels could he have paid his debt of vengeance with a keener or opener malignancy of delight.

"There, you Highland blusterer," he cried, when the issue was decided, "have you enough or would you like more? How does it feel to get a drubbing?"

"You ought to know, who have had it so often," I retorted; "but as to this day's work, we will reckon for it yet. To-morrow we'll see who crows loudest."

"We will," he laughed, with a more sinister expression than I had ever seen in his face before. "For once you and I agree. And when the reckoning comes there are muircocks I know whose crow will not be so cruse as it is to-day."

He came up to me with a devilish gleam in his eyes and snapped his fingers in my face. "To-morrow," he hissed, "I'll show you what'll be to-morrow. See, I'll crush you like that!" and he stamped and ground his heel in the dust. "A poor crawling thing like you setting yourself up before me!" Then he stood off a step, and broke into a laugh of derision; but checking himself he bent forward again, saying in a tone of simulated compassion, "After all, as I'm a Christian I ought to pity you. There is a shilling for you—take it. Before seven days are over I dare say you will find it useful."

Such was my amazement at this speech and the sudden change of his manner, that I mechanically held out my hand and took the shilling. But its touch, which was as a sting in the quick, restored my senses and I flung the coin back in his face.

"You may insult but you cannot degrade me," I cried, a hot, moist, prickly sensation springing to my eyes. "What your meaning is I cannot tell. I only know that being yours it must be spiteful and malicious. But before the seven days of which you talk are over I will repay your affront with interest. And in the meantime I will say, in the spirit of

Timon, it is a pity you are not good enough to spit on."

My outburst awed the throng that had gathered about us, and I strode away in the midst of a dead silence, the picture, as an eye-witness afterwards told me, of fury incarnate. It could not, however, keep Peter's tongue long silent.

"Ha, ha!" he cried, mockingly, ere I had gone fifty yards, "so the beggar would ride on horseback, would he? Don't forget that pride goes before a fall. The pauper who refuses alms to-day may to-morrow dispute with the dogs for a bone. Even a Highlander may find it hard to feed on his pride."

I turned quickly on my heel under a frantic impulse to go back and rend my tormentor on the spot. Perhaps it was the vision of jeering faces that deterred me, for the crowd was chiefly made up of his friends, or it may have been an acute sense of my physical disability, but I only called out in a frenzy of passion, "They laugh best who laugh last. I'll silence your tinkler tongue yet!"—and held on my way, my rage so furious that passers-by stared at me, my brain throbbing with the fellest purposes of revenge.

Poor fool! One brief moment's prescience, one glimpse of the future and the keen-edged sword that Fate held imminent over my head would very speedily have checked my passion and turned my mind to other things than petty aims of vengeance. Yet such foreknowledge would not have diminished my sense of wrong. For my enemy's evil influence was predominant, and little as I guessed it, was to shape my whole subsequent career.

On reaching my rooms I found a letter from home awaiting me. The superscription was my father's, a circumstance that at another time and in a calmer mood would immediately have arrested my attention, since my mother was the invariable correspondent at Glenrae. But just then I had not eyes to observe. One thing, and one thing alone I saw and thought of,—the detested object of my wrath. He loomed upon my distracted mind like a portentous fate, shutting out all else. Instead of making haste to learn the news, I crushed the letter in my hand, and strode about the apartment, darkening it with violent language.

At length I tore the envelope and read the letter. The effect was as if a fevered man were to plunge into an icy flood and have all his flaming currents chilled in an instant. I seemed to have passed in a moment from one extreme of horror to the other. I had leaped, in the words of our poet, from "hell-heat to arctic cold;" from the region of anger into that of despair; and for a while I was paralysed.

At first I read incredulously, thinking that fury must have disordered my brain. Holding my head in my hand, I read again and yet again, hoping to prove the first interpretation wrong. But reperusal only brought out the fatal truth the more clearly. Then I thought that my father must have been mad when he wrote; but that hypothesis also had to be abandoned. The letter, indeed, was mercilessly sane and explicit.

It was a voluminous document, covering a full half dozen sheets of large, closely written letter paper. That I might the better understand the crisis which had come upon us, and the course of events leading up to it, my father thought it incumbent upon him to relate the history of all the preceding generations of our house. My ancestors, according to the partial historian, were men of rare virtues and splendid accomplishments, brave, generous, and well-favoured, aiming ever at keeping their honour bright, and their hall full of good cheer for their friends. Their hospitality shone conspicuous in ages more bounteous than ours; and, said my father, with a pride that had its touch of pathos, "No man of them was ever known to do what did not become a Glenrae of Glenrae." But he was constrained to add, "Though I am afraid they were not always as wise as Solomon."

The eulogy was the preface to a very bitter tale.

Bog and crag and moorland but ill fit people with a chivalrous spirit and a lavish hand; nor is the spell of prodigality to be cast off in a moment. The Glenraes having spent themselves in keeping open house began to borrow. Then insidiously, bit by bit, the estate crumbled away till only a remnant remained. "When I came into possession of it," wrote my father, with a stroke of sardonic humour, "it was like succeeding to an almshouse." The sequel was a moving tale of the incessant attacks of harpies—Israelitish usurers aided by conscienceless lawyers,—and how these harpies were now "closing in like ravenous beasts of prey howling for blood." "Wherefore it comes," continued the letter, "that things are pressing hard on us at this present writing, and I and your mother are sore distressed." There was, however, a chance of keeping the foe "beyond the gates" by temporizing until such time as I, the sole hope of the family, should be able to come to the rescue. The manner in which I was to bring relief was by beating the harpies at their own game. In other words, I was to retrieve our fallen fortunes by turning lawyer forthwith.

"After much deep deliberation," pursued my father, "the law commends itself to me as a high and honourable profession. A lawyer in our family would fairly set us on our feet again. Lawyers are all rogues, Angus, as I know to my cost; but you might get a long enough spoon to sup with the wiliest of them. Once started, once rising, none knows where you might stop. You might be my Lord Advocate yet, and go to court and make a great name and get influence, and then we could cock our bonnets, and whistle with the best of them."

This was bad enough and hopeless enough, but the pinch was yet to come. That my progress might be facilitated, I was to begin my legal career in the office of Thomas Clephane, in Dundee—that is to say, I was to put myself completely and unconditionally in my enemy's power. My father thanked Heaven that I had an opportunity of making so good a start. "I will write to your uncle immediately," he said, "and it lies secure in my mind that he will admit you on favourable terms. Delay not, my son. Let our straits be a spur to your resolution; we look to you to save us, and I am sure we do not look in vain. I have a dim memory of hearing you once say that your cousin, who will naturally be your uncle's partner and successor, is your fellow-student at the University. Cultivate his good will, and, by the grace of God, he may befriend you."

I read this letter a dozen times, dazed by its news, sickened at heart by its misplaced and tragic hopefulness. Locking the door to prevent intrusion, I sat down and tried to think. What was this burden that had been laid so suddenly upon me? What was I asked to do? Not half an hour before, Peter had publicly ground his heel in the dust to signify how he would crush me, and I had flung defiance in his face. Now I was to plead for his favour, his help, his toleration, his good will. I was tacitly to court his scorn, to invite him to heap insults and humiliations on my head. He might taunt me and tempt me, call his companions to join him in making sport of me, he might spit on me, treat me like a dog, and I could give nothing in return but the crouching subserviency which a dog owes to its master.

I sprang to my feet quivering with anger, and began to pace the room in a tumult of revolt. No, by Heaven, it should never be! Never, as long as he drew breath, would Peter Clephane rejoice in domineering over me. To be snubbed, contemned, jeered at, treated as a slave, a creature of the mire every time the humour seized him, was a prospect to be cancelled at once. He must be aware of our condition. Already he had flung at me the gibe that I was a pauper, and given me a foretaste of the treatment I might expect at his hands. My father could have no knowledge of what his proposal meant. He would not willingly deliver me bound into the hands of my worst enemy.

And then, with a subduing and sobering effect, it struck home to my heart that all this was but the rebellion of a selfish pride. The individual has his rights, private feelings have their place and value; but to weigh them against the claims of a pressing duty is impious. Could I be guilty of such impiety? Could I turn a heedless ear to the call for help from them to whom by every law of God and Nature, every tie and sentiment of affection, I owed all the aid it was possible to me to give? No, a thousand times, no. Better suffer any humiliation, better sacrifice freedom and liking for ever than turn traitor to those I loved. Help! Yes, I would help. If necessary I would go to Dundee, and be deaf and dumb under Peter's persecution. He could lay on, and I would never so much as protest.

The gloaming came, and my landlady brought a light. The cheerful glow of lamp and fire strengthened my resolution. My writing materials were on the table, and I sat down eagerly to reply that I would do in all particulars according to my father's wishes. As I wrote, my paltry objections grew less and less, till they were no more than a vague shadow at the back of my mind. My spirits rose: the prospect brightened. I was almost glad of the opportunity that had arisen to do something practical and helpful. I would throw myself into my new studies with all my soul, and—who knew?—I might yet realise my father's dream and be a legal luminary and restore the fortunes of my family. I had read of such romantic things; I would make my own life a romance.

My sheet was perhaps half full when all at once there arose a great shouting under my window. I stopped to hearken, but unable to distinguish what was said, I raised the sash and thrust out my head. The moon, which was near the full, shone in an unclouded sky, so that the light was good. Below I saw half a dozen familiar figures, and in their midst, with a leer on his face, was Peter Clephane. He broke into a tirade of reviling and mockery as soon as he saw me, asked me how I liked my drubbing, and whether I wouldn't come down and get more. I closed the window, firmly resolved to make no response. Words are but wind, and should not turn a strong man from his purpose. But the clamour waxing louder and more aggressive so that I could not write with any degree of self-possession, I put out my head again to beg them to go peaceably away. I was received with a volley of very ill-smelling slime and shouts of derisive laughter.

"That's a slight expression of our respect and esteem for a scabby Highlandman," cried Peter. "How does it taste?"

I shook off the filth with a dizzy head and a sharp constriction of the throat that made me gasp. I did not speak, I could not; but there was a fascination that held my eyes fast on the enemy. As I did not withdraw I was bespattered a second time. They were mightily pleased with themselves, and screamed in their glee louder than ever, Peter's voice being high over all. But the swelling tumult within was drowning the noise without. I did not hear what was said; I scarcely saw their mocking gestures. Lights began to leap in a fantastic maze before my sight, and there was a sound in my ears like the vicious song of a million bullets. I cleaned myself again as well as possible, my assailants screeching in an ecstasy of joy at my plight; then turning backward, I clapped on my bonnet and descended the stairs for my revenge.

My appearance outside was the signal for another and a fiercer storm of ridicule and revilement; but my passion was already running high and needed no fresh tempest of derision or abuse to make it surge. Walking straight up to Peter and looking him in the two eyes so that he flinched and fell back, I said, in a voice that was strange even to myself: "The time has come for you and me to settle some points. Come this way, and bring your friends."

At the back of the house there was an unused plot of ground, covered by a soft sward. It offered a desirable seclusion, and thither I led them. They took the thing as a fresh jest, making boisterously merry over it, little aware of the maddening electricity that tingled along my veins, or the deadly intent that had brought me there.

"Fire away, Flanagan," cried one hilariously. "Well done, hobbledehoy," chimed another. "Hold on till I get claymores," roared a third, and they were all unconscious what a fire they were feeding.

Immediately upon entering the enclosure I threw off my coat and waistcoat, slipped the braces from my shoulders to have freer play, and tightened the belt about my waist. Peter stood regarding me with a look partly of curiosity, partly of contempt.

"I think you had better strip," I said, quietly; "I want no advantage." There was no longer any thought of the crippled arm.

"Valiant words to come from so white a face," he laughed. "I swear you look as if you had just come from a gathering of ghosts."

"Get ready," I said, biting my lip in my impatience, so that I tasted the salt blood.

"Well!" he cried. "I declare the farce deepens, though I must say it seems an odd taste to want two thrashings in one day."

"Get ready," I repeated, "for fear I kill you before you have a chance of defending yourself."

He laughed outright at this, a jeering exasperating laugh. "Who said a Highlander had no spirit?" he cried. "This is worthy of the formidable knight of La Mancha." He might have been less free of his taunts had he foreseen how speedily and effectually the tune was to be changed.

He stripped leisurely, taking time to fold each article daintily as he took it off, and to keep my purpose hot his tongue was busy with sarcastic compliments to my valour. At length, bowing elaborately, he announced himself ready to receive any attention I cared to bestow upon him. The words had scarcely left his lips when he was reeling from the charge. For it was not a fight such as we used to have. It was a furious onset and a feeble defence. I can liken it to nothing but a cur struggling impotently in the claws of an infuriated tiger. He was stupefied and windless before the smile of disdain had time to leave his face. I was not conscious of his resistance. I did not feel his blows. I thought we had not well begun when he was an inert heap on the ground and his friends were calling for mercy. When he was helpless I turned from him to them; for my fury was still in raging flood.

"Will any one of you, or all of you together, take his place?" I roared.

But the challenge was not accepted, for none of them cared to fight a demon, and so, crying out about caitiffs and cowards who could jeer but had no heart for battle, I re-dressed and went back to my rooms.

With the passage indoors there came a swift and miraculous change. I had not been absent ten minutes, yet I returned to another world, a world of convulsion and frightful upheaval. My father's letter lay on the table, and beside it the unfinished reply. Glancing at them, my eyes caught the words of supplication, the appeal for aid. I sank into a chair with a moan and buried my face in my hands.

"And this is how I help!" I cried, with a choking sob. "This is my loyalty to them I love! God forgive me!" And my anger went out in a passion of tears, leaving unutterable remorse and horror behind.

Having shattered my prospects and disregarded my father's advice, as far as it was possible to do both, I felt there was nothing to be done but to go to him as quickly as might be and seek his pardon. It was not an agreeable nor indeed a promising mission, for though my father was one of the most affectionate of men, he was hasty-tempered and, when opposed, narrow and arbitrary—ay, even capable of headlong, volcanic violence, nay of downright injustice. I was thwarting him in his dearest wish, and he would not easily forgive me; but go to him I must, were it only to hear his sentence of banishment. So, with the heaviest heart I had ever carried, I set about packing at once, resolved to start by the first coach on the morrow.

CHAPTER II.

A PERSONAGE OF VAST IMPORTANCE.

About midnight I went to bed, but my rest was an agonizing mockery. "Nightmares rode on my strangled sleep," rode roughshod, and, as if that were not inhumanity enough, stayed their course to torture and dance. The experiences were such as make brave men shake like cowards and strong men weep like children. Mountains toppled upon me, ghastly screeching hags tore me with venomous claws, serpents and black dogs writhed and leaped on my breast, shapeless monsters strained to devour me, and appeared likely to succeed—in a word, a multitude of terrors encompassed and smothered me; and through it all, though I struggled to escape and cry for mercy, I was as helpless as a paralytic and as tongue-tied as a choking baby. In some dread crisis, perhaps as I was on the point of being swallowed whole, or torn, or crushed to death, I would jump up bathed in the cold lather of panic; then lie for a while tossing with aching sensibilities; then doze to start and shudder again and creep together in the dark as at the touch of evil spirits.

It was a relief when the grey dawn broke in searching chilliness, and I rose with chattering teeth to face a world that had strangely altered during the night. I was miserably sore and bewildered. My bodily injuries, indeed, were naught; but my mind beat with

a poignant sense of bafflement and disaster. Swept
from its moorings and cast adrift by the first real
breath of tempest that had ever blown upon it, it had
lost its reckoning and was groping pathetically in the
blank isolation of enveloping mists, seeking anchor-
age and some ray of intelligence to explain the confusion.

When the mists began to dissolve, turning vague
apprehensions into dismaying realities, the change
assuredly did not tend to lighten the spirits. For a
clear perception of the situation brought back upon
me all the horrors of remorse and despair. It would
be difficult to say which was the harder to bear, the
thought of impending ruin or the recollection of my
folly and disobedience. Either would have been
hard enough; together they were as the torment of
Dives. But by degrees it came to me that what is
must be borne. As I had made my bed, so I must
make shift to lie on it. The philosophy is hard but
bracing.

Happily for the unfortunate calamity has its stim-
ulus as well as its terrors. Happily, also, man is ingenious in devising excuse for his faults. I began
in the time-honoured fashion to console myself with
the reflection that I was not entirely to blame for what
had happened or was happening, that in the common
phrase I was the victim of circumstances. At the
thought the old spirit of revolt arose within me. I
thrilled to the brazen call of necessity, and my teeth
clenched in savage resentment of the cruelty and injustice of fortune. Fortified by a desperate defiance,
a determination deep as the wounds in my soul, I
swore I would make my enemies suffer. There
might be little hope of victory; but there was a
wicked gratification in prolonging the conflict and
rendering evil for evil, even to the bitter end. In
the warm atmosphere of the dawn, however, my fiery
resolution could not keep me from shivering.

My impatience to be off brought me to the point at
which I was to take the coach a good hour too early.

That space, for want of better employment, I spent pacing to and fro on the pavement of Princes Street, chewing the cud of very sour reflections. About me stable-men shouted and swore, horses clattered into place, and fussy passengers made a commotion for no reason whatever, as fussy passengers have a way of doing. At another time I might have been amused, but just then Babel and the tongues ten times confounded could not have diverted my dismal and rankling thoughts.

The morning broke brilliant and keen—caller, as they say in Scotland—with the wind coming briskly off the firth and the level sun striking with a dazzling radiance on dewy roof and tower and spire. The scene was one to lift the gloomiest out of his gloom. Misery itself, which sees most things with jaundiced eyes, could not look without a thrill of exaltation, a momentary self-forgetfulness, on the romantic city flashing in liquid brightness, as if she had just arisen, dripping like some shining miracle from the sea, and glowing, nay blazing, with a thousand colours that made her pinnacles points of fire and turned her ramparts and buttresses to opal and amethyst. Every moment brought fresh enchantments, magical effects of gold and rose and gauzy silver,—so that Edinburgh, clustering about her hills and precipices and broken into a rich confusion of iridescent peaks and fantastic pictured masses, seemed a poet's dream—a city of Fairyland. Yet already, in obedience to the conditions of her existence, she was bending her neck to the prosaic yoke of a sordid routine. Wheels were in motion that would grind her people as if they were sacrificial offerings, fling them aside, maimed and useless, and hum and roar for more, that would in due course be thrust among the iron teeth. I saw the beginning of that daily battle of life from which so many of the combatants are glad to escape to a quiet grave; saw men and women going forth to contend for food, to trample, to rob, to plunder, to deceive, as if the

decree of heaven were that mankind must live by
force and fraud, and the hand were fallen powerless
that feeds the sparrow and clothes the lily. It was
a piteous fate; yet in comparison with mine it seemed
sunny and attractive.

The castle alone seemed independent and unsubdu-
able, lifted completely above the trivial and vexatious
affairs of life. The sentinel's steel gleamed on the
battlements with stirring and quickening suggestions
of its own. I thought of the glory of carrying arms,
experiencing in imagination something of the shock
of battle and the rapture of victory. Why should I
not join the ranks of those who joyously sought renown with banners and music? What more natural
to the hand of a Highlander than the hilt of a sword?
But as I asked myself the question the trumpet
blared out its summons to mount, and so, instead of
getting into warlike accoutrements, and putting my
fortune to the arbitrament of bloody strokes, as my
Lord Stanley has it, I took my seat on the coach as
meek as any Quaker.

We rolled off with regal pomp, our flourish of
trumpets and the ostentatious gaiety of our equipage
collecting a group of gazers at even the early hour of
six. But they did not long feast their eyes on our
splendour, for our steeds being fresh and the char-
ioteer given to display, we were soon out of the echo-
ing streets and bowling merrily along the highway.
The exhilaration was immediate and exquisite.
There is something in freedom and rapid motion and
vivid sunshine and the jovial companionship of irreverent coachmen and trumpeters, and the admiration
of blushing rustic maidens, and mettlesome horses
gay with polished trappings and flying ribbons, that
even the child of misfortune cannot resist. My
spirits, chill and leaden as they were at starting, were
soon in a glow, which they retained more or less
until, with a rousing blare of the bugle and a great
bustle of welcome, we drew up at the Hound and Stag
in Perth, where we were to pass the night.

The Hound and Stag was a cosy old inn, with low black ceiling, yellow sanded floors, a cheerful display of kegs, copper kettles, crystals and other utensils of good cheer, and an appetizing fragrance diffused by savoury pans and bubbling, hissing ovens. It was a place which the hungry guest entered with expectations and left with regret and pleasant recollections. The traveller can find no such hospitable refuges now. We have palace hotels and great gilded dining-rooms, and formality and grandeur, and invisible landlords and supercilious waiters who criticize your manners and expect exorbitant tips for doing it, and flunkies in livery with the petrifying stare of Gorgons; but no comfort comparable to that of the Hound and Stag. That evening the entertainment was so royal that long ere the supper was over half my fellow-travellers were uproariously hilarious, and the host took no offence.

Being in no mood for revelry, I stole out through the town and down by the green soft banks of the Tay to have a quiet thought to myself. When I returned some of the company had prudently gone to bed; others, less mindful of appearances, were snoring serenely in their chairs, in every variety of posture possible to the human frame made limp by ardent cheer; and one or two, whom I took to be kirk elders, on furlough, were discussing the doctrine of predestination and eternal punishment in a perfectly amiable and fatuous manner over well-plenished tumblers of toddy.

There was no apprehension of fiery torments in their jocund countenances, though one of them, hiccuping violently, declared it was "an awfae thing, an awfae thing to dwall in everlasting flames and never be burnt oot."

"Ah, laddie, laddie," he said, solemnly turning a watery eye upon me. "Mind yer ways in the days o' yer youth ere the evil days draw nigh and the deil has ye in his cloots. Ance ther, ye may sing

'Fareweel to Lochaber.' Ah! it's an awfae thocht, an awfae thocht."

He emptied his glass with apparent relish, and re-filled it. "There's waur things in this world than toddy," he remarked at large, "aye providing it's no spoiled in the making. There's a deal o' skill needed in the brewing o' toddy, let me tell ye. I have said as much to oor minister mair than ance—the good man taks a gless himsel, ye ken, just for his stamach's sake, as the Apostle says—and he agreed wi' me. Ay, it's no every coof can brew toddy." He refreshed himself again, and as he was setting down his glass his eye fell once more on me. Instantly his face became grave as with a weighty sense of duty.

"Can ye tell me, d'ye think, what's the sixth commandment?" he asked, leaning across the table towards me.

I answered that I thought it forbade killing. He shook his head with a pained solemnity, nearly tipping over his glass with the point of an extraordinarily long nose as it swung to and fro like a pendulum. "In a Christian country it's waefae, perfeckly waefae," he observed tragically. "What are oor ministers aboot that the like o' this can happen? Man, it's a peety, a great peety! and yer no an ill-favoured callant ava; just ignecrant, fair lost in ignecrance. The seeventh commandment is, Thou—mark it weel for yer edification, laddie—thou shalt not covet thy neighbour's wife—it's the greatest o' sins amaist—mind Daavid, laddie, mind King Daavid and be warned—thou shalt not covet thy neighbour's wife,—get ane o' yer ain if ye like, but let his a-be—the Lord be thankit, there's wives enough and to spare for us a'; weel let anither man's wife alane: what's the sense o' robbin' him o' gear that's so plentifu'?—and his ass too—that's his cuddy, ye ken—neither his meal-poke, nor his her-rin' barrel, puir man, and least o' a' his coo and his bit lass. What are ye waggin' yer finger at me for, Tammas?" he demanded suddenly.

"I'm thinkin' ye've made a bit o' a mistake, Geordie," returned Tammas. "Accordin' to the law o' Moses—Deuteronomy—I dinna just mind tho verse and chapter—or may be it's the Sang o' Solomon—I've aye thocht it says a great deal for a man wi' sae mony wives;—seeven hunder, I think, was the number—that he could sing; anyway, it's clearly laid down that it's the eighth command-ment that forbids the covetin' o' other men's wives."

"Tammas," said Geordie, with an inane leer which was meant to be extremely stern, "I widnae hae be-lieved it. It's doonright scan'lous. I've a good mind to hae ye afore the session."

"It's my opinion ye baith deserve the session," chuckled a third, blinking unsteadily upon them. "Much good Moses and Solomon and Deuteronomy and the Carritch* hae done ye. Whan I was a lad-die, as my hurdies hae good reason to mind, it was the fourth commandment that forbade wanderin' frae yer ain hen-roost."

"Was it?" said Geordie, in a thick voice. "Man, I widnae hae believed ye were sae very igneerant. The session will hear tell o' this. Laddie, laddie," he went on, addressing me with an added lugubri-ousness of manner, "pray to bo delivered frae idle, igneerant babblers. Go home and learn the ninth commandment aboot lettin' what's no yours alane. In whatna heathen land was ye brocht up any way that yer in sic darkness?" He looked down at the table. "It's dry work convertin' sinners," he said, and with an incontinent wink he emptied his glass. "That's the stuff to wet a man's whistle," he ob-served; "we'll hae mair o't." Finding his own sup-ply exhausted, he reached across the table for another decanter. "The Lord helps them wha help them-selves," he remarked. "Laddie, here's t'ye. I like yer looks; but ye maun mind yer Carritch if yer goin' to jouk auld Clootie. Go hame and learn the twelfth commandment and——"

* Catechism.

"Is this a society for the propagation of blasphemy?" broke in a sharp voice with the disturbing effect of a thunder-clap.

Geordie paused with the uplifted glass half way to his lips, and the others turned abruptly to the questioner with faces of amazement.

"God forbid, sir," answered the landlord, unctuously. He had just crept in softly to see that his guests were happy, and was scandalized at the imputation of irreverence for sacred things.

"Blasphemy!" echoed Geordie, bringing his glass down with a decision that sent it into splinters, and trying to sit very straight. "Blasphemy! I'd like to clap my een on the man wha wid talk blasphemy to my face."

"To enjoy that privilege, then, you have only to look into the mirror," said the intruder with a fierce scorn.

"Anything wrang wi' the doctrine?" demanded Geordie, hoarsely.

"What doctrine?" said the other. "I have heard none, except it be the maundering of a licensed fool."

Geordie rose to his feet with contorted visage, but he found it hard to maintain his equilibrium, and charitable hands set him back gently but firmly on his chair.

"What's wrang wi' the doctrine?" he queried again in truculent but husky tones.

"He rides on the riggin' o' the kirk, Geordie," whispered Tammas, winking violently with both eyes. "He's a son o' self-righteousness whas portion is wi' the Pharisees. A hot spot, my certie. Better for Sodom, a heap better, in the day the elect— you and the rest o' us, Geordie—are snug in Abraham's bosom. Fire and brimstane." He grinned like an ass eating thistles. "Foreordained, ye can see it, min." He drew himself up, and faced the stranger with a shining countenance. "Like as not thae discussions are no in yer line, sir," he observed affably. "Maybe ye dinna like goin' oot o' yer depth, and when ye come to think of it, what are ministers paid for if no to save gentlemen frae fashin' about their souls? It's a kittle business, sir; ay, an unco kittle business." He smiled fatuously, evidently expecting an answer; but all he got was a withering glance of the eye. Nothing abashed, he smiled again after a vacant interval. "Weel, weel," he continued amiably, "let that flea stick to the wa'. Am sure ilka ane is free to tak a spring on his ain fiddle; and nae doot we'll a' mend as we grow better, and get to heaven wi' the lazy weaver at last. Yer very excellent good health, sir."

Geordie, however, maintained his militant mood unabated. "What's wrang wi' the doctrine?" he demanded once more, with a lurid fire in his rolling eyes. "I want that question answered. What's wrang wi' the doctrine?"

"Will ye no step up by to bed, sir?" asked the landlord, bending double before him.

"No," answered Geordie, ferociously. "No sae much as half a fit;" and he sat on glaring at the intruder, and muttering at intervals, "What's wrang wi' the doctrine? that's what I wid like to ken. What's wrang wi' the doctrine?"

Naturally the interest gravitated to the man who had so unceremoniously questioned Geordie's orthodoxy and piety. That he was a person of consequence was evident, no less from his own lofty and imperious port than from the servile attentions of mine host. He was booted and spurred, as though he had just alighted from the saddle. A silver-mounted riding-whip, and a pair of riding gloves, lay beside him on a table, and he wore the loose brown velvet coat affected by the better class of horsemen. High about his neck was a huge stiff collar, that held his head defiantly in the air, and kept his ears rigorously at attention. An imposing bunch of seals dangled from his fob, and his rosy gills and portly waist proclaimed that he was one of the fortunate people who have their bread buttered on both sides. His head was bald on the crown, and a ragged wart marred the symmetry of his nose, which, however, was flung in the air with a sempiternal snort of contempt, as if scorning common noses and their owners. His air told, he was perfectly well aware, that when he stood, his two legs supported the very pink of creation.

When I turned from my examination he did me the honour of staring hard at me; but almost immediately he brought the tips of his fingers superciliously together, and turned his eyes to the ceiling in a manner which said plainly he regretted demeaning himself with an utterly insignificant and casual stranger, and that he would certainly not do it again. As he was delivering himself silently but impressively of these sentiments and resolutions, the landlord bustled into the room with a bowl of steaming, fragrant toddy, a glass and a ladle, all of which he set down with an air of ceremonious reverence on a small table specially placed at the right hand of the great man. The great man thereupon took his eyes from the ceiling, and his eloquent finger-tips apart, and condescended to give a grunt of approval. Thus encouraged the landlord became adventurous.

"I have taken the liberty, sir," he said, in his suavest manner, with an inclination of the body towards his patron, "to put the heel of a lemon in it. I aye think lemon adds to the flavour of the best Glenlivet. Let me fill your glass, sir. There, I think you'll find that worth drinking. I had Sir Thomas Gordon of the Elms here the other day—something in India or China, I dinna weel ken which or what —a fine fellow if he wasna just so yellow, but that's the liver, sir. My word, a bad liver's——"

"An ugly companion," said the great man, taking a sip, "but, to say the truth, I'm not interested in Sir Thomas's biliary organs."

"Faith nae mair am I, sir," promptly responded the host. "A man has troubles enough of his own in this world, without fashin' wi' other folk's livers,

—but, as I was saying, Sir Thomas happened to be in——"

"Unspeakably gracious on his part, to be sure," interrupted the great man. "Yet the fact does not interest me."

"Weel, weel, sir," responded the host with a deepening of the colour in his rubicund face, "I'm sure I'll be the last to fash ye with things ye dinna want to hear. I only meant to say that Sir Thomas praised the toddy of the Hound and Stag."

"An honour sufficient to shed lustre on your family forever," said the great man, taking another sip; "you'd better have the bellman sent out to apprise the town of Sir Thomas's compliment. Meantime, if you come back in fifteen minutes, I'll have a question to ask you."

"My tongue's aye at your service, sir," replied the host, unable to conceal his chagrin. "A man like me must wag it at the will of them that pay me." And picking up his tray he marched out of the room with an injured look.

The great man gazed at the retreating figure until the door closed upon it; then he nodded his head with profound significance. "All tarred with the same stick," he said to himself, "all born bletherers;" with which sentiment, he crossed his legs, and lay back to contemplate the contents of his glass.

Punctual to the minute, the host returned, and, with an extremely solemn countenance, made his obeisance to the great man. The great man moving his head slightly, so as to have a fairer view, stared without speaking.

"You told me to be back in fifteen minutes," said the host.

"It was rather a suggestion than a command," returned the great man. "But since you are here, will you have the goodness to inform me at what hour the Highland coach starts in the morning?"

"Six o'clock sharp, sir."

"Six o'clock," repeated the great man, musingly.

"Then intending passengers must be afoot by five.
Call me precisely at that hour, if you please; and it
would be an advantage to have a pitcher of hot water
left at my door.   And, let me see, for breakfast I like
ham and eggs when there is a prospect of fresh air to
digest them, and a cup of good coffee—good, you understand! If you attempt to poison me with your
adulterations——"

"My adulterations!" cried the landlord, no longer
able to control himself. "My adulterations! Certie,
that's bonnie talk to a man in his ain hoose, a hoose,
too, that the best in the land hae praised. Let me
tell you——"

"Keep your temper," said the great man, with unruffled calmness; "possibly you may require it yet.
What I wish to say is that, if I am poisoned with
adulterations, it will be the worse for you. Perhaps
you can understand that as a matter of self-interest.
And I presume the sheets have been aired?"

"Aired!" repeated the landlord, in strident tones.
"Every bed in the hoose 's as dry as the fogg in a
lintie's nest, and as sweet as new-mown hay."

"I trust I shall find mine so," said the great man.
"If I should be so unfortunate as to contract rheu-
matism in your bed I know how to get damages."

"Nae doot yer a braw hand at sic games," retorted
the landlord, now nettled beyond endurance. "Maybe
yer ane of them that ken how to get the breeks off a
Highlandman, and the skin off a flint stane."

"There is one thing I know," said the great man,
freezingly, "a civil innkeeper, when I see him."

Having delivered this Parthian arrow, he emptied
his glass, caught up his whip and gloves, and strode
out, casting never a glance at one in the room. The
landlord, uncertain whether to follow and apologize,
or remain behind and give vent to his feelings in
profane language, compromised the matter by falling
viciously on a servant who inopportunely came in his
way. And Geordie, who still sat nursing his griev-
ance, desired once again, in a voice inarticulately

thick, to be informed what was wrang with the doctrine.

I did not see the great man at breakfast next morning; but no sooner had I taken my seat on the coach
than he clambered up beside me. The day being
chill and foggy, he was wrapped to the eyes in a
great-coat and an enormous woollen muffler, such as
the Scottish people like to hide their heads in when
the air happens to be too shrewd.

"Ugh, dear me, it's raw," he remarked to the
world at large, as he settled back in the midst of a
pile of rugs and plaids, sublimely oblivious of the
fact that he was reclining upon me, and appropriating
half my space.

We were not far on our journey when the sun
shone out warmly; the mists which filled the valleys,
and lay heavily on the wooded slopes, began to rise,
and some of the fairest scenes in all fair Scotland
opened to the sight. The landscape smiled. But
there was no corresponding token of geniality in the
face of the portentous individual by my side. He so
far responded to the benignancy of nature, indeed,
as to unbutton his great-coat, lower his muffler, and
lay himself out to the sun as if he were a bundle of
mouldy hay. But even this he did out of sheer con-
descension, and, in the process, he made me suffer.
He dug into my ribs with his elbow, he flapped his
coat into my face, he stamped on my toes, he rubbed
himself against me, finally keeling over and lying
on me, as if I had been a cushion specially placed to
save his bones. His pressure nearly pushed me over
the side of the coach, and I made a movement to save
myself.

"I'll trouble you to look after your elbows," he
said, acknowledging my presence for the first time.

"Really, sir," I retorted, not without a little heat.
"The request comes rather oddly seeing how you have
been using both me and my space."

He turned his head quickly and his eyes were as
live coals. Doubtless he expected me to crumple and

disappear in the blaze of his anger; but as that did
not happen, he said very deliberately and with savage
emphasis, as if every word were a branding iron,
"Young man, your impudence is amazing. Cultivate it; it will do much for you."

He averted his eyes, snorting like a charging bull,
while I, confounded by the striking example of the
virtue with which he credited me, could only repeat
in astonishment, "Impudence!"

"Precisely," he rejoined, nudging and spreading
himself out still farther, so that he almost cracked
my ribs against the iron rod at the side. "Precisely.
You have the effrontery of a brazen serpent."

"And you the weight of an elephant," I answered,
giving him a heave that sent him against the passenger on the other side.

"I am at a loss, sir, to make out whether you suffer
from congenital idiocy or inborn viciousness," he
cried in a burst of passion. "But I warn you to
beware. I am not a man to take offences lightly. I
don't like them, and what is more I won't have them.
Mark that for your private well-being. There is a
law in this country, young man, and it might turn
out to some people's cost that I know something
about it. A bonnie thing, indeed, that passengers
on a public conveyance should have to submit to the
will of one who makes himself a nuisance and a danger." His wrath went on increasing. "I will not,"
he roared, the wart on his nose glowing like a point
of fire. "I will not. I do not take insolence. I do
not endure assault and battery from young cubs in
stage coaches at their pleasure. Not by half a hundred miles. That is not my method of re-creating
myself. Sir, there is such a thing as justice in this
land, as you and the owner of this jolting, ramshackle
old coach may learn to your detriment. You laugh
at me," for indeed I could not keep my countenance
—"you laugh at me, but take care, sir, take care that
I do not make you laugh on the wrong side of your
mouth. I am not to be mocked with impunity."

The aid of the guard was invoked, but that functionary could discover no sufficient reason for acting on the great man's suggestion that I should be flung head foremost from the coach. The official leniency was fresh fuel to the great man's ire.

"I have only to say, then," he cried, his face a fateful purple and crimson, "that if I should have the misfortune to be injured by this person, you will be held accountable; for you have had warning of his violent intentions. Do you understand, sir, what it is to be an accessory before the fact in a criminal case? See that I am not forced to have you informed on the point."

Thus admonished, the guard returned to his bugle, blowing (as I fancied satirically) till his cheeks nearly burst, while the other passengers tittered, causing the great man to glare on them severally and individually as if they deserved thumb-screws and hot pincers. Having scowled to his satisfaction, expressed his contempt for everybody in a series of ferocious snorts, and again warned the guard of the fatal consequences which were almost certain to follow his refusal to have me bound hand and foot, he pulled out a fat note-book and began to study a page of figures, keeping, however, the corner of his eye on me. As he studied, a smirk of joy now and again relieved the blackness of his countenance. I judged the figures represented some profitable investment; but little could I have guessed what that investment was.

At length he closed the book, returned it to his pocket, and, in spite of all that had taken place, once more reclined at his ease on me. It was now my turn to appeal to authority.

"Guard," I called, "have the goodness to remove this gentleman. And make haste, please, for if I should be crushed to death you will be held accountable as an accessory before the fact. You understand what that means."

The aggressor sat bolt upright as if an arrow had pierced him, his face presaging a tornado.

"It is intolerable!" he said, with the hissing menace of a hurt snake. "But mark me, it shall not pass. I will have justice."

"It will please me greatly to have justice done between us, sir," I answered, stretching myself to the full limits of my space.

"And you shall have it, sir! you shall have it!" he cried truculently. "I pledge you my word you shall have it; and I hope it will prove to your taste."

"I trust it will prove mutually agreeable, sir," I replied; whereupon the passengers tittered again, fanning the great man's anger till I thought he must explode. But by dint of blowing so furiously through his nostrils that one irreverent passenger pretended to look for a spouting whale, and another for signs of a hurricane, he managed to save himself. By a miracle of prudence and self-control he also bridled his tongue, having perhaps discovered the futility of his threats. For the rest of the journey he punctiliously kept from touching me. Nor did we exchange another word, though he occasionally cast a malicious sidelong look at me. We left the coach together at Aberfourie, and when he disappeared into the inn I fervently hoped I had seen the last of him.

Though I made all haste after alighting from the coach, leaving my portmanteau in charge of the innkeeper, that I might go unencumbered, and taking a short cut across the moors, the gloaming had fallen ere I caught my first sight of the turrets and chimney-tops of Glenrae, dim and solitary in the midst of the dusky heath. The mountain tops were still radiant with a waning golden light, but the valleys were already awesome with the gloom which night brings to the haunted solitudes of the Highlands.

I walked quickly, my heart beating tumultuously with a dizzying alternation of hopes and fears and expectations, yet as I got out among the dark ravines, an eerie sensation crept along the spine and among the roots of the hair. At one point, where the path

dived into a lonely hollow, passing in its depth between a black tarn, said to have no bottom, and a
cairn that covered a murderer's bones, and a moor-
cock rose from the heather with a sudden cry of
alarm, my breath came in a thick gasp, and my hair
rose on my head, seeming to lift my hat with it. I
got out of that hollow, in very truth—

> "Like one that on a lonesome road
> Doth walk in fear and dread
> And, having once turn'd round, walks on,
> And turns no more his head;
> Because he knows a frightful fiend
> Doth close behind him tread."

I set down my feet firmly, assuring myself I was
quite composed, and resolved not to accelerate my
pace, yet half a regiment of the Queen's guards could
not have made me look behind.

I reached the top with a long-drawn breath of relief; and then my heart bounded afresh as the lights
of my home shone clearly before me for the first time.
Unable to contain myself I ran, leaping over ditches
and boulders almost without knowing it; but in spite
of my speed, that last half-mile seemed longer than
the entire journey from Edinburgh.

As I drew near, panting from excitement and want
of breath, Bruce, biggest of Newfoundlands and best
of watch-dogs, rushed out with a threatening growl;
but when I called, though I had been absent for
months and my voice must have been strange from
emotion, his growl instantly changed to a yelp of delight, and he flew at me, nearly knocking me down
in his joy. While he wrestled and caressed, I vainly
endeavouring to escape and get forward, my mother
was upon me with a warmer, tenderer embrace, and
a joy that exceeded his. Then my father, wondering
what all the commotion was about, laid aside his
pipe, and hastened forth to investigate. And there
we were, a solitary group, in the deepening gloom,
exchanging greetings that were mostly silent, for
somehow speech would not come.

Ah me! that was two score and five years ago. The world is all changed since then, and I am changed with it; but that home-coming is vivider in my memory than are the doings of yesterday.

CHAPTER III.

A CRISIS AND A SURPRISE.

So much had to be talked of, so many questions asked and answered, that it was far past bed-time before any reference was made to the business which had brought me home.

"We have said nothing about the subject of my letter, Angus," said my father, looking at me wistfully, "because you must be fatigued; but when breakfast is over to-morrow, we will, by the grace of Heaven, have the matter discussed and settled."

"Very well, sir," I answered, "I shall hold myself ready at your convenience."

Both he and my mother smiled approvingly at this sign of filial compliance, and having seen me to my chamber, and assured themselves that all was comfortable, they left me.

I said I was ready; but it was with the readiness of the criminal who faces the inevitable punishment, and desires to have the ordeal over as quickly as may be. Though I was weary I could not sleep. My brain throbbed like a furnace, and every nerve was aquiver. Among other scenes I might have argued myself into the solacing conviction that I was but an innocent cause of the disappointment which on the morrow must overwhelm my father and mother; but amid the old surroundings, with their eloquent tokens of affection, their subduing appeals to the heart, the sense of folly and disobedience was maddening. At times I could have risen and rushed from the house, then a feverish wish to comply would seize me; but it would vanish, leaving me in the old turmoil again.

I felt as if I must go to my father and have the miserable business ended at once. The more I thought, the more terrible my guilt appeared, and the darker the retribution that was at hand. Fortunately, however, even remorse has its limits, and at last I dozed.

I awoke in the morning, with a queer idea of having been travelling in a foreign land, and went to meet my father in a haze of uncertainty. His manner had a caressing tenderness in it that was unusual with him—a circumstance that added to my embarrassment; a further cause of embarrassment was that he introduced the business of my visit as if it were already settled, except in details.

"You see, Angus," he said, "the law has many advantages. It is a money-making business, and enables a man to fight for his own hand, in a way that brings rogues to confusion and ruin. As I hinted to you in my letter, these considerations are not indifferent to us at the present time. To speak plainly between ourselves, there are some despoiling us, who have no moral, nor, as I think you will be able to show, legal right to one farthing of our money. They harry us because we are without proper defence, because there is none to checkmate them. But I have a strong notion that the tables are going to be turned, and that these vultures will get the right-about in a fashion that will astonish them." Here my father rose, and paced the room, in great exultation. "And eh, it would be sweeter than honey to me to see these ravening sharks of the seed of Jacob, and the descendants of Ananias—by which I mean the Jews and lawyers—well stewed in their own broth. And, Angus, you're the man to do it."

My tongue clove to the roof of my mouth at this speech, and I knew not where to look for the eager, disconcerting eyes of both my father and mother.

"I am exceedingly sorry, sir, to learn of the embarrassed state of our affairs," I faltered, with my eyes on the ground.

"Yes, Angus," put in my father quickly, "we are

embarrassed, fearfully embarrassed, but our fortunes
may be restored quicker than we think." And the
dear soul in his confidence came forward, took my
hand fondly in his, and looked in my face in a way
that stabbed me to the marrow.

"I would do all I could for the family credit," I
said.

"The right sentiment, Angus, if rather haltingly
spoken," said my father, with an encouraging pressure of the hand. "Come, my boy, give your courage
tongue. I know it is in your heart to help us, ay,
and in your head too. You will be as cunning a
lawyer as the best of them. You have it in you.
This is only the blateness of a boy."

"There is no sacrifice in the world that I wouldn't
make, sir," I responded; "but——" And there I
stuck with my tongue paralyzed.

My father stared at me for a second or so, then he
dropped my hand, and his brow contracted. The
crisis had come, the evil I had feared was upon me.

"That word sounds strange in my ears, Angus,"
he said, with a strain of harshness in his voice.
"When I proposed the law I did not anticipate any
talk about sacrifices."

"Oh, sir," I blurted out with a frantic desire to
precipitate matters, "I wish I could tell you in a word
what I have to say. I cannot do as you wish."

I would have gone on, but the look he gave me
brought me to a sudden and dead halt. He stood
regarding me for a little, with eyes that seemed to
question my sanity.

"Eh, what's this?" he said, in a voice strange with
amazement. Then his anger flashed out. "You cannot do as I wish!" he cried. "Indeed, indeed, indeed! you cannot do as I wish? That is very pretty,
very dutiful, very becoming from son to father; isn't
it, now? You cannot do as I wish?" And he kept
on repeating the words, and giving them a false
meaning which I was powerless to set right.

"And since such is the case, sir," he went on,

throwing himself into a chair, "perhaps it is not too much to ask what your own proposal is?"

I faltered that I hadn't any, and held my breath for the effect. It was electric. With an energy I had never seen in him before, my father sprang to his feet and began to stride about the room, or rather to stamp, his face a thunder-cloud, his breathing a series of angry snorts. As I stood quaking in every fibre, my mother gave me a look which seemed to say, "My dear, unfortunate boy, what does all this mean? Have you taken leave of your senses?"

"I can scarcely believe my ears," cried my father, when he had got over the first spasm of rage, "I doubt my very senses. A son of mine telling me, in the very crisis of fortune, he will not lift a finger to save us. That is intelligence to make the ears tingle. 'I cannot do as you wish,' says the beardless Solomon to the foolish greybeard. That's good; the world's improving. There can be no doubt we are advancing. Before long old men will be taking lessons from babes. Cannot do as I wish. This is what colleges and professors do. Go out, sir, and get me a hazel rung till I teach you obedience. By my faith, Wallace Glenrae will not be disobeyed in his own house."

"Do not agitate yourself so," pleaded my mother. "Angus means no disobedience, I'm sure. You haven't given him a chance to explain himself."

"To be sure, to be sure," said my father, "we have not heard his explanations. I'll warrant they're very ingenious and convincing, coming direct as they do from that nest of Jesuits, the College of Edinburgh."

Then, after a turn or two more about the room, he threw himself again into a chair. Thinking that now was my chance to speak, I began very humbly—

"If you listen, sir, I'll try——"

"Listen!" he thundered, leaping to his feet as if I had struck him, "listen to you. No, the listening shall be on the other side. And this is what I have to say, that you shall obey me without troubling about explanations, or you shall go out of this, bag

and baggage, to reap the fruits of your independence.
I am master here yet, and, by the Powers above, I
will have no explanations when my authority is challenged."

"I only wanted to tell you," I ventured again.

"On your peril, sir, do not attempt to argue with
me," he returned, with an access of wrath; "I am
none of your patent logic-choppers. But I know my
own mind, and it is this: that you shall do as I wish,
or within three minutes you shall darken my door for
the last time!"

And I verily believe he would forthwith have thrust
me from the house had not his attention been arrested
by a knock at the outer, or hall door, a loud imperious knock, that seemed to announce a person of uncommon importance. The next minute the door of
our apartment was opened, and in walked—my bump-
tious travelling companion of the preceding day. He
was all smirks and smiles now, as he reared his portly
figure in the doorway, and looked about him the very
embodiment of good nature. My father, being taken
aback in the midst of his passion, stared for a moment, without a word of welcome or recognition.
Then suddenly he cried, "Thomas Clephane, by all
that's wonderful!"

"Troth, just the same, cousin," returned the visit-
or, complacently taking my father's outstretched
hand. "And glad to see you hale and well, though,
to say the truth, a wee thought ruffled about the
comb, so to speak. And this is my good cousin
Janet, no doubt," beaming upon my mother, and ex-
tending a puffy hand. "I am glad to make your acquaintance, cousin, and gratified to find you well.
Many a time have I thought of you all, many a
time." Then spying me—"Ah, whom have we
here? A familiar face surely. Dod, as I'm a living
man, my stage companion, whose pretty wit and
lively manners I found so entertaining on the
wretched journey hither. Well, well! this is a pleasure, to be sure," grasping my hand and nearly

wringing it from the wrist. "Who could have thought of this? But the unexpected's ay happening; little know we what a day or an hour may bring forth. And to think that yesterday we dunched each other in our daffin, never dreaming we were the same blood. Your looks tell me I'm right in taking you for the heir of Glenrae. Home from college, likely. I've heard of ye from Peter. Faith, Peter says ye're an unco scholar."

"It's a pleasure to me to welcome you to Glenrae," interrupted my father. "And it was wholly unexpected."

"Pleasures are aye sweetest when unexpected, cousin," returned Mr. Clephane, urbanely. "What's expected is discounted, enjoyed before its time, so to speak, like wind raised by *post-obit*. I was in the country-side, and could not leave without looking in at Glenrae. And I'm lucky in finding you all together and doubly lucky in finding an old friend"—returning his radiance upon me; "though, to say the truth, what the minister called him escapes me."

"Angus," said my mother.

"To be sure," said Mr. Clephane, laughing. "My memory's no worth a preen, as Bobbie says. I might have remembered what Peter has so often told me. 'Father,' he has said, 'there's not the like of Angus Glenrae in our University. Mind you what I tell ye, he's born to make his mark.' But the fact is that old folks are so much fashed wi' the world, the flesh, and the devil, their minds get slippery and lose the grip o' things. I hope the college days are not over, Angus. It's an auld saying, and a true—stick to the school—(the schule, we said in my halflin days)—and the school will stick to you."

"It's a curious coincidence," said my father, when the voluble Mr. Clephane had been induced to take a seat, "that we should just have been talking about a profession for him."

"A very important matter, cousin," responded Mr. Clephane, with deep gravity of tone and countenance. Then assuming his sprightliest manner, and looking at me, he added, "The most important except getting married, aye make that exception, Angus. Faith the lasses take the lead, will we nill we. Solomon with all his glory—I mean all his wisdom—couldn't resist them, and when he failed who's likely to succeed? What's this the poet says? there's nae poetry in law, cousin, and I'm clean forgetting the warblings of the muse, but anyway he means that in camp or grove love's supreme. A man meets his fate when he meets his wife. Mind that, Angus. But about the profession, cousin—excuse my digression into the realms of sentiment and romance. Lawyers go there but seldom, and, truth to tell, dinna feel ower well at home when they do make an excursion. What's to be Angus's profession, if it's a fair question?"

"There's a difference on the point," answered my father. "I'm for the law, partly because I remember your own prosperity, cousin, partly because a lawyer might be useful in the family; and he's—well! he's against it."

"Hm—ha," said Mr. Clephane, stroking a purple double chin. "Dear me, that's unfortunate; and yet it would never do for us all to be of the same mind. There are many ways of making a living, cousin, and the laddie has his own tastes, nae doot. As to the law, it's with it as with many another thing—those like it best who know least about it. At the best, it's a slippery game, in which ten fall for one who keeps his feet. I have sprachled through— I'll no deny it,—but wi' the skin o' my teeth, as tho man of Uz says. I'm not sure I'd advise another to follow in my steps. Each for himself. Only don't forget, Angus, what the proverb says about the wilfu' man needing to be unco wise. But dinna let me interfere: dinna let me come between father and son." Whereupon Mr. Clephane rubbed his hands and smiled, thus figuratively washing them of the whole business; and the subject of talk was changed.

When Highland hospitalities had been dispensed, Mr. Clephane and my father went out for a walk, leaving me behind. I was not sorry, since their absence gave me an opportunity of speaking with my mother, who, good soul, was on tenter-hooks on my behalf. I told her my whole story unreservedly, and she sympathized, as only a mother can. I also told her the history of my relations with Peter, which startled and amazed her.

"It is a shame, Angus," she said, with the tears gleaming in her dear eyes. "But Mr. Clephane probably knows nothing of Peter's behaviour, and, at any rate, for your father's sake, we must uphold the honour of Glenrae. It must not be said he came here, and was ill received."

And then, with many a caress, she told me she quite understood my unhappy position, and that she would do what she could to re-establish me in my father's favour. I could see, however, that the loyal heart was deeply troubled. She would fain have seen me obey while pledging her word as a partisan. My blessings on her memory.

As fate would have it, when my father and his visitor returned, they were accompanied by a neighbouring laird, Sir Thomas Gordon, of the Elms, of whom the reader has already casually heard from mine host of the Hound and Stag. Meeting the baronet in the course of their walk, my father, with a touch of the impulsive generosity, the fantastic sense of honour and sociality which had been the main cause of our trouble, insisted on taking him home for luncheon, regardless of domestic convenience or resource. But my mother was right glad to see Sir Thomas, and he, in turn, was unfeignedly pleased to see her, declaring, in his fine old-fashioned manner, it did his heart good just to cross the threshold of Glenrae.

Sir Thomas, my mother had told me, always gave her the impression that he was extremely lonely. He might have been happy, as the world goes. A retired Anglo-Indian official, he was wealthy, and, though a widower, he had the companionship of a devoted daughter, whose equal in beauty and goodness has not breathed since Eve left Paradise. But these blessings were mysteriously counterbalanced. There was a break in his health, and one could see it plainly, a break in his heart, two evils for which money is no medicine, and which even filial devotion can hardly do more than alleviate. Sir Thomas had both seen and done a great deal in times that history now calls stirring. He had been a prominent actor in more than one memorable and exciting scene; he had fought a valiant battle, and victory had crowned his exertions; yet he had a skeleton in the cupboard. He sighed often and unconsciously, and his habitual look was downcast. But he was not one of those who parade their woes. In company, he was cheerful in a subdued way, and always gentle and considerate. Much knowledge of men and their imperfections had not hardened him, and bitter experiences had but saddened, not soured his sweet spirit. Nor had years of authority and much honour destroyed his childlike simplicity.

I hoped that luncheon would pass without reference being made to what had brought me home; but in that I was disappointed, for the matter lay too near my father's heart to be kept out of his conversation. Sir Thomas was told of the plans that had been made for me, and how, for some unaccountable reason, I was bent on spoiling them.

"We must not be angry or disappointed if youth does not see with the eyes of age," said Sir Thomas, graciously looking at me. "Morning and evening have different lights. Mr. Angus has the fresh vision and quick intelligence of his time of life; they are not to be despised. At the same time, I am sure he will consider soberly, and not underestimate the importance of maturer judgment than his own in the decision he is called on to make. Least of all will he grieve, by any obstinacy, those to whom his welfare is perhaps dearer than to himself." And then he added, after a pause, "People's thoughts run on the lines that are most familiar to them. India occurred to me. I make a mere suggestion; how would you like to try your fortune in India?"

"No better place in the world for a young man of ability and enterprise," put in Mr. Clephane, quickly. "India is a land that flows with better things than milk and honey. It's the place of all others for making a fortune pleasantly and rapidly. I think I see in Angus a Nabob in embryo."

No one took the slightest notice of him, all the attention being bent on me. I had not thought of India; but the drowning man clutches at a straw; and so I hastened to express a desire to go to India, greatly to the astonishment of my father, and the consternation and horror of my poor mother.

"Do not make a hasty choice," said Sir Thomas, smiling kindly upon me. "Come to the Elms to-morrow evening, and we will talk the matter over at dinner. Perhaps we may have the honour of Mr. and Mrs. Glenrae's company also"—smiling upon them in turn; "and, Mr. Clephane, I shall be glad if you too will favour us with your company. Then we can all help destiny to choose a career for our young friend." And so, for the present at least, I had found a loophole from threatening evils.

CHAPTER IV.

THE ELMS—A MOMENTOUS DECISION.

YOUTH has an enviable knack of turning its back upon the troublous past so soon as a blink of hope shines out of the future.

Next day I had forgotten my woes, and was as snugly in conceit with myself, as ardent, as full of preposterous schemes as if, instead of being the foot-ball of fortune, I had been her first favourite and Grand Vizier. I passed the day zealously cultivating those aerial estates which make so fine a show in the eye of imagination, and promise so rare a revenue, and waited with impatience for the evening. Yet, when the hour came, and I found myself at the Elms, somehow my elation forsook me, and with it my confidence and self-possession. The ordeal of the introduction to Miss Gordon put my wits utterly to flight, leaving me with hot gills and an uneasy foreboding that I was going to make a fool of myself.

When we sat down to dinner I was still haunted by this fear, and consequently very flustered. It would have been unspeakably grateful to me to slink into an obscure corner whence I could watch without attracting attention, but a perverse fate placed me disconcertingly close to the dazzling young hostess. It may seem an odd thing; but in the distress of the first fifteen minutes, had there been the choice, I would gladly have resigned my seat to charge upon a blazing park of artillery; and I would sooner have fought ten men than address a voluntary remark to her. To find her so much as looking at me was to be struck with a ridiculous palsy that sent a nervous tremor all through me, as if there were an electric battery in her eyes; to be directly addressed by her, was total overthrow of the wits and paralysis of the tongue.

That was during the first half-hour of our contact. By degrees, I came to feel that, notwithstanding the flutter of fright she caused me, it was good to be near her, and listen to her wondrously vivacious and penetrative talk, and watch the flying shadows of thought on her superbly moulded and expressive face, and the gleam of her raven hair, and the sunshine that rippled in dimpled cheek and chin, and the sparkle of her dark eyes—eyes which were equally ready to laugh in joy, or melt in pity, or flash in stern indignation and rebuke.

At this point the novelist would have his opportunity; but I am not going to attempt a description of my heroine's beauty, a formal portrait being to me

a thing clean out of the question. She was twenty
and a child of the sun and the peer of any queen on
earth, not surpassed in loveliness by her whose face

> "launched a thousand ships
> And burnt the topless towers of Ilium."

There was a time when I would not only have said
as much, but maintained it with my sword.

Dinner had not long begun when my business was
introduced.

"It is not a thing to be lightly decided upon," said
Sir Thomas, seriously. "You are at a time of life
now, Mr. Angus, when every act, every decision is
momentous; our acts and decisions, indeed, are always momentous, but they are peculiarly and particularly so in youth, when we give the tone and bias
to our whole later life. A hasty or an unwise decision in early years, too often involves a life-long regret. I hope you have well considered with your
father and mother?"

"As to that, Sir Thomas," chimed in my father,
ere I could speak a word, "his mother and myself
have come to no decision in the matter. To be perfectly candid, we have not been consulted. But he
is free to choose. If he thinks it will be to his advantage to go to India, let him go to India. He will
be the likelier to succeed if he decides for himself."

"My sentiments exactly," said Mr. Clephane em-
phatically. "I have a son of my own, and I say,
'Peter, my boy, choose for yourself. We are all endowed with different tastes and different faculties.
Therefore, choose for yourself.' I make no doubt
that Angus is quite competent to select a career for
himself."

"Probably he is," responded Sir Thomas, quietly;
"yet most of us are wiser at sixty than at twenty."

"And India is so dreadfully far away, Sir
Thomas," put in my mother, tremulously.

"Why, as to that, cousin," said the lawyer, with
an unctuous smile, "*Cœlum non animum mutant,*

qui trans mare currunt, crossing the seas does not change a man's nature."

"A great truth," observed Sir Thomas, with just a touch of irony. "Yet what does not change the nature may be a strain on the affections. India," turning to my mother, "is far away. Many a weary mile lies between us and it. The fact is not to be forgotten; but I was once young myself, and went abroad—and—and if youth were to come back to me, would probably go abroad again; and when you come to think of it, if the young were always to take the counsel of the old, the world would have come to a stand long ago." He said this in the kindliest manner, not as a reproof, but as an encouragement to my mother, whose dear heart was faltering at the prospect.

Seeing my opportunity, I stammered what I regret to have to confess was hardly the truth, namely, that I had given the matter careful consideration, and was fully resolved to go to India.

My mother said nothing; but the dinner had little relish for her, and she and Isabel left the table early. There was silence for a little while after their withdrawal.

Then Sir Thomas said, "Since you have decided then, Mr. Angus, if it would not be prying too much into private affairs, might I ask—if I am impertinent, pray tell me so—what your plans are after your arrival in India? I have a special reason for asking."

To this I was forced to confess that I had not thought out my plans, that, in fact, I had no plans at all.

"Youth trusts to luck," said the lawyer, over ready to thrust his tongue in where it was not wanted. "Fortune favours them who have the pluck to show they don't care a rap for the jade."

"I trust, Glenrae," said Sir Thomas, turning to my father, and ignoring the lawyer's remark, "that when you have heard my reason, you will not deem me intolerably selfish. I wished to ascertain that Mr. Angus had fully made up his mind before intruding any personal concern of my own, lest his generosity might lead him to neglect his own interests."

"You are quite incapable of doing anything from selfish motives, Sir Thomas," returned my father, quickly and cordially. "Whatever be your reasons, I am ready to wager they do you honour."

"You are extremely good to express such sentiments," said Sir Thomas; "but I am afraid my motives in this instance are selfish."

"Then, Sir Thomas, I shall be very much surprised indeed," responded my father, promptly.

"You are too generous, Glenrae," said Sir Thomas, "but you will be better able to judge when I have explained my reasons for being inquisitive. The fact is, I am anxious to find some trustworthy friend going to India who would—well—who would undertake a delicate family mission for me."

My heart jumped at this. What could the family mission be? And would Isabel be interested in it?

"There are those in India," continued Sir Thomas, after a short pause, "of whom I should very much like to have intelligence." He stopped a moment in evident embarrassment; then he went on, while we all listened intently, "I think it is generally supposed by my friend and neighbours that Isabel is my only child, but that—I speak in confidence, gentlemen—is a mistake. She has a brother Donald— Donald Gordon—and it is of him I would fain have news. The young man himself is not addicted to letter-writing, and my correspondents in the East seem somehow or other to have lost sight of him. It may be that he is dead," and there was a quiver in his voice. "If so, it would be some satisfaction to know it. And to be brief, I thought that if Mr. Angus were going to India, he might possibly be able to look Donald up."

"Gad, Sir Thomas, Angus is just the very man to

do that," put in Mr. Clephane. "I'll warrant he'll find your son. It is a mission to suit one of Angus's adventurous spirit. I only wish I could substitute my own son. But Angus is not to be superseded. I envy him his opportunity."

"We all envy the opportunities of youth," said Sir Thomas. Then turning to my father with a smile, "You see, Glenrae, my motives are selfish after all!"

"As I was ready to wager, your motives do you honour, Sir Thomas," answered my father, stoutly; "and he were no son of mine who, going to India, would not exert himself to do what you wish."

With that my father looked at me as if to say, "There now, speak up. There's something to your taste perhaps."

"I need hardly assure you, Sir Thomas," I said, clearing my throat, for my excitement was great— "I need hardly assure you, that if ever I set foot in India, my first business will be to find Donald."

"Thank you, Mr. Angus, thank you," responded Sir Thomas, while his voice shook and his eyes glistened. "Thank you. Only pray remember that should you change your mind you will not let this generous promise to me in any way interfere with your own projects. I will not accept your service on any other condition."

"Never fear, Sir Thomas, never fear," answered my father for me. "Make yourself quite at ease on that score. If he changes his mind he will tell you so frankly."

"My heart's thanks to you, Glenrae," murmured Sir Thomas. "You have made me fifty years younger. My spirit—ah me! but there—there. Shall we join the ladies? I dare say they are feeling rather lonely." And we rose and left the room.

"My dear Isabel," cried Sir Thomas, with the glee of a boy as we entered the drawing-room, "come here, child, I have news for you." She rose instantly and met him with a pretty look of expectation on her face.

"Mr. Angus is going to India, and will search out Donald," continued Sir Thomas. "There's news to gladden your heart, my child!"

Isabel turned towards me, her eyes gleaming with a dewy, wistful brightness, and her hands shaking with a sudden tremor, so that I would fain have taken hold of them to comfort her.

"Oh," she said, advancing a step nearer me and speaking in a low voice, which I fancied was meant for my ear alone, "if you could only get tidings of my brother, I cannot tell how grateful I should be. But the news that you are even to try seems too good to be true. How can we ever thank you—what can we ever do to repay you?"

And I, with my hot face and leaping heart, certainly could not tell her.

The joy that gave Sir Thomas and Isabel new life, lifted me also to an exquisite pitch of buoyancy, but when they were radiant with hope and happy by anticipation of family reunions, my dear mother's face blanched, so that my gladness was checked by the duty of comforting her. In this office Isabel came to my help with the sweet words and winning ways that were all her own; and by dint of our unceasing perseverance in looking at the sunny side of things and keeping the dark out of view, by our dwelling on the chances of a young man who was not afraid to face the world, and had health, friends, and a modicum of brains to back him, in a little while my mother smiled through her tears, owning (with a fervent embrace) that it was good for young men to go out among their fellows and try hazards with fortune. "Few have such friends, Angus," she said, looking towards Isabel, while clinging to me; "and I would not stand between you and distinction; far less would I hinder you from doing a worthy action." And then she and Isabel laughed and cried together, while I chewed my thumb in a corner, and there was an end of objections.

It must be understood that I was not to go solely

as Sir Thomas's emissary to seek out Donald. Precisely the reverse was the case. Primarily I was
going on my own account, to push my own fortune;
and Sir Thomas's mission was, as he was pleased to
put it, "a mere act of charity done to a stranger out
of the goodness of my heart." Yet in truth the
charity and goodness were all on the other side.
But for Sir Thomas's potent and timely aid I should
have gone away in disgrace, empty-handed, and
without hope. As it was, my benefactor—for such
I may well call him—not only furnished me with
letters of introduction to the best known and most
influential men in Bombay, but wrote batches of private and special letters in my behalf which I did not
see. My career was to be a mercantile one, that, on
mature consideration, being thought to afford the
easiest and speediest way to affluence for one of my
talents.

"The richest Europeans in India are merchants
and bankers," said Sir Thomas, "and they are all,
as the saying is, self-made men. The days of the
East India Company are over. There are no fortunes being made in that service now, though"—in
a significant voice—"it was not always so. But
India is a wide field, and these letters, Mr. Angus,
will, I think, put you in a position to choose according to your tastes. I have no advice to offer except
not to be in too much haste to decide."

For what Sir Thomas had specially at heart all
provision was made both in letters and in money.
Of the last there was to be absolutely no stint. I was
to spend as much and as long as I should think proper,
or, in other words, as long as there should be the
faintest hope of tracking Donald.

"My bankers shall have full instructions in the
matter," said Sir Thomas, "and in the mean time
we must not forget preliminary expenses." Whereupon he insisted on my taking in ready money and
bankers' drafts, a sum that seemed to me a fortune.
Finally, as I was in great glee with my prospects,

and protested against delay, it was arranged that in exactly three weeks from the date of my home-coming, I was to sail from London in the steamship *The Pearl of the Orient*, commanded by Captain Rogers, who, being a friend of Sir Thomas, was charged to provide for my comfort on shipboard.

And so the ultimate decision was made. I was to lift anchor and set sail for the unknown, as so many did before and so many will do after me. How I fared there, how the reality belied all dreams and anticipations, how fate mocked at wisdom, made naught of forethought and a plaything of me, it will be the business of succeeding pages to relate. None of us could have imagined what was ahead of me; and it was well we could not. Coming events cast no shadow before, and in the mean time I was eager and happy.

How the three weeks passed it would be hard to tell. Living insubstantially on air, sedulously dreaming dreams and seeing many visions, I seemed to have no part or lot in the prosaic life of the world about me. The world about me knew nothing of the poetic and romantic raptures that swelled my breast and gave a bounding elasticity to my step. I led an existence of my own, impalpable, ethereal, and rosy as the dawn when the sun comes without mist on a summer morning. Were not all the glories of conquest before me? and, more entrancing still, was there not the wild possibility that one whose name I scarcely dared to breathe, even to myself, might help me to bear the weight of that crown of victory that shone afar off on the steep heights which I was to climb? That was really the thought that gave zest to all my enterprises. I saw my name blazoning in the public prints; I saw men, women, and children looking up to me with wonder and admiration; I saw flags flying; heard crowds huzzaing in my honour, and the glorification was very sweet; but it was as nothing to the vision of the radiant being who took her place beside me to share the homage of mankind.

I am not certain whether she had come down from heaven expressly for my sake, or by the special favour of Providence I had been exalted for hers. That is a detail of no consequence. The chief thing was that we stood together on the shining eminence and that her beauty was worshipped and my merits extolled in the same breath.

"Sentimental bosh!" exclaims the practical reader. So be it, my friend; we are not going to quarrel over words, but pray tell me, whose was the delicious experience, yours or mine?

I was a frequent guest at the Elms and saw a good deal of Isabel, whose presence I learned to bear without shrinking or shaking. She talked to me of her life in India, but most of her brother, for whom she had an affection amounting almost to idolatry. There were times when I wished she could spare a trifle for somebody else. But that was a wish I had to keep to myself. It evidently did not occur to her that there was any one outside of her father and brother of whom she might appropriately think with a little tenderness. I could not help considering it an extraordinary oversight on her part; but the matter was delicate, and no suggestion as to the bestowal of any fraction of her regard passed my lips. Nor is it likely my counsel would have availed, even had I ventured to offer it. Women and princes, I have noticed, like to have their own way. But this is between ourselves.

"They may tell you stories about Donald," she once said. "They may say he was a scamp, and all that, for it is easy talking. But don't believe them. He was high-spirited; that was his fault, and my father crossed him. His worst sin was to become a soldier when his friends wanted him to be something else, and the records of the War Office show he was no coward. He saved the British colours when the enemy broke a British square, and has more than once been mentioned in despatches for valour in the field. If he had remained in the army he'd have got almost any rank; but he hadn't peace to do that, and it's since he left it we have lost trace of him."

She never missed a chance of speaking about him. He seemed to fill her whole soul, to be her only thought, a circumstance that, as I have hinted, secretly piqued me not a little.

"Oh," she would often break out in the most irrelevant way, "if you could only find my brother, if you could only find Donald, I should be so grateful to you. But indeed, indeed,"—and here she would look in my face till I thought I saw visions of heaven—"I will be just as grateful to you if you never find him. Words cannot express your goodness in trying."

Then I would reply that if Donald were in India I would find him, a speech which always brought me a rapturous smile of thanks and further visions of Paradise.

I will pass swiftly over the preparations made at Glenrae for my departure. My dear mother took care that my outfit lacked nothing it was possible for her to procure, and even my father softened towards me, busying himself with my affairs and seeming conscience-stricken for having been so stern with me.

"You do well, Angus," he said one evening when we chanced to be by ourselves, and his voice was husky—"you do well, Angus, I have no doubt, in following your own instincts. When you go so far away—for to a home-keeping man like me it is so far away though it is still in God's universe—when you go away, do not forget that we are left behind, and you'll let us hear from you. And as to the other thing, we may find a way out of our troubles. God bless you, my boy. We are all in His hands." And he could say no more.

At dinner on the last evening, Duncan, the coachman, who was also gamekeeper, factor, forester, and general factotum, and had served the Glenraes man and boy for fifty years, got out his pipes and serenaded us in his most stirring manner.

"It is for Mr. Angus," he explained. "He will be going away, God bless him, and be a big man with black servants, and maybe Duncan will never set eyes on him again. And, God bless him, he will have the pipes to his denner whatever, just as loud as auld Duncan's lungs can blaw. Ay, will he too." And so lustily did Duncan blaw, that not a word of conversation could we have during the whole meal. When his pipes were silent, however, and the dusk had fallen, and we three—my father, my mother, and myself—sat together, there was earnest and affecting talk; but no syllable of it will be set down here, for it was for ourselves alone.

Next morning Duncan drove us to meet the stage in the ancient family chariot, which threatened to keep me at home by breaking all my bones and dislocating all my joints. This antique vehicle—a sort of Noah's ark, furnished with springs that would not yield under the roughest bumping, and set on wheels as stout as those of a gun-carriage—had served the Glenraes longer than the memory of living man extended, and was the pride of Duncan, notwithstanding the rude shakings it gave him every time he mounted its box.

"Your new-fangled kerridges will be bonnie things for play," he would say, sententiously, "but they will be going to splinters in a week. I think this will be going to last for ever. They will not be able to make the like of it nowadays."

It was drawn by a team almost as venerable as itself, and certainly as lean as Rosinante—a team, too, most decorously indifferent to any idle manipulations of whip or rein in which a frivolous driver might indulge. It did not, however, take us more than twice as long to drive to Aberfourie as it would have taken me to walk, a fact on which Duncan did not fail to congratulate both himself and his horses.

Early as was the hour, Sir Thomas and Isabel were

waiting, and greeted us with a fervour that was almost silent. Isabel held in her hand a tiny parcel and two little bunches of white heather, on which she looked down from time to time, as I fancied, with some embarrassment. At last she came close to me, and with a soft emotion suffusing her cheek and shining in her eyes, she said—

"This is a miniature of Donald, which may help you to identify him. It is in the uniform of a soldier. And this," handing me the bunches of white heather, "is for luck. One is for Donald—you see I expect you to find him. The other," and her voice fell to a mere whisper, "is for yourself. It will keep you in mind of the old home, and perhaps I may see them both again."

There was no time to reply, for almost before she ceased speaking the shrill notes of a bugle broke upon the morning stillness, and a minute later the stage coach came up at a handsome pace, the horses fresh and mettlesome, and shaking their heads as if eager for the road. All at once half a dozen people pounced upon me as if intent on squeezing the breath out of me. My dear mother clung to me longest and closest, and indeed flatly declined to let me go until the guard had warned her twice. She released me with a passionate kiss, then stood motionless and speechless, gazing at me and weeping silently, as a woman will when she feels the cables of her love slipping. My baggage was already up, farewells were hastily taken, and I mounted to my place, feeling as if I were in an unfamiliar region of mists. Suddenly old Duncan scrambled up beside me, holding a green bag in his hand.

"Take it," he said huskily, pushing it into my arms. "God bless ye, take it. It will be the siller pipes I learned ye to blaw on. Ayont the seas ye'll can gie a skirl at times to mind ye of old friends, and when ye come back ye'll can march to your own quick-step, and maybe Duncan will be there to fling his bonnet in the air. Hooch aye! God bless ye—

God bless ye!" and a tremulous hand patted me on the back as if I were a baby.

Then Duncan leaped down and stalked back to his horses, daring any one to say he was not perfectly calm and self-possessed. He turned once, waving his Glengarry, then climbed on the box and sat as stiff and grim as a bronze image; but I knew that the furrows in his cheeks were streaming.

In another minute the driver of the stage had gathered up the reins, flicked the prancing leaders with his long whip, and we were off. I gazed back, waving my hand to the little group by the inn door till we rounded a bend in the road. Then, seeing none too well, I turned, setting my face resolutely forward.

CHAPTER V.

THE SEARCH FOR DONALD GORDON.

On the journey south, my spirits being now mounting like mercury in the sun, I could not resist the temptation to spend an hour or two in Edinburgh in the delectable diversion of making my old comrades envious. The achievement was not difficult. A few significant hints and the sight of my letters and drafts brought every man of them as near to bursting as the frog in the fable. Some envied me the money, some the adventures, others said it was the beautiful combination of both that took their fancy, and all agreed I had certainly been born with the coveted silver spoon in my mouth.

"It's one of the shameless tricks of Madam Fortune," said an embryonic divine, slapping me on the shoulder. "Here you go out there to ride elephants and shoot tigers and order bronze-faced lackeys and enrich yourself from inexhaustible treasures of gold and gems, while I am left to wrestle with harrowing problems in theology. It's enough to make one forswear divinity."

I was to write them volumes about the wonders of the Indies, and was to give particular information on these two points, namely, the feeling inspired by a wounded tiger charging full upon you when your gun is empty, and what I thought of the heathen gods—from a financial point of view.

"I believe," remarked one with a taste for finance, "those unconscionable pagans make themselves deities of the finest ore set with precious stones, while we haven't cash enough for an afternoon's outing. Just send us a god, Glenrae, till we see how the heathen abomination would melt in the crucible of a Christian goldsmith."

They escorted me in a body to my coach. For being prosperous now acquaintances became friends. At parting I received a unanimous injunction to mind my liver and be on my guard against the encroachments of pride, when, as a nabob with a retinue of slaves, I hobnobbed with the dusky and luxurious potentates of the East, and the start was made in the midst of a riotous burst of cheering.

Only one thing marred my enjoyment. I had it set in my mind to give Peter Clephane the soundest drubbing he had ever had in his life by way of remembrance; but as he happened to be absent in Dundee, my virtuous intent did not blossom into action.

Arrived in London, my first business was to find Captain Rogers. He had heard from Sir Thomas, and received me with great affability and consideration, undertaking to have me bestowed in the best part of the ship, and to let me see something of the town before we started. In me, as I distinctly remembered, our sight-seeing expeditions produced perhaps as much bewilderment as pleasure. I wandered through the seething, roaring desert of the illimitable Babel, eager to learn and admire, yet feeling so utterly out of my element, so much confounded by the din and smoke and rush, by the ruthless self-assertiveness and indifference that seemed to characterize men and things alike, by the squalor and splendour—so grotesquely blended and tragically contrasted—in a word, so dazed by the distracting throb and tumult of a nation's mighty heart, that I had neither wit to observe properly nor power to enjoy.

Yet there were times when the mystic charm of wandering among storied and historic scenes, and treading, as it were, in the very footsteps of heroes with whose fame the world had rung bore in upon me through the confusion. Beyond all question I was in a realm of romance—a realm full of astonishing things, some to be contemplated with wonder, some with amusement, and not a few with awe and reverence.

I stood on the grave of genius in Westminster Abbey, meditated among the sepulchres of kings, loitered in dim cloisters suggestive of a departed world, and read the essence of England's history on mural tablet and time-eaten monument. It was affectingly solemn and still in that community of the dead, so solemn and so still one could hardly believe that but a few yards off was the confounding din of the restless city.

I looked dizzily up at big St. Paul's, with its swelling dome and glittering cross crowning the height of Ludgate Hill, and thought of the time when the Roman eagles flew there and strange gods were worshipped where stands the Christian sanctuary. Rounding St. Paul's Churchyard I thought, too, of the time when a peaceful "river flowed down the vale of Cheapside," where now are adamantine pavements and the throng and roar of multitudinous traffic. I visited the Tower, not without a little chill of horror at its grimness and grisly associations. I looked down from London Bridge on the black swirling waters of the mighty river, in whose sullen bosom disappointment and disgrace have so often sought and found oblivion. I watched the coming and going of the rich City merchants whose argosies are on every sea, whose operations rule the marts of the world; the streams of vehicles, the thronging processions of men, women, and children, wondering much whither they were all bound and what they could all be about. Turn where I might there were immensity and uproar, the clatter of hoofs, the grinding of wheels, the confused blending of cries delivered in a thousand varying voices, from the piercing treble of the huckster calling his petty wares to the savage deep-chested growl and snarl of the quarrelling omnibus driver or carman,—a chaos of noise that (I was told) ceased not day or night.

Some famous men I saw also, and of one in particular I must tell. Captain Rogers had taken me to Hyde Park to feast my eyes on the greatness and fashion of the metropolis. As we went along marking this and that notability, and making our own comments, suddenly the captain caught my arm. "Look, look," he cried, pointing with his finger; "there's the greatest man in England, ay, sir, or in Europe."

I looked and saw sitting upright in a modest brougham a very old lean man of gentle aspect, with straggling white hair, a colourless face, and a hooked nose.

"That's the man who trounced Buonaparte, sir. That's Wellington," added my guide eagerly.

I needed no more; my blood was on fire at once, and, dragging Captain Rogers with me I ran after the idol of my boyhood. Fortunately he proceeded very slowly, being impeded by the press of admiring people and the duty of acknowledging their courtesies.

"Don't be up to any nonsense now," whispered Captain Rogers, gripping my arm. "Remember where you are."

"Have no fear," I answered excitedly, "have no fear." But from the manner in which he held me it was plain he had much fear.

We passed the Iron Duke, turned and met him; then getting as close to him as was possible, I doffed my hat and bowed. Turning half round he smiled upon me with a little nod. In another minute he

5

was lost among the crowd, and I saw him no more; but among my memorable bits of memories remains that passing glimpse of the Victor of Waterloo.

When the time came to sail, the river sides were thronged with people to witness the spectacle of our departure; for that being near the beginning of the era of steam, our start was a matter of public interest. It was still thought a miraculous thing to see a huge three-decker sailing off with never a stitch of canvas set, nor any visible means of getting forward save by a wheel that frantically churned the water into foam; and if it was strange to the spectators on shore to see a big ship going bravely on independently of wind and tide, I must own it was rather disquieting to one at least of those on board to be caged up on the waters with a belching, pounding, wheezing, screeching, fire-demon, that seemed to be crying out in eternal agony and struggling with all its frenzied might to burst its bonds and wreak destruction on all about it. Often in the night have I lain listening to it in its miniature pandemonium, never silent, never slumbering, never for one brief moment at peace, but for ever wrenching and writhing, for ever setting up the same inappeasable cry of labouring pain and the same terrible threat of vengeance. Nowadays we have grown so familiar with the fire-fiend that, as it were, we stroke him complacently on the back; but I never come near him in steamer or hissing locomotive without a shudder at the thought of the vengeance he may one day wreak on the world.

But in that fresh experience, curiosity and interest soon mastered fear. There was gladness in the ease and speed with which our flame-fed slave carried us down the river and along the coast of Kent, and past "the tall white cliffs of Dover," the last prominent spot on which the exile's straining eye rests when he is leaving England for the East, and the first on which it wistfully falls when happily he returns. The sun was going down in a soft suffusion of colour as we entered the strait, casting a glamorous iridescent light on the receding land and the sails of the many stately ships that were bearing gallantly up and down, some like ourselves outward bound, others, their wanderings for the present over, bound for the home we had left. I stood on the deck gazing backward till the land melted into darkness; then Captain Rogers quietly slipped his arm in mine and we went below to supper.

The *Pearl of the Orient* made a quick and prosperous passage, landing us in Bombay in a day less than the time reckoned for the voyage before starting. You may be sure I did not allow Sir Thomas's business to lag.

Having presented my letters of introduction and undergone a brief but fiery course of hospitality, I set vigorously to the work before me, assisted by the numerous friends of my patron. I had no difficulty in discovering that Donald Gordon had been in Bombay some eighteen months before, and had suddenly disappeared. But whither he had gone, whether he had departed by land or by sea, or been despatched by the hand of the assassin, no one had the least idea. There were of course conjectures in plenty. He might be hunting in the jungle, or taking the cool air among the hills, or trafficking with oily natives in another town; he might be in China, or Japan, or Australia, or the South Sea Islands, or Peru, or in the interior of some enterprising shark; the possibilities were endless—but there was only one certainty, that he had completely slipped all his friends in Bombay.

In endeavoring to trace him I did all that a man might do for his best friend. At the peril of my life and against urgent and earnest advice, I explored the plague-spots of the native city—spots which disseminated all manner of foul and festering disease—salaaming and embracing and swearing brotherhood with loathsome and astonished Hindoos and Parsees, and assuring hawk-eyed hostile Moslems (whose full-

er acquaintance I was to make by-and-by) that beyond doubt there was but one Prophet and Mohammed was his name. I roused suspicions concerning
both my sanity and my honesty by the way in which
I interrogated wealth and lay in wait on Malabar
Hill. I haunted temples, dodging imprudently
among idols till I incurred the wrath of the bloodthirsty Siva,* whose apostles followed me with murderous knives concealed in their garments to exact
atonement for my sacrilege. I consorted with riotous sailors of all climes and many profane tongues,
till zealous missionaries shook their heads and spoke
gravely of contamination. I frequented bazaars,
public gatherings, and questionable places of recrea-
tion, and did many other things which respectable
people, under ordinary conditions, would have studiously refrained from doing.

But of none of these things did I tell my correspondents at the Elms or Glenrae. Nor were they
informed that I had invoked the aid of the police
and of every detective, public and private, in the
city, and that we had all failed to find so much as a
single clue.

In my first report, then, I had nothing better to
send than hope, of which I was no niggard. I
stated, truthfully enough I trust, that I had already
learned something about Donald; also, I fear not
quite so truthfully, that I was not without reasona-
ble ground for thinking that he and I should shortly
have a dish of curry together.

Had I written what was in my mind, I should
have said frankly, that so far as could then be seen,
there was not the remotest chance of being able to
trace him. Perhaps the better course would have
been to say that. I saw this more clearly when the
letter was gone, and I had stronger reason to con-
clude he must be really dead.

I argued in this way: Donald Gordon has a multitude of friends in Bombay, and if he wished to leave

* The Hindoo god of destruction.

he would certainly have told them of his intention, and the direction he purposed to take, and what he intended to do. There is ample evidence that he never breathed a syllable to one of them of any plan for the future. Moreover, there is a considerable sum of money standing to his credit with his father's bankers; he knew it had been lodged there for his use, and considering his extremely precarious and slender means of living, and the almost absolute necessity of money to a European in the East, is it probable that he would decline to take advantage of this provision which had been made for him? Then there is the curious circumstance that he was last seen a few hours after he must have received the banker's letter apprising him of the deposit which had been made to his credit. Supposing this letter was seen by others, would not the money be a great temptation to a needy villain, who might take the risk of attempting to secure it by getting rid of Donald, but finding the thing impossible as he proceeded abandoned the project ere any one became aware of its existence?

All this I reasoned with myself over and over again, and the more I reasoned the firmer became my conviction that Donald Gordon must be dead. He did not die in the orthodox fashion, else there would be a record of his death, but there was no evidence that he ever left the city; and he was not it in now.

I laid my conclusion before the bankers and some others; they all said it was plausible—"only," said one, "you forget Donald's pride. He was the proudest man I ever knew in my life; indeed he was silly in that way." And to be sure there was Donald's pride to be taken into account. But it did not aid us. At the end of two months I had exhausted my own ingenuity, and that of all my friends and assistants, without coming on a single trace of Donald. If he were dead, he was buried beyond hope of discovery; if he had gone away, he had most effectually covered up his steps, had indeed left as little track as a shadow leaves. There seemed to be nothing for it but to abandon the search, write my dismal report, remit Sir Thomas his money, and turn to my own concerns. My friends admitted it really was the only thing to be done.

"Indeed, Mr. Glenrae," said Mr. Macdonald, a banker at whose dinner-table the matter was discussed, "if it were a financial speculation, depending for return of profit on the finding of the volatile Donald Gordon—who, for aught I know, has the power of making himself invisible—I am bound to confess I would have nothing to do with it. It seems unquestionable that Mr. Donald has gone, desiring no further news of his friends; and I think you are right in giving up the chase. And now that you have disposed of Sir Thomas Gordon's business, might I ask what your plans are for yourself?"

I was obliged to answer that I had no definite plans as yet, having been so absorbed in the hunt for Gordon that I had had no time to think of myself; but now I would certainly look out for an opening.

"As to that," said he, "there is a desk at your disposal in the house of Macdonald, Mactavish, and Mackintosh—good Scots names all of them, you will observe—any time you may feel inclined to begin work. The emoluments will be sufficient to enable you to live pending the finding of something better, should you not take kindly to figures and a three-legged stool."

"I have had some knowledge of Highlanders," put in Mr. Matheson, one of the merchant princes to whom I had a letter of introduction—"I have had some knowledge of Highlanders, and I hardly ever saw one of them feel at home at a desk. Put a gun, or a sword, or a tarry rope, or anything else that means fresh air and activity, in their hands, and they're as much at home as a rabbit in a sandhill. But that's not saying that Mr. Glenrae would not take kindly to banking. If he's after rupees he will for his own sake;" and Mr. Matheson cast a glance of intelligence at his friend.

I hastened to say that I was very grateful to Mr. Macdonald for his generous offer, and that, with his permission, I would keep it under consideration for a day or two.

"Quite right, Mr. Glenrae, quite right," said Mr. Macdonald, cordially. "Look well before you leap, especially in this land of deceits; though, to tell you the truth, and never flatter, you have done so well in this Gordon business that I should like to catch you. However, I say again you are quite right to avoid a rash decision. A false step involves a change; and —though the proverb says that changes are light-some, it adds that only fools are fond of them. I am not one of those who pin their faith to proverbs—good or bad. If a rolling stone does not gather moss it often gathers what is a great deal better than moss—an auriferous coating that we are all glad to admire. But too many changes are not prudent, so don't decide hastily. It's a poor business getting out of the frying-pan into the fire, and back again from the fire into the frying-pan. Avoid it."

"And that you may have an alternative, Mr. Glenrae," added Mr. Matheson, "let me say that in a week or two, I have a vessel starting for Jedda, and that you are welcome to a free trip if you choose. It will enable you to look about, and give you an opportunity to think out your plans. The trip will not take long altogether. It will be a holiday to you if nothing more, which after your hard work as a detective will, I dare say, be grateful. What do you say to that, Macdonald?"

"Capital," answered Mr. Macdonald. "Let Mr. Glenrae go by all means. The followers of the Prophet are worth cultivating, and the trip will widen his horizon if it shouldn't put many rupees in his pocket. Scotsmen like a wide horizon, Mr. Glenrae. I'll wager a singed sheep's head you'll find some of our countrymen guarding Fatima's tomb and making the job pay."

He laughed softly as a man laughs who has good reason to enjoy his own jest.

I thanked Mr. Matheson, as I had thanked Mr. Macdonald, saying that as the ship was not sailing immediately I would think the matter over. But the suggestion pleased me, whereas, though sincerely grateful to Mr. Macdonald, I was not in love with the idea of perching on a stool.

The upshot was that I declined Mr. Macdonald's offer, and decided to visit Arabia in Mr. Matheson's ship. The kindly banker would not, however, take a final answer, but said that the post should be kept open till my return, as ships and tarry sailors might by that time have lost their attraction. If he has kept his word, there has been a vacant desk in that establishment for a very long time.

The decision made, my next piece of business was to write home—a long letter to Glenrae, and another to the Elms. The Glenrae letter was out of hand with no effort; but the one to Sir Thomas was a different matter entirely. I felt a great pity for the poor gentleman, which I durst not express, lest he should die of heartbreak; so that my communication had to be somewhat of the nature of a diplomatic despatch. Unhappily, the task of composing it called for gifts with which I was but scantily endowed. I wrote the letter and rewrote it, and again wrote it; then took it to bed to dream over, undoing the whole thing on the morrow, and going through such agonies of composition as do not make me envy the life of an author. On the third day my patience was exhausted, and the clumsy essay in diplomacy was posted. It tried to make out that there was abundant hope for the future, while there was also a sufficient reason for abandoning the search at present; but I fancy it could not have imposed on anybody. To put the better face on the thing, I fabricated a little fiction about the severe heat telling on my health, and being advised to take a short sea-trip. I trust I shall be forgiven, for the motive was good; and I know that, acute as must have been Sir Thomas's disappointment, it was not any acuter than my own; for if his hope was centred in Donald, so also was mine.

CHAPTER VI.

DISENCHANTMENT AND DESPAIR.

WHILE the *Bird of Paradise*—such was the alluring name of our gallant brig—was being loaded with a cargo of cashmere shawls, cocoanuts, drugs, glass beads, and other articles of merchandise likely to suit the cultured Mahommedan taste, I was so closely engaged with my own concerns and the urgent hospitality of Sir Thomas's friends, that I paid but scant heed to the men with whom I was to sail. I had a vague notion of a picturesque medley of dusky children of the sun who would be likely, in the course of the voyage, to discourse of many marvellous things, and discover traits at once new and interesting. But at sea, and within the narrow confines of a two-master, one is impelled to take an active individual interest in his companions; and so it came that as soon as the towers and spires of Bombay had sunk out of sight on our weather beam, I was eagerly and curiously studying my surroundings, and the characters of officers and crew.

Never was mortal more swiftly or completely disenchanted. Perhaps it was because I was young and foolish and ignorant that I had so gaily cherished illusion, perhaps it was the fine name of the brig that had given me exalted and gorgeous ideas; but I had anticipated a holiday sail on sunlit seas in a sort of Cleopatra barge, with companions fitly representing, if not the pomp and magnificence, at least the poetry and romance of the Orient. My punishment for indulging such fantastic reveries was speedy and condign. The *Bird of Paradise* bore as much resemblance to the ship of my imagination as a hedgehog bears to a leopard. In plain truth, she was an ill-smelling, leaky old coal-bunker, with a crew of the most villainous-looking desperadoes that ever swung from a yard-arm. What their past had been it required little shrewdness to guess. A child could have told that whatever pleasure, whatever romance there could be in sailing with the dregs of Asiatic pirate crews, of men who, for reasons to be comprehended by the simplest, had found it expedient to lay aside for a little their natural vocation of cutting throats, such pleasure and romance were mine. Naturally, I was amazed to find such men on Mr. Matheson's ship, but the explanation came later. I had forgotten that the Scotch are frugal! and did not know how Asia pours her scum upon the sea.

My security, such as it was, lay in the fact that, among themselves, there was not the least evidence of good will. They regarded each other with open aversion, at times even with savage hatred. Sullen, suspicious, and incommunicative, in all their lives they had probably never known what it is to smile out of pure good nature or innocent hilarity. For their features were fixed in a perpetual scowl which nothing could soften. Towards each other, as towards their officers, they had the sulky, defiant demeanour of caged beasts of prey, and, no doubt, they had a sense of imprisonment. Off duty or on, they indulged in no freedom or jollity of intercourse. No stories were told, no songs were sung. You would have listened in vain for the hilarious laugh or the jovial ditty from the forecastle; but if you had hearkened close you might have heard mumbled threats and deadly curses in plenty. The spirit was that of a chain-gang working at the point of the bayonet or the muzzle of the rifle. Misfortune, failure in hazardous and bloody enterprises, had brought them together, and though the proverb says that crime puts those on an equal footing whom it defiles, yet somehow these rogues were not able to fraternize.

The officers matched the crew. Though Captain Holden was an Englishman and Mr. Malcolm, the mate, Scotch, there was nothing gracious or prepossessing in either of them. The captain was short and broad, square rigged, with a tremendous breadth of beam, as a sailor would say, and his squat, burly frame had in it the muscular strength and energy of the tiger. His face, hairy as a Skye terrier's, showed no feature in particular, save the huge nose, which a long course of grog had turned to the likeness of a purple knob, and bulging eyebrows that hung over small deep-set eyes as a cliff overhangs a cavern. His visage was truculent, and his temper and voice were in harmony. His most caressing tones were the growl of the thunder, his anger was the fury of a fiend. His natural qualities, too, had been well cultivated. The broadside of oaths he poured upon his men when anything went amiss was an achievement in profanity to be remembered with a creepy shudder for a lifetime, and the gleam of his eyes, and the way in which he fingered his pistols under the stress of passion, indicated that he had no childish reverence for the sanctity of human life.

As might be expected, his career had been eventful, his experiences startling and varied. He boasted—and I am sure truthfully—that he could show more seams and scars than any other man of his size then living. "A man with a greater extent of hide might beat me," he would sometimes say, "but to the square inch show me him who equals me. By Jupiter, if I was to preach on that kind of tattooing, a week would be too short for my sermon." And you immediately assented.

The mate could not be described as being of a milder natural disposition, but only as being less fully developed. His name for cruelty was less eminent than his chief's, but he was training fast, and gave high promise of brutality. Meanwhile he garnished his speech plentifully with blood-curdling expletives, took his grog and practised assiduously on the crew. The first day out he knocked a sailor down with a marline-spike, under the very eyes of the captain, who was too indifferent even to curse approvingly. A little later he sent another head foremost into the hold (which happened to be open thus early on the voyage), without so much as casting a downward glance to see whether the man were dead or alive, and not a day passed that he did not distinguish himself by some deed of tyranny or violence.

Such, in brief, were my shipmates, and it will be easily understood how quickly and completely my dreams of a holiday voyage vanished.

It enhanced the discomforts of the situation that I fancied myself regarded by the captain and mate as an interloper, a spy, whose proper place was with the sharks outside. But on that point I was unwittingly flattering myself. Neither of them troubled his head in the least about me, nor ever came near me, except it were by chance, or in the way of duty. To be sure, the captain usually rolled out some hoarse greeting when we met in the morning, but he never delayed his step for conversation, and never once evinced a desire to know how I was enjoying myself. Only at meal-times did we come into close contact, and then I was glad to get back to the deck and the disinfecting air of heaven.

Nor was the mate much more sociable. One evening indeed he spoke to me of Scotland, but as his talk was of nothing but fallen angels fuddling in taverns about the Broomielaw and riotous orgies by drunken sailors, I did not encourage him. He left me with a feeling of profound contempt, never again making any attempt to draw me into conversation. When we met, his looks declared as plainly as looks could that I was a priggish, puritanical landsman, who

was no fit company for a jolly blasphemous seaman
like himself.

Mr. Watson, the supercargo, was the only soul on
board who took the smallest interest in me, or with
whom I cared to speak. He understood my position,
and, I think, had compassion for me. At any rate
he tolerated my amateurish views of seafaring men
and things, and sought opportunity to discover topics
we could discuss with mutual pleasure. He was
fond of talking of Edinburgh, which he knew well,
having attended the High School there. We com-
pared notes on our reading, and he was certainly not
the worse read man of the two.

"This roving, free and easy life, Mr. Glenrae," he
said one day, "has a tendency, as Burns says, to
'harden a' within, and petrify the feelings,' but I try
to keep a fresh sweet corner in my affections for the
thoughts and fancies of choice souls. After all, a
good book is better than their riotous games at nine-
pins with virtue and character, and to read about a
pretty girl is better than to go about carousing with
an ugly and debauched one. As Sancho Panza says
about sleep, God bless the man who invented books."

Books, however, were the subjects of our by-talk
only. Our conversations included India, Arabia,
and many other quarters of the globe; but oftenest
they were about our companions.

"Just look at them, Mr. Glenrae," said Mr. Watson once; "aren't they a pretty set? Haven't they
the look of having been born, bred, trained, edu-
cated, for the special purpose of giving the hangman
a job? Without the testimony of your eyes, could
you imagine that so much villainy could be condensed within a few skins, and on a small trading
brig? Old Nick would blush for them; for he—if
reports be true—is a gentleman, and it's libelling him
to suppose he would risk his reputation with such
gibbet birds. You have the felicity, sir, and I hope
you appreciate it, of making companionship with the
flower and blossom, nay, the choice ultimate fruit of

all the vices ever engrafted on the unlucky seed of Adam. Study them; you will never have such a chance again of observing finished and perfected cutthroats. Innocent folks in England talk of the Newgate Calendar and shudder. I wish they could come here to have their nerves braced. They would return home firm in the conviction that poor Jack, who was hanged for his little frolics, was a pattern of virtue and respectability."

"And how in the name of wonder do these men come to be on Mr. Matheson's ship?" I asked.

Mr. Watson screwed his face knowingly, and winked.

"Ah, ha! now you are asking questions," he laughed. "How comes the purse to rule the conscience? Mr. Matheson was born ayont the Tweed, and knows the value of bawbees. These rinsings of creation are got cheap, because they're flying from the scaffold."

"Flying from the scaffold? How do you know?"

"From experience and the modicum of wit Heaven gave me. Respectability's a thing we don't care to pay for on East India traders. And that minds me, are you armed, Mr. Glenrae?"

"As Nature armed me," I rejoined. "I did not think it was necessary to come on board Mr. Matheson's ship armed."

"Necessity's often as you take it," he said significantly. "In this golden clime it might not be necessary to wear clothes, but you do it all the same. A pistol's not heavy, and sometimes it's very handy. I always carry one, and this little thing besides;" and turning up the edge of his waistcoat he revealed the handle of a dagger.

"That's to prog them who might take a thought of progging me," he remarked. "I have found it useful at close quarters more than once. Come this way, Mr. Glenrae."

He led me to his cabin, which was office and bedroom in one. When we were inside he carefully closed and fastened the door; then getting upon his knees he unlocked a heavy iron box, which, notwithstanding its immense weight, was fixed to the floor with iron rivets.

"This is for the ship's papers," he explained, looking up with a smile of intelligence. "But you can put more than hats in a band-box. Here take your choice of these!" And he lifted an armful of pistols.

I drew back a step with a quick sensation of chilliness. The startling discoveries were crowding too closely upon each other for my nerves.

"Oh, you'd better have one," he said, in his matter-of-fact way. "It's nasty to be caught unprepared. I dare say you know something about firearms."

"I know more about fowling-pieces than pistols," I answered, taking one with a trembling hand.

"Well, well, you'll soon get used to it. Nothing trains a man with the pistol like knowing he may be turned into a target at less than a moment's notice."

"And do you really mean to say there's danger?"

"When you've been a little longer at sea, you'll spare yourself the trouble of asking such a question," he answered with a little laugh.

"I know I must appear lamentably ignorant," I said humbly; "but the plain fact is I was not prepared for this."

"Tut, tut. God bless me; don't take it so much to heart then," returned Mr. Watson, cheerfully. "We must all begin life. The best of us is born soft, you know, and continues soft till the world and the devil (people put them together and name them destiny) have done the hardening."

"Then there is danger?" I said, for that was the point on which my mind dwelt.

"There you are again," responded Mr. Watson, gaily. "That's just as you look at it. If the risk of being killed without time for prayers is danger, then a blunt man might have to confess we're not in the safest place in the world. That's a good one, Mr. Glenrae; take it with you."

I stowed the weapon away while he rummaged in the box.

"Here, will you have one of these?" he asked a moment later, holding up a sheaf of daggers.

But they were too suggestive, and I declined the offer.

"Well, well, so be it," he remarked, putting back daggers and pistols into their place. "Since you won't have a dagger, I suppose it's no use offering you a sword. No, I thought so. Well, now for the copestone of the counsel," he continued, standing erect and looking me straight in the eyes. "Don't let any one get too familiar. The moment you smell trouble draw and blaze away. If you don't kill they will; if you do kill, it's but justice anyway. If you hesitate or deliberate you're lost. And now lest they should suspect a plot let's go out." Saying which he opened the door, and we went on deck.

For the rest of that day I was hot, nervous, depressed and ill at ease, yet with a certain feeling of consequence. Firearms give courage as the saddle confers authority. The touch of my pistol-hilt thrilled me, and many a time did I surreptitiously slip in my hand just to gain assurance by grasping it.

I kept, as you may think, a vigilant eye on the crew, for though there was not a whit more danger now than there had been from the beginning, I detected treachery and a murderous intent in every act and look of the men. I expected bloodshed, and tried to convince myself I was prepared for it.

But, indeed, it was to matter little to me whether I were armed or not. The feeling of heat and depression grew upon me hour by hour. At first I naturally referred it to my conversation with Mr. Watson. But in this I was mistaken. I went to bed deadly sick, to toss in a feverish paroxysm through the long night, and next morning I was so giddy that on attempting to rise I staggered and sank to the floor. When I gathered myself together the room was whirling like a huge spinning-wheel, carrying me with it in its gyrations. Steadying myself a little, I managed to crawl back to my berth on hands and knees, my eyes wellnigh sightless, and my brows throbbing as if there were steam machinery inside. My skin burned with a prickly heat, and my throat and tongue were parched, sore, and swollen.

"I am in for it," I groaned; "God in heaven! and in such a hole as this!"

And presently, when Mr. Watson looked in to see why I was not getting up, my worst fears were confirmed.

"I'm devilish sorry to see this," he said, after examining me and hearing my symptoms. "Don't be frightened, but you've got the fever that Portuguese chap died of. You must have brought it on board with you; it was raging in some quarters of the city. I'm devilish sorry, we're so ill off for medicine, or indeed for anything that a sick body needs. But we'll do our best; and mind, if you go and die on our hands, I'll never forgive you. I'll make you snug, and then I'll send the captain to see you."

In the course of half an hour or so, the captain came in and looked at me for a moment, as he would at a sick beast.

"Going to kick the bucket, youngster, eh?" he said, in a voice as hard as the nether millstone. "Keep her head to the sea, and you may ride the storm, though I kin see you're pretty bad. Mr. Matheson might be worried if you was to go off on his ship." Then he asked some perfunctory questions and left me.

A little later the mate, too, came in, and his kindness was, if possible, more cruel than the captain's callousness.

"There's no saying how this may go, you know, Mr. Glenrae," he said, after lying in his throat by saying he was sorry for me. "Fevers on board ship are like simoons in these seas; you never know what's to be the upshot. On East India traders, too, sick

C

folks have less chance of making port than their friends could wish.   There's little room, evil smells, no resources, and the devil for physician.   If you have any message you would like delivered to your friends, or anything to return to Scotland, I am at your service.   Maybe there's some relics you'd like returned or something of that sort."

A man may be dying, but it hurts him to be brutally told so.   For the first time in my existence I appreciated the boon of life, the simple privilege of continuing to be and of the sovereign balm of sympathy.

I shook with fright and great beads broke out on my brow.   Yet neither sickness nor fear could keep off anger.   To die with fortitude, to renounce hopes, schemes, ambitions, to lay down life in its rosy morning hours when the world is full of promise of bliss, to do this at a moment's notice and with resignation is possible, but it is not in human nature to be grateful for cruelty.   The disease had not yet wholly mastered my spirit; there was one fierce spark left, and so, rising on my elbow and speaking in a voice that trembled and quivered, I ordered the man off.

"Go!" I said.   "Let me never look on your face again.   And when you come to die, pray you have a better comforter."

He went without a sign of compassion or contrition, indeed with a smirk of disdain, and I, falling back with a feeling of being forsaken by God and man, lost heart, and a scalding torrent soaked the coarse blankets.   And in that moment of dire punishment, as if present evils were not enough, there smote upon my conscience the lightning-like stroke of an accusing memory.   The thwarted plans of my father, the unheeded sorrow of my mother, were as arrows of fire in my soul.   Fate had, indeed, permitted me to please myself, but she was now exacting payment, and it was my life.

I had a feeling, I say, of being forsaken, but in the graciousness of Providence I had a friend even now. Not long after the mate left me, Mr. Watson returned, gave me some medicine, spoke cheerfully to me, telling me to keep up my heart, for that many a man had had fever on shipboard and lived long years after to tell the tale. But I could see that out of his humanity he was dissembling his real thoughts, and so I determined, if possible, to get at them.

"You have seen cases of this sort before," I said. "Is it serious? Be plain and tell me if you think I have a chance to pull through."

He seemed unwilling to answer the question, which of course was an incentive to me to press him.

"If you don't answer," I said, "I'll know it's because you're afraid to tell me the worst."

"You know the old proverb, Mr. Glenrae," he returned, slowly, "that while there's life there's hope."

"Just so," I said,. "and that in cases like mine doesn't mean much, or rather it means a great deal."

"I will not mislead you, Mr. Glenrae," he rejoined, shifting about uneasily on his feet. "I think you have a bad attack, and this is a foul hole, and we are without proper remedies. But then you are young, and have a good constitution, and that, as any doctor will tell you, is worth gallons of drugs."

"Thank you," I said. "I wanted your candid opinion."

And now when I thought there was no chance of life, I grew calmer. Indeed, my fear almost vanished; for as the wind is tempered to the shorn lamb, there is hardly an evil but brings its anodyne with it.

Mr. Watson left me abruptly, but presently he came back carrying a book in his hand. By this time I was posting hard to the stage of dreamy indifference, and thought he was going to employ his leisure in reading a story to me. But it was a Bible, not a story book, that the good soul held in his hand.

"Well, mate," he said, with an odd falsetto inflection, as he sidled sheepishly up to my bed, "I have been a good many years out of Scotland, and have forgotten much of the training of my youth and the customs of my native land; but the memory of them all isn't quite gone, and I am going to do now what I think your mother would be well pleased with;" and, sitting down on the edge of my berth, he began to read.

His voice had a tremor in it unnatural in one bred to the sea. He coughed a good deal, too; indeed, he seemed to have infinite difficulty with his throat; and when he looked at me, it was furtively, from the corner of his eye, as if he wished to evade my gaze. I remember dimly wondering what could be the matter with him, and why he was acting so strangely. I don't think I had the least idea that his emotion was for me; I don't think I any longer connected external events or circumstances with my own condition or existence. I have an impression that I tried to comfort Mr. Watson; for he moved my pity. Then as that mood passed (all my humours were fleeting) he got mixed up in the most fantastic fashion with scenes and persons he had never seen or heard of; and there were moments when I could have laughed outright at the incongruous figure he cut. And then he would pass out of my reckoning altogether, and I would find myself suddenly in the midst of old friends, or performing some prodigious feat of strength and agility such as mortal had never attempted before. I leaped from lofty towers without hurting myself, scaled precipices hundreds of feet high at a single bound, wrestled a score of men at once, and triumphantly threw them all, fought wilder beasts than were ever known at Ephesus and did many other marvellous things to my own perfect joy and satisfaction.

Occasionally I got into ugly scrapes, but my supernatural dexterity got me easily out of them all. Again I would change my identity with the facility of the hero of a fairy-tale, to revel in phantasmagorial antics that the sane imagination cannot picture. Sometimes I was myself, and sometimes I was somebody else; but so far as I can recollect I was never for an instant a fever-stricken wretch on board a poisonous ship.

I came back from one of my flights to find Mr. Watson on his knees by my bedside. His attitude dimly suggested distress. I understood from him afterwards that, putting out my hand, I patted him encouragingly on the head, telling him not to take misfortunes so much to heart; that his troubles would blow over and leave him happier than ever. And then I have a vision of a figure, with streaming eyes, bending over me and nervously twining his fingers in mine. Yet oddly enough the first words I can recall were singularly at variance with his appearance.

"Damme if I've played the parson for years before," he laughed, furtively drawing the back of his hand across his eyes; and then, as if fearing an answer, he hurried away.

It might be that same evening, or it might be some days or even a week later, for I have but a vague and confused memory of that period, that he rushed into my cabin with a deathly face, and, in an extremely excited manner, began to bawl something in my ear. I thought his behaviour very extraordinary, and told him so. But he only bawled the louder and the more frantically. Trying hard to make him out, I discovered presently that his incoherent talk was about the brig. What he wanted to tell me, however, I could not in the least guess. "Now, it's a pitiable thing," I said to myself, "to see a nice respectable man in drink. The poor fellow hasn't the remotest notion what he's saying or trying to say."

Catching the word "waterspout" I connected it at once with familiar waterfalls in the Highlands; these again, by a natural sequence, with angling expeditions and baskets of trout, and so on through a long train of memories. I was recalled by a sudden jar which made the brig tremble and vibrate to her centre. "What is that?" I demanded.

"They are firing cannon on deck to break it," he roared. He made ludicrous grimaces at me as he bellowed, but for the sake of friendship I let that pass.

"Don't you think that a very foolish thing to do?" I asked. "Clearly I am among madmen!" I reflected. "I only hope their insanity is of the harmless kind."

"Good God!" yelled Mr. Watson, with a face that was comical in its terror., "The brig is going down. That gun was fired to break the spout."

The announcement made no impression on my disordered brain.

"Going down!" I repeated, amused at the illusion. "Why that is stark, clean impossible. Try and pull yourself together."

"For Heaven's sake, Glenrae, rouse yourself," he cried again in a shriller, more fearful voice than before. "I tell you we are going down. There's not an instant to be lost."

As he spoke the brig lurched violently, so that I was hurled against the back of my berth. At the same time there was a deafening noise as of thunder and splintering wood. What Mr. Watson's words failed to do the shock did. I sat up awake, conscious, terrified, and burning to know what was happening.

But before I could ask a question there was another crash, as if a sudden blow had rent our timbers, and the brig flew up at the bows like a fisherman's punt when a heavy weight is swung on behind. I had my sconce dented in the bunk, and Mr. Watson swept the floor with his back like a kind of incontinent besom. When in the rebound the stern went up in turn I fell back to my place breathless and helpless, and the supercargo, scrambling to his feet with the cat-like agility of a sailor, made desperately for the companion-way. Then for an instant the vessel seemed to lie still, but the next she was reeling and dancing like an eggshell in a boiling caldron. Now she would rear from the bows, now from the stern, then tumble on her beam-ends, careening till mast and keel must have been level, then rebound, then spring, shaking herself like a thing demented with pain, and all the while she cried and groaned in every timber with a terrorizing, human-like sense of the pangs of dissolution. I clung to my bunk with all my feeble might, unable to discern anything clearly, yet conscious, in spite of darkness and terror, of the swish of water rushing through the open door.

After a while Mr. Watson came back, his face ghastly, his manner maniacal. I looked at him beseechingly for news, for in the tumult I could not hope to make myself heard. He did not keep me long in suspense.

"Smashed by the stern, smashed all over," he shouted at the pitch of his voice, bending over me as he held on by the side of my berth. "The spout hit us, carrying with it masts and rigging, and now we're reeling in the grip of a tornado. The fury of the pit's let loose on us. Wind and fire and water, heaven and hell and the sea, all contending against us. And worse than that we're waterlogged, and the infernal crew threatening to take to the boats. Captain's keeping them at it with the pistol. Keep you still, I'll come back again."

I could say nothing, I could do nothing, only lie and listen to the raging of pandemonium, and speculate what would come of it all. Presently Mr. Watson returned, his face whiter than ever.

"The brig's done for," he shouted. "The first blow killed her. It's terrific. I have been through simoon and tornado, and never saw anything like this. They're going to batten down, though Heaven knows why. I must run. But don't you be frightened, I'll not desert you."

He bolted up the companion-way, and the hatches closed with a bang.

I passed an eternity hearkening in the darkness, which the lightning made lurid, expecting every moment to feel the suction and hear the gurgle of death as the ship went down. But we were dying hard.

By-and-by I began to think that the fury of the tempest was abating, and that the movements of the brig were steadier. Then I wondered why they were keeping me closed down there like a rat in its hole. Another eternity passed ere there was any evidence that I was remembered. At last the hatches were thrown open, and I looked with joyful and frantic anxiety for Mr. Watson. To my horror he did not come. Sicker with fear than disease I got to my elbow to listen. In a momentary lull of the blast I heard the rattle of ropes on the ship's side, and then a splash as if some flat-bottomed object had struck the water. A terrible fear, a terrible suspicion struck into my vitals, and, weak as I was I rose, and groping my way through the darkness to a port-hole thrust my face against the glass. There were boats alongside, and the officers and crew, who looked like demons in the livid light, were struggling and fighting to get into them. With the frenzy of death, twisting and tugging and tearing, I tried to open the port, but the screws were stiff and my fingers nerveless, and I failed. Then, my face hard against the glass, I shrieked as only a lost man can shriek. The next instant the glass was in shivers, and I was imploring those without not to abandon me. But the tempest drowned my voice; no one heard, at least no one heeded me. One by one, in the hellish conflagration of sea and sky, the boats rowed away, leaving me alone on the sinking brig.

CHAPTER VII.

I ABANDON HOPE.

BY the glare of streaming fires I could watch the boats driving deliriously before the wind, which still blew with hurricane force. To any eye but that sharpened by the terror of despair the flying, leaping specks would not have been distinguishable from momentary rifts in the careering billows. For in that terrific scene nothing was distinct, nothing individual; there was no ocean and no sky, but high and low a whirling chaos of foam and spray, with gleams of ghastly green in the breaking mountains and of hellish lividness in the swirling chasms and shattering crests.

The noise was as the shivering roar of heavy batteries pouring death on each other at close range, and the light as the hurtling blaze of their belching muzzles. Sea and thunder crashed together as if heaven and earth were bursting in universal wreck, the wicked hiss and shriek of the tempest rising dominant at times like the screeching of demons drunk with the exultation of havoc. The frenzied waters—racing, reeling, tumbling, eddying with the drift of a Highland snowstorm, and the booming confusion of ten thousand tide-rips—spun and tossed the brig like a top or a cork. And she, like a sentient thing, seemed demented with pain and fear. Now she would poise shuddering on a white crest high in air, so that I looked into a horrid gulf dyed as with blood; the next instant, plunging with dizzying velocity down a yawning steep, she would crouch in the hollow of a great wave, as a hare might crouch in a cleft of the earth from pursuing hounds, until the curling breakers, with frothing, crimson lips and hideous hissings, coiled in upon her like monstrous snakes burying and crushing her in their folds. Then, groaning and shaking, she would wallow in a caldron of yeast, canting now to one side, now to the other, so violently that she must have threshed the surges with her masts. Again she would be pitched aloft far into the blinding rack, to be hurled back, pounded and battered as with steam hammers, and sent headlong into a dancing avalanche of surf. She would recover with the tottering stupor of a creature stunned or half drowned; and there would be a momentary pause; but only because the infuriated waters were gathering for a fiercer and deadlier attack. Rallying in piled-up, wreathed masses, as if the ocean were heaving from its utmost depths to gather force, on they would come again, their angry combs bent forward in ravenous anticipation of prey, their towering fronts mantled by ragged foam, to fling themselves once more upon her in crushing cataracts and torrents that tore and wrenched.

Every moment I expected—as far as expectation was possible—she would founder. How she lived was a marvel. A right good sailor she must have been in spite of her ugly looks and her evil name; for never surely did craft survive so mad an onset by the spirits of storm and destruction.

Smothered and pelted, now deep in billows that strove with a living force and fury to tear me away, now beaten to stupefaction by the driving spray, again dashed from side to side so furiously it is a wonder my bones were not ground to powder, only the vice-like grip which the fear of death gives could have held me in my place. My fingers, indeed, were like a dead man's in tenacity and fixedness: they might have been cut or broken; they could not have been loosened. If you have ever felt the clutch of a drowning man you may partly understand the tensity of my grasp. And holding thus in the midst of distracting buffeting and uproar, I shrieked as often as I had vent and wit, shrieked till my voice failed me and my cry sank to a hoarse gasping rattle, that tore chest and throat as raw as if they were being scraped by a rough-edged instrument. The situation gained an added poignancy and cruelty from the fact that all my powers, physical and mental, were absorbed in feeling. I could suffer but I could not act. Had I been myself I should have been on deck in an instant and head first into the surging wilderness in pursuit of the treacherous crew. My fate would have been soon decided; for the swimmer did not exist who could that night have escaped the devouring maw of the sea. But there would have been a moment's satisfaction in battling, and a speedy end to suffering. As it was, I could not so much as make an effort; so I stood there with my head thrust through the port-hole, battered, crushed, choked by the pitching ship and the breaching seas, yet frantically straining to hold on and to hail the quickly vanishing boats.

Every fibre in my body trembled with a mortal weakness and terror. My fingers were getting cramped and palsied, my breath was gone to a gasp; yet ever as my strength waned the desire to shout for succour became the more frantic. Have you ever seen a spent animal panting with open mouth for a little air in its extremity? Even so I panted then, with distended but voiceless lips. I would have given a million worlds, had I owned them, for the return of my voice, just for one instant, to make an appeal for help that would rise above the howling and breaking of the storm. But the storm maintained its supremacy.

In a sudden darkness the shock of a tremendous broadside hurled me back with a bellyful of salt-water. I scrambled up sputtering, to be hit and knocked down again; the second time I rose with greater difficulty, and, clutching desperately at the port-hole, looked over the flame-lit waste. There were no boats; either the sea had swallowed them or they were hidden by the storm-scud. In either case they were lost to me.

An excruciating anguish of mind and body came upon me; a horrifying sense of being left alone and face to face with death. Yet it could not be. Gracious God, I was not to perish thus! For one moment despair gave me maniacal energy, and I found my voice in a wild yell, not the sharp cry of simple fear, but a delirious and convulsive outburst of the whole being, as if the doomed wretch would overcome Fate by vehemency of appeal and fierceness of protest. Then all at once a giddy sickness seized me, my head got light, sea and ship flew round together, the din fell to a far-off murmur, buzzed and died, and I, losing my feeble hold, sank splashing into the water on the floor.

I came to my senses drifting to and fro like a piece of wreckage in the eddies of a flooded river, and half crawling, half swimming and in utter blackness I got back to my berth. I was no sooner in than I was out again, floundering and spluttering on my back. Recovering myself with a mighty effort, I managed to regain my tossing bed, and as I strove to keep in it, suddenly there came back to me with terrific and appalling vividness the realization of my position. To feel was to act instantly and with the concentrated energy of every faculty and fibre.

I leaped up, to be knocked on the head, and sent once more floundering and spluttering on the floor. Ere I could find my feet the flood came pouring through the open port full in my face, sweeping me across the cabin; then, as the brig canted, it poured out, dragging me back and lashing me against the side.

By degrees I got my breath and my feet, and thrusting my head through the port-hole with such frantic precipitancy that the jagged edges of the glass ripped my neck and shoulders, I strained my eyes for some object or sign of hope. As well might Dante's condemned shades have looked for happiness in their Inferno.

The heart did not beat that could have dared to hope in face of that titanic and unbridled fury of the sea and the storm. The whirlwind and the lightning, the thunder and the crashing gulf of waters, mocked at the idea of escape. And I had but to look on the convulsed and scudding desolation, the Phlegethon of flying rolling mountains wreathed with fiery foam and often spouting like volcanoes, to feel the blasting force of the mockery. The powers of darkness and the deep, of fire and tempest, were in possession of the world, and in a frenzy of elemental frolic were tearing it into fragments, whirling and tossing it in an indescribable jumble, which was as the riot of hell itself.

My crowding impressions were such as may not be

set down in words. One moment it seemed as if the riven ocean were bellowing in agony; the next that it was animated by a host of furies, and roared in the glee of devastation and destruction. There is no shape of horror it did not take, no sound of terror it did not simulate. A million trumpets were inciting its legions to the charge, a million voices were answering in shrieking ecstasy, a million arms were reaching to clutch and destroy the brig, a million eyes were watching in triumph for the inevitable catastrophe. To say that the elements had broken loose, had burst every bond of restraint, would in no wise express the sense of demoniac hate and hostility that was upon me. To my distraught fancy there was an inspiring directing will behind the raving savagery. Every leap was made in fiendish and intentional ferocity at my life. Every sucking swirl was meant to drag the ship to her death. The uproar increased rather than diminished. As before, the breaching seas choked and the scarlet drift blinded me; and sometimes, too, I had scurrying reflections of a drawn horrified face, more awful than the anger of the elements.

Gripping with all my might I strove to hold on. But what was my puny strength, what would have been the strength of ten thousand men, against the rage of winds and waves? Hurled back by a stunning blow as from a giant's fist, I was thrown sprawling on the floor. I lay for a little in a sort of stupor, then managing somehow to pick myself up, I crept once more into my bunk.

Heaven alone knows why I got there. It may have been from some vague notion that bed was the proper place to die in; or perhaps I acted from a mere involuntary effort to evade the cold black water that seemed to be following me with lethal intent. Whatever might be the reason, the refuge profited me but little; for with every plunge and lurch of the brig I was deluged.

Of the drenching indeed I was not conscious; but

the cruel element coiling, lapping, sucking, now in vicious spurts as if to force me into the grave, then softly and insidiously as if to bear me off by stealth, then crawling over me as if to discover an entrance to my vitals and despatch me where I lay, made me pant and quake with icy dread.

In such a turmoil of feeling, coherency of thought and accuracy of sensation were alike impossible. Yet on one point—if on one only—my mind was preternaturally clear—that I was dying for my transgressions, dying alone and forsaken, utterly without comfort or consolation. If ever sin came back accusingly on mortal it so came back on me in that fearful hour when the deep was roaring for my life, and the trampled and staggering brig appeared every moment to be yielding it up. Yet it was hard, excruciatingly hard, to accept the fiat of inexorable justice, so disproportionate seemed the punishment to the offence. Was there no pity or mercy left in the world? Could no man of the many millions that lived stretch forth a saving hand to me? Did those whom I had wronged and disobeyed know that I was perishing in the grip of the ruthless sea, and, if so, would they not plead for me? Was there no deliverance? the recoiling flesh asked; no plea, no prayer, no form of repentance that would avail? No, no; I had chosen my course, I had pleased myself, and this was the result, to die where no human eye could see, no human arm aid, no human heart pity; past hope, past care, past help.

I tried to pray, and the prayer was the cry of a lost soul for mercy—"Father in heaven, save me, save me! Thou who commandest the raging of the sea to cease, keep me from perishing."

But Heaven answers in its own way and its own time. I saw no sign of intervention or leniency, and in the insanity of the castigated sinner I revolted. If I was doomed, why this lingering torture? Could I not be allowed to die quickly? Why had my late companions not thrown me overboard or drawn a sharp blade across my throat? They were devils enough to do it. Why was I selected for sacrifice to a blind vengeance? Were my sins greater than the sins of multitudes who were well and happy? And so the impious questions multiplied till the rebel broke down in a gush of tears, which I hope were accepted as a token of penitence.

When the fit had passed, I closed my burning eyes, feeling that no light would evermore fall on them till that light rose that shall not fade away. Ere the morrow morning I should be "deeper than did ever plummet sound," coffined in the black hulk of the engulfed brig, and no mortal should ever look on my grave among the green and slimy things that strew the Indian Ocean. Well, well!

> "We cease to grieve, cease to be fortune's slaves,
> Nay, cease to die, by dying."

I lay quiet now, save for the pitching of the berth, for there was no longer any motive to move. The tempest was evidently abating, though the waves still leaped madly against the ship's sides, sometimes making clean breaches over her. I wondered why she held so long afloat. But, doubtless, she was going steadily if slowly down. She would sink gradually for a while, then, in a crucial moment, when the flood should have gained a proper hold, she would go down with a quick, dizzy gurgle and swirl. I could anticipate the vertigo of the descent and my own sensations in the embrace of death. There would be a momentary, convulsive effort to hold back, a gasping for breath, a brief pain as of one choking, a sudden giddiness fading swiftly into unconsciousness, and then absolute peace. I wished that the ordeal were not so long delayed. I wished that the hurricane might blow anew, and that the billows would rise in their utmost rage and overwhelm us at once. For the suspense was as the pangs of many deaths.

But no fresh hurricane came, only, after a great

while, there was a loud splash by my berth side, followed by a sharp cry that made me start in alarm, though why I should be alarmed, who had nothing worse to fear, nor better to hope, than death, is a question I cannot answer. Start, however, I did, with a frightened look into the blackness of darkness about me, to see what uncanny thing this might be that was disturbing my parting hour.

I could, of course, see nothing, but presently I understood, from the splashing and squealing, that the rats were prowling around, and were greatly disgusted at finding the cabin floor under water. As for me, I was glad of their company.

"If the creatures could only speak to me," I said to myself; "if we could only exchange sympathies, and converse together on our fate, there would be some satisfaction even yet."

And as I lay listening to their interchange of sentiments, mostly, as I guessed, expressive of disappointment, I thought of the marvellous instinct, amounting almost to intuition, which is attributed to rats in regard to sinking ships. An old story occurred to me. A vessel had foundered in mid-ocean, the crew took to the boats, even like the crew of the *Bird of Paradise*, and as the last man was stepping off, a company of rats appeared, and, without ceremony or hesitation, leaped into the boats with the men. The ship was going down, and they knew it. My companions were doubtless endowed with this instinct also; what if the brig were not sinking after all? It seems an absurd thing to take any comfort from the actions of rats, and yet a wild hope that I might still be saved thrilled through my heart. One hope begets another. I went on to think that since the brig was settling down so very slowly, she might keep afloat till we should be discovered. A drowning man clutches at straws, and hope, as the poet says, springs eternal in the human breast; springs, too, with no regard to time or circumstance. Here was I, in the direst extremity in which man could be placed, busy with schemes of rescue and happiness.

The thought that I might be saved kept with me through the long hours of darkness, and when the morning light returned, and found me in no worse plight than I had been in at sunset on the previous evening, my hope strengthened to an absolute belief in my ultimate escape. My physical strength increased with my mental, and when the sun was fully up—the sun I had not expected to see again—I leaped from my bed to welcome it, almost forgetting my fever. Had I Shakespeare's gift of expression ten times over, I am sure I could not half tell how sweet, how transcendently glorious it was, after that night in the tomb, to feel the warmth and mystic potency of the returning light.

In the first great burst of joy, I wondered why I should ever have been depressed, so inexplicable do despair and dismal thoughts become to us in moments of supreme exaltation. My heart welled into my eyes in thankfulness as I drank in the full, deep draught of happiness; and yet I was so full of wonder, that, more than once, I doubted whether the whole thing were not a vision, a trick of the imagination. It was as if Plato's fantastic dream were realized, and, after ages of immurement in nether darkness, a man were brought forth to behold the rising sun for the first time. Yet the illustration is incomplete, for, while Plato's supposititious character would have been overwhelmed with awe, I was filled with gladness. The creature of Plato's dream would have veiled his face in terror before the sun's majesty; I thrust mine forward in eager and rapturous welcome. I had risen from the dead; here was the joyous exuberance of life again, with all its hopes and teeming possibilities. It was worth while being at the point of death to learn how sweet it is to live.

I saw the east kindling with a divine illumination that was as the light of a resurrection morn. Higher and higher the blaze of glory rose, till the flood of

life had mounted to the zenith, spread with rosy au-
roral promise, and possessed the entire heavens.
Death had vanished. The world was born anew,
fresh, lusty, jubilant as on that primal morning when
the Omnipotent said, "Let there be light." When
the great orb showed the edge of its flaming disc, a
golden shaft shot straight across the ocean to the
derelict brig. It came like a kiss of salutation, a
benediction, a promise of life. Then, as the sun rose
slowly, monarch of the world, and the waves of light,
inexpressibly beautiful and holy, came rolling towards
me, I was ready to cry out in worship. O God, how
sweet is life after death, paradise after the pit!
There are those, miserable fireside philosophers, who,
from the depths of easy-chairs, ask, with sapient wisdom, whether life is worth living? Put them in
danger of losing it, and I dare say they will find an
answer to their silly question.

With my new-found strength, I tried the screws
which had baffled me in the night. Joy succeeded
joy; they yielded, and the brass rim opened, thus
giving me more space. Then I thrust out my head
well up to my shoulders, and drew a long breath,
which was as meat to the starving and drink to the
parched. Again and again I sucked in the delicious
cordial, feeling its grateful stimulating effects in the
uttermost atom of my frame. When I had inhaled
till I was dizzy, I leaned forward as far as I could,
and feasted my eyes on the glittering water, now
rolling lazily in big, smooth billows that rocked the
brig as gently as a mother rocks the cradle of her first-
born.

I know not whether it was the peculiarity of my
disease, or whether the new-born hope gave such
fresh vitality to my system as enabled it to throw the
fever off, or whether it was owing to an extra dose
of quinine I had taken from a box of pills which Mr.
Watson had left me, but, from that time, I began to
improve rapidly. True, after the first delirium of
joy had passed, there came a short period of depres-

sion and relapse, but I strove to keep up my courage, and the feeling of convalescence soon returned.

My improvement may be judged from the fact that, ere long, I began to think there are worse things in the world than a morsel of food. I got out of my berth, and, after some rummaging on hands and knees, I discovered a box of biscuits, for, happily, I had ample provisions on board, the crew, at their departure, having been more afraid of drowning than of starving. My fare was rather dry, and not such as might be supposed to suit the taste of a sick person; but I gnawed with so much relish, that, when the first biscuit was done, I took up another, which was likewise finished. Then I took a drink of water, laved my neck and head, and felt vastly revived. So wondrously was I restored, indeed, that it occurred to me to go on deck and take my reckonings, and see how the crippled brig looked, and perhaps hoist a signal of distress; but, that proving an enterprise still beyond my strength, I had another mouthful of fresh air, and returned to bed. And lying there, I tried to judge of the ship's condition by her movements. But these guided me to no conclusion, save what I might have arrived at without taking them into account, namely, that, since she had floated through the storm, she might continue to float in the calm, and that I might still be saved; so my courage remained good.

That day I passed in a sort of dream, suffering somewhat from thirst, which I frequently slaked, but otherwise almost free from pain. My head, which had troubled me sorely in the earlier stages of the disease, was now clear, albeit occasionally rather light. I continued to enjoy the boon of fresh air, having by this time opened every port I could get at, and it proved a very effective medicine.

When the sun again fell, I was lonely, but untroubled by the multitude of horrors which had weighed upon me all the previous night. Nor on this second night was I doomed to darkness. During my peregrinations in the day, I had found an oil lamp, which, after careful trimming and lighting, I swung from a rope in the centre of the cabin. On the approach of night I lighted it; then lay and waited for the rats, feeling certain they would repeat their visit. Nor was I disappointed. After a while I heard a suppressed squeak, then a furtive scraping, and half a minute later a whiskered gentleman peered cautiously in to see how matters might stand. Being in a fantastic humour, I called on him to enter, which, of course, had the effect of sending him scampering into the darkness. But presently he came back, bringing a companion with him to keep up his heart, and the two standing just outside the door, cocked their heads very wisely and surveyed the apartment. Then they retired as if for consultation, then came advancing boldly into the centre of the floor, but catching sight of me they flew off in a panic. When they returned after the space of some minutes, they were accompanied by numerous friends, and the entire body reconnoitred, now advancing, now retiring, and all the time keeping up a running commentary of squeaks. I threw a shower of crumbled biscuit (with which I had provided myself) on the floor, and they made off again; but plucking up heart, presently they came back, and with many cautious looks and squeaking whispers began tentatively to nibble. The second shower disturbed them less than the first, the third less than the second, and the fourth hardly at all. By the time the sixth fell, they were quite at home and feasting royally. I should say the whole company did not number more than a score, though to judge by the chatter there might have been several hundreds. The banquet lasted for fully half an hour, and I am sure the host derived as much pleasure from it as the guests. Having finished the feast they slipped quietly away, judging it good manners evidently to take their departure with as little fuss as possible.

Next night they returned with increased confidence

and good will, and indeed, every night so long as we remained on the brig, they came to cheer my solitude, and eat their supper. We gradually got so familiar that towards the close of our strange companionship, they evinced no timidity whatever in my presence, but ate as if I were a proved friend and benefactor, hardly even getting out of my way when I moved about the cabin. Had we continued long enough together, I am confident I could not only have turned them into staunch comrades, but taught them to romp, to gambol, and perform tricks. For a rat has affections and intelligence. As it was, they knew my evening whistle, and would come with pretty looks of expectation to have their meals, and depart with becks and squeaks of gratitude. I have been with many men who were far less companionable.

Meanwhile, the *Bird of Paradise* continued miraculously to float. Many days passed ere I could make a survey, and ascertain the actual damage she had sustained, or what stress of weather she might still be able to stand; but after the first day it became manifest that if the crew had not been cowardly in leaving her, they had at least been precipitate. But as I grew accustomed to the loneliness (my hope keeping strong), I was not sorry they had gone; indeed, as time ran, and I was still safe, my fear was that they might spy the brig and return. The wish that I might never look on one of them again, Mr. Watson only excepted (and he, I knew, must have perished), grew with my growing strength, and my strength increased apace. For some time the fever troubled me in the evening, but hope and a good constitution, with some grains of quinine per day, gradually overcame it, and within a week I was able to make my way, with comparative ease, about the lower part of the ship.

It might be on the fifth or sixth day from the time I was deserted that I managed to crawl up the companion-way, and surely never shall I forget the

strange ecstatic feeling that came over me on stepping again into the sunlight and the open air. It
was lonely and desolate enough, Heaven knows, to
find one's self the only soul on board a derelict ship
in the midst of the ocean, but even with desolation it
was returning life, and I was glad beyond expression. I stood for a while at the head of the stair inhaling the balm; then I turned my attention to the
brig.

She was as ragged and battered as any craft that
ever encountered and survived a hurricane in the
tropics. The jibboom was gone, the broken foremast
hung over the side entangled in a mass of shrouds
and rigging that it had pulled down, the unfurled
sails were hanging in ribbons, showing that the blast
had caught us unexpectedly, and found us unprepared, and the deck was strewn with wreckage. I
could not discover, however, that the hull had suffered very seriously. There were sprung planks and
boards, indeed the bulwarks were smashed, and the
after-deck was a mass of splinters, but as the injuries
were mostly above the water-line, they might not
mean much. The most serious damage was to the
steering gear, which was completely wrecked. The
brig lay heavily to one side like a vessel running
close hauled, and she was going so slowly that there
was scarce a ripple at her cutwater. My examination
cheered me; so long as the weather held fair, I was
safe.

The survey finished, I sat down on the booby hatch
to take the air. The ocean was asleep, there was not
a sound in all the wide solitude, nor, so far as I could
see, any living thing to break the eternal silence.
The brig was all alone, "a speck on sky-shut seas,"
and a very insignificant speck too, when you come to
think of it. I wonder if any man ever before sailed
those seas in a plight like mine, or was so utterly
alone, since Robinson Crusoe built himself a hut on
his island?

I suppose it is evidence of the inherent cupidity of

human nature that very soon I began to think how I should dispose of my goods in the event of my being picked up, or of my drifting into some port. Would the profit be honourably mine, or ought it to go to Mr. Matheson? Yes, it should be his since he owned both ship and cargo. I decided to sell the goods, return to Bombay, hand him over his money, report the conduct of his men, and turn to my own affairs. My experience had not yet taught me the folly of speculation. Providence had decreed that ship and cargo were to be disposed in a manner that I little expected.

CHAPTER VIII.

A GREAT SURPRISE.

TEN days must have passed thus in the utter solitude of an unfrequented ocean, days, however, not of depression and despair, but of tranquil joy and gratitude, soothing alike to mind and body after the shocks and perils of the tempest. A little while before, I could have dreaded nothing more than this desolation; it would have seemed hopeless and maddening. But deliver a man from the grave, and the desert will be to him as a fruitful and umbrageous garden. Now indeed, except for the loneliness, my situation was one that might have provoked the envy of men who hunt happiness, or struggle for bread in dusty noisome cities.

After the thunderstorm the air was cooler, and when there chanced to be a breeze, its pervasive and delicious balm was like a foretaste of heaven. Morning and evening, too, the orient spread its flaming pictures along the sky for my sole delight, and the glistening iridescent sea, lately so terrible in its fury, caressed the ship's side with a liquid murmur of endearment. Slowly and softly the brig heaved on the long foamless swell, without so much as a suggestion of the reeling agonies she had just passed through.

On deck, I had my improvised awning of sails and tangled rigging, under which I dozed and dreamed when I was not cooking or eating, or watching the flying-fish. Company would have been grateful, but I had got back my life, and that was more than company. Moreover, I lacked nothing, for, as already stated, the ship's stores were practically untouched, so sudden had been the crew's departure. With plenty of meat and drink in a world where so many people have to go on short commons, one should not complain; and as for society, if it was wanting, there was none to thwart my humours or break my meditations.

A chief part of my pleasure was in the books left by Mr. Watson. "Rob Roy" was there, and truly it would have seemed a ridiculous thing, could any one have seen a miserable ocean waif holding his sides at the humour of Bailie Nicol Jarvie. I fear the gallant Rob himself was not a pattern of morality, but his daring Highland spirit was captivating; and if he lifted cattle when he should have been saying his prayers, he did well when his back was to the wall. Others also of Sir Walter's books I read, among them being "Ivanhoe," which is surely the best romance ever written. "Don Quixote" I had too, a book which I found as rich in the golden grain of practical wisdom as in the elements of perpetual laughter; in a word, the product of a soul of sunlike radiance and universality, though the geniality had its sable tinge, as if the writer knew well what it is to dwell in the dusky chambers of sorrow. "Robinson Crusoe" likewise fell to me then, and I dare say the resource and ingenuity of that immortal castaway gave valuable hints for the ordering of my own mode of life. Besides these, I had some numbers of old reviews, which were good reading for the wigging they gave unlucky authors, some of whom have since, however, unaccountably achieved fame. I had also a publication called "The Posthumous Papers of the Pickwick Club," which, I understand, is more familiar to the present generation than its Bible. My blessings on the memory of Boz for the fun and heart he gave me in that dismal time. If ever a more amusing person than Mr. Pickwick came from a creator's brain it was the Knight of La Mancha alone, or perhaps Jack Falstaff; while Sancho Panza and Sam Weller ought to march down the generations hand in hand, as the most diverting henchmen who ever sinned their souls from loyalty to fantastic masters. There was likewise an almanac, which I thought might be available for its weather forecasts; but whether it had been written for some other quarter of the globe, or was merely a humourous effort, its predictions never had the least bearing on the weather in the Indian Ocean.

I had yet another resource, still more fruitful of enjoyment. When the books palled, forth would come Duncan's silver-mounted pipes from the green bag (which was guarded as if it were gold), and I would blow myself into a species of intoxication. Now it was an old air my mother or my nurse had crooned to me in the dim far-off dawn of memory; then, being a little sentimental, a wail of lament, maybe Rob Roy's pathetic "Ha til mi tulidh" (I return no more); again a pibroch opening with the weird dirge-like measure of a coronach, but every moment quickening in time, till the excitement and ecstasy of it carried me clean out of myself, and away from all thought of forsaken seas and derelict ships. By a natural transition, this would lead to a quickstep, a reel, strathspey, or Highland fling.

All the while, I was back in the Highlands, in the glee of a harvest home, or a gathering on the green of a summer's evening, cheering and urging the dancers, whose whirling tails and gleaming knees showed the energy of the response. I could hear the resounding "hoochs," and sharp thumb-cracking of the men, as well as the panting, joyful, half-frightened soughs of the lasses, as they were swung off their feet in the fury of the fun. Or again, it might be a plumed

and kilted company marching with springy step to
the strains of "The Highland Laddie," or "The
Pibroch of Donuil Dhu," or "The Campbells are
Coming," or "Blue Bonnets over the Border."

And then, at the impulse of uncontrollable exaltation, up I would get to strut about the deck with as
proud a stomach as if I were playing clansmen into
the heart of their enemies. Nor was strutting always
enough. For, oblivious of physical weakness, I often
caught myself skipping about in the mazes of a country dance, or leaping in the Highland fling, or prancing in a bout of the sword dance, the fingers unconsciously going on the chanter. It would be hard to
tell how many times I went over "Reel Thulachan,"
and "The Reel of Tulloch," and "Ghillie Challum,"
and "The High-Road to Linton," and "The Auld
Wife Ayont the Fire," and "Dainty Davie," and "The
Marquis of Huntly's Farewell," and "Sleepy Mag-
gie," and such-like tunes, trying, not always success-
fully, to keep time between the dancer and the piper.
The exercise usually continued till I had to give up
for want of breath, and did more good than all the
physic doctors could have poured into me. And indeed, to this day nothing heartens me like the drone
of the pipes bumming in my ear, though I fear this
will be reckoned a rude taste by the refined young
gentlemen, who know so much about pianos, things of
mystery to me. Yet old Duncan often declared I had
notions of music, and could make the pipes utter
emotion and sentiment in a way that sometimes
stirred him, though he owned I was no hand at the
warblers.* But since there was none on the brig to
criticize, my deficiencies did not in the least spoil the
pleasure in my own melody. There was but one
drawback to the performances, that my companions

* The true piper will stake his life on his warblers or grace
notes; anybody can play a common tune by sticking simply
to the air, but a man must be a born piper to introduce
variations with skill. It is in the management of these that
art lies.

fairly abhorred them. No sooner would they hear me screwing up the drones for a bit of piping, than they rushed off squealing to hide in the darkest recesses of the ship. Since then, I have learned that nothing jars on the sensitive ear of a rat so much as the music of the bagpipes; he will go through fire and water to escape it. That is why, in the Highlands, when rats get troublesome, it is a common practice to call in the aid of a piper in driving them off. The device never fails.

The *Bird of Paradise* lay dead as a log without guidance from helm or impulse from sail, but she kept afloat, and that was a reason for thankfulness. As there was no compass, it was impossible to judge the course save vaguely by the stars, and as the heavenly bodies had never been much among the objects of my contemplation, my reckoning was wild enough. But my conclusion was that we were making, or more correctly drifting W.N.W., for what wind or current there was seemed to be in that direction, and that barring accident or the good fortune of being picked up, I should sooner or later touch somewhere in the neighbourhood of the Persian Gulf. This pleased me little, for I knew the entire region to be infested by bands of pirates, who, should they discover us, would make short work of both me and the brig. But being powerless to alter the course, I had to drift on, trusting in Providence for safety.

One evening there sprang up a breeze in our larboard quarter, which for the first time since I had been left alone, pushed the *Bird of Paradise* to something of a pace.

"I'll take it as a good omen," I said to myself. "If she keeps at that I shall soon arrive—somewhere."

I sat on deck that night longer than usual, partly to keep a sharp look-out, partly to enjoy the bracing breeze. It could not be called a clear night, but there was a strange light on the sea, half aerial, half phosphorescent, that would have made a sail visible at a considerable distance—had one chanced to come that way—which it did not. About eleven o'clock I went below, and, having fed my family of rats—a thing I did as regularly as I said my prayers—turned into bed. I lay long awake, however, with a premonition that something was going to happen. It was not by any means a painful feeling, rather a dim vague intuition that some change was impending, and would come speedily. However, I fell asleep after a time without disturbance of any sort.

The sun was already level with my peep-hole windows when I awoke. After dressing leisurely, I went on deck to go through the usual morning exercise of sweeping the ocean for a sail. At first I could discover nothing, and concluded I was still alone; but presently, taking a second look, I descried the tiniest black speck—as it might be a floating hat—between me and the horizon. My heart gave a great leap.

"Now, what the deuce is that?" I found myself saying with quickened breath. "It doesn't look like a sail—no, it cannot be a sail. If I were anywhere in the track of civilization, I should say it is a buoy; but a buoy where ships never appear to come, would be an impossible piece of absurdity."

I gazed with all my might, rubbing my eyes when they were dazzled and smarting, and going at it again like one whose hope of salvation depends upon his accuracy of vision. My curiosity increased without bringing me clearer knowledge.

"Perhaps it's some monster fish taking the sun," I said aloud as if I had listening companions. But no fish that I had ever heard of was fond of being broiled alive. It did not move nor show sign of life. "Flotsam—jetsam—ligan——" I went over the possibilities. "Pieces of wreckage, goods sunk by pirates, to be found again at convenience." Neither theory was satisfactory, and my anxiety became feverish. "It's the old man of the sea," I thought, frivolously; "or a mermaid—no, it is too black for a mermaid, the creatures are fair."

But I was too painfully concerned to give way to a

whimsical spirit; so in right earnest I conjectured and stared and stared and conjectured, propounding theories to myself and immediately rejecting them, rubbing my eyes when they saw double, taking a turn about the ship to ruminate, making a childish compact with myself not to look again for fifteen minutes, and yielding in fifteen seconds to the spell of the black speck. I gazed till I saw double, treble, quadruple, till my head was swimming and a thousand objects were leaping and whirling fantastically on the light-grey horizon; then thinking it prudent to stop gazing for a little, I went below for breakfast.

It was a hasty, perfunctory meal that morning; for in less than five minutes I was on deck again palpitating with excitement. The black speck was still on the glittering plain, distinct, motionless, mysterious as ever. The gentlest breeze blew in my larboard quarter, and in my eagerness I ran to the helm, forgetting that it was a splintered wreck as potent for its purpose as the tail of a moulting hen. Then, finding it was to be a game of watching, I hurriedly rigged a hammock out of the tangled cordage and sails, and climbed into it, intent on discovery. Hours passed without bringing enlightenment. The burning sun beat down on a shimmering brazen sea, whose metallic sheen made me giddy and nearly blind. The breeze died away, and the brig lay idle; in all the vast silence there was not a sound save the thumping of my own heart, nor a visible object save that aggravating black speck.

By-and-by I went below, with a misty idea of luncheon, immediately rushing back on deck more eager than ever. Hardly had I swung myself into my place when I leapt down again, calling out as if the immense vacancy were peopled, that beyond doubt the thing moved, and was growing bigger. Then after awhile I saw something like the flutter of a flag; and I understood the black speck was a boat with a man in it. And he saw the brig.

"Ye-hoo!" I cried with a leap of joy. "Deliverance at last!"   And I ran about the deck like one possessed, shouting, "Deliverance!—deliverance!" and could have wept for joy.

But all at once a chill struck me to the marrow and put an end to my rapture.   What if this were some of the crew returning?   For one brief moment my mind was blank with fright, but the next I had taken my resolution.   Swift as ever man prepared for an enemy, I got two pistols and a musket, loading them and laying them beside me ready for use.   Then I went to Mr. Watson's strong box, smashing the lid with an iron bar, and taking thence the longest sword I could find.   That being of a good weight and sufficiently keen, I selected a Turkish dagger and a long sailor's knife, with two more revolvers and some ammunition.   Then I arranged my armoury, and waited for the boat.   It was now close enough to enable me to discern that there was but one man in it, a discovery that gave me confidence.   With such an arsenal and the natural advantage of my position, the deuce was in it if I couldn't take care of myself.

The man was rowing hard, and the boat came quickly over the sleeping water.   When he was within hailing distance, I stepped to the bulwarks and leaned over.   In the same moment, resting on his oars, he turned to look at me.   My first care was to find out whether or not he was one of the crew, but a very brief examination sufficed to show he was not. He began to pull again, and I, thinking my warlike preparations slightly overdone, hastily put my weapons out of sight, reserving just a brace of pistols and a dagger to meet emergencies.

My visitor did not come close alongside, but held off a little distance, as if doubting the reception he should receive.   He was an Arab, and showed signs of distress.

"Row up," I called in English, never expecting him to understand that language.

"God is merciful," he responded joyfully in the same tongue; and with two or three vigorous strokes, he was alongside. Then for a minute or so we silently took stock of each other. I was not enamoured of his looks, and perhaps he was just as little in love with mine.

"You seem rather in a bad way," I remarked, speaking first.

"Allah is a mighty scourger!" he said, with a shrug of his shoulders.

"So He is," I replied. "How do you come to be alone and in such a plight?"

At this he worked himself into a sudden rage, gesticulating wildly, and talking brokenly of villains and robbery and outrage. His story was that he had been in command of a ship laden with a valuable cargo, that the pirates had plundered him, killing his crew, and that it was only by the greatest miracle he had escaped with his life. On my inquiring how he happened to know English, he replied fawningly that he had learned my beautiful tonuge in Egypt and in Africa.

"An Arab slave-dealer," I concluded at once.

But his misery was plainly very great, and I could not do less than take him on board.

"Praise be to Allah for His mercies!" he exclaimed, clutching at the rope's-end I let down to him.

He climbed with the agility of a cat, pouring out thanks and blessings as he ascended.

"Bi takdir an tatakallam bil Arabi," he said with questioning eyes when he reached the deck. "La, la!" he exclaimed as I stared in uncomprehending wonder. "You do not speak the tongue of the Prophet. Inglizi, Inglizi (English), it is the speech of brave men, yea, of heroes and conquerors. Are they not my brethren? Do I not love them as my own soul?" and, profuse of honeyed words, he insisted on embracing me in the most fraternal manner known to his exuberant race. He laid his forehead against mine and threw his arm over my shoulder, clasping my side with the other, and laying his chin first on my left breast, then on my right, striking my palm with his, and giving other novel and embarrassing tokens of esteem and friendship, all the while invoking the choicest blessings of Heaven upon my head. Then he kneeled with his face towards Mecca and repeated the Hizb-el-Bahr, or prayer for safety on the ocean wave. His devotions over, we raised his boat, which was a crazy kind of coracle.

CHAPTER IX.

MY VISITOR TAKES STOCK.

It will be thought that our common straits would have drawn us into a bond of sympathy. Here we were, a pair of forlorn waifs, met on the high seas, each with the marks of dire misfortune behind and ahead, such a prospect as might have made us tremble and cling to each other for support. But on one side, at least, there was not that fellow-feeling which, according to the poet, makes us wondrous kind. On the contrary, there was grim suspicion, that soon came very near to aversion. Abram ben Aden might be an injured saint, but his appearance rather suggested a villain down at heel. So I judged it best to keep my distance and let him understand that familiarity on the part of strangers was not among the things I liked. My attempts to give him that impression, however, were not strikingly successful.

He was mightily surprised to find me alone, and could not express his astonishment when he saw how the brig was laden.

"Now here's a wonder beyond anything man ever dreamed of!" he exclaimed, with a covetous gleam on his lean, swarthy face. "You alone master of such riches as this! By the holy Alborak, there must be a tale here surpassing in marvel any told by Scheherezade."

But I was not to be taken in the snare of even so

artful a fowler as the Arab seemed to be. Pretending to make light of his wonder and ignoring his deft interrogatory, I laid my hand on the hilt of my revolver with a wink of significance, remarking that a man might get very rich if he had only the heart to dare. He looked at me for a moment with curiously questioning eyes, which began to glow in their dark depths.

"'Tis the best thing I ever saw!" he said meaningly. "Did you do it alone and by magic?"

"Alone and by magic!" I repeated with a swagger. "And why not?"

"You are a hero!" he exclaimed, overcome with admiration. "Blessed be the day that I am permitted to gaze on you! To take a ship is a great thing. It is a deed of valour worthy of the song of poets. Twenty men, to whom blood was a joy, have failed in it, and you have succeeded alone. Yet your face is as smooth as a woman's. War and blood have not set their stamp upon it. When you are older, your name will be the terror of the sea. I tell you, I have come upon a great marvel. And you have all this"—with a comprehensive wave of the hand—"as the reward of your courage—enough to build a palace and buy slaves and have the pleasures of a sultan. How did you do it?"

"The fool opens the windows of his mind to the passer-by," I returned, taking a turn about the deck, "but the wise man shuts them."

"By my faith, you are as prudent as you are brave," he remarked laughingly, though I could see my reply had cut him. "A secret is in my custody if I keep it; but if I blab it, 'tis I that am prisoner. A wise proverb, and yet there is another that has wisdom also. Conceal your secret only from such as are known to be indiscreet, but impart it to him who has the prudence to keep it."

"We talk of proverbs and forget the duties of hospitality," I said. "You must be in need of rest and refreshment."

8

"Ju'an atshan (holy prophet), how my inwards crave for food and drink!" he replied warmly. "These many days and nights have I endured sun and moon without a morsel of bread to stay my stomach, or a drop of water to cool my burning tongue."

"Then," I returned, "you suffer from three things for which talk is no cure—hunger, thirst, and weariness. Let us see what refection may be got out of the ship's larder."

"May Allah grant you lifelong bounty and the Prophet receive you in the home of the faithful!" he answered, in a burst of fervent piety. "The brave are ever generous," he added, following me down the companion ladder, convinced that I was the king of buccaneers.

He ate ravenously, devouring the victuals in such huge mouthfuls that he would certainly have choked had his throat not dilated like a serpent's under the pressure. He washed down the solids with copious draughts, first of coffee, then of rum, which he happened to discover when the meal was half over.

He was draining a cup of the latter, when, as if under the impulse of some powerful emotion, he jumped to his feet.

"The Genii scourge my memory," he exclaimed, bowing elaborately towards me, "that would let me forget the customs of your brave people—yea, customs that put courage in the heart and make the bonds of friendship strong. A votre santé, Moosoo," says he with a grin of intelligence. "Ah, Fransawi, Fransawi, it is good, but better is Inglizi. Here is a health to the next throats we do cut, dammee. Send them to Davee Shone. That is it; the ocean chest of Davee Shone. 'Tis the language of heroes whose words are like flames of fire, and whose swords thirst for blood as the sands of the desert for water. Verily, I tell you they are a great people; they make the sea one big grave—no man may count the tombs." He leaned forward confidentially. "And you are the greatest and mightiest of them all. What numbers have you——" and he mimicked the slashing of a windpipe. "Nay, nay, these things be secret," he added quickly, as he perceived a shade of resentment on my face. "A man thinks alone of the blood he sheds. We know what it is to take a ship. Crews of laden ships will be fools, and what can the rover do but give them to the sharks? Ah, 'tis a great game. I swell at the thought of what you have done."

He resumed his eating and drinking with renewed voracity.

"Paradise!" he remarked between the gulps. "But for the blessedness of this feast, I could believe it all a vision. Men do not banquet like this in visions; 'tis too satisfying for dreams. If I do not return thanks day and night, and remember your name perpetually, may Azrael drag me to the uttermost depths of the pit."

When he had eaten beyond the capacity of three ordinary Englishmen he once more turned a beaming countenance upon me.

"Afdalt, sahib," he said, smacking his lips. "That is the—ah, yes, I know—the grub, 'tis fit for the Great Sultan. Good is the kahwa,* and the sailor wine is as a pleasant heat at the heart. But we tarry. By the mother of Mohammed, we will go and behold thy wonders. The thought of them stirs me so that I cannot sit still. Mighty and great is the corsair—ha, ha! He goeth out into the deep for riches, and lo! his hands are full of gold. He hasteth away, and leaves no more trace than the wind. Come, sahib, come."

And nothing would content him but an instant and complete survey of the brig. For the purpose of exploration it was necessary to get a light; this I gave to Abram ben Aden, making him precede me, so that he might not be tempted to take me unawares from behind. I have observed it is a good plan to keep a doubtful guest always in front of you.

* Coffee; also coffee-room.

As we made our examination, coming on pile upon pile of stuffs from the looms of India, he was ready to burst, though striving to hide his covetousness by eulogistic speeches.

"You are greater than Ran Dahid, whose prizes made him so rich and powerful that he married a prince's daughter," he said once. "For he had his crew, and you are alone and but a youth. It is a great day for me when I am permitted to be your slave and learn your methods."

He had knowledge of such things, but he had never known the bravest rover to take a prize like mine single-handed.

Again I made light of my achievement, treating the taking of a ship as if it were but the amusement of an idle hour. I swaggered a good deal; but I am sure that, in spite of all my bravado, I looked but an indifferent pirate.

When we returned on deck, the wreckage which he had not noticed at his first coming on board, caught his attention.

"You have been amid the terrors of the deep," he remarked, "and yet, perchance the tempest has favoured you."

"You speak like a magician!" I replied.

"Nay, by the Prophet's beard, you are the magician!" he said quickly. "You ride the storm to fortune. The anger of the sea, which destroys other men, befriends you; the very elements are your slaves. A magician indeed you are. Yet, the ship is hurt. The helm hangs useless as a broken bough, and there is nothing to guide the ship. Over yonder is the Persian Gulf," he added significantly.

"I know it," I answered carelessly.

"There you may be among friends," he ventured, with a look of intelligence.

"If I am among foes the worse for them," I responded.

"Verily, I believe it," he said with unction, showing a disposition to embrace me again.

Thoroughly confirmed in the belief that I was a man of desperate and bloody deeds, he grew confidential, entertaining me with an account of some of his own exploits as freebooter and corsair, and dwelling with the relish of a devil on scenes of cruelty and death.

"Then you lied when I took you on board?" I said sternly, interrupting him in the midst of his narrative. Even a sea-robber may have his code of honour, and for the present my foible was to hate lying.

"Could I guess your trade from that girlish face?" he asked, with an impudent grin. "You might be a missionary ship."

"I am no liar," I said severely, while conscience whispered, "Impostor."

"And I swear by the rover's flag I will follow truth," said the rascal, with a broader grin than ever. "Are we not brothers, and should not our souls be as dials in the sunlight? Yea, and I love the brave Englishman. In Egypt and Africa have I not known him, and in the Persian Gulf have I not seen with joy his skill in slashing off heads? He is the angel-demon of the world. He will make good the black Ethiopian, and sell that which maketh the eyes red and the feet to fail, and take ships, and make himself rich with what others have gathered. I love him as a very brother!"

Naturally I was gratified by this high and impartial testimony to the noble qualities of my countrymen.

A moment later, in his rummaging, Abram ben Aden came upon my armoury.

"What a warrior you are for one whose beard has yet to show itself!" he exclaimed with some excitement. "Here are weapons for a whole ship's crew." And selecting a sword, he drew it from the scabbard, and began to feel its edge.

"Not so fast," I said, stepping up to him. "These are dangerous. You talk of magic, let me warn you of the magic there is in these weapons."

"Yea, I believe in their magic," he answered complacently, "but is it not the magic of the arm that wields them?   I know a blade when I see it.   Choose you one, and we will have some sport.   May I perish if I am not forgetting the ring and the gleam of steel. See—see how it bends; 'tis a well-tempered blade. Yea, and it is light in the hand."   And he made a circle of sunbeams about his head.

I stepped back, my hand instinctively seeking the hilt of my pistol, and said indifferently that I was not in the humour for sport.   With a shade of disappointment and vexation, he thrust the sword back into its sheath and returned it to its place.

We had an early supper, and went early to bed, my guest getting a closed-off berth to himself.   I lay awake until I heard his stentorian snore; then I crept softly upstairs, and gathering all the weapons together, carried them down and hid them in my cabin. It was better that Abram ben Aden should not be tempted to do mischief while I slept.

CHAPTER X.

ALONE ONCE MORE.

WHATEVER evil designs Abram ben Aden may have harboured in the secret chambers of his heart, his bearing towards me was the essence of courtliness and friendship.   My own brother could not have been more solicitous for my happiness and welfare, nor the most loyal of henchmen readier to do me service. When, from some chance expression of mine, he discovered that I was just recovering from a mortal illness, he broke into fresh chantings of my valour and fortitude, and insisted on taking on himself the duties of cook and general personal attendant.

"It is not meet that heroes should do the work of slaves," he said.   "Leave it to me, who am but a common mortal.   I am happy in serving so valiant

a master, and so generous a benefactor, one whose
deeds should have been the inspiring theme of the
peerless Kaab-el-Albai * himself."

A blunt man like myself is at a grave disadvantage
in dealing with a courtier.   In spite of his fine words,
I mistrusted my guest as much as ever.   That he
coveted my possessions I knew, and that he had designs on my throat I more than half suspected; yet
I could not resist his advances nor deny his sallies of
wit and humour the meed of smile.   He was insist-
ently and infectiously light-hearted; for he took life
like a gambler's game, in which success and failure
should be accepted with equal equanimity.

He had other popular and charming qualities besides.   To the *aplomb* of the man of action, and the
peculiar knowledge of the man of the world, he united
the imagination of the poet and the happy audacity
of the born romancer.   His adventures had been many
and marvellous; and no man was ever his own Homer
to finer effect.   He had seen more with his two bodily
eyes than I had ever dreamed of, and he invested his
tales with a glamour that professional story-tellers
would have envied.   I do not think his recitals were
remarkable for a strict adherence to fact, but there
could be no question of their fascination.   His talk
was like a sojourn in the land of enchantment, amid
flowers and fragrance, and fair women, and palaces,
and gold, and precious stones, and heroic exploits,
and all the raptures of the brightest realms of fancy.
He made the "Arabian Nights" tame, and Baron
Munchausen a commonplace falsifier.

To give variety to the entertainment, one day he
proposed that he should teach me Arabic.

"Know that Abram ben Aden, though a rover, is
likewise a master of literature," he said, with a superb flourish of his arms.   "The poets are his espe-
cial delight.   They are greater than the magicians;
they are as a flame in the soul which illuminates the
universe.   But how is the adventurer, the corsair, to

* The famous Arabian poet and favourite of Mohammed.

carry the poets with him? Why, here"—tapping his forehead—"here is the chamber in which the poets have their abode! And here"—producing a greasy volume from the folds of his dress—"is what the Prophet gave the faithful as a consolation till they are translated to Paradise to make eternal love to the houris. You are an infidel, but what of that? You know what joy is, you also know what sorrow is. You have feelings, aspirations. You are a man. You hope to get to heaven. I will show you the way, and while I show, you shall learn the Arab's tongue. Come, my merry infidel! You shall yet converse as a brother with the children of the desert." And with an air of having the erudition of Alexandria at his finger-ends, he forthwith began my instruction.

He proved a good teacher, and I was not an inattentive pupil. One rule my tutor made and adhered to rigidly, and that was that we should talk nothing but Arabic. It was a sore trial of patience at first, but I persevered, and in a week (such was my diligence) was able to converse with tolerable fluency. The second week I was deep in the Koran, and able to follow my teacher in his recitations from the Arabian poets; the third week I was reciting myself. Abram ben Aden was delighted with his success.

"By the Prophet's mule," he said, "I will have you in Paradise yet! Your speech already is as that of one bred in the desert. You have the Arab's tongue, and next will come the Arab's faith. We will drink of the milk and clarified honey of Paradise together, my gay one; yea, and behold the black-eyed damsels reclining in the shade of pleasant gardens beside sweet fountains. Cheer thy heart, for one of them may even be thine when thou hast had time to repent of thy sins."

I said it was unspeakably good of him to take so deep an interest in my eternal welfare; and he replied nothing would grieve him more than that the bravest rover that ever set foot on the deck of a prize should at last be denied the bliss of the faithful.

As a diversion to our studies he lured me, rather against my judgment, into a daily bout with the sword.

"It will keep your hand and eye true," he said insinuatingly. "Let the master practise on his slave. Methinks you take joy in the ring of the steel. All brave men do. By the sword of Sikandar-el-Rumi, there is the stuff of a fighter in you! This ship with all its plunder, shows it; yet you will not let your blade drink your servant's blood."

It was not likely I would, but there was no assurance that my servant would exercise a like restraint over his blade. Indeed, on second thoughts, his proposition seemed to me a ruse to try my mettle and wheedle me into an overweening conceit with myself that would give him his opportunity. Happily I was not entirely ignorant in the use of the sword, for my graver studies had been interrupted, perhaps too often, by prolonged fencing bouts. But then I was far from thinking myself an expert; so that it was no light matter to stand up before a man of unknown skill and suspicious motive, whose greatest delight it might be to spit me at the very first go off. Nevertheless, I had given my consent, and it would have been both folly and cowardice to go back. So, putting on my stoutest front, I stood up, though the naked, wicked flash of our weapons in the sun caused me a nasty sensation. It was but momentary, however, for the demand on every faculty of mind and body was too keen to leave me time for fear.

I soon discovered that Abram ben Aden was a skilful swordsman, with a sure and rapid eye, great length and suppleness of arm, a wrist like a swivel, and the confidence which comes of many triumphs. My first efforts were very cautious, as you may suppose, no hint being lost on me, but we were not long at it when I rung him blow for blow, and I ended the early encounters in a glow of satisfaction. We were both nimble as goats, and I believe a spectator would have said the fencing was lively. For an hour each day we exercised thus, and my companion's good humour continued unabated.

We lived this life for a month. During all that time the weather was glorious, and we enjoyed it undisturbed. The brig floated lazily along, whatever wind there was being mostly steady in the same quarter. Not a sail nor a soul did we see, and I had but the haziest notion of our whereabouts. If Abram ben Aden was better informed, he kept his knowledge sedulously to himself.

He seemed, indeed, too intent on providing entertainment to give a thought either to our course or our destination. We told tales, and sang songs, and ate and drank, and fenced, and studied, and, all alone on a derelict water-logged ship, led the most delectable existence imaginable. My companion fairly adored me. He anticipated my wishes, spoke unceasingly of the unequalled deeds I had done, and more than once showed a strong disposition to fall down and worship me.

"I have been a rover," he would declare, with the unction of a man saying his prayers, "but may Azrael seize me this moment if I speak not the truth in saying that never have my eyes seen a man who matches you in bravery and good fortune. And you are but a youth," he would add in the most engaging tone.

This continued till I began to fancy I had enchanted the man, that he was verily my slave, and I had only to exercise my magical power to bend him to my will as completely as the most docile and obedient genie in any Arabian tale of wonder that was bent to the will of a happy prince. I dare say I plumed myself on my ascendency, I dare say I put on airs, and I have no doubt whatever that Abram ben Aden, most adroit of courtiers, most subtle of flatterers, saw through me, and took my measure with perfect accuracy.

One evening, in our fencing exercise, I thought he pressed harder upon me than ever before, and that his blade rang with unaccustomed sharpness. But the quickened movements only made my blood run the faster, for, by this time, I was both confident and dexterous. We went at it as much in earnest, perhaps, as any two men who ever crossed blades for amusement, and I remember the thrill caused by the thought, "What if he is trying to kill me?" My opponent was the first to cry halt; he was flushed and out of breath, and I fancied that under his everlasting smile there was a feeling of vexation.

"By the right hand of the Prophet, you are a gallant swordsman!" he cried, recovering his breath. "Your eye is the sun and your stroke a flash of lightning. I would not fight you for ten shiploads of gold. The man who fights you puts his life on your swordpoint. As a jest, you have taken my wind away, and, by the breath of the desert, I am hot. Come, thou champion brandisher of steel, and let us refresh ourselves. A cup of that sailor wine would give me back my strength."

Ordinarily, we put away our weapons as soon as our exercise was done; but this evening we took them with us, and they lay across our knees as we ate and drank.

"Are we enemies?" cried Abram ben Aden, laughing immoderately at the idea of two peaceable and friendly men sitting down to meat armed as if for battle; yet, somehow, we did not lay the swords aside, and when we went to bed we still had them.

I slept soundly that night, and was late in awakening next morning. On reaching the cabin, I found that Abram ben Aden had not yet risen, and, thinking to surprise him, I crept to his door. It stood ajar, showing an empty berth made up as it had been left the day before. I whistled softly, then going quickly on deck, looked for his boat. But it, too, was gone!

CHAPTER XI.

SETTLING ACCOUNTS.

HERE was an unexpected turn of the wheel of fortune—a new mystery to rack the mind, or give an added relish to life, just as you might chance to look at it. I was not at all sorry to find my companion gone, nor, in truth, greatly surprised; but his departure might portend more than it was pleasant to speculate on.

His character was pledge enough that he had not gone away from any pious motive, nor to do good by stealth. Too much of a knave to be a fool, a consummate rascal in the widest acceptation of that comprehensive word, despising moral scruples, insensible to gratitude, insatiably avaricious, bold in planning and ruthless in executing, I felt he must be bent on some scheme that boded neither me nor the brig any good. I recollected with peculiar and not very agreeable sensations, how he had pressed me in our bout on the evening before, and how, on finding himself fairly matched, his chagrin had broken through his well-trained smiles and courtier-like air of compliment. To be deprived of his company was a cause for rejoicing, for his absence relieved me of a constant source of suspicion and danger. But better a present evil than a lurking enemy; with your eye on the foe, you can defend yourself; but when he may spring upon you like a tiger in the jungle, at any moment, from any quarter, back, front, side, or oblique angle, the constant apprehension is apt to fret the nerves. And indeed the legions of black thoughts came trooping back upon me with such disquieting effect, that, unchristian as it may sound, I would have given my left hand to be able to run Abram ben Aden through with my sword, and there and then make an end of him. But, as it was, I could only conjecture, and conjecturing on a matter of life and death is positively the most unsatisfactory exercise in which the human mind can engage.

You may be sure I kept a sharp look-out that day, remaining constantly under my awning, save when I ran below to douse my head, which had a feverish tendency, or swallow a mouthful of food or drink. But the day passed, and no boat or other object hove in sight. I saw neither landmark nor watermark, nor even so much as the flash of a sea-bird's wing—nothing but the dreary, blinding glitter of the eternal ocean plain.

The darkness came, came at a stride, as Mr. Coleridge says, for in the tropics there is no twilight, but a leap from light to darkness, as if the night were lying in wait, and pounced upon the world as upon long-expected prey. The stars came out like points of lambent flame in a fleckless, grey-blue sky, and by and by the moon rose with a sense of sovereignty, a majesty and magnificence never equalled on land. Higher and higher she mounted, her white, unveiled radiance nearly obliterating the stars in her path; and she smote with almost as cruel a stroke as the sun. There is a promise to the righteous that the sun shall not smite them by day nor the moon by night. The smiting of the sun dwellers in a temperate clime may partly understand, but the smiting of the moon, never. You must go to the East, and experience her addling, withering blight, to comprehend the fact that a hard Arabian moon will drive a strong man stark mad in a single night, if he lie unprotected from her light. Even with me under my covering she seemed to be sucking at my vitals.

Weary with watching, and, to say the truth, more than a trifle worried, I fed my rats and went to bed. I lay long awake, in spite of fatigue and the soothing lullaby of lapping waters. At length I began to doze, frequently starting up, however, with a vivid impression of hearing Abram ben Aden calling my name. Rising on my elbow, I would hearken, panting with excitement; but, the great silence being unbroken,

save by the low, sweetly blended voices of wind and
water, I would lie down again, to be honest, with
something of the frozen feeling of a frightened child.
Once I was constrained to get up and look out, first
on one side, then on the other.   But the deep serenity
of nature was undisturbed.   The moon shone resplen-
dently, and the sea, gently crisped by the breeze,
sparkled like fretted silver, or glowed with phosphorescent fire.   The night wind, soft and warm and
odourous, caressed my face and head with a wooing
murmur that would have been delicious, had I been
in a frame of mind to enjoy it; and far aloft the
stars palpitated in their azure setting with a sort of
tender compassion.

Ah! mystery of mysteries, how came all those
splendours to be above me?   And how came I, of all
the millions on earth, to look up at them from such
an utter desolation?   Did I need the lesson of human
feebleness more than any one else?   Was my pride so
stubborn, my disobedience so great, that I had to be
sent out here, a second and lonelier Ishmael, to be
humbled and corrected?   If the sins were many, truly
the punishment was sore.   Faint and trembling, I
leaned against the side for support, and as I rubbed a
clammy face my heart in its anguish and despair
could have burst out in that desolate and piteous cry
that went up from Calvary, the cry which vents the
concentrated misery of a lost race: Yet is not God
the God of mercy, is not God the God of love?   I had
scarcely asked myself the question when, as if by celestial impulse, my mind flew back to a heathery brae-
side, and I was nestling from threatening perils in
arms that compassed me safely about.   As one whom
his mother comforteth!   The wounded animal seeks
its lair that it may die in peace; the wounded spirit
turns home that it may be strengthened and solaced,
were it only by mere recollection.   But for that divine memory, that swift flight through space and
time, I might have gone that instant, and leaped from
the bulwarks into the flood below.   It was an impo-

tent mood, the mood of a coward, if you like; but let those who have been similarly tried say if their hearts have never failed them; and let those who have not beware what fate has in store for them. "They jest at scars who never felt a wound," or in the words of the ancient moralist, "In the thought of him that is at ease there is contempt for misfortune."

I returned to bed by-and-by, falling asleep at length on a resolution to be up next morning with the sun. As it turned out, I was astir in advance of my time. Just as the first glimmer of dawn flickered on the sea, I was startled by a noise of ropes upon the ship's sides, a scurrying of feet on the deck, and a tumult of contending voices in shrill confusion all round. Quick as thought I tumbled out of bed, threw on my clothes, stuck a brace of revolvers in my belt, grasped my sword, and bounded up the companion-way. At the head there was an abrupt and uncomfortable stoppage, for no sooner did my foot touch deck than a score of gleaming scimitars were circling about my throat, in a fashion fit to turn the blood to ice. A throng of swarthy, fierce-eyed, vociferating villains pressed and brandished their weapons so truculently, that I could have sworn to a chilly sensation of steel in my windpipe, though as yet no one had actually touched me. Divining that the rascals were Arabs, I demanded in the Arab tongue, and in rather gasping accents, what this sudden invasion and hostile display meant. At this, a familiar voice called out—

"Enlarge thy turban, friend; great is the bountifulness of Fortune to her favourites."

There was a sardonic laugh from those whose blades were closest about my neck; then one, who seemed to be the leader, pushing a little forward, said sternly—

"This ship is ours! If thou art in love with thy life, surrender; if thou art tired of it, resist. Speak quickly!"

The logic of this laconic speech being perfectly irrestible, I immediately answered—

"Since I value my life, notwithstanding the difficulty of preserving it, I surrender. Will my friends lower their swords? There is no need for so much hostile steel at the throat of a defenceless man."

"When thou hast given up thy weapons," said the spokesman, curtly.

"They who do me the honour of this visit belong to a brave and chivalrous people," I rejoined, remembering Asian manners; "I know their history, and the valour of their deeds, and the songs of their poets. I am a stranger, alone and at your mercy; my arms are my sole possession, I pray you let me keep them."

"Nay, by Fatima's eyelash, arms in thy hands are as poison in the adder's tongue," cried Abram ben Aden, coming forward so that I now caught sight of him. There was a diabolical fire in his black eyes, and his face bore an insolent leer of triumph. The look of him put all my fear to flight, and in its place kindled a sudden and savage desire to be revenged.

"That man," I said, pointing in scorn and anger at him, and forgetting the fate that was so imminent, "that man has betrayed me. He has brought you here to plunder. Is it not so?"

Perhaps it was the unexpected audacity of my mien and question that made them answer so promptly and frankly, but instantly a dozen of them called out, "It is so."

"I have taken this viper to my breast," I cried, "and he has stung me. It is a base thing that stings the hand that helps it. By the honour of your fathers, by your love of vengeance, I charge you to leave him to me. Let it be seen this day how treachery and ingratitude can be requited. We two have eaten salt together; now he clamours for my life. It is his if he can take it. You will grant the prayer of a forsaken stranger that no hand but his enemy's be raised against him."

All this while, the Arabs were swarming upon deck, and pushing and crushing and craning to see me, and catch my words. Their looks encouraged me.

"The ship is yours," I went on, still more boldly. "I yield it without a murmur, only let me put my life against the life of this son of a dog."

"Why do we waste time?" demanded Abram ben Aden, savagely. "Let his infidel throat feel the edge of a believer's sword. Who is he that he should bandy words with us? Off with his head; to the sharks with his carcase, and let us to the spoil."

"Thou art as wise as the goat of Akhfash, Abram ben Aden," said the man whom I took to be the leader. "Thy tongue outspeeds thy wit as the lightning leaves the desert caravan. He has yielded the ship to us. He is ready to put his life upon thy blade-point if thou wilt grant him a like privilege in return. A fair bargain, by the memory of Sikander-el-Rumi. Many a time hast thou boasted of thy skill with the sword; thou lovest revenge as well as any man. Here is thy opportunity to show thou possessest one and canst take the other. . . . What think ye?" addressing his comrades. "Is it not as I say?"

"It is as thou sayest," came quickly in chorus from the two-score eager men.

Inspired by this favourable change of sentiment, I strode forward, and before he could raise a finger to prevent me, caught Abram ben Aden firmly by the beard.

"Last night we ate salt together," I said; "it was the vow of friendship: to-day I spit in thy vile face; it is the vow of eternal enmity," and suiting the action to the word, I spat full in his face. It is the greatest affront you can offer an Arab, or indeed to any man of the Moslem faith.

"Thou shalt rue it!" he shrieked, stamping with rage, while he wiped his face. "By the holy Prophet, thou shalt rue it! Mark me, son of an infidel dog, my sword will slake its thirst ten times over in thy blood. I will hew thee in pieces; I will scatter thee to the winds, so that no man can gather the fragments."

9

In an instant I was back with my sword at the guard ready for the attack.

"Thou hast there the sword I gave thee," I said. "Crown thy baseness, and scatter me."

"Thou art a fool!" he hissed. "There are better things than letting the blood out of thy foul Christian body. I will take revenge for this defilement, yea, revenge that will not so much as leave thy name among men; but not now."

"Hear how a coward can speak," I said to the crowd. "But give us room. Either he takes his revenge now, or I take mine."

"Yea, leave them room," rose on all sides, and the mass pushed back, making a vacant space in the middle. On the one side stood Abram ben Aden, his lean dark face like a fiend's, his knotted throat and swarthy chest heaving with a short convulsive motion, his half-parted lips white with bubbling foam, his fingers nervously clutching the handle of his sword; on the other was I, motionless, deadly pale, I am sure, but with a fixed determination to die or have vengeance. I was perfectly calm, probably because the hazard was so desperate. The gaze of all those alien eyes was as nothing; as nothing, too, was the chance of being killed. Thought and purpose and feeling were concentrated on a single terrible idea. If I had come thus far to die I would not quit the scene for nothing.

I made a movement forward, and Abram ben Aden squeezed back, saying it was of more consequence to secure the booty than to turn aside to put a toad out of existence. But the circular human wall was solid, and he could not get away. As he struggled ignominiously, I advanced and struck him on the cheek with the flat of my sword.

"If there be aught else I can do to affront thee," I said, "name it."

He glared like a baited bull as I stepped nimbly back a little; then, thinking to rush in and end the encounter at a blow, he sprang at me with the headlong ferocity of a tiger. But he had miscalculated. Swerving slightly, I caught his blade on mine, and the sharp, fell ringing of steel announced to the remotest of the spectators that two men were fighting for their lives.

We got every opportunity to slay each other according to our own methods. The crowd preserved complete silence, showing no disposition to interfere. There was no commotion; the drama of death went on without sound, save what was made by the whistling, clashing swords of the combatants; for the Arabs, being undemonstrative on such occasions, take the sight of blood and the issues of life and death without excitement or horror or pity.

I have no recollection of the particulars of the fight. I only know that, for my part, I went at it with a single simple purpose, that I had no thought of fancy swordsmanship, nor; indeed, of anything else, save not to yield while I could draw breath.

My opponent had the first blood. By some accident or clumsiness on my part his sword in glancnig off mine struck my shoulder, peeling it. But the wound, though it bled freely, was a flea-bite, and if it had any effect at all it was to spur me on. From that moment I pressed the harder, forcing my antagonist back inch by inch to larboard, the crowd giving way in that direction. He fought as a cornered devil might fight, but, in spite of his fury, or perhaps because of it, I kept pushing him steadily before me till, at last, his heel was against the vessel's side. Finding himself at the wall he uttered a great oath, the first word he had spoken since we engaged, and plied his weapon with such swiftness and force that it was a marvel I escaped being slain on the spot. No doubt it was my reckless calm that saved me, though it is fair to add it was materially aided by his ignorance of point-play or the advantage of the thrust. At any rate, by meeting him at every point at once, as if I had the eyes of Argus and the hands of Briareus, I was able to maintain my ground; nay, was able to keep his back glued to the brig's side.

Blood flowed on both sides, yet the sight of it did not relax my resolution, if resolution it can be called, which was a blind determination to have my sword in my opponent's vitals, or his in mine. One of us two must die; that was the fell verdict. So we fought, not to show our science, but as men fight who are bent on killing each other in the shortest possible space of time. I had but to look into his eyes to see the fate intended for me, and I dare say he looked into mine and read with equal clearness that meant for him.

There was no device known to either of us—and Abram ben Aden must have cursed himself for my dexterity—to which we did not resort. Yet the advantage hung in the balance; and the stolid gravity of the spectators was giving place to a restless impatience to see one of us finish the other.

The breathing was becoming hard and fast, and there was some risk we might be deprived of the satisfaction for which both of us panted by our very eagerness and violence in trying to get it. That some such thought must have flashed across Abram ben Aden's mind was quickly made manifest by his manœuvring. Blowing and staggering as if in the last stage of exhaustion, he suddenly swerved, apparently with the intention of flight, at the same time making a very feeble defence. The ruse nearly gave him my life. For an instant I thought I had him, and my whole being thrilled with unholy glee. But the light in his eyes and my knowledge of his crafty ways speedily put me on my guard again and restrained my ill-timed exultation. Well for me that they did. Scarcely had I recovered myself when Abram ben Aden, with a great roar, and strokes that fell like lightning, charged upon me, pushing me back and nearly running in under my sword. But he had delayed the onset just a second too long. Had he made his rush immediately on the heels of his retreat, I had been a dead man. But he took too much pains to mislead me. Deception had o'erleaped itself and opened my eyes.

But he was quickly to make amends for his mistake in tactics. He had been a savage before; his failure turned him into a fiend. His sword sang in my ears like a nest of hornets, and his blows fell like a shower of missiles. Overborne by an onslaught that was the very fury of the pit, I went steadily back, though exerting all my strength and skill. Abram ben Aden had got his second wind, which was stronger than the first, while I was done. The end must be at hand.

This curdling thought had just been forced upon me, when, in one of our most furious moments, my antagonist's sword broke without warning in his hand.

My blood became as fire at the sight, and I must have swelled with the consciousness of victory. Now, in very truth, I had him. He was mine—mine to do with him as I would. Escape was impossible; no power under heaven could rob me of my revenge.

But the elation was just a trifle premature; the calculations a trifle too confident. There were two things I failed to take into account—the valour of the desperate, and the resource of a self-possessed rogue, who had spent his life in shedding blood. Quick as his own evil thought, he plucked a crooked dagger from his girdle, and swift as the swoop of an eagle he was upon me. He came very near sheathing his blade in my body. But, more by luck than skill, I struck the weapon from his grasp, and it flew over the heads of the crowd into the sea, while a writhing horror shot across Abram ben Aden's face.

I suppose a devilish rapture leaped afresh into mine; for, with a despairing cry upon the name of Allah, he shrank back, impotently shielding himself with outspread hands; and, being balked in his effort to get away, clamoured aloud for mercy. Mercy! mercy to the serpent that has stung you, yea, the mercy of swift and violent death, the mercy that would not only kill, but tear and rend and scatter the

fragments to the winds—even such mercy as he would
show to me.

Drawing in my breath deep and fierce, I paused
just an instant to gloat over my triumph.   My enemy
would have been a piteous sight to any one not beside
himself with the madness of destruction.   His hor-
ror-struck, blood-shot eyes protruded as if they had
been half plucked out, and left hanging upon the
edges of the sockets; his gnarled throat and wrinkled
chest laboured hideously with the rasping, spasmodic
action of a beast in the throes of a sudden agony; and
his knees knocked together like castanets.   But to
me, in my flaming state, his distress was joy unspeakable, such electric, diabolic joy as the destroyer
feels in the supreme moment of victory.   I could
scarcely believe that Heaven had delivered the black-
hearted ingrate and betrayer into my hands.

To make certain of satisfying my fury upon him,
I would despatch him at once.   This full cup of bliss
must not on any account be imperilled.

I stepped forward, sword in air, to cleave the cringing thing in two.   But the blow never fell.   Even
with all my passions raging, I could not take advantage of a creature so abject.

"I have broken your sword," I said in a hoarse rattle, "now I will break your neck:" and, dropping my
weapon, I sprang at him.

The next instant we were reeling in deadly wrestle.
He was a grown man, strong, sinewy, and uncommonly active; I was but a stripling, soft of bone and
muscle; yet my arms were no sooner about him than
I knew which of us was master.   We rolled and
swayed to and fro, I doing my best to squeeze and
shake the wind out of him and he striving, like the
foul fiend, to get at my throat; but my hold was firm
if my breath should be short; and, besides, I was at
familiar exercise, whereas the game must have been
strange to him.   When I judged the wind to be
pretty well out of him I drew him close to me with a
sudden jerk, my elbows hard on his ribs, my left knee

at the joint of his right leg; then, carefully maintaining the bear-like embrace, while putting forth my whole strength, I bent him back and he turned over like a willow sapling. The next moment the fingers of my left hand were fixed like hooks of steel in the links of his throat, while the right clutched the lower part of his body, and, before he could recover, I lifted him high in the air and brought him down with all my might on the edge of the bulwark. He yelled in the excruciation of the pain. But a sort of Pythian frenzy was upon me. It was death or nothing. In an instant he was up again, but finding him limp and listless in my hands, instead of bringing him down with a second crash, I hurled him headlong from me, as a thing not worth attention, and he fell into the sea with a splash like a log.

CHAPTER XII.

FIGHTING FOR THE BOOTY.

I TOOK no heed whether he sank or swam, nor indeed so much as cast a glance after him; but, turning quickly on my heel, picked up my crimsoned sword, wiping it roughly on a coil of rope that lay handy. Then, making my best salaam to the pirate leader, and speaking as well as a blown man might, I said, "You have graciously granted my prayer and the satisfaction for which my soul yearned; in token of submission and gratitude, I now sheathe my sword in sight of all." And, suiting the action to the word, I shot the weapon into its steel scabbard, with a clash that could be heard all over the ship. The chief bowed grimly in return, but without speaking a word; then, courtesies being at an end, he gave the command, and the looting began.

Leaning against the companion head, I watched the wild rush and scuffle for a minute; but being greatly hustled and buffeted, and feeling faint besides, I tottered to a secluded corner, where I sank with a reeling sensation on the deck. Huddled there, pretty much like a bundle of old clothes, I mopped my face, and tried to discover the sources of the many streams of blood that seemed to ooze and trickle all over my body. There was, perhaps, no great effort made to staunch the flow, for I was far enough gone to be careless. What did it matter? Might I not quietly pant out my life there and be done with it? And even while the thought was in my mind, the brightness of the sun was suddenly overcast, as by the duskiness of death, and the clamour of the robbers died away in my ears.

I must have been some time in this state of collapse, when the brig grated harshly on the bottom, careened slightly, lurched and lay over, fast aground. The queer grating sensation, as of the pricking of a million small pins, roused me, and I staggered, half awake, to my feet. The first thing I saw was Abram ben Aden being hauled dripping by two men into a boat. I rubbed my eyes, wondering how he came to be in need of help, or to have companions to render it, and finding no answer, called out as lustily as I could, "Hello! What's the matter there?"

He heard and looked up. At sight of me the fire of hell sprang anew into his black eyes, and his thin features gathered in a malevolent scowl. Then my wandering wits began to return, bringing a remembrance of what had happened.

I should have fallen into the sea but for the support of the bulwark. In a dizzying turmoil of feelings I laid hold with trembling hands to keep myself up, my eyes fast on the distorted face of Abram ben Aden.

"God! man, are ye much hurt?" I asked, scarcely knowing what I said. "We're a pair of fools," I added, laughing and crying together.

But either he did not hear me or he was beyond speech, for he only cast a look as if to say he wished he had my heart out, and slipped into the boat, which hid him from my view.

I was fain to sit down again, my back propped against the vessel's side, and breathe myself. The commotion of spirit brought a fresh gush of blood, which bathed back and chest in a warm stream. Yet what I had just seen occupied me more than my wounds. Indeed, forgetting both them and the black vindictiveness of Abram ben Aden's countenance, I felt only an all-pervading joy at seeing him alive again. For now, being past thoughts of vengeance, and much too weak to have heart for slaughter, I realized in some measure what a disquieting thing it is to face the great last reckoning with the blood of a fellow-creature on your head. I hoped that the man whom I had so lately and so desperately striven to kill might live, even were it only to finish me. And I am sure I should have smiled inanely; who knows but I may have beamed in welcome if he had suddenly appeared, sword in hand, and intimated that my time was come? No doubt my mood of Christian meekness and charity was due to the circumstance that nature was perilously near yielding in any case. I suspect the best of us occasionally owe our piety to lack of pith.

Reviving a little presently, I began to think of my own life (since no one else seemed to desire it especially just then), and exerted what surgical skill I possessed. It was not much, and it received no aid. Lying there in the midst of a crowd, no one inquired about my hurts, no one offered help; no one, in fact, cared a straw whether I lived or died. The plundering went on with much noise and not a little quarrelling, and if the plunderers came near it was only to curse at me for being in the way.

Perhaps they could not have adopted more effective means of dispelling my lethargy. There are times when a kick, literal or metaphorical, is the very best tonic that can be administered. The rough behaviour of the pirates pricked me to a vigourous self-interest that no process of soothing or doctoring could have induced. The savage oaths and savager looks were to my spirit what the grindstone is to the knife; they turned listlessness and dulness to an activity that had an edge of anger, and some possibility of retaliation. The first result of this new found energy was the thought that to crouch there and bleed to death was most assuredly not the part of a man. So, watching my opportunity (for the companion-way was mostly blocked with thieves), I went below to finish my dressing.

Fortunately my wounds, though making so gory a show, were neither deep nor dangerous. But it was wonderful in how many places Abram ben Aden had touched me; more wonderful still that having succeeded so far he had not succeeded farther. I owed my escape to the fact, as I have already hinted, that the Arab swordsman has still to learn the use of the point.

Returning on deck presently, swathed in handkerchiefs and stray pieces of cloth, and strengthened by twenty grains of Mr. Watson's quinine, I discovered we were within sight of land. A stretch of shallow, blue-green water ran away to a sandy beach that ended abruptly in iron cliffs, which suggested hardness and barrenness beyond.

"What is the land?" I asked one of the corsairs, pointing shoreward.

"Thou shalt know soon enough," he snarled; and concluding that perhaps the fellow was right, I forbore to put more questions.

Meanwhile the unloading of the brig went on apace. A score of small boats lay round her to receive the plunder, and some thirty or forty men swore on her decks and ravaged her hold. They quarrelled incessantly, shouting, pushing, kicking, brandishing knives and cutlasses, and pouring out curdling maledictions and threats that to a less fervid race could mean nothing short of an instant intention to revel in blood, but never staying the main operations to settle personal disputes.

Islam has a Koran which straitly forbids thieving, yet the Arab is by education and example a thief. A pattern of piety when there happens to be no chance of profitable roguery, saintly in his observances of prescribed ceremonials inside a mosque or when he has leisure for prayers outside, a loud talker about the duty of obedience to God and the Prophet, he is the very flower, the perfection of brigands and bandits when he can securely lay hands on another man's goods. Nor does he regard discipline more than religion; for whatever deference he may profess for authority, pillage swiftly transforms him into a rebel. No sooner had the band about me got to work than it was a howling, disorganized mob, regardless alike of leader, order, and unity of interest.

Civilization teaches the value of concerted action; the barbarian lacks the intelligence to understand the use of combination in crime; the art and policy of a judicious division of spoils are beyond him. Consequently, in that scene of clamourous contention, each rogue simply seized and made off with what he could gather, defending his booty with tooth and claw, after the manner of his fellow-savages, the wolf and tiger. Standing idly by, I took a grim delight in noting how they thwarted and hindered themselves, and what time and energy were spent in bootless scuffling.

As the cargo diminished the struggle grew hotter and the hubbub louder. Curses and recriminations rose shrill and fierce; faces were black and swollen with avarice, eyes ablaze with anger; and it seemed the thing must inevitably end in a flood of gore.

"May the devil fly away with thee, thou son of a dog!" . . . "I will see thee in the clutches of Azrael,* thou mongrel cat, ere parting with an ounce weight to thee!" . . . "May perdition be thy eternal portion, thou foul thief!" . . . "Calamity make thy leg bare!" . . . "May scorpions eat thy heart out, thou unjust man!" . . . "By Allah,

*Azrael, the angel of death.

I will cut thy head off!" . . . "Malec* have thee eternally in his keeping!" . . . "May thy hands rot for their greediness, oh, most wicked of robbers!" . . . "Mayest thou be seethed in boiling oil!" Such were some of the stimulating cries with which the pillagers carried on their scramble.

In the midst of the strife, when the tumult was at its height, and the company so intent on clutching and tearing from each other that they had no eyes for anything else, suddenly there rang out a startled cry that sent burdens rolling on the deck and hands gripping in girdles for pistol or blade.

"Enemy, enemy!" yelled a man, who chanced to look out to sea; and sure enough there, less than a tenth of a league off, were two large boats full of men coming swiftly towards us, under the combined impulsion of sail and oar. Perhaps a sixth of a league beyond there rode at anchor a vessel of strange rig and build, from which it was plain they had come.

The crew on board the *Bird of Paradise* acted with the valour of surprised thieves. Evidently of the mind that half a loaf is better than no bread, many of them leaped into the boats alongside and tried to make off with what booty they had managed to secure. But before they could get away the strangers were among them, and in a twinkling half the boats were floating keel up. It was surprising to see the rapidity with which boat after boat canted over and emptied its contents, human and inanimate, into the sea. A push, the touch of an oar, a jerk on bows or stern seemed to do it. But skill ever gives an idea of ease; and it was plain the present performers were playing familiar parts. .The fellows in the water spluttered, bellowed, and threatened; but as the tongue was the only weapon they were able to use with any freedom, their opposition scarce counted as a hindrance. The strangers laid about them with their oars with such vigour and dexterity, such lightning-like quickness and precision, that ere one could

* Malec, the keeper of Hades.

say the thing had well begun hardly a boat remained right side up.

Having worked confusion in the water, the conquerors came clambering over the sides of the brig, their ugly, crooked swords in their teeth, and a light in their eyes that was uglier than the gleam of their steel. There was a pretence of resistance by the remainder of the first comers, but before there was any chance of slaughter they were dodging about the deck, and playing hide-and-seek about the masts. At this signal of surrender weapons were put up with a promptness that would have astonished any one ignorant of Arab ways; and with one accord all hands —first comers and last alike—fell to the old game, only that now instead of being lowered into boats the goods were thrown into the sea, which was soon thickly mottled with bales and boxes. It did not take long to relieve the brig of her cargo, and as soon as the last bale was overboard the robbers followed it to continue the scrimmage outside.

For me who remained on the brig there was no lack of entertainment. There was exhilaration amounting at times to positive excitement in watching the nimbleness and straits of the combatants and the frequency with which the booty changed hands. The incidents were often such as would have made freeminded spectators roar with delight. Now there would be a knot of men inextricably entangled, as it might seem, and just as you thought the lot must go down together, a lucky boat would dart clear. Then there would be exciting pursuit and capture, or the runaway, giving all its attention to its pursuers, would rush into the clutches of a skirmisher lying in wait on the outskirts. Again, a cluster of boats would be locked into a sort of pontoon-bridge, which would sway and rock for a while, till in the energy of the action it would suddenly tilt or careen, pitching men and goods into the water; or again, two men wrestling would lose their balance and turn over like revolving buoys, to come up blinking, spluttering,

and streaming at the mouth as if they were automatic
pumps.   Then, shaking themselves roughly like a
couple of drenched dogs, they would probably close
again to repeat the same diverting peformance.   Thus
the sport went on with endless variety of incident and
no bloodshed that I could see to mar the enjoyment.

By degrees the combatants drew away from me, for
besides the tendency of such a battle to spread, the
ebbing tide was carrying the wares out to sea, making it necessary to follow them.   It was clear that
the last comers were getting most of the spoil.   A
few of the others, dodging and watching their chance,
managed to make off, carrying freight for ballast, but
the frequent trips to and fro between the centre of
war and the anchored ship told where most of the
plunder was going.

There are no reapers with a tithe of the energy and
speed of pirates.   In spite of the time wasted in useless contention, in spite of races, captures, somersaults,
and the thousand and one egregious hindrances indulged in, as might almost appear from a spirit of
sheer frivolity, the harvest was quickly gathered, and
very soon the only floating objects to be seen were the
ship with her boats near at hand, and in the distance
other boats running for life with the tide.

As the diversion declined, my mind naturally reverted to my own miserable condition.   What was to
become of me?   Was I to be left to my own devices
with a stranded ship and no commons?   And if so,
what should I do?   Should I make my way ashore
and risk the savageness of man and beast, or remain
on the brig to await developments?   While I was
thus thinking and debating, a boat put off from the
pirate ship and rowed towards me.   Coming alongside, its crew climbed on board the brig, and, judging
it best to be civil, I received them with a profound
salaam and a cordial marhaba, or welcome.   I might
have saved my pains.   Instead of returning my salutation the leader came forward with drawn sword,
demanding to know whether there was any treasure

on board, and intimating that if he caught me in a
lie my throat would be cut on the spot. I assured
him that I knew of no treasure, but invited them to
search for themselves, since there might be secret recesses in the ship that I had not discovered.

"Thou shalt be guide," said the fellow, "and as
thou valuest thy life, a true one. It is likely thou
knowest the taste and virtue of steel."

It is perhaps unnecessary to say that I complied with
alacrity, conducting them faithfully into every corner
above and below, for the fear of death gives wondrous
fidelity. They examined very deliberately as they
went along; battering, probing, even rending the
frailer fittings and boardings, hanging upon doubtful
sounds from beam or bulkhead, and then in their disappointment turning with furious questions and men-
aces on me, as if I were responsible for their ill-luck,
or were concealing valuable knowledge. One fellow,
muttering that I was playing the innocent just a little too much, thrust at me ferociously with his sword,
saying that if I did not wish to be cut in two I had
better spurt out all I knew. Fortunately he was not
close enough to do damage, and on my answering him,
with a fervency that must have carried conviction to
the heart of a stone, that I knew no more than he did,
he passed on with a curse on my stupidity and blind-
ness. I fairly perspired with the tension of it; and
indeed there were frequently recurring moments when
I lost hope of ever getting into the upper air again.
But I was suffered to live because my death would
have profited them nothing, and because, however
strong the inclination, there was no time to be wan-
tonly cruel.

Feeling their way foot by foot, and taking nothing
for granted, they went over the whole interior of the
ship—hold, forecastle, cabin, officers' quarters and all;
questioning, contradicting, threatening, and every
minute getting more and more frightful with looks
of disappointment and rage.

My poor belongings they scattered like chaff, appropriating what they considered worth carrying away, and effectually disposing of the remainder by cutting and tearing it into shreds and then throwing the rags into the sea. Besides my clothes they took all my weapons (save a pistol I had hidden), and all the ammunition they could find, but by good chance I was able to save my mother's Bible and Duncan's pipes, Isabel's two bunches of white heather, and the miniature of Donald Gordon, treasures which, as you may suppose, were almost as my life to me. To this were added some powders and pills left by Mr. Watson. The rifling done, I was peremptorily ordered on deck, and I ascended alone.

This arrangement puzzled me, but I was soon enlightened. In a few minutes a thin column of smoke curled up through the after hatch, then another rose further forward, then another and another, till the several volumes spread and blended into a thick cloud.

It grieved me to see the brig's fate sealed in this way; we had been friends long, and she had saved me when there was no hope. But what could I do to save her?

When the fire had gained sufficient headway to ensure its speedy victory, the incendiaries reappeared, and one of them, pointing with his sword to the boat alongside, growled that I might get in. In an instant I was down and crouching meekly in the bows, where I was likeliest to be out of the way. The others followed quickly, and we rowed away, leaving the *Bird of Paradise* in a sheet of flame. Almost in the same moment my company of rats sprang into the water, and struck out gallantly for the shore. In spite of fear I could not help giving them a hearty "well done" for farewell.

CHAPTER XIII.

IN THE HANDS OF THE CORSAIRS.

IMMEDIATELY on boarding the Arab vessel we hove up anchor, set sails, and flew away to sea with a smart breeze on our port quarter. The ship was a queer one, but it was soon proved that, however odd in appearance, she was an uncommonly swift and graceful sailer. She carried three masts, lateen sails, and a jib. The fore and main masts were without tops, or top-gallants, and, of course, without caps or cross-trees. The long slender hull was jet black, and, what was strangest of all, the upper deck was sharply convex, with level gratings running round the sides. The convexity, as I afterwards discovered, was meant to make a ready way for water to the scuppers, or in times of stress for blood; while the gratings, by obviating the slant, made the footing firm, a matter of importance in storm or action. She carried no colours: nor did any inscription, such as ships usually bear, give a hint of her port or nationality. Finally, though light, she was well armed.*

Every stitch of her ocherous canvas was·crowded on, and beautifully she swept along, heeling and dipping under the bellying sails, the bright green water swishing from her gleaming sides, and the snow-drift flying from her fore-foot in a way that would have been pure ecstasy to one with an untroubled mind. Even I felt the gladness of the rushing, arrowy motion, though on the whole the speed was more ominous than inspiring, seeing the dubious tune to which I might be made to dance at the end of the trip.

The strain of dark uncertainty was somewhat relieved by the diversion of studying the crew, who

---

* The vessel was the dreaded xebec, the terror of the high seas when Algerine corsairs flourished, and still of evil repute on the coasts of Arabia.

10

were a living epitome of the fashions, past and current, of pretty nearly all the nations of the earth. Probably no company of equal size ever displayed a like variety of costumes; assuredly none could be more innocent of ablutions or on more distant terms with the tailor. It was impossible to say which gave the greater distinction, the diversity, the dirt, or the tatters. There were Arab shirts reaching to the ankle, Indian turbans, Syrian combazes, European jerkins, top-boots, jerseys, hats and frock coats, Persian gowns, breeches of all known cuts and countries—in every degree of foulness, in every stage of decay and raggedness—jumbled together as if some malicious artist had tried what effects of incongruity and grotesqueness, what outrages on taste and decency he was capable of achieving.

The captain might have challenged the world to match him as an example of the ridiculous. He was elaborately arrayed in a steeple-beaver, strongly suggestive of the defunct missionary, in spite of its jaunty ostrich plume and tarnished silver band; a coarse woollen shirt, smeared like a hog in autumn; a leathern girdle, from which depended a sword, a brace of pistols, and a crooked dagger full of significant purple stains; Turkish trousers that had originally been crimson, but were now of more hues than the makers of Joseph's coat ever dreamed of, a pair of red boots that must once have had their splendour on state assemblies and gatherings of grandees; and sashes enough of various colours to furnish a regiment of sheiks. The decorations were thickest in the rear; indeed, when the gallant captain turned his back, it might seem that some mischievous sprite had clapped a porous plaster on a certain part of his person, so oddly mixed were the incrustations of tar, grease, paint, and other adhesive susbtances. No sense of absurdity, however, disturbed his serene self-consequence. He paced the deck with as proud a step, as high and keen a look as if he were an Admiral of the Fleet in faultless uniform, and the evidence of a hundred victories blazing on his breast. He seldom condescended to any familiarity with those about him, never with me crouching in my corner.

We tore along at an incredible rate, and were soon beyond sight of land, though for a good while the smoke of the burning brig showed our starting-point. Whither we were bound I could not guess, and durst not ask. I was free to conjecture, if I pleased, that our course was for some happy haven not far off, though appearances rather suggested a cruise for less desirable things.

By-and-by we hauled our wind and began to fetch in a backward direction. But we had not gone a league when we bounded off on another tack; and for the next hour or two we tacked and changed so frequently, running close-hauled as if for our lives, and dropping off as if in sheer perversity, that I completely lost my reckoning.

It was wonderful how that strangely built ship behaved, how sensitive she was to the gentlest pressure of the helm, how clean, quick, and graceful were all her movements, and how she rushed on her course when she got her head. In spite of rather rough seamanship, only once did she make a mistake. Through a too hasty luff she happened to come dead into the wind's eye, and for the space of a second she hung in irons with loose sails. She seemed to shake herself with vexation like a highly spirited horse thrown on its haunches without reason, turned quickly half round, caught the wind again, and then, with her yellow wings spread to their utmost went skimming along like a sea bird.

It was now well on in the afternoon. The sun, though scorchingly hot, was near our level, and the water had a sheen of purple and crimson. I was beginning to think we were to have a night at sea, when the captain gave the order to put the helm hard down; we swung round and sped on a landward course, sailing free and very swift.

"We shall make land a good hour ere sundown,"

said the captain to his chief officer, giving me the
first authentic information of the day.

By this time my faculty of curiosity had lost its
edge, but at the mention of land I sat up to keep a
look out, and in less than an hour we sighted the
shore. Its general character resembled that of the
part we had left earlier in the day, though I soon saw
we were not returning to the death scene of the luckless *Bird of Paradise*. Instead of a shallow beach
the water ran close to high rocks penetrated by
rugged gorges, into which the sea flowed. No port,
town, or human habitation was to be seen; but that,
all things considered, was not surprising.

We shot into a narrow opening under the darkening brows of toppling cliffs, and immediately the sails
fell together with a flap. Almost before they ceased
fluttering they were in and furled. Then a boat was
lowered, half a dozen steel-sinewed men got into it
and rowed, pulling the ship by a cable. Light and
of small draught, she followed easily, and in half an
hour or so, after manifold windings, we came to a
rude jetty hewn, as it appeared, out of the solid rock.
Here we disembarked, the vessel being made fast to
a rough stone pillar.

As we leaped from the bulwarks to the ledges of
rock that formed the pier, my heart fluttered like a
bird's with conjecture and apprehension, for it was
plain that a crisis was at hand. To guess what it
might be was enough to make the stoutest tremble.
The black precipices, the yawning caverns, and hoarse
roar of warring waters, were of evil suggestion, but
of far darker import than any menace or ugliness of
nature were the lowering faces of my companions.
These men had shown during the day by a hundred
expressive tokens that they resented my presence
among them, and now I fancied I caught them casting sidelong looks at one another, then at their
weapons, then at me, as if settling by such glances of
intelligence the manner of getting rid of me.

With quaking limbs and the direst forebodings, I

fell into line at the bidding of the captain, and we struck single-file into a craggy path, at its best no broader than a sheep-run in the Highlands, and in places so narrow as scarcely to afford foothold for a weasel. Looking upward from the bottom, one could not imagine how it scaled the overhanging precipices that frowned upon us in vast swellings and juttings with the savage, solitary pride of the inaccessible. If the ascent did not prove utterly impossible, it was because every man of us had the feet of a goat and the sinews and agility of a monkey.

Glancing ahead our ribbon of a path looked like a series of broken lines scratched by a madman's chisel as it wound in crazy coilings and twistings, now rising vertically a dozen feet of smooth slippery stone, now dropping treacherously into a fissure that went down black and yawning to the tormented sea, ceasing suddenly, and again appearing beyond some perilous projection that a chamois would hardly have attempted to pass. As often as not we were on hands and knees, scraping with toes and clutching with finger-nails, as we crawled over some slippery mass, like ants on the polished knob of a glacier, or scrambled up a jagged rock the points of which cut and rent like sharpened flints, or slid down face inward twice our own length to a scarcely perceptible crevice, forming a fresh starting-point. I was bred a hunter, and knew what it was to scale cliffs and tread dizzy ways. I had followed the fox to his lair when the hounds had turned tail, and robbed the eagle's eyrie when the hardiest of my companions stood beneath me holding his breath in awe. But the self-possession and free spirit of audacity which prompted to such hazards and gave them relish, were utterly gone; to speak the truth, I shivered like one suddenly taken with an ague, and a hundred times nearly lost grip and footing and felt myself toppling. At such times I would pause, clutching wildly at any point or inlet on which finger or foot could lay hold, to be struck roughly with the butt-end of a musket, and told with many imprecations to go on.

It was not, as I have said, the terror of the place alone that appalled me. To go leaping and scrambling on a hair line along the brink of a tumbling, hissing gulf that sent the spumes of its wrath high up in clouds, with no outlook or hope of escape, was indeed disconcerting enough, yet scarcely of itself sufficient to take the heart out of a born mountaineer. The tremours and shakings, the alternate spasms of heat and cold were due (I trust it is not cowardly to confess it) not to the threatenings of cliff and chasm, but to the hostile weapons that gleamed in front and rear, and might at any moment be dyed in my blood.

How easy it would be to prod me there and send me toppling mortally wounded into the abyss, to be ground as between millstones at the bottom! A sudden stab in the back, a push, a giddy, headlong fall, and the deed would be done, and no word of it need ever get to the outside world. More than once, as my mind dwelt on this, I clung to the rocks, shuddering like a child in mortal fright. The gruesomeness of the situation was enhanced, too, by the eerie shadow of night. Here and there buttress and jutting promontory flushed into rose, and shone in gold and amethyst; but these points of radiance only gave a hideous emphasis to the deepening gloom of the gorge. They were like the ghastly mockeries of a world I had once known, but was never to know again.

I am no judge of how long or how far we had struggled when, on turning a sharp angle, we came upon an open space, or circular ledge, of the dimensions of a small room. Here we stopped, our sides heaving like the flanks of a spent hound, and the best of us glad to breathe himself.

Whether by accident or the unsuspected design of those about me, I stood on the outer rim, the very edge of the wall that fell fifty fathoms sheer to the surging, unsounded depths beneath. Under that unaccountable species of fascination which lures a man to gaze on the horrible and awful, I bent forward and looked into the black pit at my feet. With a swimming head I drew back. I had not taken a step when I was seized roughly from behind. An icy horror froze my blood, I gave a great gasp, and my knees knocked violently together. The fearful moment I had been anticipating had come. Shutting my eyes I thought of Heaven and home and friends as in a flash, and had just sufficient presence of mind to breathe a prayer.

But, contrary to expectation, I did not feel myself hurled into vacancy. They bandaged my eyes, and bound my hands to my sides, and, thus made helpless, left me standing. I shut my lips tight, and my eyes also, although they were covered, and awaited the fatal thrust and giddy whirl into space. Not a word was spoken. I heard the rustle of garments and the rattle of arms, and away below, the sullen muffled voice of the sea brooding in the wrath that was to kill me, but other sound there was none. The ill-boding silence was more terrifying than the menacing tongues of a hundred enemies, ay, or even than their swords. Could my captors not do the deed at once, and be done with it? and if they simply desired my death, why all this stealthy secrecy? Were they devils to make my last moments a sport and a mockery?

In the crowding fears and agitations, the idea flashed upon me that they meant not only to slay, but to torture me. I thought of all I had read about living men being flayed and cut into bits by savages, and my flesh crept and shrank as if at the touch of the knife. It was only by keeping teeth and lips clenched that I managed to hold from venting my agony in shrieks.

To my great astonishment and unutterable relief, the procession began to move on again, I being given the muzzle of a musket to direct my steps. Bruised, cut, bleeding, and panting with fear and fatigue, I stumbled often, causing my guide to curse savagely and threaten to pitch me head foremost down the cliff. I could not help thinking that if he were blindfolded he might go just as clumsily, though I had to keep the opinion guardedly behind my teeth.

Presently there was another brief halt, and I could hear the Arabs in whispered consultation. Then I knew that part of the company went one way, and part another, I sticking to my gun barrel as if it were my sole hope of salvation. Another breathless clamber followed, doubly trying to me in my blinded condition, and in a little while I understood from the free play of the air that at last we had reached the top.

I had hardly time to wonder what was coming next, when one of my guards spoke.

"We wish to be rid of thee," he said bluntly. "Listen well to my words; for they concern thy very life. While we were yet far down the gulf, some said, 'Cut him in two, and cast him to the fishes;' others, and well for thee they prevailed, answered, 'No, rather let him live, if so be he go not to come back. If he return, then shall his blood be upon his own head.' Now we are merciful. We will lead thee to a place of safety some distance hence, and there leave thee; only if for the space of one hour thou triest to free thine eyes from their covering, then as surely as thou doest it, thou shalt die ere thou hast time to look twice."

Without waiting for a word from me he gave the order, and we went on again. The ground was broken and uneven, but after the pit sides we had climbed, it was like the Queen's highway.

We may have marched for an hour, when we stopped. I was made to sit upon a stone; then they untied my hands, admonishing me to remember the penalty for disobedience in respect to the bandage on my eyes, and having given me my pipes, which in a surprising spirit of generosity had been taken care of, they left me.

I sat there for a while with perfect loyalty, acutely

mindful of the injunctions and admonitions I had received. I kept my hand tight on the green bag; in the stress of terror just gone through, I had forgotten it; but now that it was returned, its touch had for a moment something of the solace of an old friend's presence.

Partly to amuse myself, partly to compute the flight of time, I began to count the seconds, but it proved a weary process, and was given up, only, however, to be begun again, and again stopped, and yet again resumed, to be finally abandoned in despair. In the usual reckoning, an hour is but sixty short minutes; that hour was an eternity. With stoical resolution, though anything but stoical indifference, I tried to sit stock still, imagining the while a hundred levelled spears at my side, ready to be plunged into me at my first movement. The ordeal kept every nerve aquiver; every sense in a flutter of dread.

The disciples of Zeus have a pretty doctrine about arming "the obdurate beast with stubborn patience, as with triple steel." I hope they are able to do it in crucial emergencies. To me, seek it as I might, the stubborn patience would not come. In vain I pricked the will, in vain recalled lofty maxims about the duty of bearing pain heroically. It is glorious to shine as a hero; but at times exceedingly difficult. I cannot be of the God-like race for the harder I strove for fortitude, the faster my power of endurance ebbed.

I started and fidgeted, listened, held my breath, shivered, shrank together and perspired; the air was full of ominous sounds, and horrible slimy things seemed to be crawling over me. At last the agony of blind suspense became insufferable. Come what might, I would have my eyes free.

With trembling hands, and a caution that was amazing in such burning impatience, I raised the bandage and glanced from under its edge, first on one side, then on the other. Seeing no watcher I tore the cloth off, and got to my feet, looking round with more care and deliberation.   Not a soul was about.   I was alone, absolutely alone.

There was just light enough to enable me to discern I was in the middle of a wild desolation of gorges and piled-up cliffs rising in the dim distance to what appeared to be a range of mountains.   More for variety's sake than from any definite object, I took up my pipes and began to walk forward from the sea.   But some falls and frequent trippings, with sudden glimpses of a yawning world of blackness at my very feet, made it plain that to proceed in such a chaos of crags and clefts was to risk my neck at every step. Weary, faint, and in no heart to face unknown dangers, I sat down again, my back against a big stone, to reflect on the new turn affairs had taken.

Hunger fell upon me with the fierceness of a beast of prey.   Most people, I suppose, have felt a sharp craving in the stomach, but mine was a burning pain that soon became a maddening anguish.   You are to remember that I had eaten nothing that day, that I was active and had the importunate appetite that comes with a full recovery from sickness, when nature is spurring to make up for lost time.   Yet all I could do was to tighten my waist-belt and think yearningly of the hard tack of the *Bird of Paradise*, and dream ineffable dreams of the sumptuousness of home.   Let me tell you that they who dine on such fare are not likely to die of repletion.   The sting of the sword or the bullet is keen, but give it to me before the inappeasable pang of starvation.

The stars began to come out presently, very large and lustrous; and I suppose, to the proper eye, full of poetry.   By-and-by a silvery lightness fell on the landscape, and a little later, the white moon rose in a sapphire sky, revealing the haggard dreariness of the scene as clearly as if the time were noon-day.

I got to my feet, and some strange birds that had their dwelling among the fastnesses of this desert flocked about me in evident curiosity: then flew away screaming at my invasion of their retreat.   No other living creature did I see or hear. Too weak and drowsy to make any effort for succour, I crawled into a shady spot beneath the ledge of a great rock, and in spite of trouble and pain, soon fell asleep.

I awoke near the dawn chilled to the bone, for the dewy night air in those parts is shrewd, and fallen together like an empty sack. The pain of my stomach was excruciating, being for all the world like a living, consuming flame in my inside. To the tortures of hunger, too, was now added the torture of thirst, and in all the black riven wilderness there was not a drop of water. More disheartening still, there was not a sign of human abode or occupation anywhere to be seen. The temptation was strong to lie down and rest, but as that would be madness if I wanted to save my life, I staggered on once more, ignorant of my direction, and in the last ebb of hope.

Weary hours passed; hours full of indescribable agony of mind and body. The sun came out, a huge white-hot furnace, enveloped in a pale haze of its own heat. The earth blistered and cracked under my eyes; the rocks were scorching; it seemed as if fire and famine were blackening the land together. A slight wind blew, but it was the poisonous breath of the crater or sulphur-pit let loose to destroy.

Gasping to suffocation, and dreading sun-stroke, I hid in a deep cleft; here I lay a while in shade, but very soon the sun smote in upon me till the walls were like glowing iron. Crawling out, I sought another refuge which, in turn, became an oven, forcing me to change; and so, for the best part of that day I went from place to place among the rocks seeking shade, and all the while getting fainter and more parched, from want of food and water.

Late in the afternoon I resumed my march in sheer desperation. But it was woeful, heartbreaking work. I had got past the stage of acute pain from hunger, but the thirst was a worse agony than ever. Fortunately the hot, noxious wind had fallen about noon, so that I breathed more freely; but it was still the struggle of a dying man. And, indeed, if relief did not come quickly I should soon cease to be in need of it.

By degrees the country grew less barren and forbidding. Grass began to appear, at first in scanty brown patches, but gradually getting greener and more plentiful. This heartened me a bit, and ere long, to my infinite joy, I came upon a man herding a flock of goats in a little valley that nestled among the cliffs.

He was mightily astonished at seeing me; and his demeanour at first was none too friendly. But my wretched condition must have touched him, for when I came tottering and rolling down the slope to where he stood he stepped forward to meet me with words of pitying inquiry. I saluted briefly, and appealed to him in Heaven's name to let me have drink or I should die. In an instant the Christian soul was vigourously milking his best goat. I watched till the skin was half full of the frothing, creamy milk, then, unable to forbear, I snatched it from him, and drank till I choked. After slaking myself I had some dates from his wallet, and felt wondrously revived. And for his charity he had as grateful thanks as ever came from the heart of a perishing man.

When we came to talk I told him only such parts of my story as I thought he could understand. He was greatly amazed, breaking out into frequent ejaculations at the relation of Abram ben Aden's treachery, and the pillaging of the pirates.

"And what is to become of thee?" he asked suddenly.

"Only God knows that," I answered. "But if thou wilt add to thy goodness by directing me to the nearest town, I may perhaps find a way of returning to my own country."

This he gladly did, but before he would consent to my departure I had to take some more milk and dates. Nothing loth I feasted a second time, the goatherd joining me in token of good will. Then, with ceremonious embracings and many vows of amity, we parted.

Rekindled hope is the best of all cordials. I had drunk of it and now pushed on a new man, reanimated in body and in spirit. In two hours I was climbing a range of hills beyond which lay the town that happened also to be the capital of the province; in an hour more I was on the top, and Moses, beholding the promised land, could not have gazed forward more wistfully. Pausing for a moment, my eyes shaded with my hand, I looked down upon a verdant plain, dotted here and there with dark palm groves, and the patriarchal flocks and herds of Arabia. On the farther side, embowered among clustering trees, was the town I wanted to reach. With a fluttering breast I went on again, bounding down the slopes almost as joyously as if I were descending the steep braes above Glenrae.

CHAPTER XIV.

STILL AT ODDS WITH FORTUNE.

I was soon swinging light-heartedly along in grateful shade, among the orchards and gardens and tinkling watercourses that skirted the town—a very Eden after the desert I had passed through. The people flocked about me as I went, some eying me with darkening brows, some regarding me with simple amazement, others of a deeper curiosity turning in their walk to follow me; and I could hear them debating what kind of outlandish barbarian this could be, who had unaccountably found his way amongst them. I felt very much like a monster on exhibition for the entertainment of the vulgar and the idle: yet, remembering the necessity of prudence, I was at great pains to be civil. Salaaming and saluting incessantly, I invoked peace and the best blessings of Heaven on all and sundry; but the marhabas or welcomes were disap-

pointingly few. Had I known the full significance
of an Arab's failure to return a salutation, I should
probably have made more haste to get out of the town
than I was now making to get into it. But ignorance is a wondrous preserver of men's spirits.

Judging it best to refrain from asking questions, I
pursued my way at a venture through squalid alleys
that writhed and twisted like endless snakes, turning
upon themselves in eternal windings and circlings,
with the sole object, as it seemed, of bewildering and
distracting.   They led anywhere and everywhere;
but dodged a definite conclusion, being thus no inapt
emblem of the tortuous Asiatic mind.   The scents
were pungent, and of the kinds that make one fain to
hold one's nose. If these were the "Sabean odours
from the spicy shores of Araby the blest," then let it
be put on record that in spite of the mighty authority
of Milton, Sabean odours are never likely to be popular among people imbued with a prudent love of sani-
tation or endowed with delicate nostrils.

Packs of lean, hungry dogs, too, kept sniffing at
my heels in a way that was sorely vexing.   There
are notoriously ill-conditioned dogs in Turkey and
Greece—Constantinople swarms with them; they are
worse than the brigands in the mountains of Attica.
But of all the despicable, degenerate curs in existence, the starveling hounds that prowl about Arabian
towns are the basest and most degraded.   Without
owners, greedy partakers of all that is vile and forbidden, "the filthiest beasts that banquet upon offal,"
despised and maltreated, marauders by inheritance
and by necessity, they have long lost every vestige
of canine morality. In contemplating an assault they
do not bark at you, nor show their teeth: such
honesty might put you on your guard. They sidle
up to you with the averted look of incurable depravity, pretending to take no notice of you, yet all the
while carefully selecting the juiciest part of your leg.
Even when they have selected their point of attack,
they will not fly at it; but wait patiently for their

opportunity. When it comes, presto, their fangs are in your calf, and they are off with their mouthful before you have time to turn. These brutes kept me continually with one eye over my shoulder, and the other down by my side, for I was ever afraid of the tooth of a dog. Sometimes the people made a pretence of remonstrating with them; but I think there would have been less sorrow than gladness had I been worried to the bone.

The squat box-like shops and bazaars were littered with a miscellany of goods exceedingly strange to European eyes. Variegated cloth, red and yellow slippers, saffron, sandal-wood, glass beads, mirrors, swords, files, razors, ropes, bells, saddles, butter and various nameless kinds of oil and grease used for anointing the head and body, water skins, coffee-pots, brazen pans and kettles, and many other stuffs and trumpery were strewn about in hopeless confusion. Standing by the doors, or sitting cross-legged on palm-leaf mats, in the midst of their wares, waiting with heavy eyes and languid mien for the customers who never appeared to come, were the merchants. One and all they stared hard at me, and most of them came into the street to look after me, with muttered guessings and comments. I have no doubt there were muttered curses as well.

To my surprise, the orchards and gardens ran almost continuously into the centre of the town, and who would was apparently free to enter. In variety and richness they surpassed anything I had ever seen, and indeed seemed rather like the concentrated luxuriance of a whole country than the natural growth of a single spot. There were clumps of feathery date trees, Indian palms, pomegranates, orange, apple, apricot, peach, and fig trees. Another tree there was, too, more famous in Arabian song and story than any of these—the balm tree. Like so much that is good and famous, it is not beautiful; in fact, it is ugly and scraggy and, were the eye the sole judge, contemptible, but those who know its virtues think little of its mean appearance.

In striking contrast to the dark olive foliage were the blazing tropical flowers, many of them of inexpressible glory and brilliancy. But what touched me beyond anything else were some clusters of magnificent roses that flung their fragrance on the air unmindful of the general noisomeness, at times indeed, making one forget it. The sight of that common English flower, so familiar and so lovely, stirred the emotions as not all the splendours of the Orient could stir them. It was like the greeting of an old friend in a strange land.

In some of the gardens people were drawing water from deep wells with leathern buckets, others scooping it up from slender stone-rimmed watercourses. At sight of such plenty I began to get hungry and thirsty again, and so tempting was the fruit that presently I found myself meditating a robbery. But at every gate I decided to wait till I reached the next, and in this way, a thief at heart, an honest man from fear, I went along feasting my eyes, but grievously vexing the stomach, which protested ever more and more vigourously. It is an ill experience to be famishing in the midst of plenty.

On turning one of the many street corners, full of the thought which most engages a hungry man, I entered a square in which was assembled a great crowd. A glance made it plain they were holidaymakers. In the midst was a man wearing, over the usual shirt, a gay parti-coloured mantle, and a scarlet vest with wide sleeves like a bishop's gown. His head was fantastically enfolded in a flaming handkerchief, in the voluminous twists of which there were stuck three bobbing peacock-feathers. He was seated on a camel as gorgeously caparisoned as himself, and was shouting and gesticulating with many wild grimaces, the people responding to his sallies of wit and distortions of countenance with resounding bursts of merriment.

"A professional story-teller," I said to myself, and it proved I was right.

The fellow seemed master of his business, for all were eager and excited, save only the gaunt, sorrowful camel, which was sunk in a gloom no mirth could brighten. Perhaps, like harlequin, it was too familiar with jests to be much cheered by them. I had not watched the performance more than a minute when the clown noticed me. He stared for a second in amazement, but quickly recovering the professional insolence, he pointed a leering finger at me, calling upon the assemblage to look at the rare curiosity that had opportunely appeared for their entertainment. Like one man they wheeled about and fastened their eyes upon me.

At this I turned quickly on my heel to walk off, considering it the safest policy to get out of the way with as much speed and as little fuss as possible. But the story-teller hurling a stinging gibe at me about my courage—a quality I would let no man make a jest of with impunity—I turned again and faced the throng, my heart already beginning to bristle in my breast. There was a moment's silence, then the buffoon on the camel began a running commentary on my looks, my dress, and spirit, enlivening his remarks with witticisms that made very free with my feelings, and sent the listeners—all save one—into convulsions of laughter. He capped his insults and insolences by inviting his audience to step forward and examine me for themselves. The next minute they had formed a ring about me, taking care, however, to keep some distance off, as if I might be an animal of uncertain temper. But a perky youth, in rich cloak and many-coloured sashes, eager to set an example in temerity, and make sport for his fellows, ran up and probed me in the ribs with his riding-stick.

It was wonderful how the old fiery spirit of retaliation came back on me. Quicker than thought I whipped out my pistol and covered the fellow's head.

11

He ducked, dodged, and disappeared like magic. Disappointed at his celerity in getting out of sight I took aim at the clown.   He, too, had an antipathy to such target practice, and, like a flash, was off his camel and hiding among the crowd.   A thrilling pause followed as the people, fallen silent, stared in wonder at me, then at one another, then at the camel standing as saturnine and stupid-looking as ever, apparently quite unconscious of its master's sudden desertion.

Satisfied with having frightened my molesters, and anxious to prove my pacific intentions towards the company in general, I returned the pistol to my belt. Seeing this the chap-fallen story-teller sneaked back for his beast, taking care as he led it off to keep its body between him and me.   The crowd hesitated a moment, as if uncertain which performer to patronize, then went trooping after the clown in evident expectation of further diversion elsewhere.   My impulse was to follow and spoil the fun; but, remembering the discretion which is the better part of valour, I turned aside and went in another direction.

I had not gone a hundred yards when I felt a gentle touch on the arm, and, looking round, found at my side an elderly Arab of venerable and benignant aspect.   As my eyes met his he bowed with a cordial gravity and held out his open hand.   Glad to find any one so friendly I also bowed and laid my open palm in his, waiting for him to speak.

"I was in the midst of the concourse when the jester derided thee and made the people laugh," he began in a kindly tone, "I saw thee pull out thy weapon and aim at the fool who smote thee with his riding stick, and I trembled for thy safety, for assuredly hadst thou slain him thine own blood had watered the ground. When the jester slunk away and the people followed I hastened after thee to speak with thee, and if thou be in need of aught I possess, now of a surety it is thine.   If thou art an hungered thou shalt eat, if thou art thirsty thou shalt drink, if thou art weary thou shalt wash thy feet and rest. Said Achmet hath himself been a wanderer, and knoweth the distress of a stranger in a strange land."

Greatly surprised, though thrilling with joy and gratitude, I replied, "I am indeed a stranger in a strange land, cast on the shore like driftwood, to be tossed and made the sport of fate. But thy kindness puts new spirit in me."

"Art thou hungry?" he asked, looking in my face.

"Hungry, thirsty, and spent," I answered.

"Come with me, my son," said the Arab, graciously. "I would fain know who and what thou art, and how thou camest hither, where I doubt if any man of thy nation ever set foot before. But long tales fit not a craving stomach. When thou hast eaten and rested, peradventure thou wilt tell me thy story."

He led the way, I walking by his side in silence, for it is contrary to Arabian etiquette to make a tired man answer questions. We wound for a long distance through circling streets, then turned aside under the shadow of clustering palms into a small but luxuriant garden, fragrant with flowers and musical with babbling water. From the garden to the house was but a step.

A black slave met us as we entered, and, at a word from his master, brought a pile of cushions to the Khawah, or reception-room, for me, placing them near the stove, which is the place of honour. Then, bringing water, he took off my shoes and washed my feet, a piece of attention that was strange but exceedingly refreshing. After a while came the food. This consisted of a large piece of boiled mutton, a kind of batter made of ground wheat and melted butter, boiled rice, fresh dates, figs, sour camel's milk, and coffee—from the best Arabian berry, that never by any chance comes to Western lands. The abomination that deluded Englishmen gulp down as coffee an Arab menial would not deign to put to his lips. The truth is

that the untravelled Briton never sees, not real
Mocha, because it is a thing of the past, but the choice
fruit of the coffee tree; what passes with him as such
is only the refuse of all the plantations of Arabia (and
often of plantations outside Arabia) gathered in the
interest of shippers, and greatly to the prejudice of
occidental palates and stomachs. The pale flavour-
less berries sent to Western Europe and America are
to the rich, brown, aromatic berries valued by Eastern peoples what the sour crab-apple is to the luscious
nectarine. Yet the swells of London and Paris drink
the muddy mixture served to them as coffee with
symptoms of delight. Truly ignorance has its enjoy-
ments and consolations. As for myself, my nose
never comes over a cup of the English preparation
without causing me a spasm of disgust.

The meal was all brought in together heaped on one
huge wooden trencher, and what had been on the fire
was eaten scalding hot with the fingers, for the Arabs
scorn the frivolity of knives and forks. I found no
difficulty whatever in reverting to the methods of
Adam. The batter I could make nothing of, since it
was like putty in my hands, and the mutton seemed
none too cleanly dressed; but on the rice and fruit
I fell with the furious zeal of a famishing man, being indeed as empty as a dry well.

The meal finished, literally finished, for Arab hospitality enjoins that a guest shall eat while a morsel
remains, we washed our hands, an operation that was
highly necessary, and went into the garden to smoke
the pipe of peace under the umbrageous cover of date
palms.

I cannot express the luxury of reclining in that verdurous scene watching the sun descending to "his
chambers" in the west. Put mind and body at rest
after racking both; let fruits and blossoms and green
masses of foliage take the place of a baked and blasted
wilderness; after a raging fever of thirst let water
splash and sparkle in fountain and stream; instead of
torrid noxious blasts let

> "Gentle gales
> Fanning their odoriferous wings, dispense
> Native perfumes, and whisper whence they stole
> Those balmy spoils, "

and above all, let a sense of human cordiality and sympathy replace the distress of the outcast, and you may dimly conceive my feelings of quiet joy and deep content. Everything was in unison with my mood—from the mystic splendours of the encircling mountains to the soft beauty and incense of the golden mellowy groves close at hand. We spoke not a word, for the Arab has more wisdom than to interrupt the sensuous enjoyment of the kayf* by talk. In delicious silence we saw the gold waning, and the rose flushing, and mountain, plain, and tree shining with a shifting glory that was like an effluent flood of light and colour from the open doors of Heaven. Then down dropped the sun, darkness rushed upon the land, and we went inside. Said Achmet lost no time in reminding me of the promise to tell my story.

He listened to it with the immovable countenance of the sphinx, sucking quietly at his pipe, his eyes fast on the ground. When the recital was over he raised his face to mine.

"Thou hast been in great peril, my son," he said, "and such as thou never couldst have escaped except the hand of God were with thee. Of a surety thou art reserved for some great work."

I asked him if he had any idea who and what the men were who had plundered and fired the brig, and almost truculently he answered—

"Dogs and thieves and murderers, and, if it be possible, worse. I know them, the evil offspring of Cain. They have had their polluting hands on me— they have made me suffer. Their deeds reek with iniquity. They are men, look you, whose heads

---

* Kayf, intoxicating and passive delight; "the troubles of conversation, the displeasures of memory, and the vanity of thought," are held to be unpleasant interruption of the kayf.

should not be on their shoulders; that is it. But let us not talk of such vile dogs; it is not good; it polluteth the mouth to name them."

Finding him so strangely moved I was at a loss how to proceed, but at a venture I inquired the name of the town.

"The city is called Marabel," he rejoined. "Thou shalt know it all. It is not so mighty a city as Bombay; neither is it so rich. Yet it is a famous place and we are ruled by a great prince. It will please me to present thee to him. But perchance I may inquire what thou meanest to do?"

"How can the driftwood cast on the beach know what the next wave will do with it?" I answered.

He smoked a little more thoughtfully at this, as if he were pondering something.

"We are a people by ourselves," he remarked, slowly, after the space of a minute. "For ages, too many to be numbered, we have been what thou seest us. I have travelled. I know what changes are in other parts of the earth; but we change not, save to go from youth to age, from our mother's care to the darkness of the grave. As the son is so was the father, and so the father's father, even to the generations afar off when the patriarch Abraham built the Holy House of Mecca; and Job, after manifold sufferings, was enriched for keeping his soul's integrity, and numbered the increase of his flocks and herds and gathered the overflowing gold and silver from his threshing-floors—gold from that which was for wheat, and silver from that which was for barley.* The children of Ishmael have been the same since the beginning, like the sun and the moon and the stars. Yonder hills, my son, have yielded more to time than the seed of Hagar, and the sea has been further moved from its place than they. As a people we

* The Arabs believe that Abraham built the Caaba, and that after proving the righteousness of Job, God sent two clouds which rained gold and silver on his threshing floors till they ran over.

abide by ourselves. No ships go from hence to far lands; wherefore if thou desirest to return to thine own country it may be hard for thee. And I grieve to tell thee that sojourning has many perils—for my people are incensed against the face of a stranger. Three moons have not passed since an Egyptian spy was slain and torn asunder in a public place, and the blood of a Persian, who came seeking what was not his, is yet wet on the ground. Yet let not these things dismay thee. I know an evil countenance when I see it; thine pleads for thee, therefore shalt thou abide with me. Moreover, a man of thy nation once gave me my life. It would be a long tale to tell, but I remember it to his race for ever. For all these things tarry with me for a time, and while I have store thou shalt not want. And if thine ears are open to counsel there is one thing more I would say."

"Speak," I said earnestly. "If thy wisdom equal thy goodness it will indeed be well with me if I attend to thy counsel."

"Mortal knoweth not what may come to pass," said the Arab, solemnly; "only God and His holy Prophet. This, then, is my counsel: that thou make thyself as one of us. Already, to my astonishment, thou art master of our tongue. As thou canst be an Arab in speech be one also in apparel. Thus far honour our country, and be assured it will stand to thee."

"It shall be as thou wilt," I answered.

Said Achmet got to his feet with an eager smile.

"Good," he cried. "See if I make not as likely a follower of the Prophet of thee as the best of them."

Whereupon he began hastily to search out the clothes that were to effect my transformation.

He was fastidious in having me orthodoxly arrayed. My long shirt was spotless white, my turban was of fine yellow silk, my mantle was black and gold, a gorgeous scarlet sash, that would fitly have adorned a queen, encircled my waist, and my naked feet were put in costly sandals.

"By my faith, as genuine a child of the desert as ever I set eyes on," exclaimed Said Achmet, when I was habited in my flowing robes. "But one thing thou yet lackest."

He ran into an inner room and brought forth a small silver-hilted sword, supported by a richly wrought, variegated belt of camel's hair and leather, set off with silver edgings.

"Thou shalt wear this," he said warmly. "It once belonged to the head of the Faith himself, and never before dangled by the side of an infidel. Nay, nay; what said I? Thou wilt pardon the unthinking haste of the tongue. Not an infidel, an alien; that is to say, a stranger such as thou art."

Partly to cover his confusion, partly to show the heartiness of his friendship, he insisted on investing me with the badge of honour himself.

"Fit to be a sheik, by the glories of Al-Raschid," he said, stepping back in admiration when he had buckled on the weapon. "I tell thee that great are the swordsmith and the maker of garments. Who conferreth distinction like them? Thou art no longer as straddling tongs. Thou hast the grace of the waving palm; thou bendest as the willow by the brook. On a war-horse thou wouldst be the bravest of warriors; yea, and in the shadow of the court, in the place of judgment, who could so fitly deliver laws? In every line and look of thee, save mayhap in the fairness of thy face, thou art a son of Ishmael. And the Arabian sky will quickly take that fair cast out of thee; then of a truth thou shalt be as ourselves."

He walked deliberately round me, noting with words and beams of delight each point of resemblance to the true-born Arab. He could not enough admire, though I suspect his pleasure in my galllant equipment was due rather to his own share in it than to the dignity or naturalness with which I carried it. Suddenly he got grave.

"Thou remindest me of them I would fain have

about me," he said, with something of a sigh. As if to explain his change of manner he added, "I had three sons. One sleepeth beneath the green waves that bore thee hither; one lieth deep under sands heaped upon him by the fingers of the lone desert wind. The third is even now doing battle, or it may be he hath gone the way of his brothers. My heart is solitary at the thought that I may never look on him again. And thou art so like him. He resembled thee in youth, in suppleness, in bearing, in goodliness of appearance; his eye had the hardihood of thine, and his arm the same readiness to strike."

His comparisons were cut short by an imperative knocking at the door, which replaced his look of sadness by one of alarm.

"What meaneth this?" he said with bated breath, as he bent his ear to hearken.

The knock was almost instantly repeated with an added imperiousness and emphasis.

"It must be a summons from the Prince," he said, glancing at me with an expression of anxiety as he rose to meet his visitors.

It was as he suspected. A dozen of the castle guards, armed to the teeth, clustered about the door, and it was evident they were excited. Said Achmet endeavoured to temporize, but he was peremptorily ordered to stand aside; and the men, with weapons drawn, pushed past him. Without a word they seized me and began dragging me towards the door. The idea of resistance comes strong upon one handled so unceremoniously without cause, and I had swift thoughts of trying the quality of Said Achmet's silver-hilted sword. He perceived the danger and rushed to my side.

"As thou valuest thy life, resist not," he whispered hurriedly. "The Prince has sent them to take thee. Go, and rely on my aid."

In the grip of a dozen armed fanatics it would indeed have been folly to make opposition. So, merely begging that I might be permitted to take my green bag

I quietly suffered myself to be thrust into the midst of a bristling clump of spears. The greatest malefactor on earth could not have been more jealously guarded or more ignominiously hustled. I had just one word of encouragement. In passing through the door I got a whisper from Said Achmet that he would be at the castle by sunrise on the morrow to testify in my favour. His meaning was not clear, but it was solacing to have even one friend at so dubious a juncture.

The winds seemed to bear intelligence of my arrest. No sooner had we quitted the garden than we were in a clamouring crowd, bearing links that shed a grotesque and lurid light on the strange scene. As I knew that in Arab towns the inhabitants are rarely abroad after sunset, the demonstration was proof of unusual, indeed of extraordinary commotion. That I was the cause of it was speedily manifest.

The people pressing about us, speculated aloud on the doom that was in store for me, and their auguries were anything but cheering. What was more disquieting they once or twice showed a disposition to take matters into their own hands; if they had done that I have a notion this history would never have been written. As I listened to their shoutings and mutterings I had a very vivid remembrance of Said Achmet's tale of the Egyptian and Persian.

"Here may be the very place where they were killed," I thought to myself as we went along. "Here their blood may have been poured out; these walls may have echoed their dying groans." And sometimes, in sudden flares and sweeps of the torches, the crimsoned ground had gruesome suggestions of violent deeds and untimely ends.

On reaching the castle walls—which were surprisingly thick—we entered through a narrow gateway, flanked with towers, to a sort of esplanade crowded with soldiers. Then we entered an outer court, passing through another narrow gate to an inner. This also we traversed. Then we passed through several crooked corridors till we came to a gap in a dead wall. Into this I was thrust. A door was banged and bolted behind me, and I was alone in utter darkness. A moment's groping proved I was in a windowless dungeon—probably a condemned cell.

CHAPTER XV.

ON TRIAL FOR MY LIFE.

HUDDLED in a foul hole, which admitted neither light nor air, I tried to imagine what might be the outcome of this fresh entanglement. One thing seemed certain, that I was to be kept fast under bolts for the night. It seemed equally certain that in the morning, if a pestilential air did not finish me in the meantime, I should be led forth to a mock trial, and convicted by overwhelming evidence of uncommitted crimes, for I knew the ingenuity of the Asiatic mind in contriving plots and charges. What would follow —the judgment and form of execution—were matters that could be foretold with disquieting accuracy. It was a pinch at which a wise man would have betaken himself to his prayers, in anticipation of crossing the dark bourne, and even the most obdurate sinners have thought of the good policy of repentance.

The prospect, however, gave me less concern than might be imagined. Assuredly Fortune was using her teeth and claws upon me with implacable malevolence. But her persecutions were beginning to lose something of their poignancy. Like a vain woman, Fortune loves to show her power, and, like a meddlesome one, she must have a finger in every man's pie, making it sweet or sour according to her whim and humour. But when one has, as the poet puts it, looked on his own funeral procession, he may smile at her efforts to inflict pain. He is then getting beyond her range. To that stage of apathy I was fast approaching.

The ignominy of the thing troubled me most. To

die once is the fate of all, and death, as wise men have ever taught, may be made glorious.   But to be shut up in a hole like a rat and then probed out to be worried by bloodthirsty hounds, is not to close the fifth act of one's play with any dignity or glory.   If they would only put a proper sword in my hand, then I might leave my memory green, and furnish a tale worth telling to their grandchildren.

In spite of what has been said, I must not boast of a mind at ease, for when at length outwearied nature claimed her boon of sleep, I was constantly starting up with a throbbing heart and a clammy brow.   To be rid of the plaguing dreams, I decided at last to keep awake; as the best means of doing that I crept about the cell, entertaining myself first by guessing its dimensions, and then by feeling its walls inch by inch with my hands.   This diversion lasted but a little while, and then I fell back on my own thoughts.   If I was in durance, they, at least, were free enough. With the vagary and volatility which have ever distinguished them, even in the midst of pressing perils, they flew to other days, to old scenes and familiar faces.   Time reversed his movement; the past became the present; dead things started into life, and the absent and the distant were brought near.   Every brae and bush about Glenrae, every bend of the road, every burn, almost every tuft of heather, every dear figure, my father, my mother, old Duncan, and the rest rose before me with the vividness of reality.   Sir Thomas Gordon, with his brown face, was there too, and so was Isabel, looking as I had so often seen her, with her melting eyes and her abundance of glossy hair.   I trembled with a feeling, half of joy, half of superstitious awe, as I looked from one to another of the visionary company.   It was pleasant to see them all as of old; should I ever see them again?   The meeting was gladsome, but would it be the last?

In some agitation of mind I rose, and my foot struck against the green bag.   It was an electric link connecting me in very reality with those of whom I was thinking. I picked it up, drew forth the pipes, hurriedly tuned them, and the next instant was playing Highland airs with might and main. Very weird, and strange, and thrilling sounded the music of my native hills in that close subterranean cell, thrilling as the grasp of a friend in the day of adversity, strange as the Gaelic speech amid Arabian sands. I played till I knew no fear, and forgot all danger, till there rose within me a spirit of resistance that would have defied the united power of all the Caliphs from Abu Bekr to Mustassim.* My jailers beat upon the door with the butts of their muskets to demand silence, but they might as well have whistled to the charging lion. Heedless of their pounding, indeed scarcely hearing it, I played on, the wild slogan of the clans almost bursting the walls asunder. Faster and faster danced the fingers of the piper, ever more and more furious swelled the strains that never yet failed to give the strength of ecstasy to a Highlander. It was the pipes that won Waterloo, that saved Lucknow, that broke the Russian swoop at Balaclava. On reeking fields of gore their scream has made men forget death, and banished the thought of yielding. What they had done in the stress and havoc of battle they were now doing in solitariness and darkness. With their music in my ears I could dare anything.

All at once the door opened, and a reflection of faraway sunshine dribbled freely in. A band of grisly warriors stood without, grasping their weapons, and bearing countenances on which there was a singular mingling of ferocity, distrust, and apprehension.

"Come forth," said one, stepping a little in advance of his fellows. "The great Abou Kuram waiteth to hear the charges against thee."

For half a second I held my breath, wavering whether or not to put up my pipes. Then, with a fierce gathering of all the defiant elements of my nature (and I have been told they are neither few nor

* The first and last of the real Caliphs. Under the Mamelukes there were, properly speaking, no Caliphs.

trifling), I blew again, harder than ever, and swept forth, my chanter discoursing so bravely that the Arabs fell back with their fingers hard in their ears. Perhaps it was out of charity, or it may have been from fear to meddle with a thing so unearthly, but the guards suffered me to have my own way, and I took it like a gamester who ventures his last frail chance with a light and brazen confidence, as if ruin were to be averted by levity.

We passed along darksome, devious passages of treacherous suggestion, then through an open circular court, whence we had a glimpse of enormous walls stoutly bastioned and buttressed, and of massive towers flanking arched gateways, then into another large court surrounded by balconies. All the while I blew with unabated defiance and independence, much to the amazement of the assembled people, and to the obvious terror of not a few who clearly regarded the skirling of the pipes as the screeching of evil spirits. My tune on entering was the "Highland Laddie," and a very singular figure I must have cut, with my bandaged head, my puffed cheeks, and trailing garments. I had a fantastic feeling of being a second Macpherson, marching victoriously to death to my own quick-step, and I dare say the bit of bravado sustained me. It had, at least, the good effect of keeping me from thinking too much; for thought at such times is no upholder of courage.

Though it was yet little past the dawn, the court, was densely thronged with citizens and soldiers, for the Arabs are abroad with the sun. On a raised seat facing the entrance sat the Prince, benches of stone and beaten earth that ran round the sides were occupied by courtiers, castle officials, and the more prominent citizens, while the common people and the soldiery, some with bristling arms, and some without, elbowed each other to find standing room as best they could.

Marching with my proudest step into the centre, I abruptly ceased playing, and saluted my judge. He did not return my salute, but, sitting motionless as a statue, watched me with sharp eyes and contracted brows.

For an Arab he was uncommonly handsome. In the prime of life, he was tall, broad-chested, clean featured, and bore himself with the imperial mien of the Cæsars. His hair was jet black, his eyes, also black, were as keen as the falcon's, and more determined, and his countenance in general expressed haughtiness and inflexible resolution. Just then it was inauspiciously severe.

He was arrayed with regal splendour. Over a gleaming white shirt he wore a Cashmere robe richly embroidered by the artists of Delhi, and above that again, a small, delicately worked cloak of camel's hair—a distinction reserved for sheiks and princes alone. His tasselled turban was of the finest red and yellow silk, gorgeously brocaded, and was fastened by a fillet of camel's hair inwoven with gold and silver, and blazing with precious stones. His leather girdle, worked with gold and set with brilliants, supported a gold-hilted sword and a steel and ivory handled dagger flashing with jewels and embossed and inlaid with the precious metal. His feet were in crimson slippers, on which were bound elaborately decorated sandals.

There was an uncomfortable silence as he examined me minutely from head to foot. On both sides of him sat his ministers, ugly, crafty, pitiless-looking dogs, with a sort of grin of expectation on their faces; but none dared to disturb the Prince's scrutiny. Presently he gave a signal and without a word the guards pushed me closer to him. For a moment he scrutinized me again, and his eyes had in them the leaping lights of a hawk's when it bends over its prey.

"Thou hast the face of a Christian, an infidel, and the garb of an Arab, a believer," he said sharply, at length. "How cometh it?"

"My lord," I replied, with a profound bow, "a generous and charitable man of this town bestowed these clothes upon thy servant."

"His charity was ill at ease, methinks. What is his name?"

.I hesitated, not wishing to compromise Said Achmet.

"Thou wilt find it best to be quick with thy answers," said Abou Kuram, sternly.

"His name," I replied, "is Said Achmet."

"Said Achmet!" he repeated in surprise. "Thou meanest to tell me Said Achmet sheltered and clothed thee?"

"He succoured thy servant when he was in need," I answered humbly.

"Go, bring Said Achmet," he called out. "By my word we will see into this matter of harbouring strangers."

Three men instantly bent themselves to the earth, and hurried off to arrest my benefactor.

"Whence comest thou, and what is thy business?" he asked, turning to me again, and looking rather through me, than at me.

As briefly and succinctly as possible, I told him my tale.

His lip curled, and his eyes danced as he listened.

"It is a likely story," he remarked sternly, when I had finished. "How comest thou, an utter stranger, and as thou sayest with no desire to come hither, to speak our tongue?"

I told him of the tuition of Abram ben Aden.

"Thou seest yonder tower," he said significantly. "It is not many days since it was adorned with the head of a spy who added lying to his other virtues."

"As my lord liveth, I speak the truth," I returned earnestly, for it was a hardship that my proficiency as a linguist should stand against me.

"Never liar yet, but was as true as the Prophet. Thine own ears shall hear the confirmation of thy words."

Whereupon he called the witnesses. They appeared in appalling numbers, with appalling testimony, delivered with the glibness and assurance of actors who had well conned their parts. I had anticipated much; the reality was beyond my wildest conception, beyond anything, indeed, that the sluggish Western imagination could conceive. Speechless with amazement and horror I heard the damning evidence heaped up that would have convicted with a jury sworn to acquit. At times I was almost moved to indignation at my own villainy; for I had difficulty in remembering that I was the scoundrel depicted, so atrocious above all belief were the crimes I had committed. Never did odious rogue swing from gibbet or yard-arm, or dangle from castle wall with half the felonies on his head that I bore.

I was the emissary of a hostile power scheming to conquer and enslave. I had been caught spying by honourable and respectable men, whose word was as far above suspicion as Cæsar's wife. I had sought entrance to the castle in order to assassinate the Prince my judge, and so clear the way to the throne for a foreign usurper. Failing in that, I had tried to bribe others to do the foul deed, and the actual money I had given was exhibited by the recipients. These and other enormities far above any ordinary capacity for crime were triumphantly brought home to me. There could not be the shadow of a doubt that I was a rare monster of wickedness, a disgrace to the species, and assuredly deserving the cruelest death that judge and executioner could devise.

The clown appeared against me with proof of guilt sufficient to hang ten honest men, and the impertinent youth on whom I had drawn backed him up with a readiness and resource that I must have admired had he not chanced to be swearing away my life. After them trooped half the population, each with a darker tale and clearer demonstrations of felony than the other. It was wonderful how one man could have sinned so much, how one head could have planned and plotted so much wickedness. Long before my accusers were finished I was loaded with a

12

mass of iniquity and infamy, sufficient to drag a
score of saints to the uttermost deeps of perdition.

My judge had an easy task. He had to determine
no question of guilt or innocence, no delicate balancing of points was demanded of him; he had simply
to decide what should be done to an infamous wretch
who should be defrauded of his deserts by hanging,
beheading, drawing and quartering.

Abou Kuram did not move a muscle during the
fateful recital. Sitting with clenched lips and drooping lids he scarcely seemed to hear. But when the
pitch was exhausted, and I could not possibly be made
blacker, he turned on me the face of victory.

"Art thou satisfied with the testimony?" he asked
grimly. "Thou seemest a man of much integrity.
Of a very truth thou art a pretty fellow."

"My lord," I blurted, with a gulp, for in spite of
my early bravado the sweat of terror was now breaking upon me, "my lord, they are liars, every one."

"And thou alone speakest truth. Yea, that is
likely. Thou couldst not lie were all thy interests
clamouring for a falsehood. And thy heart is as
good as thy tongue is true. Thou hast been at the
pains to learn our language, and hast faced perils in
coming hither, and put on our clothes, and spied and
plotted out of a pure desire to befriend us. Thou art
a very prodigy of goodness. Thy secret plannings
and bribings are all for our welfare. Thou yearnest
to do good by stealth."

For the first time he laughed, and it was a laugh to
curdle the blood. When the judge cackles in irony
the prisoner may well quake.

Quickly recovering his austerity of manner he
looked me over with eyes that penetrated to the core
of my being.

"Doubtless, some one is present to testify to that
goodness thou displayest so strangely," he said.

In my bewilderment I had forgotten Said Achmet,
but now I turned anxiously to seek his friendly face.
A chill went to my heart as I searched the crowd in

vain. He had not come; he would be too late. But just as I was about to break out into an incoherent protestation of innocence, in despair of a favourable word, there was a movement among the people, and my witness entered between his guards. Advancing with respectful bearing to the front he made a low obeisance, and stood with bent head and body to hear the Prince's pleasure.

"I thought," remarked Abou Kuram, very slowly, "that Said Achmet was of those we could call friends."

"There liveth not a man this day who could wish my lord better," returned Said Achmet, in a low but fervent voice.

"Yet thou givest refuge to spies and enemies of the State."

"Heaven forbid thy servant should do such a thing."

"But thou hast done it."

Said Achmet's eyes nearly started from his head.

"My lord but jesteth," he said, after a pause, during which he scarcely breathed.

"My faith, 'tis a jest that may cost thee thy head," answered Abou Kuram. "Look on this fellow and tell me what thou knowest of him."

Said Achmet briefly related the circumstances of our meeting and his reasons for taking me in and giving me clothes.

"Thou art a man of honour, Said Achmet," observed the Prince, "but thy pity hath blinded thee. Dost thou know aught else of him?"

Said Achmet in a few sentences repeated the tale of misfortune I had told him, Abou Kuram listening with palpable irritation and contempt.

"I doubt not he had trouble in getting hither," said the Prince, "and the reason for his coming may be judged by his readiness to endure dangers and hardships. Thinkest thou it was for sport he encountered those perils by sea and land, or from a wish to do thee and me a favour? In spite of thy years and thy

wanderings thou art but a babe, Said Achmet. A
feigning tongue imposeth on thee, and thou art
moved by the woe of the deceitful. Hast thou never
yet learned that words are easy as the wind, and
often as false. This fellow hath come to spy, and the
wages of the spy is death. Thou mayst go in freedom, Said Achmet, but another time see thou let not
thy compassion make a fool of thy judgment. Methinks it is time thou wert learning to discern between friend and foe."

Said Achmet, again bowing profoundly, retired
without a word. As he went out our eyes met for a
moment, and the look he gave me was full of compassion. It was but a glance, yet it seemed to express as plain as words could the sorrowful conviction
that I was beyond hope or help. The intelligence
struck me with something of the cold dismay which
the refusal of an expected pardon might bring to a
man sentenced to be shot or hanged.

"Is there any one else to speak for him?" demanded
Abou Kuram, in a loud voice.

The crowd swaying violently, craned its neck for
an answer. None came, and the judge turned to me.

"Thou canst not be old," he said, surveying me for
the fiftieth time. "Thy face hath the bloom and the
comeliness of youth, yet already thine acts reek
with iniquity, yea, they are as carrion to the nostrils. Under what master thou hast learned thy
guile and how thou hast the heart to practise it, I
know not, but thou art a match for the hoariest
headed transgressor alive. We have had some of
thy kind here lately, and they did not return to
the place whence they came. Thou hast heard the
tale of thine iniquities; what thinkest thou is thy
due?"

Before I could give any opinion in the matter—indeed my tongue was not at all ready—one of the men
seated on Abou Kuram's right interpolated.

"A needless question, my lord. Cast him to the
dogs, and let them tear him alive. Then let his

gnawed head be perched on the topmost tower as a
warning to spies and other malefactors."

He was a leather-faced rascal, with small deep-set
eyes, very close together, the mouth and jaws of a
bloodhound, and the shifting sinister expression of
the hyena.

There are brave and elegant gentlemen, adventurous, kid-gloved, satin-waistcoated heroes, who can
dispose of the fear of death in an epigram. Un-
luckily for myself I am not so happily constituted,
and it was with a sudden chill of blood and marrow
that I now turned to the minister. The hate of hell
was in his lowering fanatical face; the spirit that
makes the Moslem a fiend in the fray; that impels him
to cut out an enemy's living heart and stamp its
quivering life under foot; that in jealousy, anger,
revenge, or statecraft makes him subtle, crafty, ruthless, diabolic, an instigator of foul deeds, a secret assassin or an open murderer as the occasion may require—such a spirit gleamed sullenly from every
lineament of the minister's cruel and repulsive visage. Crouching there, his hand upon his crooked
sword, he watched me as if he fain would spring
forward and cleave me on the spot. His hideous
countenance and glittering eyes fascinated me as the
serpent fascinates the fluttering bird it is about to
destroy. My tongue was frozen. With a tingling
sense of innocence and wrong in every atom of my
being, I could not utter a word in self-defence or vin-
dication. I could do nothing but gaze enchanted
upon the devil that had so suddenly confronted me
in the form of a man.

Fortunately Abou Kuram had thoughts and a
mind of his own. He made no reply to the minister's
suggestion. Perhaps being human he pitied me in
spite of my bad character, for I must have presented
a moving picture of distress; perhaps after the fashion
of the great, he hugged the idea of absolute power.
At any rate he made a diversion which set my heart
leaping with tumultuous hope. A small thing you

will generally notice is of great effect in an extremity.

"What is that instrument on which thou madest music?" he asked. "Nay, rather," he added quickly, "on which thou madest witches and genii screech."

With palpitating haste I answered it was named a bagpipe in my country, that it put the power of victory into warriors, and the fleetness of fear into the heels of their enemies.

"I said it was the scream of demons," he remarked, with a chuckle. Then suddenly his expression became one of deep thought; he seemed to be trying to recollect something. "I have it, I have it," he cried, sitting up with a beam of intelligence. "In thy country are the men naked about the legs?"

"Partly, my lord," I answered, in astonishment.

"They have been to Egypt, have they not?" he said eagerly, "to Cairo, Alexandria—they have looked on the desert and sniffed its sands. They have likewise been to India; they have pulled down princes, established empires, uprooted ancient laws, and made new ones, said prayers in a strange tongue, that no man could understand, and gone to battle with great cries. Have they not done all this?"

"My lord speaketh the truth," I said, more and more amazed.

"They are called——" He pressed his brows as a man will to aid his memory.

"Highlanders," I shouted, beside myself with excitement.

"Nay, nay; not that—that is not it. I will remember; yea, I have it. Dust thou not recall the tale of that Egyptian?" turning to his minister; "naked Scottish devils—that was it. They leap like lions, and roar like bulls of Bashan; yea, they have the voice of the wild ass, and their tread is like an army of horsemen that maketh the earth to tremble."

"My lord is right again," I cried.

"Wert thou naked when Said Achmet took thee in?" he asked.

"No, my lord."

He seemed disappointed at this, but his face lighted up again as he said—

"At any rate, thou hast the screeching demons with thee. We have leisure this morning. Thou shalt give us some of the war music of thy land."

"If my lord will cause room to be made for me," I said joyously.

"Cause room to be made for thee! Why, dost thou swell with playing?"

"Nay, my lord; but the piper must walk to and fro to play well."

"Thou callest thyself a piper. I have heard of the company of prophets with pipe and tabret. Perchance we shall have thee prophesying as well as making music." Saying this, he waved his hand with a laugh as a signal to the soldiers to clear a space. "Make room," he called. "Hearken to the music that putteth courage in the hearts of the naked Scottish devils."

The next instant the wondering people were being hustled back, and the pipes were squealing in the process of tuning up.

You may be sure that, if ever piper played with all the zeal and skill that were in him, it was then. The consciousness of the great prize at stake was diffused like an electric current through lips, and lungs, and fingers, through head and feet, and all that lay between, giving fiery energy and ardour to both the soul and body of the performer.

Yet, in spite of this earnestness and the acute sense of momentous issues hanging in the balance, I could not help being tickled by the ludicrousness of the situation. Very absurd it was to me, an Arab in garb, a Highlander in feeling, to go sailing about in flowing skirts, bursting my cheeks for the favourable verdict of judges who had never seen or heard a bagpipe in their lives, who did not know one tune or note from another, and who would be quite likely to decide with overwhelming unanimity that all my merits were faults, and all my faults merits, and who were prejudiced and incensed against me. It was like putting Harlequin on a trial of skill before a jury who had never seen a play, who detested the theatre and its traditions, and, above all, fervently hated the performer. Yet I gave them the music of my native hills with all my might—all the marches, strathspeys, reels, pibrochs, coronachs, all the solemn tunes and ranting airs, all the rousing battle pieces and the melting funeral wails I had ever learned or heard, with many more that were improvised on the spot. I thought my playing would have charmed the soul of a Macrimmon; my vanity even then made me proud of my crowding warblers; I had flying thoughts of the delight of Duncan could he have heard me; in fine, to my own mind, I was surpassing myself in all kinds of music, both grave and gay, and playing nobly enough to win the plaudits of the best judges in all Scotland. But Arabs are not Scotsmen. The glances I managed to cast with the tail of my eye showed me either a listless and apathetic or a frowning audience. The predominating expression in their faces was unquestionably one of disgust. Rollicking airs and solemn psalm tunes—"Tullochgorum" and the "Old Hundred," "Jenny's Bawbee" and "Martyrdom," "The Laird o' Cockpen" and "The Land o' the Leal," "Macgregor's Gathering" and "Roy's Wife," had precisely the same effect—an ominously unfavourable one. I played charges that would have made the "Black Watch" or the "Cameronians" howl for blood, and pibrochs that would have made a Highland bailiff sit down and cry, and lilts that would have sent the young men and maidens of a whole village skipping on the green; I strode, I doubled, I danced, without moving a single individual to enthusiasm. There were plenty of black looks; but if any one gave a sign of encouragement I did not see it. Yet I blew on, blew livelier or fiercer, as the case might be, for the incentive to keep going was strong. I walked with my drones in the faces of the ranks that lined my path—

a thing that was unwise; I pressed as near as possible to Abou Kuram and his ministers—a thing that was unwiser still, for the pipes at close quarters are more than any foreigner can bear with equanimity.

I was in the midst of my parade, when, in advancing towards Abou Kuram, I noticed the leather-faced counsellor at his right wriggling as if in dire pain. Paying no heed, I came up, wheeled, and marched back; but, before I reached the other end, there was a sudden cry, and, with a rush, the people closed in, almost knocking the pipes out of my hands.

CHAPTER XVI.

MOMENTOUS INTELLIGENCE—MY LIFE HANGS IN THE BALANCE.

PRESSING forward with the rest to discover the cause of the sudden commotion I saw old leather-face on the floor engaged, apparently, in the singular diversion of trying to curl himself into a ball. His head was bent between his knees, and at the moment of my catching sight of him he seemed to be making prodigious efforts to clasp his feet about his neck. Failing in that, he began a series of rapid gyrations as if he were making experiments in the principle of spinning tops; but just as he was on the point of demonstrating how neatly the human figure may be made to revolve on its head, he shot himself out to his full length with every limb and muscle rigid. In this attitude he lay for a second or so, then groaning piteously he began to roll over and over, his hands clapped hard on his stomach and his knees again spasmodically seeking his neck. A glance told me the man was in convulsions.

As I stood peering over the shoulders of the first rank of the crowd, his rolling eye caught mine, and his face, already hideous with anguish, blackened with hate. He was still sufficiently master of himself to be venomous.

"Ah, thou son of a mongrel witch, thou spawn of Satan, may the fangs of the serpent and the claws of the vulture be in thy living heart ere this day's sun go down!" he screeched, spitting and pointing a clenched fist at me. "Thou hast bewitched me with thy devilish arts. To thee I owe these gripes of death; I owe thee, too, my curse. Thou shalt have it, and may it drag thee to perdition."

And rousing himself with a diabolical effort, he cursed me body and soul, till, what with his frightful contortions, and the fiendishness of his imprecations, I felt as if a stream of minute icicles were trickling down my spine. He had to take breath in the midst of his maledictions; then, gathering himself again as he recovered a little, he turned to those about him, and in the same screeching voice demanded my instant execution.

"He is in league with evil spirits," he cried. "Slay him, slay him, ere he work more harm with his unholy spells. I say, slay him!" he shouted still more fiercely. "If he escape, my curse be on you all!"

His words were as a breeze to a smouldering fire. Immediately a deep ominous noise, like the growling of hungry lions, rose about me, and I thought I had escaped the sentence of Abou Kuram only to be torn by a mob of vengeful and superstitious fanatics. And, indeed, it might have gone hard with me had it not been that a fresh spasm came upon the man on the ground, so that his groans and screams of distress diverted attention from me. I could be slain at leisure; it was imperative that the sick man should be attended to at once.

He was plainly in mortal agony. His face was livid and his twisting mouth covered with bubbling foam. He kicked as one distracted, and threw his arms about, and rolled from side to side, and curled himself up like a hedgehog, and beat his head on the stone pavement till, to preserve his brains, he had to be held by force. And through it all he alternately execrated me and called on God and His holy Prophet for succour and mercy.

A slave was hastily despatched for a fakeer or priest, who in Arabia ministers to the body as well as to the soul. He came in a little while, very dirty, very deliberate, and very sour, as if his chief function were to make the sinner's dying moments as miserable as possible. His medicine was strange, and his mode of administering it such as to make a whole man sick. With ceremonial slowness he first produced a greasy copy of the Koran from the filthy recesses of his dress; following a long pause came a reed pen, which was minutely examined; then came another interval as if to give the suffering man plenty of opportunity to remember his sins and groan, and after it a tiny highly polished board was drawn forth from the mysterious folds of his robes. In due time there followed a small box containing some sort of paste, with which the board was rubbed white. On the page thus prepared, the priest wrote in his fanciest penmanship two verses from the Koran; then very leisurely, as if promptitude in cases of sudden sickness were of all things most strictly to be avoided, he washed the paste off the board, mixed it, adding a liberal proportion of dirt from his own fingers, rolled it into a ball, and gave it to the patient. The man took the loathsome morsel eagerly, and swallowed it whole, nearly choking in the process.

For a minute or so he appeared to be actually relieved, but presently another spasm coming upon him, he writhed and cried out more distressingly than ever. The priest gazed down at him with impassive, unpitying face. The resources of science and religion were exhausted, and no more could be done. As for the sympathy of man, that was useless. If the minister was to die, well, he must die; no use trying to thwart the designs of Providence. Accordingly the patient groaned and prepared for death, the priest standing stolidly by to witness his exit.

"It is God's will!" said the fakeer, and the gaping crowd acquiesced.

Now, as the reader knows, I owed the minister no love. But I could not see him die of pure ignorance and superstition. Making, therefore, a profound salaam to Abou Kuram, I asked if I might have the privilege of trying to save his suffering counsellor. He looked at me keenly as if doubting my motive, then, with a gesture which meant the thing was hopeless, he gave his consent, probably thinking it mattered little in whose hands a dying man went off.

Laying aside my pipes and tucking up my shirt sleeves, I called for a copper pan such as I had seen used by Said Achmet. Filling this with wheat, I placed it, with Abou Kuram's permission, on a fire of charcoal that burned in an inner room. When the wheat was as hot as I could bear it on the back of my hand, I emptied it into a small linen bag for want of a woollen—then quickly unfastening the minister's clothes, I forcibly laid him on his back (for he resented my interference) and placed the bag fair on his stomach. He yelled out that I was inflicting the pangs of burning on him out of malice, and struggled to get away; but I held him down, and presently, as the heat reached the centre of pain, he lay quieter.

"I will save you," I said to him encouragingly, "but you must lie still. When you are well again, then you will be my friend."

He snarled that he never would be anything but my direst enemy; yet as bagful after bagful of the hot wheat was applied, he grunted with satisfaction, and at last confessed himself almost free from pain. Then remembering a small package of Seidlitz powders which Mr. Watson had given me on board the *Bird of Paradise*, I drew the paper from the bosom of my dress, where I kept my valuables. By good luck, a few of the powders still remained. Mixing a double dose, I held it to the minister's mouth, urging him to drink as fast as he could swalllow. He obeyed, and I thought he would have choked, so strong was the gaseous stuff in his throat and nostrils; but a sharp smack on the back partially restored his breath.

"It was worse than the fakeer's verses," he gasped, looking up at me for the first time, through the water that welled from his eyes. "It hath tried me sorely."

But I told him to be of good heart, for that now his cure was nearly complete, and to be sure in less than half an hour he was rid of his colic and was moving about, looking shamefacedly from Abou Kuram to me and from me to Abou Kuram. Heaven was gracious; I had saved and conquered my enemy.

"Truly, this is the greatest marvel mine eyes have ever looked on," commented Abou Kuram, scarcely able to credit his senses. "Hast thou any more of that magic thing?"

"A little, my lord," I answered with a bow, "and if my lord will deign to accept it, his servant will be for ever honoured." Thereupon I presented him with all that was left of Mr. Watson's Seidlitz powders. "If at any time my lord should feel a griping in his inner parts, let him take two of these. They will cure him."

"By the beard of the Prophet, I feel a griping even now;" and with that, he called on me to mix my drugs there and then, and let him have them.

Nothing loth, I asked for some water and a clean glass, and with a greater air of importance than if I had the lore of the entire College of Physicians at my finger-ends, prepared a second potion, Abou Kuram watching every movement. When it fizzed to the proper pitch, I handed him the glass, telling him to drink quickly, or the virtue of the draught would be lost. He drank as if for dear life, his nose buried deep in the foam; but ere he reached the bottom, he had to pause for breath. He spluttered a bit with the fumes in his nose, yet determined to do his duty, raised the glass again, and swallowed the contents to the dregs.

He handed it back to me with a wry face.

"I hope thou hast not poisoned me," he gasped, wiping his eyes. "Thou makest me shed tears like a woman."

"Let my lord have no fear," I answered. "That is a physic, which will surely drive away his pains."

"'Tis poisonous to the taste," he said. "By the bold Alborak, I am swelling," he cried all at once. "I shall burst asunder. This will tear skin and bone apart. Phew, ugh, bagh! was ever such a tempest in man's interior? I could drive a ship with the wind thou hast put in me."

"That but shows how much my lord was in need of a physician," I answered humbly.

"Oh, I shall surely burst asunder," he repeated. "They will be gathering up my fragments this minute. Why hast thou put a devil with fanners into me, to blow me to atoms?"

But the fit passed off, as such fits will, leaving Abou Kuram, as he declared, such a comfort of body and clarity of mind as he had not experienced for years.

"Thou art a marvellous physician," he said cordially, "and by my faith thy hissing medicine is a potent one. For a while, I knew not whether it would kill or cure. Verily I thought another sat in my place, and that he blessed thee for thy skill in getting princes out of the way."

"Be it for ever far removed from me, to hurt so much as a hair of my lord's head," I said fervently.

"Nay, thou hast proved thy good faith," he answered with a smile, "at least, in this instance. 'Twas but a moment I doubted; and by the merciful Prophet, it is well for thee it was no longer, or the best part of thee should now be meditating upon yonder tower. If thou lookest a little to the left—a little farther—thou wilt see a fellow grinning down upon thee. Yea, there he is. How he stareth! Methinks from the whiteness of his pate, the kites have been pecking at him; a foul liberty with a man of his consequence. He was a spy, and we have put him where he may see all that taketh place. He consented unwillingly, averring, with tears and supplications, that

so lofty a perch ill accorded with his lowly disposition.
A humble-minded man as thou seest! but the State
is courteous to such strangers as he; and so he has
been awarded our highest pinnacle all to himself. I
would his friends knew how he has been honoured."

He laughed lightly, as if the beheading and quartering of men were a titillating little joke of the rarest relish, then reverted abruptly to my affairs.

"It puzzleth me to make thee quite out," he said
with a twinkle. "Thou hast an innocent face; if it
were not that faces can lie with the unction of an
angel, I could almost believe thine; yet remember,
the proof of thy wickedness is clear as yonder sun,
though many a bright tale cometh from a darkened
and perjured imagination. We will inquire more
into thy deeds and thy history. Meantime, I would
know more of thy magical arts."

He was proceeding to examine me in the mysteries
of medicine, and I was considering what plausible
stories I could concoct when suddenly there arose a
riotous commotion about the outer gate. Stopping to
hearken, we heard a voice vehemently demanding ad-
mittance to the Prince on business of urgent importance both to himself and to the State. At this, one
of the chief officials of the court ran out, returning a
minute later with a haggard, anxious, travel-stained
soldier who had evidently just flung himself from the
saddle. The stranger salaamed very low as he entered, and, walking direct to Abou Kuram, handed
him a letter.

"From Amood Sinn, my lord," he said, bending
again.

"How fareth it with my brother?" asked Abou
Kuram.

"Ill, my lord," answered the messenger. "He hath
had evil fortune; he hath sustained defeat."

"Defeat!" repeated Abou Kuram, quickly. "Thou
speakest strange words. Art sure the heat of the
desert hath not made thee mad?"

"My lord will find what I speak written by Amood

Sinn's own hand," answered the messenger.   "Three days and three nights have I ridden across burning sands without drawing bit or bridle in order to let my lord have the letter.   My mare which standeth without is ready to fall."

"Go, wash her feet and drink the water,"* said Abou Kuram, "and when she hath had food and drink see to thyself.   My servants shall give thee whatever thou wilt ask; only be within call should I desire to question thee further."

The man made his obeisance and withdrew.   As he went out I noticed that Said Achmet hurried after him with signs of great agitation—a circumstance which I ascribed to the importance of the news that had been brought.   But there was another reason, as shall presently appear.

The next minute Abou Kuram rose with the open letter in his hand, and a profound silence fell on the assembly.   There was a grim look on his face, and his eyes shone with a sort of dusky, lurid fire.

"This concerneth not me only, but all of us," he said, in a voice that was firm yet had a tremour of emotion in it.   "The war hath gone against Amood Sinn; the conqueror of the earth hath been defeated by Yumen Yusel and now calleth for immediate help. Will he have it?"

There was a momentary pause of suspense, partly because of surprise at the unexpected tidings, partly because each man waited for his neighbour to speak.

"Yea, verily, if it be my lord's will," cried some one, and then came the eager assent of every man present, with a shout that swelled into a thunderous roar.

Abou Kuram's face flushed, and the fire in his eyes broke into darting lights.

"Ye put heart in me and give double strength to my arm," he said.   "Who is Yumen Yusel that he

*A special mark of honour to a horse that has performed some great feat.

should triumph over us and over our allies? But ye shall hear what is written in the letter."

And after a long preamble he read as follows:—

"The soaring eagle hath fallen and been trampled in the dust. An evil day hath come to Amood Sinn. His pride hath been humbled, his mighty bow broken, and strangers and enemies triumph over him. Know, my beloved brother, that I write with the bitterness of death in my heart, for my people, vanquished and beaten, have run like sheep before wolves. Deign to hear how this calamity hath befallen me. We met the army of Yumen Yusel in pitched battle four days ago. They were as naught to us, yea, we counted them as dust which the wind scattereth. On the open plain we placed ourselves between Yumen Yusel and his mountains, thinking to cut off his retreat and annihilate him. But, alas! how shall I write it? The victory lay not with thy servant. The enemy hath beaten us with great slaughter, and taken many of our camels with much provisions and water-skins, so that we are like to die of hunger and thirst. This overthrow we could not avert. My people strewed the ground with dead and beat drums and shouted with shouts of victory. Yea, verily, their spears drank blood to the half of the staff. But, suddenly there came a rush like a whirlwind, and a man on a great black horse, with a band as fierce as himself, flew into the thick of the battle, and fought so much like evil spirits that our men were affrighted and slain in heaps and overcome. The man on the black horse had a sword like the sword of the angel Gabriel, and he clove men in twain as I would cut a melon. Where the spears were thickest there was he, yet he was without scathe. He received a hundred spear-thrusts, yet was there not so much hurt on him as the prick of a pin. If he be not Satan, I do not know an evil spirit when I see it. Wherefore it came that, finding an adversary against which neither steel nor lead nor the bravery of man nor the fierceness of horse could avail, and the slaughter being very sore,

13

my army fled in dismay. The enemy pursued, falling on our camels and tents, and we are utterly despoiled. Yumen Yusel hath declared his intention of ravaging the land from the shores of the Red Sea, which swallowed up Pharaoh and his chariots, even to the Persian Gulf, and eastward to the great sea which stretcheth no man knoweth whither. With speedy aid we may yet overthrow him and bring his head to the ground, and so save thee and thine scatheless. I pray thee come quickly with as many armed men as thou canst spare."

The details increased rather than diminished the wonder and consternation of a crowd just then as sensitive as mercury in the sun. A tense and painful silence fell when Abou Kuram ceased reading, horror and awe and surprise being expressed in every lineament of the thin, eager, tawny countenances that clustered about the Prince. He was himself the first to speak again.

"We will put a curb in the nose of this mountain lion," he said proudly. "We will tame his arrogance, and make a mock of his pretentions. We waited for tidings of victory, and lo, we have tidings of defeat, and plans of unbounded conquest. We shall see, my brothers, if these things come to pass. Our kingdom and our lives, with the lives of our wives and little ones, our cattle, our horses, our camels and all that we have are at stake. But we are a fighting people; the spear and the sword are as fit to our hand as the gauntlet, and methinks this man Yumen Yusel boasteth somewhat early in the day. And to say truth, my brethren, I am curious to have a look at Satan at close quarters."

A shudder seemed to run through the throng at this touch of levity; but they liked the undaunted martial tone of their ruler's speech, and responded with a vociferous clamouring for immediate action.

"How many men can follow me to battle?" asked Abou Kuram, turning to an officer on his right.

"We have five thousand fighting men ready to draw spear and sword to-morrow," answered the officer. "If two thousand remained in charge of my lord's possessions three could march at my lord's back whithersoever he cared to lead them."

"Be it as thou sayest then," replied Abou Kuram. "Give thou the captains orders to prepare immediately for war; and as soon as the messenger hath washed and eaten, bring him hither that I may question him further."

The officer saluted and went out, nearly all the people in the court trooping after him. But the next instant they surged back like a recoiling wave at the heels of the courier, who had responded instantly to Abou Kuram's commands.

My friend Said Achmet struggled to keep close to him, and I noticed that the old man's face had a peculiar light in it, different altogether from the downcast look it had so lately worn. The cause of this change was soon explained. Squeezing close up to me as the courier was being interrogated, he whispered joyously, "He is my son of whom I told thee, Tabal, my son. Hath he not a goodly appearance, and a moving intelligence? Thou shalt know him. And thou—thy fortune is mending. May it grow prosperous from this hour."

And then he moved off with an air of indifference to prevent suspicions of undue intimacy.

Meanwhile Abou Kuram was closely questioning the messenger.

"My brother attributeth his overthrow to this man on the black horse," he said.

"And of a surety he is right, my lord," answered Tabal.

"Didst thou see him—I mean this invincible warrior, this second Gabriel who smiteth his enemies with a flaming sword so that they become as the dust of the earth?"

"See him, my lord!" said Tabal, quickly. "Yea, and felt him. 'Twas a miracle that his blade did not make two of me. My flesh gathereth on my bones at the thought of him."

And then, with the volubility of his race in moments of excitement, he launched into a description of the man on the black horse, from which it appeared that that person of demoniac strength and valour was at the very lowest estimate fifteen feet high, and six across between the shoulders; that his arms and legs were of such prodigious length and thickness as no mortal had ever measured; that his sword was longer than any two spears put end to end, and so heavy that the three strongest men in Amood Sinn's army could not lift it; that it killed at the slightest touch, and emitted lurid flames at its owner's will; that he could fire a hundred pistols together, and shoot down half an army before it had time to understand what he was about; that his eyes were balls of living fire, and that he rode a horse which was as clearly as himself a product of the nether regions; and, finally, that neither steel nor lead availed in the least against him.

Abou Kuram was almost the only man in the assembly who was not struck limp with superstitious dread. While others listened with gaping mouths, and widening orbs he had a look in which I thought amusement and indignation and a vehement desire for battle were blended.

"I must see this evil spirit," he said grimly. "Methinks it would be a curious exercise to measure the length of his flame-breathing sword, yea, and the strength of his great arm. Thou mayest go and rest," he added, "while I get ready for war. Thou shalt be our guide."

He looked round the throng, and his eye fell on me.

"We had forgotten thee," he said with an unconcerned smile. "By the holy Prohpet thou art a most potent magician. Thou hast beaten the fakeer at his own game, what I have never seen before. Yet they tell dark tales of thee, and in truth thy marvels smell of the black art. It may even be," and a twinkle lit up his swarthy face, "that thou art brother to

this angel of destruction that we have just heard
of. Heaven gave thee some intelligence; therefore,
it must be clear to thyself thou deservest death;
and, as time and business press, it were well, methinks, to give thee thy due with all speed. How
wouldst thou have it if thou wert to choose?"

This was just the sort of speech to make one laugh
on the wrong side of one's mouth; yet, judging it best
to keep a brave face, I answered quickly—

"Fighting by my lord's side."

The reply surprised him.

"That thou mayest the more readily deliver me to
thine infernal ally on the black horse," he said after
a brief pause. "That were to grant a favour indeed."

"If my lord believeth I mean aught dishonest," I
said, "let him strike me down where I stand. I desire no better answer to my accusers than an opportunity to fight in my lord's cause. Where words are
of no avail let deeds be the witnesses. One tongue
must be dumb before an hundred tongues, but two
hands and a trusty sword, with the right spirit behind
them, may tell the truth with convincing eloquence."

"These are brave words from so girlish a mouth,"
he remarked, "and brave words are ever pleasing to
a right ear. But it still remaineth clear thou shouldst
be hanged or have thy head cut off. Methinks I
should feel easier if I saw thee looking down from beside the Egyptian fellow. Yet again, to slay thee
were to destroy the stuff of a right good soldier.
Thinkest thou I could depend on thee after the testimony that has been offered against thee?"

"I have but one answer," I replied, trembling with
excitement. "If my lord doubteth, he has there
his sword, and let him strike my head from my
shoulders."

"I have ever more faith in the face than the
tongue," he said, looking his keenest at me. "The
tongue speaketh many languages, and, indeed, the
face, too, is apt in feigning, and yet, methinks, I can
interpret thine. Besides, thou art already acquainted

with perils, and, moreover, a most magical medicine
man. Where is our good fakeer? Oh, ho, gone.
Offended at thy skill. 'Tis the way of physicians.
They are as jealous of rivals as women. And 'tis
something in thy favour that he will hate thee.
Mightest thou not save a prince in the hour of trouble? Yet I forget not, if there be truth in many
words, thou deservest instant death. I will put a fair
question to thee, let thy life hang on the fairness of
thine answer. If thou wert in my place and I were
in thine, what wouldst thou do?"

"Use thine aid to crush mine enemies," I replied
promptly.

"By my faith, bravely answered," he said, with a
chuckle. "Thou wouldst use me to crush thine enemies, showing thou art a man of penetration; for, indeed, I am a soldier bred, though sitting here in idle
times to see rogues put to death. Thou wouldst use
me to crush thine enemies, and in sooth thou wouldst
do well. For I tell thee I never hear of war but my
sword trembleth in its sheath with a desire to cleave
heads. But should I do well in trying to use thee?
Perchance, my dove might prove a scorpion. It is
not a time to take risks. Shall we hang thee or use
thee? Quick, for business is urgent."

"Do thy will, my lord," I replied, with a low bow.

"That is a plain answer. I will take thee at thy
word and hang thee. 'Twere a sore scandal and an
eternal cause of laughter to my foes if, having a spy
in my hand, I let him go. Wherefore, thou hadst
better say thy prayers," and his manner became stern
and serious. "As I am an upright judge and the
guardian of my people's welfare, thou owest a debt
to justice. Let it be discharged with all haste. I
have already tarried too long over thee."

CHAPTER XVII.

A SUDDEN CHANGE OF FRONT.

So all my rosy hopes were blown to the winds again.
Fate had cut off the last chance of escape, and I
could look for nothing but immediate death. For
I had heard something of the portentous mysteries
of statecraft that make such havoc of the conscience
of rulers, and understood that behind the personal will
and inclination of Abou Kuram were reasons of such
fearful cogency as no prince who valued his power
and security could ignore. However friendly my
judge might be at heart he was not a free agent, but
merely the instrument of a tyrannous system, which
sentenced and slew with ruthless disregard of the
sanctity of private thoughts. This was driven in
upon me with staggering emphasis when the leather-
faced ingrate I had relieved of his pains, humbly venturing to commend the wisdom of his master's speech,
enlarged on the absolute necessity of preserving the
State from foreign intrigue at all hazards, and at
whatever cost of blood; and ending up with the proposition, "Let my lord decree death forthwith, and
while he despatcheth weightier matters, I will see this
rogue executed."
But we had both mistaken the force of Abou Kuram's character. A weak man is the slave of his
office; a strong man is its master and director. Perhaps it was the working of humanity in his breast;
perhaps it was a sudden conviction of my innocence;
or, what is more likely, it may have been a prince's
dislike of dictation and interference that influenced
him; but he unexpectedly took a course of his own.
"Words of wisdom drop from thy mouth as honey
from an honeycomb, Abdallah," he said, with a hard
look at his counsellor. "Foreign intriguers and spies
must indeed be given to the fowls of the air and the

beasts of the earth. It is my duty and privilege to guard the State; I will take care they are not neglected. Again, business, as thou well sayest, presseth hard, and in order that thou mayest give thy mind to other and more important affairs, I will myself execute justice on this stranger. Get thee forth with all haste; and thou, Koor Ali, who will command next to myself, go with him, and take no rest until my army be ready for war."

The two men bowed very low and hastened forth. He watched until they had gone, with a clamourous mob at their heels, then, turning to me, he said briefly—

"I have purposes that will astonish thy friend Abdallah. Thou shalt ride by my bridle rein, and we shall see of what stuff thou art made. Nay, nay, no speeches," as he saw the fulness of my heart coming into my face. "This is a time for action. Besides, thou mightest find cause to repent of thy fair words, for if thou shouldst prove false, thou shalt die the most horrible death Abdallah can devise to atone for this present clemency."

With that he turned abruptly to a fawning official, and said in a brusque tone, "The stranger will have need of food; see thou to his wants; and thy head answer for his safe keeping." Whereupon, rising quickly, he swept majestically into an inner room, without giving me the opportunity of saying a word of thanks.

My first impulse was to sit down and sob aloud. It seemed that nothing else could relieve my pent-up feelings; and, indeed, a careful observer might have noticed an unusual moisture about the lashes, which I wiped furtively while trying to jest with my attendant.

The rising sun, they say, is worshipped; and certainly the favour of a prince insures many smiles and obsequious attentions. The demeanour of the people towards me changed as singularly as my shifting fortune. Those who had spat on me with foul imprecations but an hour before, now saluted me with loud ejaculations of friendship and blessing. Many a man would probably have valued the tokens of goodwill more than I did. I had been defiant to the mob in my adversity; in my triumph I hope I was not insolent; but assuredly I was in no mood to respond with any cordiality to the greetings of people who, if Abou Kuram's humour had been different, would have shouted themselves hoarse with joy at seeing my head slashed off my shoulders.

The sight of one eager face, however, among the many fawning ones, gave me a genuine thrill of pleasure. Said Achmet had haunted the place all the morning like a perturbed spirit, and now, on the first opportunity, he came running forward to congratulate me on my new lease of life. I had not much to say, but I gave the good soul's hand a hearty Christian wring, and he did not resent it, though to shake hands with an infidel or stranger is pollution to the ordinary Mussulman.

When sorrows come, says the poet, they come not in single spies, but in battalions. Once or twice in a lifetime, a few happy mortals have the sweet experience of finding joys, too, come trooping in companies. While my benefactor and myself were in converse together, to the further delight of us both, word came from Abou Kuram that until the troops were ready I was to be his guest or Said Achmet's, just according to my fancy. Needless to say what choice I made, nor how deeply grateful I was to Abou Kuram for this fresh sign of his graciousness.

Said Achmet carried me off with as proud a heart as if I were the greatest man in the land, and treated me with a tenderness that mere greatness could never have evoked. Indeed, if I had been his own son risen from the dead, he could not have been more lavish of the caressing attentions in word and act that the tremulous affection of an old man delights in, or evinced a livelier regret at the parting that was near.

For the most part of three happy days I was with

him, listening to wondrous tales of the diabolical prowess of the man on the black horse from Tabal, or discussing the prospects of the campaign with him, or drinking in the wise and varied discourse of my host himself, as we sat inhaling fragrant essences in the shade of his garden palms.

How far off all that is now, and how strangely tinged with mystic hues! Said Achmet has long since gone to his account,

> "And on his grave with shining eyes
> The Syrian stars look down,"

but the memory of his benign refuge remains with me as a beautiful dream of a day on an azure summer isle after the beating of tempests on the main.

The preparations at the castle went on with more bustle than speed, for it appeared to be the determined object of every man to get into his fellow's way and thwart him in his work. The scene was one of constant confusion and uproar; night and day the hubbub went on, waxing ever louder and shriller, till it seemed like pandemonium come again; but at length order began to rise out of chaos, and even the novice mind could see that the preparations were really going on. Men came hurrying in from outlying districts. Horses and camels were got ready, swords, spears, and matchlocks were furbished up, ammunition was laid out, water-skins were filled, provisions were loaded on snapping, grunting pack-camels—a hundred pounds to every beast—and all the while the soldiers badgered, shouted, jested, and blasphemed in a way that might have moved the envy of any Christian army in the world.

On the morning of the fourth day a messenger came to me breathless, saying that Abou Kuram was seated in the audience court, and wished to see me at once. I hurried off, Said Achmet accompanying in some excitement, fearing that liars and intriguers had been at their loathsome work, and had succeeded in turning him against me. But I was quickly reassured;

for when I entered his presence with palpitating heart and hesitating step, he beckoned me to him with a gracious smile, bade a cushion be placed for me, and proceeded to inquire in his most affable tones, and, as I thought, with covert glances at Abdallah, who sat close by, about my health and welfare.

"Time, perchance, hangeth heavy upon thee," he said. "But thou shalt soon have sport enough. Ere the sun go down again we shall be on the march to meet Yumen Yusel and his helper Satan. We shall see how thou canst sheathe thy sword in flesh; 'tis a merry game, and methinks there will be plenty of it going."

And then in the hearing of all he repeated that I was to ride by his bridle in the character of physician and personal attendant, and that I was to be mounted on a favourite mare from his own stable. Abdallah sat looking on the ground with a clouded brow and compressed lips, but dared not speak a word. The crowd gaped and beamed on me as one basking in the favours of an all-powerful prince, though doubtless puzzled by the change of sentiment that conferred on me my distinctions.*

"Thou wilt find the little Fatema of the purest Kohlani breed," he went on, addressing me; "in shape and spirit unequalled outside the stable in which she stands. In her veins is the unsullied blood of the Prophet's own mare. In fleetness as the deer, in courage as the lion, in gentleness as the lamb, in beauty as the gazelle, in intelligence as the serpent, she will be to thee both a companion and a protector, obeying thy wishes ere thou hast time to express them. She will carry thee bravely to victory or fly with thee swifter than the wind in defeat. She will nurse thee when thou art sick, rejoice with thee when thou art glad, she will be thy lover and thy slave. See thou prove worthy of her. And now there is but

---

* An Arab can confer no more signal honour than to present a guest with a horse of high pedigree. A wife from his harem is a small thing in comparison.

one thing more: when thou seest the sun looking for his bed in the west, come hither, and thou shalt find her ready for thee."

He waved his hand to signify the audience was at an end, and rising, passed into the interior of the castle.

"Verily the great Abou Kuram hath shown thee favour beyond example," remarked Said Achmet, as we returned for a little to his home. "I think thou hast thy fair face to thank. The truth of nature will overturn many lies. As for the enterprise on which thou goest, it accordeth well with thy adventurous heart. The scent of danger is to thee as the scent of prey to the lion. Thy gladness is shining in thine eyes. I would I could see thee again."

"And may I not return to Marabel in triumph?" I asked.

"Truly thou mayest; but something tells me thou wilt not. It was pleasant to sit with thee over the evening pipe or plucking the ripe fruit, while hearing thee talk of thy country and adventures. But the bitter must be with the sweet. All things have an end, and that which once was becomes but a dream. The time of parting is at hand, and I shall lie awake on my bed at night thinking of the stranger who came from afar to cheer me in my solitude."

"And the stranger will think of thee with gratitude," I returned. "It is all he has to offer, and thou hast it in full measure. Wherever he may go, whatever may be his lot, he will remember thy kindness in the day of his trouble."

"It is surely enough," he answered in a low voice. "When thou returnest to thy people, tell them that beneath the burnoose there beat human hearts. And now one last favour I ask of thee: thou art now a man of influence. I commend my Tabal to thy care; and the Lord prosper thee."

"May my best friend forget me if I forget thy son," I replied, and he thanked me with gushing eyes.

Early in the afternoon, in accordance with Abou

Kuram's orders, Said Achmet, Tabal, and I went to
the castle, which presented a scene of frantic commotion.   An esplanade or parade ground in front
was thronged with gaunt, fierce-visaged troops, some
on foot, some mounted on horses, and some on
dromedaries, wheeling and plunging and rushing to
and fro with maniacal yells and brandishing of weapons.   On first catching sight of them, through a vista
of palms and tamarisks, I thought that either they
had suddenly gone stark mad, or that the enemy, following up his successes in the field, had pushed on
and captured the castle.   It added to my amazement
when Tabal, seeing what was going on, bolted forward, shouting at the pitch of his voice, as though
he, too, were magically bereft of his wits.   Having
no inclination to advance among the flying spears, I
was meditating flight when Said Achmet touched me
reassuringly on the arm.

"It is the Arzah,"* he said, with a smile.   "They
are getting up the courage of war; methinks it will
be bad for the enemy."

Whatever might be the issue there was no denying
the imposing ferocity of these preliminary antics.

The men were armed with a variety of queer
and uncouth weapons—ancient matchlocks, pistols,
spears, swords, javelins, and daggers, which flew
and flashed promiscuously, as if a company of madmen had somehow possessed themselves of half a
dozen armouries, and were enjoying themselves after
the manner of Bedlam.

As soon as we were seen approaching, a band of
horsemen dashed to meet us, whirling their swords in
air so furiously that in spite of Said Achmet's assurance that the display was mere sport, I was under a
sore temptation to show them a pair of clean heels.
Happily, I was saved from this disgrace; for just at
the crucial moment when their lances seemed to be
dropping for the charge they wheeled with incon-

* A war dance performed before going forth to meet an
enemy.

ceivable quickness and dexterity, and dashed back the way they came, yelling till the courts rang. Two or three times this manœuvre was repeated, each time with a madder dash and a quicker turning, then drawing up suddenly they faced us, saluting with a rigid precision that was in striking contrast to the wild evolutions they had just gone through.

They had scarcely turned to get back to their original positions when a great shout went up, and Abou Kuram, superbly mounted on a grey charger, came curvetting and prancing on the esplanade with drawn sword. His appearance was the signal for another outbreak of the entire body of troops, horse and foot. Yelling and flourishing and throwing their weapons, they circled about him rather as if he were a captive for whose blood they thirsted, than a commander whom they wished to honour, while he rode quietly through the maze, sitting his high-mettled horse like one born to the saddle. By-and-by the tumult died down, and Abou Kuram, still riding about, noticed Said Achmet and myself. With two or three bounds of his leaping steed he was beside us.

"Here thou art," he said, smiling down upon me. "It pleaseth me to see thee punctually, according to thy word. Hast said farewell to the good Said Achmet? For the time has come to mount and be off."

"I am ready, my lord," I answered.

"It is well, for the shadows grow long and the sun is hastening to his bed. Bring the little Fatema," he said, addressing a slave. "She waiteth for her master."

A minute later my little mare, fully caparisoned, was led ambling into the parade ground. Addressing her, the slave made a pretty speech to the effect that she was going forth to great honour with the fair-faced stranger; that she was to obey his will, and that she would have her reward in a care that would preserve her from all ill-treatment, and that she would have dates to eat and sweet water to drink when the perils

of the desert were past. The intelligent brute whinnied as if to say she perfectly understood him; then the
bridle rein was formally delivered to me, and she
took a step forward as if acquiescing in the change of
proprietorship. I stroked her gently as a token of
good will, rubbing her face, and speaking encouraging words in her ear, after the Arab fashion. Having thus made an agreement I fastened my green bag
carefully to the saddle, embraced Said Achmet, and
mounted.

"Have my words exaggerated her excellence?"
asked Abou Kuram, eagerly, coming close to me.

"Nay," I replied. "My lord has not spoken half
the truth."

"And thou wilt see she is as good as she is beautiful," he said; a prophesy that was fulfilled to the
uttermost, as this history will show.

Many who have never set eyes on him have been
eloquent in praise of the Arab horse. Poet and
painter and romancer have vied in delineating his
matchless excellences, physical and mental. But it is
not until you have eaten and slept and fought with
him on the desert, on the battle-field, beside the black
tent in the green pastures, until you have been his
intimate friend and comrade, and learned to appreciate his coolness and courage, his power of endurance and gentleness and intelligence and loyalty, that
you can know his many high qualities. Yet perhaps
only a poet could describe my Fatema. For in her
were surely combined the perfection of equine virtue
and beauty.

Never anything more lovely, more dainty and
proud, moved on four legs.

She was neither big nor heavy, but her muscles
were of whalebone, and her bones of the finest tempered steel. Her limbs, indeed, were like wrought
metal in the firmness, cleanness, and grace of them,
and the trunk in exquisiteness of curve and symmetry
of parts was such as a sculptor may have dreamed of
but has never matched in bronze or marble. The sum

total of that animate loveliness,—the silken bay coat, the softly sloping shoulders, the buoyancy of the curved back, the fiery pride of the arched neck, the full round haunches, the rich sweep of mane and tail, the sharp, daintily-poised ears, the broad forehead and the fine muzzle, and, above all, the spirit of the alert, full-orbed eye,—is beyond the power of any artist save Nature herself; nor does Nature take such pains anywhere out of Arabia.

When Fatema found me in the saddle, she began to glide through the giddy maze with an ease and fluency of motion that to me were like a foretaste of heaven. I plumed myself on my horsemanship; for one of the few things I learned thoroughly as a boy was to stick on the back of anything that could take a bit between its teeth, and no doubt I had now the conceit to hold up my head as a fit rider for the noblest of steeds. But, indeed, an old wife could have sat that supple, mincing creature with security; though the upward glance of her eye, with its intimation of suppressed fire, told that, under different conditions, she could behave in a totally different manner. I was afterwards to prove how her temper and behaviour varied with varying circumstances.

Presently the muezzin began to cry plaintively from the minarets, and soldiers and citizens trooped off to the mosques to pray for pardon and victory, leaving only a few men to look after the beasts. As my company in worship would defile the sacred places of Moslem, I also remained behind.

When the worshippers returned from their devotions the baggage-camels were put into line and examined by the officers, the horses and dromedaries being made ready for their riders while the examination was proceeding. Then came supper, and, in honour of the great occasion, many sheep were slaughtered and roasted whole over big fires. The hissing carcases had hardly time to take a brown crust when they were torn asunder and eaten in huge mouthfuls by a ravenous host, who washed down the burning meat with copious draughts of goat's milk. As I did not care to enter the lists in such a contest I contented myself with a piece of doughy bread, some dates, and a cup of coffee.

When the meal was over, a curious and characteristic ceremony was enacted. A calf, only a few days old, was led into the open space and killed with a sword, its blood being made to flow inward towards the castle. The animal's life extinct, every man who was to accompany the expedition stepped solemnly over the body, which was then burned so that no dog or other unclean beast might eat any part of the flesh. This is supposed to bring good fortune, and an Arab army could not be induced to take the field without first observing the sacrificial rite. The calf safely cremated, the men immediately mounted their camels and horses and wheeled into place; then Abou Kuram, going to the front, delivered a short oration on the glory of war and the bravery of his soldiers, which evoked uproarious applause from the flattered. Ere it died away the kettle-drums were rattling and the cymbals clashing the advance, and amid vociferous cries of "God save Abou Kuram!" "God give the victory to Abou Kuram!" the strangely assorted mass swung slowly into line. The huge serpentine procession wound tediously through the narrow tortuous streets in which two camel-men found it hard to march abreast, but its tardy coilings were enlivened by the caperings and shoutings of the mob who ran in front of us and hung on our heels, and, to their own immediate peril, squeezed and pressed on both sides of us. On the outskirts of the town the people stopped, finding the pace on the open ground beyond their capacity in running, so they stood there and yelled forth blessings and good wishes, which we acknowledged with resounding cheers. As we deployed into open order for greater ease in marching, I caught a last glimpse of Said Achmet, who stood apart waving both his arms as if to signify he had a

14

double interest in the receding column. Tabal and I waved our farewell in return, and from me there went with it a heartfelt benediction.

CHAPTER XVIII.

THE MARCH.

THE details of the march need not be narrated at length. Our journey lay over scarred and blighted ground and across sandy plains, and in and out among circular sand-hills,—loose impermanent heaps which the winds of the desert twist and curve and fling about in their wanton, lonely sport, desolate heaps that hide the bones of the perished traveller, and are for ever moving their formless lips with a silent, stealthy motion, to suck in and overwhelm the living. No man knows the deep treachery of mother earth till he has wrestled with the noiseless forces of the desert.

The pace, however, was brisk, for man and beast were fresh and eager; indeed it was a perpetual surprise to me how the animals made such progress over the elusive path. The camels, swinging at a steady trot, had much the best of it; for when the hard hoof of the horse sinks and slips, the elastic spongy foot of the camel spreads like a web, and he passes as easily and safely over drifting sands as a snowshoer over smothering wreaths. It was then I first understood how truly the camel deserves its title of the ship of the desert: for as ships pass easily along their liquid way, so the camel glides with sure and facile foot over his unstable course of sand. Yet the horses, too, had uncommon lightness and skill, seeing that every step forward was a half-step backward.

To the horseman the first sensation of a desert ride is as if he were poised on springs of ineffable delicacy, which swayed gently on the slightest pressure. Much of this luxurious ease is due to the yielding track, but something also to the springy motion of the Arab horse. To the saddle nothing whatever is due, since it is merely pieces of the hardest wood roughly nailed and bound with thongs of rawhide. On an English horse and a macadamized road it would reduce a trooper to helplessness in an hour; and, indeed, with all the suppleness and softness of the true Kohlan, Arab saddlery soon galls and blisters the inexperienced. Being as hard as the wood they bestride, the Arabs themselves suffer no discomfort.

On the first night we marched steadily till set of moon, then halted for food and rest. I could not half admire the quickness with which the fires were lighted with withered grasses and shrubs, and the good-humoured alacrity of the cooks in preparing the meal. To be sure it did not call for any elaborate exercise of art, for the rations consisted of nothing daintier than coarse flour, salt, dried dates, and coffee. The cooks took two or three handfuls of flour apiece, poured water on it from a skin and kneaded it into a dirty dough with dirty hands. It would be profane in an Arab cook to have clean hands, and so he keeps them religiously filthy, thus giving those who eat his preparations the benefit of many unsuspected ingredients.

The dough, which was thoroughly wet perhaps halfway to the centre, was beaten out into thick cakes which were laid on the glowing embers and covered with hot ashes. They were left thus till converted into a sodden soapy paste, then taken out and eaten as hot as they could be swallowed. I nibbled the edge of one; but finding my teeth stick in it I ate a handful of dates, took a drink of water, and then, wrapping my burnoose close about me, threw myself on the ground and slept the sweet sleep of the weary.

It seemed I had not lain five minutes when the kettle-drums were beating the *reveille*. The grey dawn was only beginning to glimmer, but already the camel-

men were quarrelling with their grunting beasts, and
our bakers were busy with the glutinous compound
they called bread. We hastily swallowed some
mouthfuls of it straight off the burning coals, with a
few dates and a drink of musty water apiece, and
were off again.

For a while the air was deliciously cool and refreshing; and the glories of the opening day in the
lone wilderness as the sun broke through his curtain
of white mist, were such as a man beholds with awe
and remembers with reverence. But the blazing orb
soon turned the dewy freshness to a sweltering, blistering heat, exceedingly trying to the nerves and temper of men toiling through shifting sands and conical
tumuli of volcanic slag. Yet no man complained,
only as we mopped our streaming faces the conversation lagged, and here and there a man gave a low involuntary moan. Save such intermittent noises, and
the dreary monotonous sift, sift, sift of animals' feet
in the sand, there was not a sound. When the sun
mounts in his might, desert travellers are apt to fall
silent.

Towards noon, when we had almost reached the
point of utter dissolution, we gained the crest of a low
ridge, whence looking to the north-west we saw what
evoked a cry of gladness from nearly every throat in
the company. It was an oasis, a tiny spot of green
with a clump of trees in the midst, shining like an
emerald in a broad drab setting. We knew there
was a well there and Tabal, with the privilege of a
guide, suggested we should halt and replenish our
water-skins. But Abou Kuram answered curtly that
we were not yet in need of water, that the time for
rest had not come, and that in forced marches men
had to think more of speed than of comfort.

There was a general look of disappointment at this
speech, which urged Tabal to appeal again, and to
advance reasons for stopping.

"When I desire thy counsel I will tell thee," returned Abou Kuram, shortly. "Look thou to the

way, and leave the rest to me. And methinks thou hadst better mend thy pace."

After this no man durst speak, and keen as was the disappointment, there was no murmuring, only the men sat a little more grimly, and prodded a little more viciously with their riding-sticks. As we passed, many a man turned with yearning eyes to the verdurous spot, thinking, perhaps, he should be dead ere reaching another.

If the forenoon had been hot the afternoon was the breath of living fire, yet we toiled·on, dissolving and open-mouthed, and wondering how long we could stand the burning lances of the sun.

I speak of the rank and file. As for Abou Kuram, he seemed to be oblivious of heat or thirst or fatigue. How I envied him! While my mouth was cracking he was evidently as cool and moist as a ripe pear. Koor Ali, who rode beside me, must have noticed the painful twitching of my lips, for, looking in my face with an expression of concern, he asked if I was thirsty.

"As dry as a baked brick," I croaked.

Koor Ali's son, Ahmed, a lad about my own age, rode beside us, and on hearing my raven-voice, burst into a fit of laughter.

"What art thou laughing at, Ahmed?" demanded Abou Kuram, turning slightly in his saddle. Ahmed pointed to me.

"The stranger croaketh with thirst," he said, "ere we are half-way over the desert."

I tried to explain, but failed; my mouth was as a rusty machine that had not moved for a century.

"Give him thy water-skin, Koor Ali," said Abou Kuram, "lest he faint. It were ill to die in the desert," he added, smiling at me.

The water was dingy and beginning to smell badly, but just then a stagnant pool would have been sweet, and I took a huge gulp. Taking another, I held it in my mouth for a minute, then squirted it out, sending it, as if by pure accident, over the sprightly Ahmed.

"By my faith, I like not to be spat on by an infi-del!" he cried, grasping his spear as if to have at me.

The laugh was now on my side, though I perceived the danger of indulging in it.

"'Twas but an accident," I said apologetically. "Yet it is good, and will cool thee."

I tried to propitiate him by handing him his father's water-skin to drink, but he disdainfully declined.

"Nay; I am not a babe like thee," he said. "Thou shouldst have brought thy mother with thee," and he tossed his head as if he were safe from the weakness of thirst in a desert land.

Three mortal hours of panting toil and dripping sweat had yet to pass ere Abou Kuram ordered a halt, and then it was but to dismount, swallow a mouthful of dry dates and foul lukewarm water, and scramble into the saddle again. Through the broiling after-noon we stewed and gasped, never drawing rein till sundown, when we stopped for prayers and the even-ing meal. I had scarcely eaten when I was asleep on the sand; and my eyes appeared to have just closed when those abominable drums were beating the order to mount and march again. Words cannot tell how sore and tired I was, or how I longed to lie down and be at peace. The feeling was as if some one had pounded me limp and nature was slowly stiffening up again, with the joints all out of place, and every mus-cle and ligament stretched beyond endurance. But as the Arabs said nothing of fatigue I would have cut my tongue out rather than complain.

Five days we panted on through scorching sands under a flaming sky, and five nights the bright Ara-bian moon lighted us on our trackless, hurrying march. By the third day man and beast were show-ing decided signs of exhaustion. Camels lay down, refusing to rise, and were left to die, sometimes with their burdens on them, sometimes with their throats cut, if there was time to aid them in going off; the horses lagged with low heads and protruding tongues, and men dropped suddenly from their saddles with strange stertorous noises, and lay as senseless as logs. Two went raving mad, one of them succeeding in killing another and himself ere his comrades could cut him down. Hollow graves, which the jackals and hyenas could reopen with a scratch of the paw, were scooped out for the dead, and their camels given to others. The young soldiers shook and looked anxious, for sudden death and unceremonious burial are disconcerting to unseasoned nerves; the old ones clenched their teeth, growling that war and the desert were not for children; and Abou Kuram, self-possessed, but a trifle grimmer than at starting, spoke roughly about the delays. So the cavalcade toiled wearily on, yearning so fervently for rest that it forgot glory, yet stolidly enduring the harshness of fate. But, indeed, an Arab is a wild cat in vitality, and more than a wild cat in the capacity to bear pain uncomplainingly. We pressed silently and faintingly ahead, counting the beads of sweat as they rolled down, and wondering how many of us the desert would swallow ere we got a chance of taking it out of the enemy.

At last we left the sands for alkaline lands, scantily clothed with hard, sour grass and sapless, diminutive shrubs, and gradually ascending to a range of mountains that crossed our line of advance north and south. It was somewhere within those ramparts that we expected to find Amood Sinn and his discomfited army. Being now close upon the scene of the late battle, we had to exercise double vigilance; for Yumen Yusel would naturally be on the look-out to prevent aid from reaching the man whom he wished utterly to destroy. Nearly all the cooking was done by day; so that there might be no fires at night to indicate our presence and position; and when we lay down to rest the number of sentinels was doubled. But we reached the foot-hills without molestation, and thankful that we were likely to be able to pick ourselves together before being called upon to fight.

As it would be at once extremely dangerous, ex-

tremely difficult and tedious to take the whole body
of troops to the rendezvous appointed by Amood Sinn,
Abou Kuram decided to send Koor Ali forward with
an escort to ascertain whether it would not be possible to effect a junction of the two armies outside the
mountains. It was near sunset when we arrived at
our halting place, and as soon as the moon rose, Koor
Ali and his little band set forth, Tabal still leading.

According to the guide, we might expect them back
at the latest by noon next day. Noon came, however,
without bringing them. The afternoon wore slowly
on, darkness fell, prayers were said, and supper was
eaten, and still no Koor Ali. Abou Kuram was getting impatient. After a forced march across the
desert, it was exasperating to be kept waiting at this
stage. The camp lay down to sleep, moon and stars
kept their vigil, morning broke, and still no tidings
of the absent ones. Abou Kuram strutted sullenly
about the camp, recalling his stock of Arabian oaths.
Noon came again, and again sunset, supper, and prayers, yet there was no sign of Koor Ali and his escort.

I am afraid Abou Kuram went through his devotions with a preoccupied, inattentive mind that evening; at any rate, the first thing he did after turning his
face from Mecca was to pour a flood of objurgations
on Amood Sinn, on Koor Ali, on Tabal, and all concerned with them. But that did not bring them, and
once more the camp lay down to rest. The commander, however, did not lie down. Long after his
men were snoring at the sky I watched his dark and
solitary figure moving to and fro in angry, uneasy
expectancy.

"There shall be a reckoning for this," I heard him
mutter once. "Woe betide the man who causeth this
delay."

He was still walking about when I fell asleep.

I was enjoying a happy dream, when all at once,
in the black darkness, I was roused by the crackle of
fire-arms and the shrill voices of excited men.

"The enemy! the enemy!" they shouted, as I

sprang up, rubbing my eyes. "The devil on the black horse, with ten thousand demons at his back." And then all along our front there was a momentary line of leaping fire, which showed our scurrying men confusedly trying to get into fighting order. To our astonishment, and perhaps also to our relief, there came no response to our volley, nor could we hear any movement outside our own lines, though we hearkened with ears that would have heard the stealthy tread of the panther.

"The enemy has run!" said some one exultingly. "Our fire has given him fleet feet to make off." And that instant, as if in answer to this boast, there was the vicious ping of flying lead in the air, and some of our men dropped screaming to the earth. We delivered another volley blindly into the darkness, then waited, with pounding hearts, for a rush, but, contary to all usage, it did not come.

Savage at the double disgrace of being fooled and taken unawares, Abou Kuram ordered a sortie; but the party had not gone twenty yards when another shower of bullets fell upon us from the opposite direction. The foe was making a circle and peppering us at his will. A second sortie party was instantly sent out; but, like the first, it came back without making any discovery. Only some said they had seen a terrible apparition on a black horse of gigantic size, and that steed and rider breathed blue flame. So the army stood there in the inky night, nervously handling its weapons, cursing all sons of Belial who made war at unearthly hours, and supplicating the protection of the Prophet. The Prophet was evidently gracious, for there were no more of those ugly surprises that night. The foe, content with a moderate amount of fun, had gone off unscathed to chuckle over his success and get ready for a big fight.

Abou Kuram knew it was coming; he knew, too, that the enemy, flushed with triumph, would be exceedingly tough to deal with; and the knowledge incensed him afresh against his dilatory ally. But intelligence was at hand. Just as the morning star was fading out of sight, Koor Ali and his little band were at last spied emerging from a defile in the mountains. Abou Kuram watched them with never a word, but his face was set, and in his heart were the elements of a fearful explosion.

As Koor Ali approached, we saw that he was accompanied by a stranger of rank, whom we judged to be an emissary from Amood Sinn. At sight of him Abou Kuram became sterner than ever.

"Behold, now we shall have a feast of words," he said to me, "and we shall be talking idly when we ought to be driving Yumen Yusel as the mountain wind driveth chaff."

When, at length, the company drew up, he received their salute coldly, and listened with a mixture of scorn and haughty impatience to the florid speech which the envoy hastened to make. The many expressions of personal goodwill with which the oration was interlarded he acknowledged stiffly; indeed, the responses were so ungraciously made, one with half an eye could have seen it would be far more congenial to him to draw his sword and fall furiously on this man of smiling face and fine words, than to stand and listen. Koor Ali, perceiving the temper of his chief, and well knowing what it meant, advanced with the object of making his report, and so cut short the palavering. But he had not uttered a dozen words, when Mohamed ben Eldad Hassam (such was the stranger's imposing name) interrupted him.

"Peradventure I may be permitted to say to my lord's brother," said the envoy, beaming upon Abou Kuram with a feline softness and craftiness of expression, "that as to the delay which hath occurred the good and gallant Koor Ali and his followers, who showed the courage of lions in coming to us, are in nowise to blame."

"My lord ought not to trouble himself with such small matters," returned Abou Kuram, with the slightest of bows and the faintest of smiles. "They become not his rank. Besides, he is weary, and needeth rest."

"I am indeed weary," responded Ben Eldad, with unruffled urbanity. "And it is because of that I would speak in behalf of Koor Ali; for may I never have the holy joy of sitting in the Prophet's presence, if he hath not driven us as if we were things of iron and steel, and not men of simple flesh and blood."

"It is not proper that my lord should thus add to his weariness," interrupted Abou Kuram. "Let him withdraw to my tent, and have his feet washed by his servant's slaves, and food set before him, and take the rest of which he is so much in need. Koor Ali will himself tell his story," and with an imperative manner that was not to be resisted, he led Mohamed ben Eldad Hassam to the retirement of the tent. In a minute he was back again.

"Now," he said to Koor Ali, drawing himself up with soldierly sternness. "We will hear what thou hast to say. Wherefore didst thou tarry so long, and what tidings hast thou brought?"

Koor Ali gave his story briefly and clearly. To begin with, he said, they did not find Amood Sinn at the place appointed, an excursion of the man on the black horse and his marauders having driven him deeper into the mountain. This change of situation involved an arduous search of forty-eight hours, and when at last Amood Sinn was found, it was skulking among the rocks as if he were a fox, with his army scattered he knew not whither.

"His heart was as the dust under our feet," pursued Koor Ali, "and he railed upon the evil spirit on the black horse who had come to destroy him. I asked him if he intended to let Yumen Yusel harry his kingdom, and carry away his horses, his cattle, his camels, his wives, and his little ones, and he answered, 'If it is the will of God.' 'Nay,' I replied, 'that is but the voice of a craven fear. We are come hither to help thee with a great host, and are we to go back because thou liest among the rocks, afraid to

come forth and give the enemy battle?'   Whereupon
there were shame and confusion on his countenance,
and he arose and said that of a surety they would
fight.   'But how shall I prevail on my men,' he
asked, 'for they think these are evil spirits leagued
against them?'   'Gather them unto one place,' said
I unto him; and he sent out messengers and gathered them into one place; a great hollow in the midst
of the mountains.   'Speak unto them,' I said.   'Nay,
it will be better if thou speak unto them,' he answered, 'for they no longer heed my words.'   Whereupon, I stood forth on a rock and spoke to them, and
told them how my lord had come to help them; and
hearing this, they took heart, and shouted with a
mighty voice that they yearned for vengeance, and
were ready to do battle with Yumen Yusel and the
man on the black horse.   And I, thinking it well to
take them while the spirit was strong upon them, bade
them come down to join my lord, whereat Amood
Sinn, trembling greatly, said, 'Nay, it is better for us
to remain here until all things are ready.'   'Thou art
more afraid than thy men,' I said.   'They are but
common soldiers,' he answered; 'the enemy seeketh
not their life, but mine.   Peradventure if we go down
with thee, he will fall upon us by the way, and slay
me.'   Whereupon I, answering, said that forasmuch
as no battle could be fought among rocks and gorges,
they must come down to the plain.   If they did not,
then would my lord return to Marabel, and Amood
Sinn's possessions would go from him and his pos-
terity for ever.   And being again sore ashamed, he
consented to come down, and now lieth yonder, close
by the foot of the mountain, awaiting my lord's be-
hest."

"Thou hast done the part of a brave man, Koor
Ali," said Abou Kuram, when the recital was at an
end.   "I was wroth at the delay, and now my anger
is kindled against Amood Sinn.   Thou hast done
right well in taking the cowardly dog by the ear, and
dragging him to the foot of the mountain.   We have

been surprised here, and a battle is at hand. Get thou things ready, Koor Ali. We will move to meet Amood Sinn. And now I must go to Mohamed ben Eldad Hassam. He lieth ill at ease in my tent, full of excuses for his brave master and peradventure for himself."

"Yea, it is likely," returned Koor Ali. "My opinion is that he cometh to spy my lord's strength. He will return, if thou let him, to report to Amood Sinn, and if my lord's army be not enough in their eyes they will betake themselves to the rocks again."

"We will see if there be no sand for his eyes," said Abou Kuram, significantly, turning towards his tent.

The warning which Koor Ali had given was well timed; for sure enough, when Mohamed ben Eldad Hassam had washed and eaten and rested and paid Abou Kuram the regulation number of compliments, he proposed that he should get an escort and precede the troops, in order that Amood Sinn might be preparted to receive their illustrious general in a fashion becoming his rank. But Abou Kuram had not studied diplomacy for nothing.

"My lord troubleth himself too much," he replied with an insinuating grace that was wonderful to behold. "We are soldiers, and will be satisfied with a soldier's welcome. We are not come hither for feasting and ceremonies, but to destroy Yumen Yusel and his evil ally on the black horse of whom we have heard so much."

Mohamed ben Eldad turned his eyes to heaven at this, mentally invoking its protection.

"Thinkest thou steel or lead will avail upon him?" he asked. "'Tis hard to kill Satan."

"If he come in our way we can but try our weapons upon him," answered Abou Kuram.

"Thou speakest like the valiant man thou art," said the envoy, sweetly. "Wherefore I would again crave my lord's permission to return in advance of the troops. My royal master will be sore displeased if he be denied the opportunity of preparing for my lord's reception."

"The good Amood Sinn knoweth we are coming," said Abou Kuram, suavely, "and thou needest not fear for his princely beneficence. We do not look for ceremonies with the foe in sight. Besides, see, the troops are even now ready to march. It were folly for thee therefore to hurry away."

After that Mohamed ben Eldad could not further persist, but his disappointment and chagrin were manifest to all. He and his master were committed to the chances of another battle.

CHAPTER XIX.

AMOOD SINN'S BRAVERY.

WHEN early in the afternoon the two armies effected a juncture, the aspect of the allies was such as might well have made Abou Kuram pause ere joining them in battle against so formidable an opponent as Yumen Yusel. The rest had given our men back their spirits; the toils, the burnings of the desert were forgotten, and every heart beat high and fast for the chance of spoil and glory that was at hand. Amood Sinn's troops, on the contrary, though they made a fine show of valour and enthusiasm at our approach, were as miserably draggled and downcast as any men that ever crept out of the mire after a trampling by the enemy, and all their brave play-acting, their shouting and brandishing of arms could not hide the sense of disaster that was upon them. To put trust in the intrepidity of such deplorable losels was like relying on the valour of a company of scarecrows.

Amood Sinn himself rode out to meet us, gallantly mounted on a richly caparisoned · charger, and attended by a suite in magnificent draperies and a blaze of variegated colours. Nature had given him a soldierly figure, and in his gorgeous and imposing dress he would have looked the *beau ideal* of a military leader, but for the irresolution of the restless eye and a general air of despondency that even the pomp and pageantry of his state could not altogether dispel.

The meeting of the two princes, however, was extremely cordial, both dismounting and embracing in the presence of the assembled host. But when the preliminary civilities were over, and Abou Kuram showed a disposition to come to business, Amood hesitated, made excuses, and then, all at once, became excited and hysterical. Launching into a distracted tale of the supernatural, which any old wife in Scotland would have been ashamed of, he declared he had had the clearest ocular proof that the man on the black horse was none other than Satan himself.

"As for Yumen Yusel," he cried, flourishing his sword, "he is but a child in war! Were he here now I would shear off his cowardly head as a swift reaper taketh the ripe barley. But can man prevail against the devil?" And he cast a doleful look at Abou Kuram as if to say, "It's really useless, you know, risking our lives."

"Perchance he is not the great Satan himself, but only a little devil," replied Abou Kuram, who, while not without his touch of superstition, held Amood's fancies in contempt. "I long to set eyes on him, if he be Satan, that I may know his looks, if he be aught else, that I may make his body a sheath for this sword."

"Is my brother mad?" asked Amood, with deep concern.

"Yea, mad with a thirst for battle," answered Abou Kuram. "Will my brother give orders to have his men made ready?"

But Amood had still a multitude of pretexts for delay. For one thing, Abou Kuram and his gallant army must be feasted ere fighting could be so much as thought of. The march hither had been long and arduous, and ill befall him if it should ever be said he had forgotten how to be hospitable to his friends.

Abou Kuram, however, was too familiar with guile to be inveigled. With a manner that was the pink of courtliness, yet had in it more than a suggestion of imperiousness and austerity, he declined festivities, saying that feasting would be sweeter after victory, and that he would joyously eat the carcasses of a hundred sheep when Yumen Yusel and his satanic lieutenant were crushed. He was aided and abetted in his policy of action by Ismael Numar, Amood's second in command, a brave and capable officer had he been free from the trammels of a pusillanimous superior. Amood yielded a reluctant consent, the kettle-drums and cymbals clashed and rattled together, and the troops marched out to bivouac on the plain.

The chosen spot reached, Amood Sinn desired to have a vermilion tent with luxurious state appointments set up, insisting so strongly on what was due to his exalted rank that Abou Kuram was forced to point out in undiplomatic language how exceedingly awkward luxurious vermilion tents might prove in case of a surprise or a night attack. So, murmuring bitterly about the unprincely discomforts of a campaign, Amood moodily ate his supper, said his prayers, and lay down beside the smothered fires to study the starry sky and await what further evils fate might bring. The soldiers lay armed by their harnessed beasts, gnawing at mutton bones like a colony of dogs, while Abou Kuram, vigilant, active, and more than a trifle angry, moved about, giving rapid instructions and speaking words of stern encouragement.

Slowly the silent night wore on. The big bright stars twinkled fitfully; the moon sailed majestically out into the empyrean spaces for a little, and then went her imperial way, leaving a darkness that was full of vague dread and awesome suspicions. The men, casting their mutton bones from them, sat up with a quivering tension of nerve and muscle, and felt their weapons. Mentally they were counting the minutes till the light should appear; for this was the terrorizing interval of blackness when stealthy spears might stab without affording the victims a chance of retaliation.

An Arab attack sometimes comes with the roar of thunder and the rush of the simoon, sometimes with the secrecy and hush of death. When the troops were beginning to remark with bated breath that there was to be no molestation from the enemy, and were daring to think of rations, all at once fierce yells and a spluttering fire broke from the outposts. In half a second more a ring of flame engirdled us. By its brief light we saw a swarm of rushing demons with levelled spears charging in among us, and the screams of pain and terror told how effectuallly they were doing their work. We leaped upon our beasts; we charged hither and thither in the pitchy blackness, mistaking friend for foe, slashing when we should have aided, and aiding when we should have slashed; and then there fell a silence as sudden as had been the tumult; for the enemy, slipping from our fingers, seemed to have disappeared into the earth. Crowding close together the army watched with shuddering expectation for another rush; then, as it did not come, recovered nerve with a hurricane of profanity.

Abou Kuram and Amood Sinn held an improvised council of war.

"Let us take to the mountains," piped the latter in the falsetto of shivering fear.

Abou Kuram laid an iron hand on Amood's trembling arm.

"The cause is thine, not mine," he said, with a quick and meaning emphasis. "Do what seemeth to thee good. Only if thou give not instant orders that every coward who seeks to fly be cut down, I and my men with me will return as we came, and thou and thy possessions can go to eternal destruction."

"It is well, it is well," laughed Amood Sinn, hysterically. "I did but jest. By this right hand the man who flieth a foot shall have immediate death for his portion. Proclaim it abroad, Ismael Numar. If there be any man afraid to fight, bring him here that

15

I may cleave the dog in two.   I decree that the man
who is afraid shall die without time to repent of his
sins, yea, die the death of a felon.   I would not go to
the mountains without revenge for the pasture lands
of Njed and all the flocks that have ever fed on them.
See thou to it, Ismael Numar, that every coward shall
be put ingloriously to death."

"My lord's will shall be obeyed," answered Ismael
Numar, with alacrity.

As the enemy did not return, scouts were sent out
to discover his whereabouts.   They came back in the
early morning with the intelligence that he lay beyond a swelling in the plain about a league and a half
to the north, and the army was immediately put in
motion to give him battle.

Keeping his counsels to himself, Abou Kuram
quietly laid his plans about the disposition of the
troops, and by a swift and adroit manœuvre, he con-
trived to get his own contingent in the rear.   The arrangement, as may be guessed, was little to the taste
of Amood Sinn.   Finding himself unexpectedly where
the fighting promised to be hottest, he came to Abou
Kuram with a fine air of graciousness and a profu-
sion of honeyed words to beg his "great brother" to
accept the post of honour in the van.   But the great
brother's modesty would not suffer him to assume a
glory that properly belonged to another.   By all the
right of war, all the prerogatives of fame and achievement, the distinction of leading to victory should fall
to the lion-hearted Amood Sinn, whose deeds of valour
were a theme of inspiration to poet and warrior
throughout the length and breadth of the land.   It
was a lesson in guile that would have benefited any
courtier in Europe to note how those two expert dis-
semblers wheedled and palavered, and how mean and
worthless each made himself in comparison with the
other.   Abou Kuram protested he was but as the dust
under the hoof of Amood Sinn's charger, and Amood
Sinn swore a solemn oath he was not fit to bind the
spur upon Abou Kuram's heel.   Abou said that

Amood was a second Sikander el Rumi, and Amood that Abou was in strength and courage as Gabriel himself. So the soft blandishments and subtle self-depreciations went on as fervently as if each man were convinced he spoke gospel truth. But in the end Abou Kuram was not to be moved out of his humility; so Amood Sinn, after a useless expenditure of breath and time, had to make the best of his unwelcome honours. Having regained possession of himself by this time, he accepted the behests of fate without a ruffle in his sleek hypocrisy, though I thought there was something of a wry twist in his feigning mouth as he turned to ride to the post of danger. No sooner was he gone than the manner and look of Abou Kuram changed. His eyes glowed, his brows lowered, and his lips were compressed to an ominous thinness.

"Our brother lieth with a rare persuasion to-day," he remarked dryly to Koor Ali, as they watched the retreating figure; adding, with a sudden truculency, "By my blade-point, I will drive him into it. I tell thee he shall fight, or if he fly, he shall find a worse foe in front than behind. Should the eagle prove a barn fowl, by my faith, instead of saving we will help to pluck it." He paused, looking over the assembled army. "Doth it not seem to thee there is victory in the looks of these armed men?" he asked.

And such, indeed, was the martial and imposing array, that it might well have made a poltroon into a hero. For the spirit of battle was once more animating the plumed and bannered host that covered the plain like a sea, its colours aflame and its arms flashing like thickets of steel in the early sun. The allies had fled to the mountains like sheep before wolves, they had been found broken, dejected, utterly demoralized, because they were without a leader, and it was with difficulty they had been brought back. But now, side by side with an army that was fresh and sworn to conquer, they were renewed in heart, and savage for revenge and plunder. So they danced about on caracoling horses or straddling camels, tossing spears and whirling swords and matchlocks to the maddening incentive of pipe and drum and cymbal and a tumult of whoops and howls.

"That is the thirst for blood," said Abou Kuram, contentedly. "Ride forward, Koor Ali, and help our brother to make haste in getting into battle array. Tell him we must possess that height," pointing upward. "It will be worth a thousand men."

Panting for action, Koor Ali galloped to the front with the message, to find Amood Sinn giving instructions about lighting fires to roast some sheep and goats that had been taken in the mountains. Koor Ali instantly wheeled his horse and rode back to Abou Kuram to report, Amood following distracted at his heels.

"My brother is impatient," cried Amood, when he came up. "The men need strength for the toil and heat that are before them. Wherefore not light fires and cook our booty?"

Abou Kuram answered that the men had dates and water ready to their hand, and would have the better wind by going on short rations.

"When the battle is won, my brother will perceive they could eat with more leisure and satisfaction," he added with a grim politeness that admitted of no dispute.

Ill pleased, for he had resolved to hearten himself with some handfuls of good mutton, Amood Sinn once more returned to his place, and the men, without dismounting, hurriedly washed down a bunch of dry dates apiece with a draught of lukewarm water. The meagre meal was hardly swallowed when Koor Ali was careering to the front again with instructions to Amood to form and make for the height without further delay.

The swelling in the plain, behind which lay the forces of Yumen Yusel, had the appearance of an enormous billow thrown up in some upheaval or convulsion of nature, and solidified and fixed as it rose. It was the only elevation in the plain, and much depended on our possessing it. Once upon the crest or ridge, we could make our arrangements for annihilating the enemy at our ease, and with all the advantages of a superior position. Then, when all should be ready, we would spring upon him, crush him, mangle him, sweep him off the face of the earth, and leave him neither name nor inheritance among the sons of men. It was an excellent plan, all that remained was the execution.

Scouts were thrown out in front to prevent surprise, while the whole force was pushed vigourously on to be ready for any advantage that might fall in the way of brave men. Abou Kuram hurried up the rear, and tried to bridle his impatience.

"It galleth me to be behind," he remarked, "when I fain would be measuring swords with this champion on the black horse. Perchance I may have an opportunity."

Perchance he might, and in case he had, we all felt it would be well for the lieutenant of Yumen Yusel to have his prayers said in advance.

A second detachment of horsemen was thrown out, and went spurring up the slope as if determined to snatch all the glory of victory to itself. Seeing it coming, the scouts, who were now well on, struck spurs to their horses, and a fierce thrill of expectation vibrated through the main body as it, too, quickened its pace. It was going to be exceedingly awkward for the foe lying unconscious on the other side of the billow. That was as clear as the sun that flamed in the heavens.

The scouts were riding their hardest, and in another minute would be on the top. As they neared the ridge, we held our breath, the whole army seeming to pause for a signal. The scouts lay flatter and flatter on their horse's necks, and the dust rose in a denser line behind them. Presently they halted, as it appeared very abruptly. Had they discovered the lurking foe? The solid mass below gave a great united gasp that was as the sough of the wind in a forest, and waited with leaping pulses.

The stoppage, however, was a mere precaution; for two or three of the scouts, slipping from their saddles, and flinging their reins to their comrades, hurried forward on foot, bending low as they ran. The army below looked up, panting like hounds on the leash. A deep murmur rumbled on the air, swelled into a hoarse growl, sank, and died away—the cry of vengeful men for blood. The commanders, excitedly gripping their hilts, moistened their dry mouths to give the order for a rush; the trumpeters hung with trembling trump to lip ready to blow the deadly blast; the men listened and looked in bodeful silence. It was the thrilling stillness that preludes the storm. Next minute the thunders and lightning of a curbed vengeance would be let loose, and Heaven help the vanquished.

The scouts, now crouching like tigers in sight of their prey, crept softly towards the crest. The enemy must be lying in fancied security, as he had been seen at the dawn. Swiftly and with bitter self-upraidings he would rue his supine inactivity when he woke up amid disaster and death. Our scouts were within a few yards of the top, and our hearts thumped with a devilish rapture of expectation.

From the front, Koor Ali was waving his sword as he looked back for a sign. Abou Kuram, tingling with excitement, waved his own in return, and in an instant a cloud of dust rose as another body of cavalry flew up the slope. The general did not intend that mad burst; yet it was inspiring to see how it acted on the army. A savage roar went up from every man in the force, and Abou Kuram tingled again as if an electric coil encircled him.

"Forward! Forward!" he shouted, making circles of light with his sword. Trumpet and kettle-drum blared and rattled, officers scurried about yelling orders no one heard, and the men, howling like an escaped menagerie, goaded their plunging beasts. And then, when all were so intent on rushing to victory and spoil that there were no eyes for what was going on above, all at once there was a crackling of musketry on the ridge, and, looking up, the very beating of our pulses suspended, we saw it dark with warriors, as if dragons' teeth had sprung up armed men. A line of white smoke ran zigzag along the top; ere we could realize what had happened, another spurted out with vicious points of fire in the midst. The scouts on foot fell to a man, and many were brought out of their saddles. A few shots were fired wildly in return, and the scouts, wheeling about, dashed back at twice the speed with which they had ascended.

In half a minute they were among the first body of horse that had gone out after them, and turned it; in half a minute more the second detachment was met and turned in dire confusion, and the whole, with a rushing pavilion of dust, came sweeping on our own advancing lines; though the enemy refrained from pursuing.

Amood Sinn did not wait for the shock. Raising his arms to heaven with the despairing gesture of a fatalist, he went about and fled as fast as a fleet horse could carry him. His men, too, urged by vivid remembrance of the past, promptly followed their general's example, and came pell-mell upon our contingent in the rear, trampling and battering with more than the madness and fury of a foe. I saw then, for the first time, that of all terrible spectacles on earth the most terrible is the first explosive burst of panic-stricken troops.

For a little, Abou Kuram looked on the demoralized mob, speechless with horror and anger, then, hastily ordering Koor Ali, who had galloped back, to stop the rabble or slay them, he dashed in pursuit of Amood Sinn, I following to the best of my ability.

"What meaneth this?" he yelled, coming up to the scudding general. But Amood Sinn could not stay for answer; so Abou Kuram throwing etiquette to the winds, clutched at the bridle and brought the flying steed on its haunches with a mighty jerk. For a moment his passion denied him utterance, and he only glared on his surprised and quaking captive.

"This is a seemly thing to do in sight of the whole army," he roared at length, and I thought he would have slain the other on the spot. "This is an example to set. Are our names to be branded with shame as if we were sick women? Get thy men about, or by this right hand I will have them speared like swine as they fly."

Amood Sinn, answering something in a quick, shrill voice about the futility of encountering Satan, tried to justify the retreat.

"How knowest thou he is Satan?" demanded Abou Kuram, scornfully. "Methinks thou wert in too much haste in getting away, to know what he is, or even if he be with Yumen Yusel."

"My brother is wroth," answered Amood, insinuatingly. "But he knoweth not what it is to come face to face with the devil."

Abou Kuram shook himself in a spasm of disgust.

"I knew not," he cried passionately, "that I came to fight with one whose spirit left him at the thought of battle. This is not a time for words. While we talk, Yumen Yusel maketh his opportunity out of thy fears and delays. Make thy choice quickly. If thou choosest to fly, from this moment reckon me thine enemy. Thou hast fair warning. I will join myself in slaughter to him whom thou calllest Satan, and there will not so much as a man of thine army escape to tell the tale of thy disgrace."

"My brother jesteth," returned Amood Sinn, with a sickly smile.

"Fly, and thou shalt see," answered Abou Kuram; and there was a look on his darkened face that was not to be misunderstood.

With a double fear now upon him, Amood turned, with what heart a hunted coward might have, to rally his scattered forces. Already they had been checked in their headlong flight by our men, who stood with a fierce loyalty by their leader's order, to stop or slay;

and Koor Ali, energetically aided by Ismael Numar, was trying to beat them back into some sort of formation. It took a great deal of exertion, and a lavish use of many kinds of language, more profane than pious, to induce the cowering wretches to accept the definite idea of fighting again. But, partly by vigourous mauling, partly by threats and coaxing and reproofs, some sort of order was at last evolved out of the shameful chaos. As it would be courting disaster to charge up the hill, it was decided to retire a little distance, marshal ourselves, and await the overtures of the enemy.

Yumen Yusel's men were now swarming like a cloud of locusts over the billow, and with every symptom of leisure and self-confidence, completing their arrangements for battle. We were to have occupied that height, but, by the chances of war and superior generalship, the position fell to the other side; so, as the Scotch say, we stood there and girned at them till they were ready to come down.

I looked intently, as you may suppose, for the man on the black horse. At first he was not visible, but presently appearing at one side, he rode along the lines at a hand gallop. A conspicuous object, all eyes were instantly upon him, and many tongues began to gabble excitedly.

"There goeth Satan!" cried Amood Sinn, in the screeching tones of fright; and he fell to cursing the man on the black horse with all the curses known to the Moslem religion, supplemented by many of his own invention. The warrior above, however, in no wise affected by the maledictions poured upon his unconscious head, continued to ride to and fro, altering formations and dispositions, and otherwise completing his preparations for the tussle that was at hand.

Abou Kuram watched his movements with the intentness of an active rival.

"Methinks," he remarked significantly, "that Satan showeth marvellous skill in marshalling an army."

"He hath the fallen angel's skill," piped Amood. Then all at once, and with intense excitement, he screamed, "See, see, they are coming! They shall destroy us utterly. Not a man of us shall escape," and he cast a look to the rear (I think in spite of himself) to see if the coast were clear for flight.

Abou Kuram shot a glance of anger and disgust upon him, but said not a word.

A body of the enemy's cavalry, consisting of perhaps two hundred lances, had detached itself, and was coming down the slope at an easy trot. When they had advanced a short distance, the camel-men also began to move towards us, slowly, and without noise or excitement.

Under the direction of Abou Kuram, who now assumed supreme command, three hundred lances cantered out from our side to meet those coming down the slope.

The conflict was upon us. Heaven and the Prophet steel our hearts and sharpen our blades!

CHAPTER XX.

THE BATTLE.

WHEN the enemy's cavalry reached level ground they divided, one troop swinging to the right and the other to the left, with the evident intention of harrying us on both flanks at once, while the camel-men, quickening their pace, advanced straight upon our centre. Our horsemen, going out at a canter, also divided to check the others, and our main force, massed after the Arab fashion, waited quietly for the attack.

All eyes were on the cavalry, moving from both sides at an easy trot, as if out for morning exercise. They made no haste and no noise; as yet there was nothing of the excitement or flurry of battle in their behaviour; indeed, to one impatient beholder, they seemed to have forgotten that this was war, that they were mortal enemies, and ought, by every martial law known to man, to be in each other's throats with the utmost possible despatch.

Presently they broke into a gallop, and my heart bounded at the thought that they were going to close. But when they should have burst into the charge, both sides wheeled simultaneously, waving their lances defiantly, and uttering shrill cries. Again they advanced, again wheeled and retired with the same truculent display of weapons, and so they went on wheeling and circling, but instead of getting closer together they drew away, until finally they must have been a full quarter of a mile apart. At that distance they brought up and stood facing each other. Had I known Arab ways better, I should have understood that now the play was about to begin in earnest. Those little preliminary flourishes that had set my heart a-beating so violently, were simply an introductory ceremony, meant partly to appease the Arab passion for show, partly to prick the courage of the combatants.

Meanwhile, Yumen Yusel's camel-men had pushed on, and were now down the slope and well into the plain. When within a musket-shot of our front lines they halted. Then, as if by magic, down went every camel in both armies, while the musketeers, crouching behind their beasts, brought their long matchlocks to the "ready." At the same moment the opposing bodies of horse that had been standing motionless, raising unitedly the fierce war-cry of "Techbir! techbir!" started towards each other at the full speed of the charge. The next minute came the shock of meeting; and far in the rear we felt the earth tremble, and heard the deadly grunt and thud and clash as the rushing columns came together. As the horsemen met, the front lines of musketeers opened fire, and the tumult and madness of battle were upon us.

For a little the cavalry rolled and reared in confused heaps; then they scattered, and riderless horses began to career in all directions; the canopy of dust spread and cleared, and the antagonists retired to their respective sides, the enemy showing unmistakable signs of discomfiture.

At this, such of our men as were disengaged raised a ringing shout of triumph, and though Abou Kuram said not a word, his glittering eyes declared his transport of joy. As for me, I stood in my stirrups waving my sword and yelling with all my might, for the hellish feeling—partly unholy glee, partly fright, partly a mad desire to kill—which seizes a man when he first sees blood actually spilt in battle, had possession of me. I quivered like an aspen, and was as dry in the mouth as if I had been in the thick of the fight for a day.

Again the cavalry on both sides wheeled, formed, and charged; again they rolled in convulsive heaps, parted with more empty saddles, and yet again re-formed and dashed at each other. It was impossible to tell which was getting the best of it, for in the dust cloud that enveloped them nothing was discernible. But there was no doubt on the point when presently, instead of forming again, the enemy's horse burst out of the dense mass, and went spurring up the hill with ours slashing and stabbing at their heels.

Abou Kuram, unable to control himself, flashed his sword in air and vociferated an order; our camel-men, slinging their muskets, seized their spears, leaped upon their beasts, and, with a resounding roar, swept to the charge. Our antagonists were as quick as ourselves. In a twinkling they, too, were on their camels, and, whooping and yelling with all the might of brazen lungs and throats, the lurching hosts fell upon each other.

The commotion of that moment is not to be comprehended save by those who have gone pell-mell into that devil's mess which men name a battle; and I, of all men, am least qualified to describe it. For although I was there what did I see? What can any one see when he is distracted by noise and confusion, and beside himself with a tumult of passions and emotions such as have never been named or classified? The leaders, I suppose, were masters of themselves; they must have been, or we should all have gone mad at once; even with their restraining and steadying influence upon us, we must have been perilously near madness. For myself, I was as far from calmness as a man may be and retain any glimmering of sanity. The thing began with fierce peals of cheering that gave me the odd sensation of having the top of my head blown off; and before the first burst was spent, the pressing ranks were rising, and falling, and tumbling upon each other like waves in a stormy cross-sea. My clearest recollection is of Abou Kuram, who appeared to be more in his element than I had ever seen him. He was here, there, and everywhere, directing, encouraging, hewing, and cutting, and ever seeking the places where perils were thickest.

My orders were to keep by his side; but they were more easily given than obeyed. A hundred times I lost him in the tumbling, whirling eddies of attack and recoil; a hundred times I was struck almost senseless in the bloody crush; a hundred times I found myself clutching in terror at pommel and mane, as the steel clashed and glanced about me; and as often I was on the point of fainting at the sickening sight of riven bodies, brute and human.

I owe it more to the intelligence and dexterity of my little mare than to any effort of my own, that I was not carved to death. To this hour I cannot imagine how I escaped, where so many better men were biting the dust. There are few things in this world more puzzling than the chances of war, and none better calculated to make brave men modest.

By-and-by I began to understand (a thing more difficult than it may seem) that the advantage lay with us. I understood it from the fiendish exhilaration of our men, from the short, deep coughs of satisfaction with which they drove their weapons home, and from the greater proportion of shrieks and empty saddles among our opponents.

The discovery acted like a drug that sets the blood on fire. To keep from going stark mad I roared myself black in the face, and rode furiously whithersoever my goaded mare chose to carry me, sometimes among friends, oftener among foes, and always with a consuming desire to see my sword run as red as the others.

All this while Yumen Yusel and the man on the black horse were posted on the ridge looking down on the battle. They might have been mere spectators, indifferent to the issue, so remote they seemed from the scene of anguish in which two armies were pouring out their hearts' blood. But when we began to gain, a mounted messenger came galloping down the slope, and spoke for a minute or so to the commander of Yumen Yusel's troops. Whatever was his message, it put fresh force and courage into the men; for, getting into closer formation, they hurled themselves upon us with a fury that soon gave them back their lost ground. But, though we yielded a little, our lances did not slacken in their work. Nay, the slicing went on with redoubled energy and oaths that were curdling to hear.

"Holy Prophet, how they fight!" cried Amood Sinn as he and Abou Kuram met for a moment in the rear. "Mine eyes have never beheld such slaughter. Look you now at Ismael Numar, how he cleaveth heads and heweth off limbs. He shall have three more wives and a present of gold for his valour. And look you, too, how the good Koor Ali layeth about him. I have been watching him, and he slayeth like one preparing for the sacrifice. There goeth a man severed in two, another, and still another. Didst thou ever see the like? He maketh stepping-stones to victory of his enemies. He shall have a dozen of my choicest slaves. And my brother, too, hath done marvellous things. I have seen his blade smiting with the stroke of lightning. He hath left the dead in heaps behind him. I will bethink me what befitteth him to receive. Yea, and I, too, have smitten the foe. I slit a fellow's ribs as a cook would cut open the ribs of a sheep. By my faith, it was fine sport."

He stopped, and looked over the sanguinary scene.

"Our men fight like lions," he said: then with a sudden change of tone, "yet thinkest thou they are being driven back? Doth it appear to thee the enemy is gaining just a little, ever so little? If we lose ground—but no," changing voice and manner again, "there they storm home. I profess Koor Ali's sword is crimson an inch deep. And there go our horsemen. Glory to the Prophet, the day is ours. Yumon Yusel's men fly—we are conquerors. They fly! They fly!"

They were not flying, but their leader had been cut down by one of our cavalrymen, and in the confusion that followed, they lost ground again.

"I told thee the day was ours," cried Amood Sinn, in a transport of childish delight. But he was soon singing to another tune. "See, see!" he cried, ere the words of rejoicing were well out of his mouth. "He cometh, he cometh: Satan cometh! We are undone. Who can withstand him? He rideth like a whirlwind, and destroyeth as a fire. My brother, we are undone." Abou Kuram made no reply, but turned his eyes to the dread warrior on the black horse, who was cantering down the slope with a band of fifty men mounted on the pick of Arabian studs. As the company advanced, it was joined by others, till the total must have been equal to half a British regiment.

A contingent promptly went out from our front to meet them, Koor Ali leading. There was to be no play this time, no circling and wheeling, no retiring and advancing for picturesque display. Lance to lance, body to body, the issue would be decided and no quarter given. Abou Kuram bit his lip in chagrin

at being forced to remain in charge of a coward in
the rear, and watched the seizing events in which he
could not participate.

The enemy's cavalry came on at a round gallop,
their pennons of ostrich feathers fluttering and streaming, their faces bent forward on their horses' necks.
The leader, however, sat his great black horse erect,
and held his sword at what I believe British dragoons
call the slope. There was something in his appearance that marked him out from his fellows, and I am
free to confess that with Amood Sinn's whining in
my ears, a thrill of superstitious awe passed through
me at the thought that he might not be mortal.

As soon as the level plain was gained, he waved
his sword quickly in the air, and the great black war
horse broke from the gallop to the charge. We
could see his fierce leap and the responsive bound
of those that followed hard behind. Before half a
dozen horse-lengths were covered, there came to our
ears a resounding double peal of " Techbir! techbir!"
for our men, too, were riding at the charging pace;
and even from our distance we saw how every
rider, setting himself yet a little forward, hugged
his lance close under his right arm. I watched
the mutual swoop with starting eyes and a thumping heart, with cold tremours at the pit of the
stomach, and a hot whirl of the brain that was as the
madness of much wine. There were fear and headlong audacity in the feeling, a fear that could easily
have made me turn and fly, an audacity that almost
impelled me to rush forward and share the delirious
ecstasy of that onset.

Nearer and nearer swept the opposing columns like
two flights of ostriches darkening the sky with dust,
the horses low and stretched as if reaching in very
eagerness, the riders alert with a tigerish intentness
of purpose. No man could have said which side sped
the more furiously or shouted the louder, none whether
Koor Ali or the man on the black horse led with the
more determined valour.

There is no resisting the magnetism of a desperate exploit enacted under your eyes; and the main bodies paused fascinated by the fearful spectacle. On both sides the riders drew in knee to knee, in order to have the greater driving and resisting power, and crouched lower upon their straining horses. The last hundred yards were covered, as it were, at a bound, and then, with a cry of vengeance from a thousand throats, a dazzling flash of steel, a shock as of clashing thunderbolts, came the collision. There was a vibrating sensation as of an earthquake, and a rumble of groanings and cursings reached us as the fighters rolled together in a dark seething heap, like the tumbling surge of two swift sea-currents meeting.

My vision was suddenly blurred, and involuntarily my eyes closed. When I opened them the combatants were through each other and wheeling for another charge. Up went the fierce war-cry again; and again came a tremendous shock and tumult, shattering the close-packed lines; but, reforming with prodigious quickness they dashed at each other again, and yet again, with an ever-increasing heap of slain and wounded weltering on the ground.

"By my father's sword, it is to be utter annihilation!" said Abou Kuram, breathing thick and fast. "They mean to kill each other out."

But almost as he spoke the enemy, bursting once more through our lines, were across the intervening space and headlong upon our main body, the man on the black horse slashing and hewing in front in a way that fairly justified the tales of his satanic character. At the same time Yumen Yusel's camelmen flung themselves upon us as if they would roll us up and trample and cut us to pieces before the cavalry could participate in the glory.

From that moment, so far as I could see, all order vanished. There is a theory that in properly planned battles things go by method and prearrangement. The idea is a pretty one for drawing-room warriors; but if there were the least truth in it no battle should ever be lost or won.   There would be no Marathon, no Thermopylæ, no Waterloo, no Alma, no Lucknow to shed lustre on the human race and give an interest to desperate hazards.   Take my word for it that a fight between two armies determined to win or die is a thing of heart-shaking surprises and riotous contempt of regulations.   The moment the common soldier, panting for revenge or frantic to save his skin, takes matters into his own hands, prophecies and prearrangements go to the winds.

The general may plan, but the soldier does the work, and commonly in his own way, and in flat defiance of orders.   In that wallowing, billowy host I dare assert there were not half a dozen men who knew their heads from their heels.   Almost every mother's son in the gory chaos cut, and thrust, and stabbed and charged, and recoiled, and roared at his own sweet will, and in obedience to what might seem, to his whirling mind, the exigencies of the occasion.

As for me, what with incessant knocks and collisions, the hubbub of rage and agony, the sharp scream and envenomed oath, and, most of all, the sickening sight of living men being sliced and laid open, my wits were so confounded I might have been in the throes of a nightmare.   I had a sword and a brace of pistols, though what I did with them Heaven alone knows.   They may have accounted for some of the enemy, but I have no knowledge of shedding any man's blood, which on the whole is perhaps a consolation in looking back from the vale of years.

In the plungings hither and thither of my mare I got glimpses of Abou Kuram making flashes of crimson light with his sword, of the man on the black horse hewing savagely where there lay the best chance of doing havoc, of Ismael Numar and Koor Ali laying about them as if they were using pruning hooks in a forest of saplings, and of Amood Sinn scurrying to and fro in abject terror, fighting the air and ever getting into the places he would have given his kingdom to be able to avoid.   I laughed at him with the

hilarity of hysteria, and, I have an idea, cried jeering words as well. But how the tide of war was running I knew not, and probably you would not have
known had you been in my place.

Once, in a furious swirl, I got knocked out of the
saddle, but with wild-cat clutch I caught something,
probably the pommel or mane before me, and was up
again in a moment, wondering in my own mind
whether I was mortally wounded or whether I was
wounded at all; and as I was trying to decide I came
upon a sight that drove all thought of self away
and made me rein up with a jerk.

In the midst of their partisans, who had formed a
circle as if to see fair play to the champions, were
Koor Ali and the man on the black horse in a hand-
to-hand fight. I do not know how long they had been
at it before I chanced to see them; but the contest did
not last long after my coming up. Koor Ali was a
good soldier and an expert swordsman, but his fate
was upon him. The man on the black horse first
tipped off an ostrich plume from the other's turban,
then some ribbons, then he shore a piece off each side,
as if showing the easy and dainty precision with
which he handled his weapon. Two or three swift
passes followed; then rising quickly in his stirrups,
with a lightning-like stroke he clove his antagonist
from crown to breast-bone, so that half fell either
way.* From the raised sword hand of the divided
man dropped the sword, but the arm itself remained
rigid in the air as if with a final threat of vengeance,
and there rose from the split throat a shriek which
haunts me to this day. Then, the horse wheeling
under a sudden convulsive pull of the bridle hand, the
body tumbled from the saddle to be mangled by a
thousand hoofs.

Waving his blood-red sabre above his head, the
victor leaped his horse straight into the heart of a
group of our men; and the hacking and hewing went

*As will be seen later on, this stroke was never learned in
Arabia.

on with redoubled ferocity amidst roars of triumph from the enemy.

Abou Kuram must have seen what had happened, for just then he tore up, his face black with passion, and riding over all that obstructed his way, made direct at the champion of Yumen Yusel. That diabolic swordsman catching sight of Abou wheeled, the two horses reared together and the blades of the riders met with a vicious clash. Both sides sent up a terrific shout; for the crucial moment had come.

Owing to the fierce tumult and crush, I could see the fighters only in partial glimpses. But it was plain that here were two men who did each other honour, plain from the quick sharp swish and ring of their swords, and from the transport of the onlookers. Win who might, there would be a tale to tell that would cause breathless awe and interest in the black tents for many a day to come.

Both armies swayed up in resistless billows to watch the encounter; for on Arabian battle-fields, the rank and file at times suspend operations to watch their betters give and take blows. It was hard to imagine, however, that they were mere spectators, for in the jam of man and beast, lance and butt end were used with the freedom of active conflict, and curse and scream still mingled. I was in a condition little short of distraction. Carried about like a leaf on boiling waters, I should probably have been done to death many times over, but for the amazing ingenuity and agility of my mare in dodging in the crisis of a press.

I judged of the progress of the fight by the varying behaviour of the partisans who were nearest the centre. Once or twice I had a terrible glimpse of two furious men reaching for each other with flashing weapons, on horses that seemed to rear and grapple like lions. But I could not tell how the advantage lay.

I was soon to know. Suddenly, Yumen Yusel's men broke into a deep roar that sent the blood dizzily to my head, and made me dash into the thickest of

the crush regardless of peril.   I was just in time to
see the end.

The man on the black horse had evidently estimated
the skill and strength of his antagonist, and had begun his old game.   Down came Abou Kuram's bobbing ostrich plume; then, so quickly that the shear-
ing instrument was a darting sunbeam, the crest of
his turban followed.   Then, both horses rearing upon
each other, there was a wild leap to either side as
the spurs went wickedly home, but ere the black
charger had well touched ground he swung rapidly
round as on a pivot.   The next second Abou Kuram,
too, was about, but as he turned, his sword arm
dropped by his side almost clean cut from the shoulder, and the sword itself went rattling among his
horse's hoofs.   The lightning could not have hit
quicker than did the man on the black horse, nor
caused keener dismay and amazement.   He made a
pass as if to run the wounded man through the body,
but changing his mind, he struck spurs to his
charger, and once more leaped in among our men,
mowing a way for himself like a reaper in a field of
barley.

The scene that followed is not to be described.
Breaking like an overcharged dam, our men rushed
in headlong tumultuous rout to all points of the compass, cursing, screeching, trampling, and stabbing
each other in the fury of their flight, and the lances
of the conquerors were hard behind, wreaking a pent-
up vengeance.

In a momentary block of the sweeping torrent,
which carried me with it as a piece of broken driftwood, Yumen Yusel's champion slashed his way
across my front, so that I saw his face full for the first
time.   My heart was thumping against my ribs with
fear and excitement, but when I looked on him it
stopped, and I gazed with open mouth.   Where had
I seen that face so familiar, so handsome, even in its
terror?   In a dream of the night, in a waking vision?
Like a flash came the answer.   That was the original

of the miniature I held in my breast. As the knowledge came to me he dashed in another direction, and
I, finding my tongue, screamed after him, "Donald
Gordon! Donald Gordon!" I fancied he turned at
the cry; but the racing, plunging tide carried me off,
and my shouts were drowned in the uproar of the
shrieking fiends who had conquered. The next minute I was riding for my life in the middle of a band
of fugitives with half a hundred cruel lances hard at
our back.

CHAPTER XXI.

THE FLIGHT.

A TOTAL and irredeemable rout with the frenzied
victors amuck among the shattered ranks of the vanquished is a thing not to be described by any one
sharing in the panic or the havoc of it. We flew as
men fly from death only—blindly, desperately, knowing neither where we went nor what we did. Wo
were possessed by one wild compulsive idea—to get
away as fast as hoof could carry us beyond the reach
of those mutilating spears: and in the distraction and
fury of fear we rode each other down without heed or
pity. Horsemen plunged into camel-men, camel-
men into horsemen; friend cursed friend for barring
the way, and smote frantically, the striker caring not
if the blood of a fellow were spilled so only he himself
escaped.

Quarter was never so much as thought of on either
side; for vengeance, fired by fanaticism, does not
spare, nor does the terror it inspires plead. The dripping lances sped like weavers' shuttles, and the
shrieks of the butchered mingled with the oaths of
the butchers, who swore because they could not clear
their points quick enough. With grunts of hellish
glee from foaming mouths, the red points were sent
home, and the victims went down screaming, to be
finished under foot.

By degrees the fugitives began to scatter, and presently I found myself tearing along in a little group of half a dozen, my heart in my mouth, and just sense enough left to know that a gush of blood was soaking my right leg. Whence it issued I had not the least idea. Nor could I tell whether I had one hurt or many hurts. Feeling in my distraught condition there was none, and examination was impossible. A moment's delay would mean a dozen lances in my body; so, heedless of wounds, I fled, with all the speed that terror and spurs could put into the fleetest steed that ever carried man from such an Aceldama. With stretched neck, and ears laid back like a hare's in the chase, my little mare seemed rather to fly than to tread the earth; and well it was I was on the back of a Kohlan in her prime, or the hyenas would that night have had one corpse more to tear.

Venturing to glance about me by-and-by, I found that I was riding alone, that no officer was within sight, nor indeed any one I knew, save Tabal, the son of my old benefactor, Said Achmet. He was a short distance to the right and ahead of me, and was urging his beast with all the might of voice and stick. I shouted to him; he turned quickly sideways, but before he saw me he threw up his arms, gave a queer cry, and rolled to the ground. Mechanically, for I was not capable of thought, I wheeled towards him, leaped down, and in a second was up again, with Tabal lying across the saddle before me. Do not stay to ask how I did it. If ever you come to be in a life-and-death strait you will find that the nerves and muscles can act independently when the wits are gone. The thing was done, and done before I knew I had undertaken it.

Starting again, I cast an eye over my shoulder, to see three of the enemy's horsemen coming full tilt upon me with levelled lances. Discerning it was to be a neck-and-neck race for life, I touched my little mare with the spurs, and though now carrying double, she skimmed along with the speed of the ostrich, quickly distancing our pursuers, who turned to easier game. But glancing backward again presently, I saw with fresh dismay three other horsemen coming at me sideways, at the pace of the tempest. From their looks I judged them at once to be Bedouins, genuine cruel children of the desert, of whom large numbers were attracted to the standard of Yumen Yusel by the glorious prospects of spoil. They had singled me out, and were riding for death and booty, evidently under the impression that my companion must be a man of rank and wealth. It was a natural conclusion that no effort would be made to save a common soldier; he would be left to die where he fell.

I looked into the face of Tabal to see whether he were dead, for he had not spoken a word since I had lifted him. If he were a corpse it would be the sheerest madness to encumber myself with him. But when I bawled in his ear he opened his eyes slowly and winked at me comically, like one awaking from odd dreams.

"Are you much hurt?" I shouted at the pitch of my voice.

He wriggled his left shoulder, and the movement brought a gush of blood.

"There," he answered faintly.

"You must sit up," I said quickly; "our lives depend upon it."

He made an effort, I assisting, and though he swayed considerably from lightheadedness, he managed, with my aid, to keep upright.

The Bedouins, meanwhile, had gained upon me, and were shouting riotously in anticipation of an easy capture. Doubtless they concluded that no horse carrying double could get away from them; but I thought to myself, with a pride which even fear could not wholly overcome, that they little knew the mettle of my Fatema. Her load once fairly adjusted, she would lead them such a dance as they might talk of with wonder for the rest of their lives. Nor did I calculate amiss. At a touch on the rein she mended her pace with an apparent ease and buoyancy that made my heart beat a fierce tattoo of joy. It was short-lived, however. I had forgotten we were in a land where horses are swift as eagles, where every hack might be handicapped against an English racer. The Bedouins, too, were splendidly mounted, and instead of abandoning the chase, came on with a double fury that threw the odds heavily to their side.

Scarcely knowing what I did, I drove the rowels deep into my mare's flanks. She turned up a reproachful eye and a distended fiery nostril, as if to say she was already doing her utmost. Nevertheless, she bounded on, her neck a little more craned, her ears a little flatter, her forefeet forging out a little further. Whatever horse could do, she would; that was the sentiment of her response.

Casting a backward look I tingled with gladness to find that, in spite of her heavy burden, she was keeping her own. But immediately I asked myself the crucial question how long she could maintain that terrific pace; for the pursuers were as hot behind as ever. With the corner of my eye I could see their horses reaching like greyhounds, their heads low, their nozzles straight out, and the black faces of the riders themselves thrust forward like the beaks of vultures. I touched my mare again. Faster and faster she sped in her arrowy flight, as if she knew the terrible need that was upon her, and close in her track came the Bedouins, like beagles on the trail yelping for blood.

The next time I turned to note their progress, I was horrified to see they were gaining upon me. There could not be the least doubt that the distance between us was diminished. My flesh crept together at the discovery, so that I must have shrunk to half my natural size. What was to be done? To fight or surrender was to be ripped on the spot, for I was hampered, and the pursuers were merciless. The sole resource was speed, and of it I was already availing myself to the utmost. Four feet could not do more than my mare was doing for me. I might save myself, indeed, but I could not abandon Tabal, the more especially that having recovered his senses, he was now begging piteously to be taken away from those gleaming crimson lances. Could my mare carry both? That again was the question of questions.

Looking mechanically round, as a man will for aid, in moments of dire need, I saw some distance to the left, and a trifle in our rear, a single horseman hard pressed by two Bedouins, companions, as I took it, of those who were chasing me. His nose was buried in his charger's mane, and his spurred heels were clapped fast to its frothing flanks. The race was bound for bound of pursuers and pursued. The fugitive seemed just able to hold his own, and with good luck might get off. But the Bedouins were not to rely on hard riding alone. Finding the reach too great for their spears, one of them quickly unslung his musket, eased slightly, and took aim. There was a crack, a puff of white smoke, and the man in front toppled over his horse's head. I saw no more of him, but a piercing scream that mingled with the yells of triumph, told all too plainly of his fate.

The horse bounded on with empty saddle, veering in my direction. On noticing this a flashing inspiration came upon me, an inspiration that sent the blood surging in a buzzing tide to the brain, so that all at once there seemed to be the voice of an infinite number of waters in my ears. For one instant I was dizzy with my own audacity; the next my resolution was fixed and definite. I would catch the horse, and either put Tabal on his back or get there myself.

Swerving slightly to head off, as men do in capturing wild animals on the prairie, I drove the spurs with all my might into my little mare. It was cruel, seeing how nobly she was already doing, but this last providential chance must not be missed from any weak sentiment about cruelty. She sprang forward with a flash of the eye, now almost as red as her nostril, and a shower of spume from her mouth.

My pursuers, quick as hawks in detecting the shifts of the quarry, must have perceived my intention, for like bolts from a strong bow, two made for the runaway horse, while the third came straight upon me. Setting my teeth, and gathering myself so as to put all my force into the stroke, I drove the rowels home again. My poor mare groaned with the pain of it, and leaped like a wounded deer. But what were her sufferings set against my life? If ever she flew, she must fly now, when fleetness alone could save; so the long Arabian spurs, which are never used save in the crisis of distress, dug deep into her again and again, and again and again she gave that pitiful groan and that desperate bound.

Horses love company, particularly when they have been trained to military service. To my consternation I saw the runaway make for the two Bedouins. Almost before I realized what was happening he was between them, and then each leaning inward clutched at the trailing bridle. My heart stopped as I expected to see him go on his haunches. But either the movement frightened him into an unexpected dash, or they were clumsy; for with a mighty jump and a furious tossing of the mane he shot free of them, and came careering on alone.

With a reeling sensation of hope and despair, I made at him once more. Taking the rein in my teeth, in order to have the free use of both hands, I helped Tabal to a firmer seat, gasping my purpose in his ear. When he was placed I gave him the rein, with instructions that so soon as I left the mare's back he was to consider me no more, but look to himself. Then, sitting a little farther back and clear of the saddle, I drew myself up into a sort of crouching posture and prepared for a spring. On came the runaway on the right. In another moment he was alongside, but too wide for our track. Tabal pulled his rein, and the animals nearly collided. Then, with something of that gathering of the flesh with which a timid bather plunges headlong into water, I flung myself upon the strange horse, intending to alight crosswise on his back. He shied, and I fell short, just managing to find the pommel with my left hand, so that instead of being on his back I was hanging by his side.

The hold was perilously slender, but the tense fingers held like hooks of iron. Adjusting my grip quietly for a moment till I got my breath, I was just on the point of pulling myself up, after the manner of gymnasts, in order to swing into the saddle, when a spear came whistling through the air, catching my horse somewhere in the hind quarter. He seemed to curl under me as the broad point pierced his flesh, then snorting with fear and pain he sprang high into the air, shaking himself so that I was nearly cast to the ground. I thought he had been struck in the vitals, and that my time was come; but after a few demented leaps he turned and bolted off in a new direction, I dangling helpless and stunned by his side.

Clinging to girth and pommel with every nerve and muscle, with every sense and faculty, bumped and buffeted, so that the wind was often knocked clean out of me, and the world seemed whirling away into darkness and nothingness, I was dragged along at the speed of lightning. To hold on for many minutes in that position was beyond human power, and to let go meant instant destruction. Had I been able to get my toes steady on the earth for half a second, I could have sprung astride the flying animal, but at that fearful velocity, the thing was beyond a tiger's agility. Yet, if something could not be done, and done quickly, I felt it would be better to breathe a prayer and let the agony end.

Small things are momentous in decisive moments; and sometimes weakness is salvation. Bit by bit the quivering grasp relaxed, and I gradually sank lower and lower, till half my length trailed on the ground.

Two or three more little slips and my enemies could work their will. A strange dizziness was already coming upon me, when my knee struck some protuberance, so that, with the hurricane speed, I bounded

like a ball. I was not yet too far gone to see my opportunity. Finding myself well in the air, I concentrated all my strength, drawing fiercely with the left
hand. The lax muscles turned to steel in the moment
of supreme need. I rose, and, holding my breath,
shot my right hand across the saddle. The hooked
fingers caught something, and the next moment,
wriggling, panting, and almost blind from excitement an exhaustion, I lay half across the horse's back.
Then, with another mighty effort, I wriggled further
up, and before I knew it, was in the saddle and reaching for the rein. As I got it a yell of rage went up
close behind, and another spear, less true in aim than
the first, whizzed past and buried itself in the sand.

The sensations of the next few minutes were such
as a man may not experience twice and live. Crouched
with my long spurs deep in my horse's sides, my heart
afraid to beat, and the cold sweat-drops falling from
my face, I pelted on, listening to the fateful thud of
hoofs and the cries and curses close behind, and knowing that the spears were levelled to strike. I felt as
the stag must feel that, straining its utmost, manages
to keep just a tongue's length in front of the foremost
hound. The least weakness, the most trivial mishap,
the breaking of the girth, the stumbling or slipping
of my horse, the slackening of the pace for so much
as the tenth part of a second, and the desert would
drink my blood.

Whither I was going, or whether there were many
or few in chase, I could not tell. I saw nothing but
a jumbled feverish vision of a low craned head of a
horse, a flying mane, and a pair of reaching forefeet
that never seemed to touch the ground, but in my
ears was a noise that told me death was riding hard
at my back.

The spume flakes flew up from my horse's mouth,
wetting my face, and soon I became aware of an
ominous heave of his flanks; now and then, too, I had
a glimpse of a red eye and a nostril, like " a pit full of
blood." It was sheer cruelty to goad him on. But

what were considerations of cruelty to one with three
fiends stretching within three yards for his life? Like
Lady Macbeth in the height of her murderous mood,
I was filled from the crown to the toe top full of direst
cruelty.   So the heavy spurs were plied as fast and as
hard as heel could drive them, in spite of the groanings and shakings of my victim.

So great was the strain of terror that it may well bo
imagined no fresh alarm could affect me.   Yet, when
a vicious cry went up, as it appeared at my very car,
betokening, as I fancied, the triumph of the Bedouins, I shut my eyes with a creeping shuddering horror that made me give a little scream.   I rode in darkness for what seemed an endless time, momentarily
expecting the thrust of cold steel in the small of tho
back.   As it did not come, I ventured to open my
eyes, but I durst not look behind.

It was now high noon, and the sun an incandescent
globe overhead.   There may have been clouds in the
sky, but assuredly there was neither shadow nor
breath of moving air on the earth.   I stewed in my
soaked clothes as if dissolving over a slow fire; and
gasped and wheezed like an asthmatic shut up in an
oven.   For the quivering, simmering heat not only
broiled the body, but was as a stinging acid in the eyes
and nostrils, and as burning fumes in the lungs.

All at once, there came a sharp puff of wind, not
sweet and refreshing, but charged with more poisons
than ever chemist dreamed of.   Looking upward I saw
a great glare in the sky, as if it were the reflection of
some vast conflagration; and even as I looked the
glare swiftly deepened till it appeared the heavens
themselves were on fire; then the fiery redness was
suddenly overcast, and a dull coppery hue took its
place, this yielding in turn, and very quickly, to a
dark purple, and that again to a deep black.   All the
while the wind came in spurts of even greater force
and longer duration.   I was wondering what all this
might mean when there burst upon my ear a great
prolonged roar, as of a mighty flood lashed to fury,

and turning to the right hand quarter I saw a portentous black cloud rushing towards me with inconceivable velocity. The look showed me, too, that I was riding alone; the Bedouins had abandoned the chase, and were now tearing off in a course of their own.

I had not taken in the situation when I was enveloped in darkness, and gasping, as if a bottle of volatile salts had been pressed to my nose. At the same time, the wind nearly tore me from my seat, and though I could see nothing, I felt that my horse had turned tail to the blast, and was drifting like a ship in a gale, or cattle in a driving Highland snowstorm. I hugged his neck, and my mantle flew over my head. Well for me it did; for this was the dreaded simoon, before which all Arabia falls down and covers its face as close as cloth will roll. I lay unable to breathe, and in exquisite torture, my horse all the while scudding before the tempest. He stumbled often, and would have lain down, but that I kept the spurs to him. Had he had his will, in less than half a minute we should both have been buried beneath a wreath of sand, to lie there until the winds came again to unearth our bleaching skeletons.

The storm passed on like a solid wall, and, as if by magic, the atmosphere cleared, though I could still see the black line of the whirlwind far ahead. I looked eagerly about for company, but found myself completely alone. No Bedouins in pursuit. No Bedouins in sight, nor, indeed, any living thing. The simoon had given me my life, but it left me desolate.

Dismounting, and looping the bridle over my arm, I walked a little bit, shaking loads of sand from the folds of my dress. My right leg, however, was so sore and stiff that I was soon compelled to sit down, though it was a long time before I had any heart for surgery. When, at length, I got sufficient command of my nerves to undertake an examination, I found myself with an ugly gash in the right thigh, from the depths of which blood still oozed. The clotted outer edges were fast hardening and stiffening, so that the

pain grew cruelly intense.   Perhaps it was because
attention was directed to my hurt that it became all
at once so sensitive, but the smallest movement now
caused a pang that cut the breath like a stab.   Besides, I was in a raging fever of thirst.   A water-skin
dangled from my saddle bow, and I reached for it in
hope of relief.   It was already cracking and shrivel-
ling in the furnace-like heat, but there was a chance
that some of the precious contents might still remain.
Now that the idea of it came to me, my whole being
called out vehemently for a mouthful of water as the
sole hope of life; nothing else could save me.

Eagerly pushing the dented sides of the skin apart,
I looked in.   The dazzled eyes saw only a vacant
blackness.   Merciful Heaven, it could not be that the
skin was empty!   I peered deeper and deeper.   My
vision must be at fault, for if I did not see water I
certainly smelled it.   Thrusting in my hand, I brought
out a handful of mud, the refuse of some well trampled into foulness by struggling perishing men and
beasts.   The skin dropped from my nerveless fingers,
and the oozy sediment came dribbling out.   Before I
knew what I was about I was sucking it for dear life;
but it stank so poisonously that I had to spit it out
immediately.   Yet moisture of any sort was too precious to be wasted, so I emptied the trickling mire
upon my baking wound, rubbing it in with my finger as a smearer rubs his tar into the divided fleece
of a sheep.   I cannot say that the application in the
least assuaged the pain.   And the disappointment of
finding the skin empty gave an acuter ache to the
throbbing of my inflamed throat and lips.   Oh, for a
single drop, just one drop, of clear, cool water, to ease
that fiery torture!   Worlds upon worlds would I have
given for so much liquid as lies on the petal of a
daisy at dawn, and worlds upon worlds could not have
purchased the boon.

I bandaged the wound, that is to say, I bound it
roughly with a rag torn from my long Arab shirt.
But what mattered it whether it was attended to or

not? Why defer paying a debt that is exacted of all men? Would it not be best to let Death distrain at once, and have done with "this fever called living"? Utterly worn out with fatigue and fright and excitement, I was tired of being the sport of destiny. To think of triumphing over her was a fool's thought. No man had done it, no man would or could do it. Why should I prolong a bootless strife? The cry of the sick heart was the cry of the ancient Celt—

"How evil was the lot allotted to Llywarch the night when he was brought forth! Sorrows without end, and no deliverance from his burden."

No deliverance from his burden! That was the sentence of old, it was the sentence still. A galling struggle, tragically relieved by momentary illusions of hope and happiness, endless humiliations, crushing defeat, and at last inevitable death. Yet it was hard to die, hard to think calmly of one's own bones being picked by those vultures which were already hovering above me in anticipation of a corpse to feed on. I was not yet philosopher enough for that.

Crouching on the sand, my head sank deep between my knees in an agony of despair, the sun beat down as if the heavens were a vault of fire, and millions of quivering arrows seemed to dart along my spine. It was rapidly driving me crazy. I was going mad with the consciousness of the calamity full upon me. Merciful God, I was to die a raving maniac in the burning wilderness! The thought thrilled for an instant in the brain, making me shiver as with a sudden chill, and then came a strange calm. *That* at least could be prevented. Drawing my sword, I felt its edge, thinking of Saul in his defeat. The blade was of Damascus steel and as keen as a razor. A moment's courage and all would be over; so sharp an istrument could cause little pain, nothing to what I was already suffering.

I learned then that a man may take his own life smiling. I turned the edge inward towards the throat, glad that I had found such easy means of escape. A

17

moment's courage, I kept saying to myself—no more —then everlasting relief. The edge touched the bare skin, and I leaped to my feet screaming with unutterable horror. No! No! I could not do that, the canon of the Almighty was clean against self-slaughter. Shaking like a leaf in the gale, with an unspeakable tumult of emotion, I fell prostrate on my face, and prayed for strength and pardon.

CHAPTER XXII.

DESPAIR AND HOPE.

GETTING back to my crouching posture, I threw my mantle over my head as a kind of screen; but while it mitigated the blaze of the sun it smothered me. Casting it off, therefore, I rose, still trembling violently, and looked about, vaguely, I think, expecting aid. Not a living thing was within sight or sound. Illimitably to every point spread the grey waste of burning sand, hot as the marl that scorched the feet of Satan in his defiant and impious journey. Above was a ball of living fire; below, an arid lifeless plain, radiating a blinding, choking heat like an infinite lime-kiln; naught else to be seen, save far away to the west, dim, pale peaks that might be the thin veil of dissolving clouds.

I tried to walk by way of diversion, but reeled and staggered, so that I was fain to sit down again. Perceiving that my horse now cast a shadow I crept into it, and huddled there, with drooping head, and aching heart, and the reproaches of conscience for company, thought bitterly of what might have been but for my own perversity.

At that moment the heather about Glenrae was in full bloom, making the air a distilled essence of honey, and the bees, with the drowsy song that had so often been a soothing melody in my ears, were thriftily preparing for winter; and shepherds were whistling and calling from crag-tops, their voices blending in a far-off music, with the barking of dogs and the bleating of sheep; and golden burns were leaping down green and purple hillsides; and over all was a soft, blue sky with masses of cool white clouds. How vividly it all rose before the eye of imagination! Many and many a time in the languorous summer days I had laved my bare limbs in those pellucid waters, and watched the flashing of silvery fin and scale as the trout darted under bank or stone, and lain on my back in some shady place, looking up at snowy fleets, touched with pink and rose, sailing on an inverted ocean. And to think of all that now! It was as the vision of Dives when, raising his eyes from his place of torment, he beheld the felicity of Lazarus. Peace brooded like a guardian spirit over Glenrae and the Elms, amid their quiet encircling hills, and the affectionate souls there were the blither because they thought I was happy and prosperous. Would no sympathetic spirit tell them of my condition? But their ignorance was part of my punishment. I had once been in paradise, too, and fell by rebellion. As we make our bed, so must we lie.

In the midst of my dream I remember that my pipes and some other things I cherished were with Tabal and my mare. But luckily, all the relics of past happiness were not lost. Undoing the folds of my dress I drew forth my mother's Bible, and with it the two bunches of white heather (now sadly withered and crushed) that Isabel had given me. The heather I put carefully back with as tender a caress as if it were a sentient being capable of feeling and returning affection. When I should have ceased from troubling it would be found next my heart, evidence of at least one faith kept to the bitter end; and, who knew, some good angel might whisper to Isabel, in a dream, that far off, and in his last dire extremity, somebody's thoughts had gone forth to her. And sometimes in the pensive gloaming, when the mind roams, she might think, in spite of the grandeur and happiness that were sure to be her lot, of one whose lonely grave she could never know, and whose love was no more than a guess to her. Futile and boyish, yet strangely comforting reflections!

The Bible I opened at random, and lo! there lay before me the wondrous story of Job.

"And now my soul is poured out upon me; the days of affliction have taken hold upon me," so my dim eyes read. But I knew the moving drama by heart. Long ago, amid far-off, happy scenes, it had been learned by my mother's side. And I thrilled eeriely at the thought that it was in this scorched land where I was now lying, under these very skies that were burning my life out, that Job had groaned in bitterness of soul.

All mankind are one in distress: the Jew and the Gentile, the civilized and the barbarian. Immediately there was established a mystic brotherhood between me and the man of Uz. Uncounted ages had rolled by since he had suffered. In the interval, things of vast and vital moment had come and gone and been forgotten; but the tragedy of the race went on. With a trifling outward difference, a mere matter of time and circumstance, Job's case was mine. Well, his afflictions were over long ago; mine also would soon end. And so moralizing and turning the leaves, I came to the gracious promise:—

"There shall be a tabernacle for a shadow in the daytime from the heat, and for a place of refuge, and for a covert from storm and rain."

And again—

"Then shall the lame man leap as an hart, and the tongue of the dumb sing: for in the wilderness shall waters break out, and streams in the desert."

And yet again—

"When thou passest through the waters, I will be with thee; and through the rivers, they shall not overflow thee: when thou walkest through the fire, thou shalt not be burned; neither shall the flame kindle upon thee."

And once more—

"The Lord will be a refuge in time of trouble."

"He shall call upon Me, and I will answer him: I will be with him in trouble; I will deliver him, and honour him."

"I will not leave thee, nor forsake thee."

It was surely enough. A prayer, oh! doubting heart, and courage even now.

The courage was urgently needed and sorely tried, not less by physical than by mental ills. Every inch of my body was a burning ache. My wound pained me more and more; my head throbbed like a steam boiler, and lips and tongue were as if flayed and laid on smouldering ashes. Not so much as the remnant of a spittle was left to moisten them. I opened my mouth and a rush of blistering air went down my throat, scorching my lungs to their roots; I closed it, and the dry flesh cracked so that the blood squirted out. Let the man who would feed fat his revenge, have his enemy sent out and baked alive under an Arabian sun in full blaze. The Inquisition never invented a torture half so cruel as that slow process of broiling by the immitigable heavens.

My poor horse was likewise in a far-gone condition. The foam was crusted hard about his mouth and flanks, his nostrils were wide, dry, and fiery, his head hung, and his black, swollen tongue protruded. Yet he remained as steady as a rock, sheltering me in his shadow. At intervals he turned and looked at me, and once he whinnied softly, as if out of pure pity and comradeship.

By-and-by there came a change. The flaming sky was overcast, the shimmering sand turned a dull drab, and after a while, dark clouds began to gather in the south. Then a tepid, relaxing wind blew from the same quarter, bringing an electric sultriness in place of the white heat. After a little the wind ceased, and a dead calm fell.

The atmosphere seemed to have suddenly grown solid, and to be weighing upon the world like a canopy of molten lead. Breathing had been a difficulty before; it was a positive pain now. My horse grew restive, snorting, pawing the ground and sniffing at the far darkness, now fast spreading and deepening.

All at once, out of the deathly stillness, came a little blast of wind that tossed the sand spitefully in my face, and passed on with a weird, uncanny wail. Another and another followed, with a low, hopeless moan as of incurable sorrow. Then silence again, so deep that to my beating senses it was audible. It was as if a great invisible host were treading the loose earth, and filling the air—an endless procession passing on into the inane. And let me tell you that the awesome sound of unshod silence is a thing to make the hair rise on the head, and the flesh creep on the bones. I spoke to my horse for the sake of company, and my words were a ghostly gibber: I shuddered at the sound of my own voice.

The darkness was soon an inky blackness. The sullen heavens were descending, and impenetrable clouds were marshalling in forbidding ramparts along the sky-line of the south. Then a lambent fire began to flicker about the outer edges of the dense masses, and presently there was borne to my ears the long roll of incipient thunder. A few minutes later, big drops of rain began to patter on the sand, sending up volumes of dusty steam.

I got to my feet with joy unspeakable. Praise be to Heaven, my cry for help had been heard and answered. I was saved—saved from the vultures and the heaping sands. Man is an insignificant atom in the scale of the universe; yet easily believes himself the object of a special providence. Here were the streams of water in the desert sent for me, and me alone. I wept with awe and gratitude.

The rain came thicker and faster, first a shower, and then a deluge. The sun was eclipsed; the dome overhead seemed to be cracking and rending as at the blast of the last trump. And indeed, to me, it was little less than a resurrection. Here was water, and water was life. The thunder roared ever nearer and louder, till worlds of wrecked matter seemed to be crashing about my head. My ears were stunned by the exploding bolts, and on my face I felt the hot smack of the forked lightning, that made the wilderness as a sea of fire. But through it all, the beneficent rain came down in sheets, drenching me not merely to the skin, but to the very marrow. With upturned face and open mouth, I slaked my baking throat; and as I drank with ten times the greediness of the fevered drunkard, I could see my horse, too, with his nozzle turned to the pouring skies.

Far into the night the storm boomed and poured. I lay stretched full length on the soaking sands, slowly turning over and over so that the blessed flood might enter at every pore. It was impossible to have too much of that Heaven's gift, and I would not miss a drop of it. Nor, while revelling in the shower-bath, did I forget to fill my water-skin against future needs.

Now and again I had glimpses of crouching forms, with eyes that matched the lightning, ready to pounce upon me; but, somehow, they never came to the spring. In the air, too, were wheeling things that would swoop down and then dart off with a cry of disappointment, at finding the expected corpse a living man.

In the early morning the storm died away, and the stars came out in a crystalline, dewy azure, that was as the cool blue bosom of a summer lake. Not daring to sleep I lay and looked up at them, meditating on the marvels they must have seen in the course of the countless ages. But though my thoughts were serious enough (and with good reason), they had not the gloom of the night before.

I had leisure to ponder many things besides the stars, such as the strange fate that had led me hither, the perils and hardships that were past, those that might still be to come, the fate of my late companions, and my own present condition. But, as you may imagine, the subject that was uppermost in my mind was the miraculous meeting with Donald Gordon; for, on looking again at my miniature, I was established in the belief that the man on the black horse was none other than he. What, in the name of all the wonders, had brought him to this strange quarter of the globe? and how came he to be fighting for Yumen Yusel? These were questions I could not answer; perhaps I did not try very hard to answer them. For I was occupied with the cardinal fact that beyond all doubt Donald was in Arabia, that I had seen him face to face, had even spoken to him, and got a hurried glance in response. But for the sudden mishaps of war, I would have declared myself to him, and he would have become my friend and protector. In the most unexpected way, my mission came near a happy accomplishment, yet, exasperating to think, had failed as utterly as if we had been as wide apart as the poles. The total failure on the verge of so dramatic a success, was another cruel stroke of that malicious fortune that pursued me so relentlessly. But, with a spark of the fire that I had thought dead, I told myself that I would not be conquered. Donald Gordon was in Arabia, and I would find him, nay more, would carry him triumphantly back to Scotland and his friends. As this bold, high project stirred me, I had a vision of two sun-embrowned men in strange, outlandish garb arriving in the gloaming at the Elms, and of Isabel, after a moment's mistrust, rushing to greet and embrace them. The delectable imagination inspired me with such heart and energy that I must have expanded inches on the strength of it.

The dawn broke sweetly over the waste with a rosy flush and a sapphire radiance, and a balm that was as a precious cordial to mind and body. The sand sparkled and gleamed like the sea, and the distant mountains stood out a definite blue-black line against the pellucid western horizon.

Revived to fresh interest in life, I began to consider

the means of escape from this wilderness, and so, having dressed my wound with wet rags, I climbed, not without difficulty, into the saddle. The question was which way to turn. Eastward, northward, southward, the unbroken expanse of sand stretched till it melted into liquid blue spaces, on the rim of the desert. To the west alone did there appear to be any prospect of succour, so, turning my horse's head to the mountains, we started on our trackless path.

For hours we plodded on among billowy ridges, my horse sometimes sinking over the fetlocks, sometimes treading firmly on the crust, and always going just as he pleased, for he had done well enough to deserve a little license. It soon got very hot again, so hot that my steaming clothes suggested a portable vapour bath aimlessly adrift in a dreary region of sand. The steam kept me moist, though it failed to keep me cool; what was more, it did much to soothe the throbbing pulses of my wound, which, in spite of the night's soaking and bathing, had still a sharp shooting pain if I chanced to move unwarily. But the excruciating stiffness that had made my leg useless on dismounting after the hunt was nearly gone.

There was no sign of life about, save here and there a fugitive jackal or hyena, running with its head down and its tail clapped tight between its legs; or overhead a hawk or vulture sharply outlined against the sky. I judged these gentry must have had a royal feast ; indeed, that it would be many days ere their gorging would be ended, and I sickened at the thought of the ravening that went on among the slain on the field of battle.

It must have been near noon, when I was again broiling in the glow of the vertical sun, that I gave a start on descrying the tiniest black dot on the ashy expanse far to the south-west. It was impossible to say whether it was dead or alive, a rock, a man, or a beast, but any diversion was welcome, and I made in its direction, quickening my pace. I had not gone far when I guessed it to be a horseman crawling to-

wards the mountains. Putting my horse to a canter
I drew rapidly near the stranger; but for a while he
held on his way, either as if he did not see me, or were
too far spent, and too indifferent to deviate in his
course. But at length he halted abruptly, then, after
gazing for a moment, came galloping to meet me.
My heart beat quick with both fear and gladness. If
this were a Bedouin, our meeting would be a tilt for
life, and I was but ill prepared for an encounter; but
if he should prove a friend—oh, joy of joys, it made
me giddy to think of the bare possibility.

On I galloped, and on he galloped. I saw him
whirling his lance, and almost unconsciously I waved
my sword in return. Then, shouting at the pitch of
his voice, he put his horse to the charge. That
rather startled me, and I was in two minds about
turning and making off; but in the critical moment
when my courage had all but ebbed, I recognized a
familiar face. Then I, too, shouted wildly, and my
horse bounded as the spurs went into his sides. The
next minute Tabal and I were hugging and embracing like long separated brothers, both of us having
leaped to the ground in order to get the closer grip.

You may be sure we had each a multitude of questions to ask and answer; but before I would hear anything of Tabal's adventures since our parting, I insisted upon looking to his injury. It was bad, he
said, but not deadly. Baring his left shoulder very
carefully, I found a shattered gunshot wound that
gave the flesh a torn and broken appearance, different
altogether from the clean lance-cut I had got. I
dressed it as gently and as well as was possible with
the means at my disposal, a service for which poor
Tabal was infinitely grateful.

"We are of different nations and religions; yet
surely we are not strangers, but friends," he said, embracing me again. "Had I seen thee now for the first
time I would have driven this lance through thee.
But henceforth it will be turned against him who
seeks thy hurt. Tabal, the son of Achmet, swears

it." And he took the oath in the most solemn manner known to his race.

That done, he played the surgeon to me.

"Thou art lucky!" he exclaimed with professional
pride when I was stripped. "By my faith, the man
who gave thee this hurt knew not his business, or
thou mightest cast away thy leg for ever. Methinks,
if I had my weapon upon him, as he had his upon
thee, he would now be food for the kites and hyenas."

"He was clumsy, Tabal," I said.

"Clumsy!" repeated Tabal, scornfully. "Nay, it
does not half express his want of skill. Having got
his lance upon thee, he should have killed thee as dead
as a roasted kid. I hold the fellow in contempt."

"Because, my good friend, he did not make an end
of one whom thou hast sworn to cherish and protect?"

"Nay, nay," answered Tabal, quickly, seeing
whither his soldierly zeal had led him. "I meant
not that. Praise be to Heaven thou art alive. I meant
that he knew not how to drive his spear. See," and
he made a thrust with his own, to show how the thing
ought to be done. "Methinks that is the way to put
an enemy into the dust. But thou art protected of
God," he added reverently, "and it maketh me glad
to be with thee. Verily, I am thy servant to do as it
pleaseth thee to bid me. And praise be to God and
the holy Prophet that we are not now having our bones
gnawed by wild beasts. Saw you ever such a slaughter as that was? Truly I think the man on the black
horse is none other than Satan himself!"

For a moment I wavered whether or not I should
enlighten him. Then I said very quietly, "The man
on the black horse is as much Satan as thou art, my
good Tabal. Listen, and I will tell thee a tale," and
I told him of my search for Donald Gordon, and the
meeting in the battle. He listened with wide eyes and
gaping mouth, thinking, I suspect, that heat and
trouble had turned my brain.

"Thou art telling me one of the tales of the magicians," he said, with something of awe in his voice and manner. "This passeth all belief."

"'Tis as true as the Koran, Tabal," I answered. "Hearken to my words: before thou art many weeks older thou shalt be as a brother to this dread warrior on the black horse."

"Nay. Heaven forbid!" exclaimed Tabal, fervently. "I would not forego my chances of Paradise for all the favours Satan can bestow."

His horror was so comical that I burst out laughing. Ordinarily I might have answered with my life for such an insult, such an outrage on his most sacred feelings. But happily Tabal was in a mood to forgive much because he loved much.

"I will put cool water on thy hurt," he said as tenderly as if he were treating an ailing and fractious child, "and on thy head, too, for the sun hath made it hot. Then, when thou art refreshed, we will talk of our adventures since the flight and the simoon parted us."

He had his way, and indeed it was exceedingly refreshing to be bathed; for I was still more than a trifle feverish. But more soothing and invigorating than the water were the brotherly gentleness and compassion of Tabal, who seemed to make himself responsible for my safety and comfort.

When we came to recount our experiences since parting, I learnt that he had passed the night like myself, alone. Like me he had thought himself doomed, had been saved by the rain, and was looking for human succour when I spied him. We went through our perils again, as old soldiers refight their battles, and embraced at the conclusion in pure exuberance of joy at being together once more.

Not the least happy circumstance of our meeting was that I got back my little Fatema, and the precious green bag with Duncan's pipes. To Tabal the bag was an object of such intense curiosity that I had to produce the pipes and give him a lilt. It scarcely ravished him, and it frightened the horses, so the

pipes were put away that I might take formal possession of my mare.   Before parting with her, however,
Tabal must needs make as fine a speech to her as ever
a gallant of the old school made to his mistress, dwelling with rapturous phrase on her beauty, her fleetness, her docility, her intelligence, and her dauntless
spirit in time of trouble, to all of which I heartily said
Amen.

Fortunately Tabal had some dates—they were really
what were left of my own—and when the ceremonious address to Fatema was over we squatted on the
sand and ate a few.   We dared not venture to eat
many, for the store was small, and it was extremely
doubtful when it could be replenished.   To make up
for the shortness of rations we had a double pull at
the water-skins, and the cooling draught was sweeter
than the choicest vintage of France.

It was again meltingly hot; indeed after the rain
the heat seemed intenser than ever.   Pungent streams
were trickling into our eyes and mouths, and coursing
down our backs and arms and legs, as if we were
patent self-moisteners that worked the better the
greater the drought.   Self-moisteners we were with
a vengeance; but the moisture could not possibly last
long.   I looked at the thin brown visage of Tabal,
thinking he must soon be converted to pemmican,
and I, too, was swiftly undergoing the same process
of desiccation.   A little while and there would not
be a drop of liquid in our bodies.

The rate at which we were changing to hard fibre
made it desirable to get out of the glare of the sand
as quickly as might be.   Tabal agreed with me that
our best hope lay in the hills to the west, and we accordingly made in their direction.   If nothing better,
their rocks and chasms would at least afford us shelter
from the pitiless sun.

CHAPTER XXIII.

BEDOUINS.

ALL day we laboured through the loose, glowing, unshadowed sands, our water bottles constantly at our mouths, our garments like unwrung dishcloths, our drooping horses in a lather. Nightfall found us still crawling on, silent, weary, and in much pain. Tabal was the worse of the two. Yet the stoical fellow never complained, nor ever forgot to comfort me when my torments wrung from me a cry or a groan.

With darkness it became cooler, and, to our further relief, there sprang up a delicious breeze. We were still wading in sandy seas, but we were now able to mend our pace a little; and indeed there was urgent need of speed, for, in our condition, another day like the last would clean finish us. By-and-by our horses began to tread more lightly and firmly; a little later they were stumbling over stones and nibbling at scrubby bushes, and we knew the water-courses were not far off. It was midnight, however, ere we had climbed far enough to feel safe for the night; or perhaps the better way to put it is that at midnight I swore I would go no farther, if the halt cost me my life. Tabal said he thought we might rest. So, un-saddling, and tying the horse's forefeet to prevent them from wandering, we had another drink and threw ourselves on the ground to sleep.

We woke with the level sun beating in our faces, greatly refreshed though stiff and sore in the regions of our wounds. Our first act was to scramble to the top of an adjacent crag and reconnoitre the situation. We looked cautiously round among the rocks, then out on the plain as far as eye could see, but nothing living was visible save flocks of ravenous birds going to and fro between the mountains and the scene of·

the late battle. Fancying ourselves secure, we descended, watered ourselves and our horses at a bubbling spring, and breakfasted on half a dozen dates apiece. Then we saw to our wounds, and the surgical operation done, we lay in the shade of a rock to think, and, for the hundredth time, discuss our adventures and prospects.

I asked Tabal what he thought would be the result of the battle we had fought and lost.

"The ravaging of the whole country by Yumen Yusel and the man on the black horse," he answered promptly. "Amood Sinn hath fattened and grown large on his neighbours, and Abou Kuram hath had immense tribute for rendering aid. Three times they have levelled the palace of Yumen Yusel and enriched themselves with great plunder. Now, methinks, it is Yumen Yusel's time to win."

"That means that the enemy will converge on Amood Sinn's capital," I said.

"Yes," said Tabal; "wouldst thou have them victorious without reaping the fruits of victory?"

A brilliant idea flashed upon me.

"Let us go to Amood's capital also," I said. "I would fain meet the man on the black horse again."

"And be cloven in two for thy pains," returned Tabal, quickly.

"Thou shouldst see us embrace like brothers," I rejoined confidently.

Tabal glanced at me with the old expression of incredulity, and jumped to his feet saying we must saddle up and get to the green valleys and rushing streams that were ahead. I was in his hands and could not dissent.

We had travelled slowly for perhaps two hours, round the shoulders of bluffs and about crags and rocks, and on the brink of dizzy precipices and over rubbly hills, when all at once we came upon a spot of such verdurous beauty it might have been the veritable garden of Eden. It lay in a deep depression, walled about by cliffs, except at one corner where there was a narrow gate-like opening.   As soon as we sighted it, Tabal, who suspected it might be inhabited, whispered me to remain quiet, and, slipping from his horse, went stealthily forward and peered over the breastwork of rock in front of us.   Returning with gestures of silence he took charge of the horses, and I went softly to spy.   Climbing the parapet I looked cautiously down the other side, and there, to my amazement, was Ahmed, the son of Koor Ali, alone and sleeping like a cherub.

Motioning to Tabal to remain still, I ran quickly to the entrance, went in, and then crept along the base of the rock, intending to give Ahmed a fine surpise. Reaching him on tip-toe, I tickled him under the chin with my finger.   He sprang up as if I had pierced him with a spear, a moving spectacle of ferocity and terror, and drew his dagger, which was his sole weapon.

"Put up thy dagger, Ahmed," I said.   "I am surely thy friend."

"Thou art no friend," he returned savagely.   "A man does not spit on his friend.   Thou hast cast the rinsings of thy foul mouth into my face, a disgrace for which thy blood will atone.   I will fight thee where thou standest, dagger to dagger, but I will not let thee call thyself my friend."

With that he wrapped his torn mantle about his left arm as a sort of shield, and put himself in a posture of defence.

"Let it be quick," he hissed.   "Stand not dallying as if thou wert afraid of thy fair skin."

"What thou sayest is impossible," I answered, drawing myself up just enough to show I was not held back by fear.   "It would be a sin in me to fight thee. I have thee at an advantage; besides, thou art in the midst of grievous misfortune."

"Thou art right," he said.   "But I will bear my grief as becometh a man, and desire not any compassion at thy hand.   As for thy advantage, profit by it. I was eager to meet thee alone, and lo! here thou art, and we will fight."

"We will not fight," I returned. "Thou art famished with hunger, and weak from fatigue; why should I kill thee in thy feebleness? I will give thee share of my food, it is not much, but it will strengthen thee; and when thou hast eaten, thou shalt rest undisturbed. If, after that, thou be of a mind to fight, I may gratify thee. Meantime, put up thy dagger."

He kept his blazing eyes on me for the space of perhaps half a minute, then, sullenly thrusting the dagger into his girdle, he threw himself on the ground without a word.

Tabal came down with the horses and the dates, and Ahmed was invited to eat. He accepted the invitation with an ill grace and a lowering glance at me. But he was in my power, and I would not let his petulance or ingratitude irritate me.

"If thou wilt sleep now," I said, when he had finished our dates, "I promise thee no harm shall come to thee."

"I am in need of no more rest," he answered gruffly.

"Concerning this quarrel, then," I said, "that thou choosest to make between us——"

"It was thou put disgrace on me," he growled.

"It was not intended as such, Ahmed," I said. "I did but jest in putting water on thee."

"Nay! by my faith, it was no jest!" he returned sharply.

"It was done in ignorance of the customs of thy country," I explained humbly.

He appeared to sway for a moment between two opinions.

"What sayest thou?" he asked, turning suddenly to Tabal. "Thou art of my own nation, and not ignorant like this infidel. Thinkest thou the Christian meant dishonour in casting water in my face?"

"Hadst thou cast water in his face," said Tabal, with the grave impartiality of a judge, "I would say thou hadst meant him dishonour. But he acted not in malice, but, as he sayeth, in ignorance. Think what that meaneth. Peradventure, if thou wert to visit the

18

Christian's country, thy ignorance should betray thee into error."

This lucid reasoning seemed to weigh with Ahmed. "It may be thou speakest the truth," he said, turning to me; "I will so take it. Only remember that if thou put disgrace on me wittingly or unwittingly again, I will kill thee where thou standest."

"I am warned, and agree," I replied; "and now, what news hast thou of the defeat?"

"The worst that tongue can tell. The troops of Abou Kuram are scattered as chaff in the wind; and my father is dead, as thou knowest. But his death shall not be unavenged. A son liveth after him. Look you here, the man on the black horse is a mighty warrior; but I will slay him if he were the very devil himself, and I had to hunt him to the depths of hell. I have sworn it, and that which I swear I will do."

It was useless to argue, so I held my peace. For a while he sat in silent anger, his hand clutching the hilt of his dagger, his flaming eyes on the ground. But looking up and finding Tabal and me watching, he rose, shook himself, tossed his head proudly, and began to talk as if he had never known a grief.

All this time our horses were feeding on the rich grass with such relish as only Arabs escaped from the desert can know. I saw Tabal looking thoughtfully at their swelling sides as if he were concerned about the matter.

"Are thy sins troubling thee that thou art so solemn, good Tabal?" I asked.

"By the holy Prophet, sins enough have I to trouble me," he answered. "Yet it was not of them I was thinking. Look you how these horses swell. If we were to be pursued, where would be their wind? Let us take them where the grass is less sweet."

"Thou speakest wisely," I replied. "Let us go."

I put Ahmed on my mare by way of cementing our friendship, and then Tabal insisted I should ride his horse.

"I have the goat's pleasure in climbing," he re-marked. "'Twill be a pastime to me."

"Nay, nay, Tabal," I said, "I will not consent to anything of the sort. I am more of a mountain child than thou art. I could scramble with delight over rocks, the mere look of which would make thee giddy. Besides, thy wound is worse than mine. Mount, my friend, and let us be off."

"Nay, not while I have two feet to walk, and thou but one whole leg," he answered.

"Tabal, do not put me to the trouble of hoisting thee by the back of thy neck and the wide part of thy breeches. Up with thee. Not a word more. Am I not leader, and shall I not be obeyed?"

Tabal laughed loudly, and, declaring I was making him as the grandmother of a hundred children, leaped into the saddle.

At first our path was no more than a fox's trail run-ning a devious and dizzy course round the base of great rocks and along the brow of beetling crags, and, at times, so steep that the riders had to dismount and almost hoist their horses by the bridle-reins. Then suddenly the aspect of the place changed, and we found ourselves in a sort of level dip several miles in extent, and giving one the impression of having been hollowed out by the hand of man.

"We must go warily," said Tabal. "Perchance we are not alone."

When he spoke we were winding among a confused mass of boulders, momentarily expecting to debouch upon the open space or plateau. I was stumbling on behind, my eyes on the ground for the greater safety of my neck, when, all at once, I heard strange voices, and looking up, saw a dozen men about Tabal and Ahmed, some pulling at the bridles, and others danc-ing round in a disquieting manner with spears and matchlocks. It required no wizard to explain the sit-uation. They were Bedouins, and we were prison-ers.

"Whence come ye, and whither go ye?" demanded

a man who appeared from his air of authority to be the chief.

"We are fugitives from the battle of which my lord hath doubtless heard," answered Tabal, who was coolest of us three.   "We have lost all."

"Nay, by my father's honour, that is a lie," said the Bedouin.   "Ye have here two as good horses as ever blessed a man's sight.   Yet there is truth in what thou hast said, for presently ye shall be without them.   Take these horses, Saba, and get ye down, my friends," addressing Tabal and Ahmed.   "And thou step beside them," turning to me, "so that we may see if ye be worth stripping.   Torn and ragged," he remarked, examining us like a Jewish pawnbroker's assistant.   "Yet methinks these garments may be worth having.   Mohamed," he called out with his hand on my shoulder, "take this fellow and leave him naught but the skin God gave him.   By my sword, 'tis more than he deserveth."

"He may strip my dead body," I said, stepping quickly back and pulling my pistol, "but not a stitch shall he have while I breathe."

"Sayest thou so?" asked the chief, with a rough laugh.

"I have spoken," I answered.

"And by that baby face of thine thou hast spoken bravely," returned the Bedouin.   "If thy deeds equal thy words, thou art a comrade worth having.   Mohamed, thou mayest leave him his clothes as well as his skin.   Heaven hath been gracious of late, and each man may in the mean time carry his own apparel.   It will be a convenience.   And now, my men, 'tis time to eat and drink.   Let us join our companions; for by this time the feast will be ready."

They took the horses and marched on, we three walking carefully guarded in the midst.   At their rendezvous in a smaller opening higher up the mountain, we found preparations in progress for the feast of which the chief had spoken.   Fires were blazing, meat was roasting, and cakes were burning among the ashes; and while the cooks were busy, others were laying out supplies of sherbet, coffee, and tobacco, things you would not see in a Bedouin encampment oftener than once in a lifetime. There were also many horses and a drove of camels, besides bundles of dresses and various other articles of merchandise—all testifying to the exceptional luck of the band in its recent enterprises. When we arrived, the cooking was held to be done, and the company, numbering at least two hundred, squatted to eat, Tabal, Ahmed, and myself being ordered to join. In appreciation, as he said, of my brave words, the chief did me the honour of keeping me close to himself, and we sat down beside the carcass of a gazelle, which had been roasted whole. As usual at such merry-makings, decency was thrown to the winds. Every man seized and devoured what lay readiest to his hand, without thought of ceremony. The chief opened the proceedings by thrusting his hand down the gazelle's throat and tearing out its half raw tongue. Taking a huge bite himself, he requested me to follow his example.

"Bite," he said, holding the still bleeding piece of flesh to my mouth. "Bite! By the Prophet's mule, never hast thou had such a sweet morsel under thy tongue. Thou wilt not!" he exclaimed, as I drew back in disgust. "Then is thy belly likely to cry out, ere thou hast more to offer it. Come ye hither," he called to Tabal and Ahmed, who were a little distance off, "come ye hither and bite. Ha! ye know how to drive the fangs," as they complied. "What aileth the other dog?"

"Defeat lieth heavy on his stomach, Suleiman," put in one of his comrades with a laugh.

"Perchance, Abd-el-Mahsin," returned Suleiman. "Nevertheless the rogue shall eat. It is my humour. Perdition to him, what is he that he should cross my purpose? Come near, thou dog, and bite," he added, addressing me. "Bite, or by our holy religion I will crush it down thy throat with the shaft of my spear, nay, I may even widen the passage with the point."

"My lord," I replied in my humblest and most respectful manner, "I have already eaten, and have no appetite."

"No appetite for such as that, thou mongrel cur! Thy vile stomach knoweth not what is good.   Had I eaten a two-year-old camel, yet would I find appetite for such sweet bread as that.   I say to thee, stick thy teeth in it."

I might have persisted in my refusal, for the look of the thing sickened me; but just then my eye caught Tabal's, which gave me a hasty but earnest admonition.   So I bit at the outer edge, where the meat was best done.

"A dainty bite, by my sabre hilt," cried Suleiman. "'Twas but a pretence.   Open thy jaws and try again, my beautiful.   That is better—so, so," he laughed.   "Now thou shalt drink, my merry one. To-morrow morning I may find it in my heart to give thee to the sun to roast and the vultures to eat; but to-day thou shalt fare as if thou wert a brother. Take that," and he held up a goblet of coffee.   "If thou say not it is the rarest that ever put joy in the soul of a child of the desert, I will tell thee to thy face thou art a scandalous liar."

I drank, and the coffee was good, so good that my lips smacked of their own accord.

"Ha, ha! my gazelle hath the right taste in his mouth yet," cried Suleiman; "that is from the store of our beloved friend and brother, Amood Sinn.   Thou mayest have heard of him.   He hath forgotten the way of victory; but he remaineth a right good judge of coffee.   Yet is it not better than his sherbet, which delighteth the soul as the smile of the houris.   Amood Sinn is a man of understanding.   He goeth forth to battle, and leaveth his good things to the needy.   My blessings on him.   May the holy Prophet give him the bliss of Paradise"—taking a draught of sherbet. "It grieveth my heart to think that Yumen Yusel and that devil on the black horse will be drinking his wine and dividing his wives so soon.   Take a cup of his sherbet, my gazelle. Ha! that is good. Thou smackest thy lips again. Now thou shalt have another bite," and the tongue having by this time disappeared, he seized the carcass and tore a hind leg off. He held it towards me and I, remembering Tabal's admonishing look, made a feint of biting greedily.

"Nay, not all! By my faith, not all!" cried Suleiman. "Abd-el-Mahsin, seest thou this? He who a moment ago would not put tooth on a tongue, is now ready to devour an entire limb. He will be asking for a whole carcass next. Yet he shall eat; yea, eat and drink," turning to me again. "Yonder is the desert, that will bring my gay one's sides together in emptiness."

So saying, he pushed the mass of meat against my mouth, and laughed uproariously because I showed symptoms of choking. But now that I was docile, the diversion of coercing me was at an end, and so, letting me eat as I pleased, he centred his attentions on himself. Never surely did man regale himself with such desperate energy. Nor was he alone in his voracity; for the entire band laid to in such an exhibition of ravening, as the civilized cannot imagine. Whole carcasses disappeared as mouthfuls, and where one minute there was meat enough to furnish a score of butchers' shops, the next there was only a heap of bones, piled for the wolf and the hyena. Tobacco and huge draughts of coffee and sherbet followed; then the gormandized camp lay down to sleep off its surfeit, the sentries alone remaining alert and undebauched. They would get their share later.

When we rose again, there was no longer any hilarity. The festivities were over, and the festive spirit gave place to one strictly devoted to business. Men who had laughed riotously at the feast, were grim and hardfaced; and amongst the grimmest of the lot was the erstwhile jocular Suleiman. He looked, indeed, as if he had never learned how to smile; and I noticed his curt orders were obeyed with a silent alacrity that told of an authority which would brook neither questioning nor insubordination. The saddling up was done so quietly, you would not have heard us a hundred yards off, and so quickly, that in half an hour after the first order was given we were in a break-neck gorge a mile from the resting-place. By express injunction Tabal and I rode our own horses by the bridle of Suleiman, while Ahmed was accommodated by the rein of Abd-el-Mahsin. Though there was no path save such as could be picked among broken ravines, and craggy watercourses, and up and down breathless steeps, the progress was swift; for Bedouin horses leap and dodge, and climb with the agility of goats. In trying moments, when we three strangers were demonstrative from fear of our necks, we were admonished to silence with the butt end of a spear, and so learned to look death in the face and hold our peace.

By nightfall, after a ride that wrenched, tore, and jolted the soundest joints and bones, we emerged from the range on a level dip on one of the spurs overlooking the plain to the west. Here we halted for supper, which was stealthily prepared, and silently eaten; for the need of concealment had come. As soon as the meal was over, Suleiman and Abd-el-Mahsin held a brief but animate consultation, the result of which was an immediate order to mount and march. By daybreak we were at the mouth of a steep and narrow defile that issued on a piece of green sloping down to the plain; and here we rested in the shadow of some tall precipices, I managing to snatch perhaps an hour of sleep.

The east was blazing in all the glory of crimson and gold, when some one prodded me vigourously in the ribs, and I started to my feet to find the company tightening girths for the road. Tabal, who insisted on being at once brother and servant to me, had my mare ready by my side. I had just time to take the rein when Suleiman gave the order to mount, and like one man the band sprang into the saddle.

At starting we divided, Abd-el-Mahsin with Ahmed and the necessary guard going southward with the captured horses and camels, and other booty, and Suleiman and the rest of us striking out to the north-west.

Before parting I managed to get a word with Ahmed.

"We may never meet again, Ahmed," I said, "and I wish to assure thee I am thy friend. Shouldst thou make thy way back to Abou Kuram, as I trust thou wilt, tell him I shall not forget his kindness, and that I commend to him the son of the valiant Koor Ali."

"It shall be done as thou desirest," he answered.

"One thing more I would beseech of thee," I added, "and that it is this, if thou shouldst chance to meet the man on the black horse, thou wilt not fight with him, nor provoke him."

"I will slay him!" returned Ahmed, fiercely.

"Nay, Ahmed, tempt him not, lest he slay thee," I said. "As for avenging the death of thy father, thou canst not right the wrongs of battle. Koor Ali fell like a gallant soldier. Lay that to thy heart. Farewell."

"Farewell," answered Ahmed. "I will think of what thou hast said."

And we parted.

It was easy to see from the demeanour of Suleiman and his men, that something big was in the wind; and, presently, an inkling of its character was conveyed in a whisper that we were bound for Amood Sinn's palace. The band swelled with elation, for the prospect was glorious; but they held their peace, and our march was as the march of the army of the dead.

CHAPTER XXIV.

IN AMOOD SINN'S PALACE.

WE pushed on with the speechless haste of men who cannot afford to waste energy on words, neither heat of sun nor lack of water being allowed to detain us. In and out among drifting dunes, across shifting ridges, over fissures that might have swallowed us all without being aware of it, through black rocks and scraggy shrubbery, dipping into valleys, climbing hillocks, skirting villages—on, on we went with never an abatement of the pace and no hint of our burning impatience, save what might be gathered from flashing eyes and keen set faces.

To me it was the old agony over again. The pangs of thirst were upon me, and my hurt was paining me dreadfully. From his uneasy wriggling and his peculiar stoop I understood that Tabal, too, was suffering. But as we had no desire to be stripped and left in the desert to console each other in native nakedness, no murmur of complaint escaped our lips.

Two days and nights this continued, with scarce a pause or remission. Our food was eaten in the saddle, and as for prayers, Heaven and the Prophet would forgive a little present neglect in view of the urgency of our business and the amplitude of the after atonement. We did not think of eating, we had no time for devotions, and such momentary halts as were permitted were wholly out of consideration for the labouring horses.

By noon on the third day we entered upon a high plateau or table-land, clothed with succulent grass and giving promise of some sort of civilization. The eagerness of the men increased. They began to strain their eyes, and whispers were passed that now we must be near the place of spoil.

We came upon many herds of goats and cattle, with

some camels, and the herdsmen, when questioned, told of the panic and revolution of war. Towards evening one of them reported having seen several bands of our own order, as well as parties of troops, that he took to be portions of the victorious army of Yumen Yusel. Suleiman listened with interest, and invited the man to become our guide.

"How shall I answer my master for forsaking the flocks entrusted to me?" he asked tremulously. "Truly he will beat me, and, it may be, have me put to death."

"We will ourselves take the blame of thy faithlessness," said Suleiman. "We have a notion of taking possession of these flocks, and thou shalt be our chief herdsman, and shalt have two slaves for thy friendliness—the sleekest that can be found, besides much rich apparel and dainty food. We are in haste and cannot tarry. Get thee hold of my stirrup strap, my gazelle—so. I know by thy looks thou canst use the feet God gave thee, and canst easily outrun a spent horse. Thou shalt feast in Amood Sinn's banqueting hall; yea, thou shalt be in Paradise ere thou knowest it. Be not afraid to grip, my brave one. And thou wilt take us by the shortest way; it will be best for thyself."

We resumed the march at a good round trot, the guide running as he was directed, and not daring to complain.

"Thou wilt do," remarked Suleiman, encouragingly. "Thou skippest like a roe on the mountains. Yea, thou art fleeter of foot than the leopard. I said two slaves; by my sword hilt, thou shalt have three."

Presently we began to fall in with rival bands of marauders, hard, fleshless, fierce-eyed rogues, who scowled and snarled at each other and at us, and rode faster and ever faster as they found more and more competitors for Amood's spoil. As they fouled and jostled in their haste there were high words and sudden gleams of steel; indeed they often behaved as if a fray were inevitable; but the Bedouin, with booty in his eye, will use much unchristian language and many savage gestures, before staying to shed blood. So they pressed together, imprecating ferociously, but nursing their private quarrels against a more convenient time of settlement.

The vulture has not a surer, quicker scent for carrion than the Bedouin for the property of the fallen or the unfortunate. From all points the children of the desert—the dirty, tawny, picturesque, warlike, cruel, generous, abominable progeny of Ishmael—were converging upon the capital of the luckless Amood Sinn, and making eager haste to divide his possessions. As we drew near our common destination the company was constantly swelling, and so was the tumult. Curses were bandied as thick as jests at a revel; and it was not ornamental swearing; for the oaths were hissed from between clenched teeth, and carried with them the intention of swift death. In the whole tumultuous mob none spoke deadlier words than the band of Suleiman.

We were in danger of forgetting our mission and breaking into gory hostilities, when, with the blood-red flush of the sunset upon them, we descried points of clustering minarets; a few minutes later the chimney-like turrets, at sight of which the famished traveller blesses himself, and the towers of a castle were drawn clear and firm against the dazzling splendours of the west. Then the children of the desert, with such whoops and howls as no throats on earth but their own can utter, clapped heel to flank, and the race became a mad scramble, with most of the features of a battle and a rout combined. It was as the descent of wolves upon an unprotected sheep-fold.

Just before the final dash orders were issued by Suleiman that if either Tabal or myself showed the least sign of disloyalty we were to be speared without question or ceremony, the justice of the deed to be considered afterwards. With the knowledge of these heartening instructions safely lodged in our minds,

Tabal and I exchanged smiles of intelligence, and rode gaily with the rest to the looting.

In spite of its forced march, and greatly to Suleiman's chagrin, his band was belated. Already the town was in the panic of a sack, and the company plied their spurs growling viciously at the thought of finding the pillaging half done. The crooked channels of streets overflowed with shrieking people who had been hunted out of their houses like rabbits out of burrows to be chased for sport and revenge in the open. Their cries on Heaven and the Prophet were pitiable, but did not detain us, for the call was urgent on every hand—

"To the castle! to the castle! In the castle is the big spoil."

Night had already dropped on us when, in the midst of a whirling and riotous press, we clattered under the frowning bastions of Amood's citadel. There was difficulty in finding a gate, and when discovered it was only by using our spears, butt and point, as was handiest, that we managed to reach it. It was closed, but a hundred shoulders and musket ends burst it at a touch, and the surging mass poured in with hideous noises. I fancy it was not properly fastened. Before our arrival the guards had been killed or overcome, or, what is perhaps more likely, had joined the looters at the first chance, and were already busy with their master's costliest treasures, animate and inanimate.

The outer court was dark and full of maniacal people, who behaved like an enraged menagerie. Dismounting inside the walls, we gave the horses over to a strong party of the most stalwart of our band, who might be trusted not only to defend, but to refrain from running off with them. Then the rest of us, following the lead of Suleiman, mowed an opening for ourselves into another court.

An Arab stronghold, as the reader may by this time be aware, is a place of vexatious courts and passages specially designed to beguile and confound. Amood

Sinn's palace was unusually rich in deceptive retreats, and now every one of them was blocked by a mob that was self-destroying, because it could neither go on nor turn back, and was frantic for plunder. The living trampled furiously on the dead and dying, and the din was as the uproar of caged beasts rending each other in the night.

In the brief lulls of the delirium, wild sounds swooped from above, and the tumbling bodies cast riven and bleeding out of windows told that work was vigourously proceeding where we particularly wished to be. Once the sharp scream of a woman rang out directly over our heads, like a shrill bugle note in the clamour of battle, telling that the pillagers were already in Amood's holy of holies. Suleiman made a remark about the harem being cleared before we could reach it, adding comments which it would be unwise to repeat.

It got horribly dark with a thick stifling darkness that you tried to ward off with your hand because it was choking the breath out of you. No man knew how or where to get a light, so, jammed in a reeking pen, from which there appeared to be no escape, we slew each other in utter horror and confusion to no purpose whatever. If the abattoir were not burst somehow none would be left to enjoy the good things that had brought us together.

At last some one got hold of a torch and kicking open a stove that smouldered in a corner, lighted it. Another and another followed suit, till twenty brands were shedding a red glare on the ghastly scene. In a swift glance we reckoned the multitude of demons against us; then, clustering once more about Suleiman, we reaped a path inward till we came to a battered staircase. Somewhere at the top of it were the secret apartments in which Amood Sinn's most precious possessions were kept, and we made haste to ascend, stabbing and tearing down all that blocked or barred the way. It would have saved much life and considerable trouble had the several bands agreed to

combine and distribute the booty share and share
alike. But no man thought of that, and probably
would not have entertained the idea had it occurred
to him.

> "For why? Because the good old rule
>   Sufficeth them; the simple plan,
> That they should take who have the power,
>   And they should keep who can."

So every ruffian did that which promised the best
and speediest return to himself.

We gained the top with the loss of only one man,
who went down clutching his slayer and bellowing
frightfully. Remarking that, everything considered,
we had done very well, Suleiman paused a moment
trying to decide which way to turn. Labyrinths of
passages ran like an intricate network in all directions: any one of them might be right, but the prob-
ability was that most of them were wrong, and it was
important to make the proper choice. As we were debating in our minds which corridor to take, and with
the aid of our weapons endeavouring to maintain our
footing, Suleiman caught a man who seemed anxious
to escape, and punched him under the fifth rib till he
screamed.

"Have a little forbearance, friend," said Suleiman.
"What do they call thee?"

"Baruk," answered the man, ready to fall in terror.

"And thy office, gentle Baruk?"

"Chamberlain of the household."

"By my faith, Heaven is gracious!" remarked Suleiman, softly. "Thou seest this dagger?" drawing
a crimson blade slowly across the man's eyes. "Take
note of its colour. It is sharp and cruel, and will be
in thy heart if we are not in Amood's most secret
chamber within three minutes!"

"How can it be?" asked Baruk, with a livid face.

"That is for thee to devise," answered Suleiman,
quietly. "Thou art at home, and shouldst know thy
way about. And I pray thee make haste, lest I be

tempted to take liberties with thee where thou standest."

"My lord would go to the harem?" said Baruk.

"Thou art a magician," returned Suleiman. "The harem and the treasury."

The man turned, making an effort to get on, but could not force his way.

"It is better to kill me," he moaned. "My ribs crack in the crush as dry twigs under the hunter's tread. Never have mine eyes looked on so woeful a spectacle as this."

He wrung his hands and would have wept, but that the point of a dagger made him leap in the air.

"Thou hast forgotten that we are in a hurry," said Suleiman. "Hadst thou not better make haste?"

He made another effort, and failed as before.

"The thing cannot be done, my lord," he gibbered in despair.

"We will see," replied Suleiman.

The dagger pricked, and Baruk yelled. Like a plunging horse, he sprang at the solid mass in front, and came back like water from a rock.

"Thou art of no avail in thy own house," said Suleiman. "Do thou guide, and I will make a way for thee."

Keeping his dagger on a level with the small of a man's back, Suleiman drove ahead, the other cowering close behind him for protection, and we resolutely supporting. Progress, however, was slow, for the light was bad, the block exceedingly great, and the fallen were troublesome underfoot. But Suleiman's dagger was very busy—quietly busy—dealing blows that were unfailingly effective, and we made steady way. Baruk wept hysterically at intervals, declaring his master would have him beheaded, and leaped like a roe at every prod from behind.

Back, far back we went along such a course as I hope never to travel again. At last Baruk, writhing as if the death agony were upon him, touched with the tip of his finger what seemed to be a panel in the wall. The next instant there was a crash of splintering wood and rending iron, and through the broken door came a gush of warm perfume. "The houries, my dove!" said Suleiman. "The houries!" The men at his back, shouting wildly, strained for Paradise, all except the guide, who groaned dismally as if he were on the brink of the pit.

Surging forward, we entered a narrow passage heavy with incense, and darkened by massy curtains. Then, bursting another door we came to a tapestried chamber. Suleiman growled at finding it empty, and was turning to have satisfaction out of Baruk, when a chorus of screams came ringing out of the remote darkness beyond. Baruk was let alone; there was fun ahead that prohibited dallying.

"The inner chamber," screeched the guide. "The inner chamber, my lord. May God and the holy Prophet protect me!" he added to himself, tragically. "Surely I shall be burnt alive for this, and never taste the bliss of the faithful. Never were the sanctities of privacy and our holy religion so profaned before."

Suleiman, in another mood, was using unhallowed language in front, because we were again in a maze of deep darkness, from which there appeared to be no outlet.

"Perdition seize thee, where art thou now, thou varlet of the bed chamber?" he called angrily to Baruk. "By the Prophet's sword, this dagger quivereth for a fleshy sheath. Thou shalt never escape alive, if there is more trouble or delay."

"Surely, my lord, I know these passages as a blind man knoweth the way to his mouth," answered Baruk, promptly. "The press is lessened. I will lead."

"Let me take hold of thy skirt then, for I have not the eyes of a cat," said Suleiman. "Thou feelest that point?—yea, that shrinking answereth for thee. Now, my gazelle, get us on if thou wouldst not be in the hall of Eblis this night."

We passed on through suffocating waves of perfume, by rustling curtains of inestimable value, over

19

Persian rugs that were like deep beds of moss under foot; upstairs and downstairs, and round more corners than Christian architect ever dreamed of. Another door flew into splinters, and we found ourselves in a gorgeously decorated apartment, illumined by swinging lamps that emitted a delectable odour, and full of struggling men and women. Crumpled, dishevelled embroideries, torn fans, broken musical instruments, and various articles of toilet were strewn about the floor; for the ladies and their attendants, not suspecting the fate of their lord, had been taken by surprise in the midst of music, gossip, and needlework.

A few of the women were negro slaves, but the majority were delicately nurtured beauties, whose manifold charms bore eloquent testimony to Amood's appreciation of diverse kinds of feminine loveliness. Fair Circassians there were, and tawny Egyptians, and thick-lipped Ethiopians, and black-eyed Arabs, with other belles of varying hue and attraction. Most of them were young; some, indeed, were mere girls; and all were plump as pullets and fragrant as musk roses.

They were in sad plight and disorder, poor things, their veils being rudely torn from their faces, their gauzy robes made into ribbons by men who were too eager for plunder to respect the sacredness of Amood's domestic circle. Occasionally the older ones fought with their captors, displaying no contemptible skill in the use of their claws; but the younger ones, to whom the mere sight of graceless strangers was pollution, shrank into alcoves and corners, panting like captured does; and were easier prizes.

Suleiman cast a swift appraising glance about the room.

"The queen—which is the queen?" he demanded of Baruk.

"She is not here, my lord," answered the quaking chamberlain.

"Not here, thou dog! and wherefore are we here?

Wouldst thou have thy blood spilled ere thou art a minute older? By this red blade, I will have none of thy tarrying and wavering."

Baruk took a step forward in quivering trepidation. Nor did he tremble without cause, for some of the women spying him were at him like tigresses, screeching that he had betrayed his trust.

"This is unseemly," said Suleiman, intervening. "Ye do your loveliness wrong."

"The wretch is a traitor," they clamoured. "He hath betrayed us. We will have his eyes out for the dishonour."

"Nay, nay, my charming ones," said Suleiman, with the most gallant air imaginable. "Ye do him injustice. Never was keeper of beauty so faithful to his trust. He hath conducted us hither, oh, lights of our souls, on the sharp compulsion of steel. We have ridden far, oh, unmatchable ones, for the joy of looking upon you, and now would ye deny us leave to prostrate ourselves at your feet which shine as the inner parts of shells on the seashore, and have the sweet odour of ambergris and sandalwood?" and he bowed profoundly.

In spite of their anger the ladies could not help smiling in a mollified way at the insinuating sweetness of Suleiman.

"Be comforted, ye who are as the stars in glory and brightness," he went on. "This guardian of your angelic slumbers hath not been false. But the times are strange, oh peerless princesses. Men are not masters in their own houses. Even the mighty Amood Sinn hath tasted defeat and is no longer able to rule his palace."

Such of the ladies as were disengaged clasped their hands, turned their eyes to heaven, and, with one accord, screamed.

"Slay me for causing you pain, ye adorable ones," cried Suleiman. "I vow we deserve death for thus disturbing your meditations. Yet must I ask one question. Is the beauteous flower, the queen, within? Business brooketh no delay, else would we tarry to sip honey off your lips, oh, ye enchantresses."

Jealousy is an ever active fire in Arab households. There was probably not one among them who would not have rejoiced in her heart to see the reigning beauty cast from the window; but deceit knows how to be discreet. Never would they permit unhallowed strangers to approach their beautiful queen, not so long as they had breath and nails to defend her. Intimating this, as many as were free bolted through an inner door, slamming and fastening it behind them.

"Make haste," said Suleiman. "We must not lose them. They will guide us whither we wish to go."

Forcing the door as if it were pasteboard, we dashed in pursuit. Along the dark, tripping ways we flew, guided by cries and vanishing skirt-tails, round innumerable angles, through countless doors, till we came upon a long straight passage. At the farther end, through a dim vista of muslin, we got a glimpse of two women whom we had not hitherto seen, disappearing at their utmost speed, with flying tresses that told of distress.

"'Tis she! 'tis she!" cried Baruk, excitedly. Then to himself, though loud enough to be audible to all, "Glory be to Heaven, she will escape. She can hide." But, suddenly remembering the position of affairs, he called again, "My lord, make haste, she is thine, so also is her companion, the Indian princess, of fabulous wealth. That is a tale of wonder. I would tell it to my lord, but there is no time. The holy Prophet preserve me!" and he groaned as if taken with a sudden pain.

Suleiman bounded past the shrieking bevy we had first encountered, the rest of us following as best we could. As we sped cries of terror rose in front and echoed shrilly in a hundred recesses. Suleiman bounded faster, calling on us to make a dash for the chief prize. The next instant we were round a corner to find the queen and her companion struggling with three men who were already setting about bind-ing them. Suleiman rushed upon the group with drawn sword, and two of the men, turning quickly to meet him, drew their long daggers with oaths of defiance, while the third, catching the women by the wrists, dragged them screeching into an adjoining room.

We crowded to Suleiman's aid, and the business would have been over in a jiffey had not the women, who were behind, come up and flung themselves blindly among our weapons. In the confusion our adversaries took to their heels, as Suleiman remarked angrily, without so much as a scratch upon them; the fellow who was engaged with the ladies, finding his attempt hopeless, dropped his hold and made after his comrades.

Thus released, the two women flew on again, in a worse frenzy of fright than ever, and we, unceremoniously disentangling ourselves, went in hot pursuit.

We gained on them, and they separated, leaping out of sight on either side of a passage as I have seen hunted rabbits disappear among whins and ferns. Suleiman, with half the company, darted after the one; I, with the rest, going on the track of the other, who proved to be the Indian princess.

We had almost overtaken her when, sudden as a tiger from her native jungles, a man sprang out of ambush, seized her, and before she could so much as cry, had her into a curtained recess. There two men made hasty arrangements to gag and bind her, but they never accomplished the operation. One went down wreaking his vengeance on the spear that pierced him, and the other shot out of sight leaving the rope twisted about his victim's arms. Faint with fatigue and fear the lady gave a little peculiar cry, staggered, and fell back, as it happened, right into my arms. Cutting her fetters with my sword I led her quietly to a divan that chanced to be near, the Bedouins crowding close about but chivalrously keeping hands off her.

"Be not afraid," I said as gently as I could when she had recovered a little. "We will do thee no harm."

She answered something in broken Arabic which I did not understand, and presently, professing herself better, she was escorted back the way we had come. The Bedouins, whispering among themselves, appraised the value of her rich attire of silk and gold and jewels; but as for me, I speculating what the trembling creature was, and how she could have drifted there.

Meanwhile, Suleiman had captured the queen, who, as he informed me with a chuckle, was worth more than all the rest put together.

CHAPTER XXV.

THE INDIAN PRINCESS PROVES A SOURCE OF MYSTERY.

THERE was still much to be done, and need of haste in doing it; but Suleiman's first duty was to provide for the safety of the ladies.

"Ye shall come with us, ye lovely ones," he said, addressing them with the grand air of a born cavalier, "and we will make you secure from the fury of man. Far have we come to deliver you from ruthless hands and ignoble bondage."

"And who instructed thee in our condition?" demanded the Circassian, flashing with queenly rage. "Thy deliverance, methinks, will be slavery, thy care a perpetual evil."

"Sweet rose of the garden," replied Suleiman, "it becometh not thy beauty to be in a tempest. Thy lord is far from hence, my beauteous one, and his return to thy lovely bosom uncertain. Wherefore shouldst thou tarry here to be abased?"

"There can be no worse abasement than going with thee," she snapped. "Leave us to such chance as fate may bring; and get ye gone, for ye are but portionless Bedouins of the desert."

"Nay," answered Suleiman, more insinuatingly than ever. "We cannot leave what hath enraptured our eyes. Make thyself old and ugly, my charmer, and we will fly from thy presence. But while thou puttest the rose and lily to shame, thou must blame Heaven, not us, if we refuse to depart without thee. And now, my adorable, there is business going on in which I must bear a hand. Will my queen therefore deign to accompany us to a place of safety, where she may be guarded from harm?"

The lady would have broken out again; but Suleiman had no more time to waste on words—

"Conduct thy mistress, the queen, and her fair companion, the gem of India, whither we lead," he said, turning sharply upon Baruk. "Is there a spot of safety about this nether pit?"

"It is as my lord seeth," answered Baruk.

Suleiman considered for a moment, then turned again to the ladies.

"Have the lights of Amood's eyes any possessions they would fain carry with them," he inquired with a courtly smile—"trinkets, jewels, costly robes? Methinks they must have. And we will ourselves help them to collect their riches. Stay ye here while we search."

Accordingly, although the queen declared vociferously they had no wish but to see the last of us, they were consigned to the care of a strong guard, of which I was one, while the rest, under the guidance of Baruk, went in search of valuables. They returned after a little with many sparkling caskets full of precious gems; loads of various stuffs of a richness unsurpassed; camel's-hair cloaks, elaborately in-wrought with gold; Indian silks of manifold dyes and patterns; Khorassan brocades; bundles of rugs and shawls; and sashes enough to furnish ten regiments of sheiks; and, more important than all, two more of the principal ladies of the household.

"Just one thing more ere we depart," said Suleiman gleefully. "There is enough of the wine of Shiraz to float a thousand ships, and, by the Prophet's beard, we go not without a share of it."

They went off again, presently coming back laden, till they groaned, with skin bottles of many sizes bursting with wine.

The burdens were set down, and Suleiman looked with joy at the pile, and from the pile to the ladies, and from the ladies back at the pile.

"It is good," he remarked. "Said I not that Amood was a mighty benefactor of his kind? There is enough here to make the black tents merry for a year."

But it was a hard question how to get all this plunder away. We had won it by force, and by force might lose it; for in such adventures as looting castles, property changes hands with unreckonable celerity.

. Suleiman stepped to the latticed window, sent it into shivers, and looked down. We were on the outer wall of the castle, and our beasts could not be far off. Suleiman's face beamed.

"There be ropes where riches so much abound, my gazelle?" he said, turning to Baruk.

"Yea, my lord."

"Take him, and bring a rope, Ali," said Suleiman to a man at his side. "Two, if thou canst find them. And make thy best speed."

Ali and Baruk were out of sight in a moment, and Suleiman went on with his instructions.

"And thou, Ibrahim, my trusty right hand, take with thee three others, cleave your way down to where we left our horses, and tell our fellows to bring them under this window; the matter will be easy. Get camels, too, if ye can lay hands on them, and our fair ones would ride the easier in litters. I will swing a lamp in the window as a signal to thee, and forget not, good Ibrahim, to make haste."

"I will not forget," said Ibrahim, choosing his companions.

In a few minutes, Ali and Baruk were back with two stout ropes, which were made fast to two spear-heads driven into the floor.

"We will slip down these quicker than the angels came down Jacob's ladder," remarked Suleiman, throwing the loose ends out of the window. "Now, my good Ibrahim, do not tarry."

Ibrahim did not tarry. Even sooner, I think, than was expected by our impatient leader, there was a sound of grunting and snorting, and low voices in the darkness underneath that made him smile.

"Art thou there, Ibrahim?" called Suleiman, softly.

"I am here," answered Ibrahim in the same tone.

"And four camels, by the memory of the great Saad.* How didst thou find them, my gay one?"

"By taking their keepers unawares, and sending them swiftly to the Prophet's bosom," replied Ibrahim.

"Malec will seethe thee in fiery brimstone for thy good deeds, Ibrahim," chuckled Suleiman.

Chattels and ladies were lowered, the latter not without difficulty, for three were timid and the fourth rebellious; but Suleiman, who was experienced and expeditious in such matters, had soon the whole four, as he expressed it, in Ibrahim's bosom below. Then slipping down ourselves, and hurriedly forming a circle about our spoils, we thrust and cut a way to the comparative quiet of an orchard, where the goods were loaded and the ladies provided with litters. This care was taken not so much for their comfort as that they might depreciate as little as possible in value.

We had not finished when dense volumes of smoke were seen ascending from the castle.

"What the Bedouin leaves the flames will have," remarked one of the men, as a sudden blaze lit up the sky.

"Idiots!" growled Suleiman, who intended to go back for more plunder. And in the next breath,

* A notorious Arab freebooter.

"Mother of the Prophet, listen to the roaring and the rushing! Our kindred will be about us like clouds of hornets; it is time to be away."

If we wished to hold our own it was time. So, mounting in the light of the burning pile, we made off with all speed.

It was not easy to escape from that whirlpool of destruction and keep our plunder intact. At the start we had to fight our way step by step, and at times the handling was so rough and the odds so heavy that it seemed we must lose all we had captured. But we kept well together, and partly by strategy, partly by a free and active use of steel, we got out at last with no more serious mishap than the loss of a little blood. To that we were by this time accustomed, and it did not hurt our spirits, though one man—evidently a recent addition to the band—made much ado about a couple of broken ribs till he was laughed and ridiculed out of his complaints.

We made straight for the desert as our safest retreat, never drawing rein till the sun was well up, and we were once more alone. Then we halted to refresh ourselves with some of the good things provided by Amood Sinn. But before there was either eating or drinking Suleiman drew up the band and made a little speech.

"We have with us four princesses as beautiful as the morning and as soft as the dove," he said, making a salaam towards the litters. "We value the gifts of Heaven, and my purpose in speaking is to let it be known that, by my life, the man who layeth a profane finger on these fair ones shall die the death of a dog. I am ready to deal with any man who disputeth that condition. But lest your hearts rebel, know there is much to comfort us. We shall feast, my merry ones. Yea, eat and drink in honour of our victories. There is a sweet savour already in my nostrils. Here are rivers of the wine of Shiraz, and bread baked in the ovens of Amood. Heaven protect him in his adversity!"

The company applauded and fell merrily to eating and drinking; the men squatted on the ground beside their horses: the women chastely withdrawn in their litters and attended by the obsequious Baruk.

The meal was not over when Suleiman and Ibrahim were discussing our next movement. Much was said in a low voice about pilgrims and caravans and the pecuniary value of ladies such as we happened to possess; and though I did not hear all, yet, by putting two and two together, I understood that more robberies were in the wind. In short, the pious of the Moslem world were then making the annual pilgrimage, and we were bent on relieving them of some of their superfluous wealth.

The caravan on which we were anxious to bestow our attentions was the one that, starting from Yemen, proceeds by the mountain course to Taif. As we knew almost to a day the date at which it would appear, we could post ourselves satisfactorily and await its coming with composure. The place of reception was in the heart of the mountains, in a deep and ugly defile where two camels could scarcely walk abreast, and a caravan could be harried with impunity. We rode hard, gained our position in good time, hid like foxes among the rocks, and prayed that the Hadjis would not tarry. While waiting their arrival I had an experience that would be worth a fortune to a story-teller.

The sun had set and the night had closed in rather dark. I had been attending to my mare, and was returning to my companions, when Baruk, sidling up with an air of profound mystery, whispered that the Indian princess wished to have speech with me.

"But beware how thou goest," he said, "a score of lances would be sheathed in thy body if thou wert caught talking to her in secret."

"What does she want with me, Baruk?" I inquired softly.

"She will tell thee. Follow me," he answered, gliding into the darkness.

The danger and the mystery were of course an irresistible incentive, and I immediately turned after him. We found the princess crouching behind a big stone, having by some pretence managed to get away from the other women. Saluting her quietly, I told her I was at her service; but instead of answering me she turned to Baruk.

"Good, good Baruk," she said in the sweetest of voices, and in broken Arabic, "gracious Baruk, go back to the litters. Say I am praying to the night; it is a custom with my people; it is a rite, say a rite, my Baruk. Fear not, I will return to thee. He," indicating me, "will keep me safe."

Baruk looked a little dubious, but he went.

"Thou art a stranger in this land," she said to me quickly, when we were alone. "In India we see thy people; but this is not India. Thy face made my heart leap in the palace. Art one of the robbers?— what do people call them?"

"Bedouins."

"Yea, that is it. Art one of them?"

A man must not trust himself unreservedly to the first minx he meets, so I answered warily. But her eager intelligence found all she wanted in my reply.

"See, I take thy hand and kiss it—so," seizing my hand and putting it to her lips. "It is sin in our religion. But I have been taught. I am a daughter of the holy Prophet; but there is more than one road to Heaven. Is that not good truth?"

I had to admit it was fairly good truth, and excellent Christian doctrine.

"Yea, yea, I know," she went on quickly, and her voice was getting thrilling with suppressed emotion. "I have been taught—more than one road to Heaven —that is what thy people say. Now listen—dost know we are guilty of a great big sin, and the big knife would cut off thy head if eyes discovered us; but thy people are brave. Art afraid?" she asked, coming so close I could hear the quick beating of her heart.

There was a rustle behind, and she turned, holding her breath.

"It is only Baruk," she said, much relieved. "Good Baruk, just a little space longer; tell them, if they ask thee, that I am safe. Thou comest from far across the sea—people call it England," she continued, turning back to me.

More and more puzzled, I admitted she was right.

"I knew," she said, with an eagerness in which pleasure and pain were mingled. "Thy face proclaimeth thy country. I know thy people—yea, one is—but never mind; that is too fast. Listen, art thou going to remain with the robbers, the Bedouins?"

Baruk came creeping back again, declaring she would be missed, and he slain.

"Thou shalt go straight to Paradise, Baruk," she replied, soothingly. "Just one little space more."

And he went away again.

"Now, art thou going to stay?"

"Not if I can help it," I blurted, almost without knowing what I said.

"That is good," she said, with a little rocking motion of delight. "There is not time to tell everything now. If thou goest, take me with thee. Let them not keep me to do their will—pollution, that is it. Thou wilt save me, and I will love thee—for ever. Listen, I was performing the pilgrimage; they captured the caravan, and slew my father. There was one—but there is not time to tell it. It was Amood Sinn that was wicked, and now I know he hath been punished, because his palace is in ashes. A battle perchance. Wert thou in it?"

I answered in the affirmative, getting ever deeper involved in the mysteries surrounding this strange woman.

"And didst thou see one there like thyself?—Hush! hush!"

Baruk came again, saying he would risk his life for us no longer.

"Good Baruk, thou wilt not die," said my companion. "One turn more—one little turn, that is it. The night is cool; thy mind will be at ease."

"Thou wilt have me speared like a goat," he demurred. Nevertheless he left us once more.

"There is another caravan coming," pursued my companion, breathlessly, "I heard it from Baruk; let us join in. Trust Baruk for his love of gold. I will trust thee in honour of thy people." And she was lost in the darkness like a shadow.

I returned to my place, and presently got a word with Baruk.

"What is this strange thing that the Indian princess sayeth?" I asked, putting my mouth close to his ear, for there was need of dead secrecy.

"Nay, I am not a magician," he answered with the oily evasiveness of the Oriental who is chary about committing himself.

"Let us have no pretence of ignorance," I said, feigning anger. "What does she mean?"

"My lord frighteneth me."

The voice of Suleiman was heard calling for some one; and in the same instant the fires leaped up, emitting a fitful light which admonished us to be careful. If we were caught consulting, our lives would not be worth ten minutes' purchase.

"Look here, Baruk," I said, "I am thy friend. What is the state of affairs? Tell it clearly."

"May I never be in such a position again," groaned Baruk. "Hark you, we deal with treachery and cruel lances. What is our blood? Nothing. What is the spoil and the price of these women? Everything. Yet we talk of that which, were it known, would make us dead men on the spot."

My thoughts were exactly like his; but a woman had asked my aid, and I could not refuse it. Besides what love or allegiance did I owe the Bedouins?

"Freedom is more than life," I said, with an audacity that was not entirely genuine. "We must not be timorous. Now look you, I am a stranger. Thinkest thou I came here to rob? We help ourselves, good Baruk, in helping the Indian princess."

"She hath untold riches; she can recompense," murmured Baruk. "Yet perchance when she was safe, she would forget us."

"And if thou remainest here, art not thou a bondman for ever? Nay, who is to hinder these fellows from taking thee out into the desert, and stripping thee naked, and leaving thee so that when the wolves were done with thy bones, they would be the sport of the winds?"

"There is much in what thou sayest."

Suleiman was calling again, and more impatiently than before.

"I will speak with thee again," whispered Baruk, hurriedly. "It is not safe now." And the darkness swallowed him.

Sauntering carelessly back to the fires, which burned red and low now, I threw myself on the ground to ruminate on all I had just heard.

We were riotously merry. There was an abundance, indeed a superabundance of food, wine flowed like water in the rainy season, and the coffee and tobacco were the best on earth.

Suleiman rising presently, went to see that the ladies were being properly attended, and came back praising the wondrous docility of the Indian princess. I smoked, looking up at the brightness of Orion, and said nothing. But in my heart was the quivering exultation of the schemer who has important business on hand, and knows that failure is death.

My next move was to enlighten Tabal. It was done in a few words, for now that the heavens were bright, the chance of private talk was small. But Tabal quickly understood all, and fervently swore a vow of fealty. To Tabal's mind there was but one serious difficulty in our project of escape.

"We go with the caravan to Mecca?" he said.

"Assuredly; it will do us all good."

"But thou art not of our religion.   Think what that meaneth."

"I am a better Mohammedan than thyself, good Tabal.   There will not be in the Great Mosque a more devout Hadji than the comrade whom thou callest Christian.   Are we not brothers?   Did not thy father put the light of the Koran into my soul?   Dost thou think I am careless about getting to Heaven?   Tabal, I will do the pilgrimage as a follower of the Prophet."

Tabal was convinced, and we parted to ignore each other very studiously for the rest of the night.

Near the dawn, when the world was black, and men were heavy, Baruk returned to me.   He had got over his wavering, and was ready for the most desperate exploit.

"We will put on the green turban* together, Baruk," I said joyfully, after listening to his promise of help. "Now tell me the name of our princess."

"They call her Ranéé."

"A pretty name," I remarked.   "Let us make her happy."

Thereupon, as briefly and minutely as possible with words, I gave him instructions both for Ranéé and for himself.   Fortunately, the simplicity of the plan of attack enabled us to make our arrangements with confidence and tolerable accuracy.

With the first blink of light, we were on the look out for the caravan; but the day had worn well into the afternoon before our scouts brought word it was at the mouth of the defile.   At the intelligence that it was coming we settled down in our hiding-place, as still as dead men, the horses being kept some distance behind, lest they should neigh and betray us. Tabal and I had many unsuspected thoughts, but as it would be unwise to express them, and it was impossible to communicate with either Ranéé or Baruk, we could only wait in silent eagerness and faith.

The pilgrims sent forward a party of half a dozen

* The badge or sign of such as have performed the pilgrimage to Mecca.

horsemen, and we were ordered further back. Suleiman himself, with one companion to act as messenger, remained to observe, their place of vantage being
the hollow top of a great rock which projected, causing a curve in the path below. Lying there flat, they
had an almost uninterrupted view of the pass, and by
deft clambering, the messenger could reach our ambush without fear of detection.

To keep us keen, and in touch with what was going
on, Suleiman sent frequently to tell us of the movements of the horsemen. We learned that passing
right beneath his hiding-place, they rode to the head
of the gorge, looked dutifully about among the rocks,
and discovering nothing, returned light-heartedly to
report the way clear. Then the caravan, wishing
no doubt to get to open ground again as speedily as
might be, swung its huge length into the defile, and
came trailing on like an endless serpent.

Suleiman, watching it closely, sent back word to
look to our horses and arms, as the prospect was glorious beyond his experience. A little later the order
for action made the blood race in our veins. Half of
us were to go to the foot of the gorge, and half to the
head, so that the pilgrims might be engaged simultaneously in front and rear, and so the readier induced
to relinquish a part of their superabundant riches.
The response was as prompt as might be expected of
men whose notion of Heaven is eternal plundering.
Almost before the words of command were out of the
messenger's mouth, we were clattering off into sun-
less chasms, and by beetling archways, and up and
down dizzy steeps that only robbers with no soul to
save, would have faced. Tabal and I were of those
who went to the foot, and fervently we prayed the pilgrims might have a good courage, and open arms for
distressed strangers.

In the course of a break-neck ride, we came often
into violent contact, and in one of the collisions, while
pretending vehement anger at the rough usage, I
managed to get a word in Tabal's ear.

20

"Whatever happens, let us stick to each other," I said, in a quick aside. "Our signal for the dash is when we see Baruk and Ranéé descending among the rocks."

"Never leech clung as I will cling to thee," answered Tabal. And then he began to abuse his horse for the son of a mule that couldn't keep his feet in a plain road; and the Bedouins, being closely occupied, saw or suspected nothing.

Reaching the bottom before the pilgrims were quite ready for us, we had to halt behind a bluff. The tail of the caravan still wriggled outside the mouth of the pass, and it would be folly to attack till it had disappeared after the body. While waiting, Ibrahim, our captain, gave his instructions briefly and pointedly. We were to rush the camel-men, throw them into utter confusion, seize as many laden animals as we could lay hands on, and make off with them to the rear as fast as steel could urge them. Such as were free would protect the others, but as many as could were to pounce on some piece of property. In short, our business was more to pillage than to fight, and if the pilgrims were not unreasonable not a man of them need lose his life.

With beating hearts and a burning impatience we kept still till the tail should have wriggled itself into the mountain cleft. As if to try our self-control, our watchers were constantly reporting that the moment for the onset had come, and then immediately contradicting themselves, to reaffirm their first intelligence the next minute. This went on until we were in a fever, and ready to rush from our concealment at all hazards. As for Tabal and me, if you have ever lain in wait with the merest chance between life and death and a frantic desire to try it, you will understand our feelings. Being apart, we could not so much as exchange a whisper, and all we had to restrain and encourage us were the muttered curses and comments of our comrades. Once a horse of keen scent neighed, and Ibrahim nearly felled the brute, thinking we were betrayed; but the tail continued to wriggle slowly on, and we breathed again. Then word came that the last man was within the pass; the next moment we were in the open and galloping furiously to the attack.

CHAPTER XXVI.

THE HOLY CITY.

THE rush was made strictly according to orders, with preconceived, that is to say, perfectly satisfactory results. Shouting "Techbir! techbir!" at the pitch of our voices, we dashed through the mouth of the defile hard upon the tail of the caravan, discharging our pieces and whirling our lances with the sudden inappeasable fury in which the Bedouin in a foray has no equal. The point of the tail crumpled up like a feather at a fierce fire, and, as we smote and seized, yelling the while to keep up the panic, there were responsive noises in front that told the cavaran had come to an involuntary halt to be robbed.

What followed the onset I could not tell in detail if I were to be examined on oath, for I had many things to think of, and thieving was the last and least of them. I saw the Hadjis jumbled together in the centre like an ice-jam in a river. I saw two clumps of spears, one in front and one behind, flashing viciously in the sun; and I saw many camels going swiftly out of the mouth of the pass in charge of new owners. These salient facts the eye took in unconsciously, without the ability to catch minute particulars.

I got the impression that the Hadjis offered but feeble resistance, and that, as I subsequently learned, was true. There is a reason for everything, and the pilgrims had a valid one for preferring their lives to their property. Human nature being sinful in spite of Prophet and Koran, caravans start expecting to be plundered, nor fail to make provision accordingly. Immemorial custom and experience have taught the Hadji that it is the will of Heaven he should suffer loss at the hands of wicked men in the performance of the prime religious duty of life. Moreover, the pious Mohammedan, on his way to the Holy City, has such an aversion to broils and bloodshed, that he would rather sacrifice a fair portion of his worldly goods than present himself at the Prophet's shrine with red hands. These things the astute Bedouin knows and profits by; the time of the pilgrimage is his harvest, and he reaps with a wide sickle.

That knowledge was acquired afterwards. Just then I had personal concerns which precluded the gathering of information. How were Tabal and I to make good our desertion in the face of so much bristling steel, backed by such savage fury? That was the pressing matter. As the crucial moment drew near the attempt seemed more and more desperate, nay, it seemed hopeless. I did not forget that we were following a woman's idea, and at that time (Heaven forgive me) I had but a mean opinion of the wisdom of the sex as a whole. The situation was of the sort that gives one a shivering in the back though the sun may be hot. So soon as we should show a sign of defection, the Bedouin lances would be after us, and in case we were caught, would stab without mercy. That was certain. Had it been equally certain how the Hadjis would receive us the matter would be simple or, at any rate, simplified. But our reception was, to put the best face on it, exceedingly doubtful, for the Arab, be he Bedouin or pilgrim, is ever sniffing for treachery and suspecting he smells it.

Another difficulty was that we could not make the dash at the most opportune moment for ourselves. We must wait for Ranéé and Baruk, and the waiting, as I was but too ready to whisper to myself, was not unlikely to be fatal. They who depended on a woman in such an affair were leaning on a broken reed. That was my feeling one moment. The next, I am glad to say, I was ashamed of it. Yet the fact stared me in the face that if Ranéé and Baruk did not come quickly our chance would be gone; we might go back with the children of the desert to shame and cruelty and violence, and it might be to lasting bondage.

The band had already distrained more than the legitimate tax—that is to say, had taken all the loose camels—and were pressing on for more than their dues, for, having the right of the strong, they were hard to satisfy.

Tabal and I, for unsuspected reasons, were well to the front, and could be minutely observed by the plundered, a circumstance that might tell awkwardly against us later on. What was keeping the idiotic Baruk? Had the coward rued his promise? If so, by all we held dear, dearly would he pay for it. We were very hot with fighting and seizing and shouting, and two of us were beginning to have tremours of despair, when at last, as we were retiring with our booty, Tabal's sharp eye espied two skulking figures slippng craftily down among the rocks. By this time the Hadjis, animated by the spirit of the wronged, were behaving in a way calculated to alarm those who meant presently to appeal to their humanity. Baruk and Ranéé made their appearance at the very worst moment. But there was no time to grumble or make comments. We must take fortune as we found it, and redeem our pledges or die.

So I gave Tabal the word, and reversing our spears to indicate we were not hostile, we drove the spurs into our horses, and bounded from among the Bedouins, calling out we were Hadjis, and praying for protection. At the same time we drew attention by pointing and shouting to the two clambering down the rocks.

Thinking, as indeed they well might, that this was but a ruse to get their ranks broken, the pilgrims hurriedly formed up, presenting a front of levelled spears and gun barrels, and faces which said plainer than any language that we advanced at the peril of our lives. And as they stood close together to receive us, there went up a diabolic shout behind; we glanced back with freezing blood to see a dozen of our late comrades at our heels, with lance shafts hugged after the manner of men resolved to slay.

The moment that followed was such as a man recalls in his sleep, with a horrid cold sweat, and a creeping of the flesh, and groanings and writhings. In front was a gleaming hedge of steel, forbidding, impenetrable; behind was more steel, already poised to strike by men to whom revenge was as blood to the lion. Half a moment more and we should be fuller of holes than a fisherman's net.

"Save us! Save us!" we screamed. "We are no enemies; but friends. For the love of the Prophet, take us in!"

There was not the twentieth part of a second to decide. The pilgrims looked swiftly from us to our pursuers. The steel hedge opened, we shot through, and it closed quickly again as the Bedouins wheeled within a yard of it, brandishing their lances, and screeching vengeance. They stood awhile vociferating, then, vowing they would yet give us to the vultures, slowly retired to look after their booty.

Meantime, Ranée and Baruk were scrambling down with the breathless haste of fear, straight upon the centre of the caravan, as being the point remotest from the Bedouins. We spoke earnestly for them, but indeed they required no pleader, their own distracted manner being ample evidence of their need. As the descent was extremely hazardous, I hurried forward to assist Ranéé, and as I ran some shots were fired from above. Poor Ranéé gave a little scream, and, losing her hold, came toppling into my arms. I put her gently on the ground, thinking she must have been hit; but a cursory examination showed she suffered from nothing worse than fright.

Baruk, however, did not escape so easily. Some of the flying slugs found a billet in his left arm, and the good man being unaccustomed to pain, cried out till the gorge rang with his wailings. But there was little opportunity to console him, for the children of the desert, having levied their tax and been balked in their revenge, had disappeared like water in sand, and the caravan was ordered to proceed. So the great snake stretched out its cumbrous length once more, making what haste it could to quit such ugly quarters. Ranéé clung to me like a scared child, murmuring how good I was, and wondering, with many ejaculations that were strange to me, if we were yet safe. I did what I could to encourage her, till a venerable man with a long white beard and a compassionate manner, thinking she might be better elsewhere, led her off to the company of her own sex.

No questions were asked of us strangers till the caravan halted safe on the open plain. Then, while fires were being lighted, we were taken before some of the chief men, and requested to give an account of ourselves. Tabal, who was a plausible fellow, with a ready invention, got through the ordeal quickly and well; but I had more trouble in proving myself a pious Mohammedan of the name of Fahd Walid. I was sore driven, and lied like an epitaph, praying the Lord to aid me. I hope I shall be forgiven, seeing what was at stake. Perhaps it was owing to my face, or it may have been from some defect in my accent; but one scurvy priest, who was the most active of the inquisitors, made a point at the beginning of doubting all I said.

"Art thou not a heretic unbeliever?" he asked, bending a pair of uncommonly sharp black eyes on me. "Art not thou an enemy of our holy religion, a scoffer, an infidel? Here, what sayest thou?" he demanded of Tabal. "Is not this fellow an unbeliever?"

"*As Lahek Allah*, may Heaven set you right," replied Tabal, with a rapt and pious expression. "Surely never man knew his Koran better."

"We will see," said the priest.

Whereupon, whipping out his Hamail or greasy

pocket copy of the sacred volume, he began to cate·
chize me with the air of one who would say, "Now
you shall see me do up this heretic."

But in my enforced leisure I had not studied the
Koran in vain.   To every question came a pat answer
in the very words of the Prophet himself, till the
priest, first amazed, then softened, and finally convinced, thrust the book back into his bosom, and embraced me as a true believer.

"*Marhaba! marhaba!* welcome! welcome!" he
said with a fervour more embarrassing than his doubt.
"I crave thy pardon for my distrust.   Thou art indeed
a worthy follower of our holy Prophet.   Would that
all his sons knew his words so well.   And now, sit
thee down.   *El hamdu l' Illah*, praise be to Heaven,
it hath fallen to our lot to rescue a believer from the
fangs of these wolves.   *Semmo* (eat)."   And forthwith we all set to work with an appetite that the exercise with the Koran had in no wise dulled.

It required constant watchfulness, however, to preserve me from lapsing into Christian barbarities and
heathenisms.   Even Tabal had to be kept out of my
inner secrets; and as to Ranéé, though I doubted not
her desire to be secret, I had a careful remembrance
of the natural weakness of a woman's tongue.

Once satisfied with our credentials, the pilgrims
made us one of themselves.   When we spoke of their
kindness to strangers, their answer was ever the
same—

"Think ye it is the will of God that any true believer should be left to perish on the way to the Holy
City?   At the gathering of the nations, when the
angels shall render their accounts of men's deeds, both
good and bad, what would be our recompense if we
were guilty of such a thing?"   And somehow it seemed
to me the spirit was one that Christians who boast of
their charity might occasionally imitate with advantage.

We travelled fast, and made our destination without loss by sickness or violence.   No Bedouin molested

us, because we were two thousand strong, and our way lay through the open where the wily children of the desert seldom attack. We went by arid strips and fertile pasture lands, among flocks and herds and herdsmen that are to-day as they were in the days of the patriarchs, and appear not to miss the blessings of civilization. We paid extortionate tolls to legalized robbers for allowing us to pass where all the world was free; and we halted for refection and prayers beside pleasant wells, that were in no fanciful sense the eye of the landscape.* And ever as we drew nearer the Holy City, the pace increased and the enthusiasm grew. We smote ourselves on the breast, ejaculating fervid passages of the Koran, and many would fain have dismounted and run, so ardent and inspiring was their joy.

At last, one evening, as we were winding among short stony ravines that edged a verdurous plain, the leaders raised an ecstatic shout, and the rest of the caravan crushing forward, with glittering eyes and a hubbub of shrill noises, beheld in a sort of valley below them the minarets of Mecca gleaming in the sun like a thousand points of fire, the Great Mosque being conspicuous in the midst.

We descended like an avalanche in a storm of dust, every Moslem of us beside himself with joy and awe and excitement; some praying, some sobbing, some shouting, some frantically beating their breasts and plucking at their robes as if to tear them to tatters, others unconsciously spurring their horses and prodding their camels to the imminent risk of many lives, and all behaving like people in a frenzy. Reaching the foot of the declivity, we burst into such a scene of commotion as could greet human eye and ear nowhere else under the wide cope of heaven.

We talk of Babel, but the credit of the real confusion of tongues belongs to Mecca. There were a hundred thousand strangers in the city, and, judging by

* The Bedouin, living mostly among torrid sands, very appropriately calls water "the eye of the landscape."

the ear, ten times as many tongues and dialects.
There were faces of every imaginable hue and shape,
from every known clime; and costumes that only a
mad tailor could realize in delirious visions of the
night. The elect of the believers were there from Turkey and Greece, from China and Barbary and Tim-
buctoo, from Egypt, Palestine, and the dark heart of
Africa, from Persia and the regions of the Indus,
from Hindustan, Malacca, and the Asiatic Isles; and
from many far-separated places besides, gathered at
incalculable cost and indescribable trouble and discomfort to worship according to the doctrines of Islam.

Yet the tumult was certainly not such as one asso-
ciates with religious festivals. Men using the language of troopers in a rage were hauling wildly at
apathetic camels that appeared to have an insupera-
ble bias in favour of standing still, and straining
titanically to stuff them in holes and corners that could
not possibly accommodate anything larger than a cat;
horses were rearing and backing and dancing, their
owners the while threatening each other with instant
death; ladies were screaming in fear of having their
litters upset and their sacred beauty exposed to the
public gaze; householders and visitors wrangled and
gesticulated as to the value of lodgings, and over all
were a million ear-splitting cries that seemed to rise
out of the very earth.

We did not a little ourselves to add to the din and
confusion; for we had a goodly number of beasts to
dispose of, and voluble tongues in our heads to argue
against the obstinacy of man and brute. It took several hours of arduous pulling and pushing and vociferating to get ourselves and our belongings housed;
but the enterprise was at length accomplished, just
as the sun, the only street lamp of Mecca, was dropping out of sight. Then, having dined sumptuously
on roast fowl, eggs, bread, and coffee—rare delicacies
after the hard fare of the desert—we lay down, to
dream of the great things that were before us.

Anxious to show ourselves patterns of piety, Tabal

and I lost no time in assuming the ihram, as a special
mark and declaration of our devoutness, taking care
to bathe and perfume ourselves in the strictest manner of the orthodox before putting it on. This famous
garment consists of two pieces of linen cloth, one of
which is wrapped about the loins like a Highland
kilt, and the other thrown over the upper part of the
body in such a way as to leave the right arm uncov-
ered. As no other garment, not even so much as a
covering for the head, is permitted while it is worn,
it makes an airy dress, specially in the evening
and early morning, when the Mecca air is often as
shrewd as that of Edinburgh.

Thus habited, we made our way to the Beitullah,
or temple, a magnificent and imposing building, with
more gates and galleries and courts and domes and
colonnades and arches, and marble, granite, and por-
phyry pillars than I had time to count.* It is con-
trived for vast multitudes of people, and the space is
all too small. Ranée we were obliged to leave in the
porch with a great crowd of her own sex; for the Moslem will allow no woman, however beautiful or pious
or exalted, to set foot in his temple. Thus the Mohammedan ladies, less fortunate than their Christian
sisters, are denied the privilege of displaying and
studying the latest fashions in church.

Inside, the pavements were full of men in every
posture of rapt devotion, some kneeling, some sitting
with bent heads, others prostrate on the floor. At
sight of these we stopped for one minute, bowing low
and uttering a prayer, then, with a solemn measured
step, we advanced five abreast upon the Caaba, keeping our eyes fast upon it. On reaching it, we stopped
again; but only for an instant. Proceeding at the
same pace as before, we went round it seven times,
reciting certain prescribed verses from the Koran, only

---

*These things are troublesome to remember after the lapse
of half a century; but, on refreshing my memory, I find that
the temple has 19 gates, that the pillars number 552, and the
domes 152. Most of the pillars are of marble.—A. G.

we interrupted ourselves at each round to kiss the
Black Stone, which, as all believed, was brought direct from Heaven by the angel Gabriel.   This was no
easy thing to do; for the worshippers crushed forward
heedless of the frailty of human ribs, or the tenderness of toes, or the uncertainty of tempers.   Consequently, the rite resolved itself into something very
like a scrimmage, to the great detriment of our persons and our piety.   At the end we broke into wild
ululations, as if lamenting the death of an empire;
but presently I discovered that we were not lamenting; we were praising.

Having done our duty by the Caaba and the Black
Stone, we turned to the Zem-zem—that is to say, the
holy well which God miraculously created for the outcast Hagar and her son, the father of the children of
the desert.   We drank of its waters, and washed in
them (for the benefit of succeeding Hadjis), but there
was one pilgrim, at least, who would have taken a
draught of Epsom salts with more relish.   The Zem-
zem may be good to wash in, but it is not good to
drink from; a fact which the Arabs themselves tacitly
acknowledge by refraining from partaking of its waters oftener than once a year.   Leaving the Zem-zem,
we broke again into plangent cries, hoping, as I fancied, to frighten the devil by sheer force of lung.

My pen halts in trying to describe with any ade-
quacy the thoughts and feelings with which I went
through those exhausting and singular ceremonies.
Curiosity and contempt and awe and fear and bewilderment were mingled, and now the one was dominant and now the other.   As a sound Christian I could
not help regarding much of the ritual as no better
than mere mummery and the zeal little above fanaticism.   Yet it was impossible to look on the strained,
yearning, often tearful faces; the prostrate bodies,
crowding every available inch of floor; the supplicating hands and eyes; and listen to the vehement out-
pourings of self-accusation, the frantic pleadings and
petitions, without a solemn emotion, nay, without

something of the genuine reverence and uplifting of the soul, which are of the very essence of religion.

My conviction of the general depravity of the Arab was fixed and immovable. He had redeeming qualities (I had proved them), but I could not forget his serpent ways, his profound duplicity, his unfathomable guile, his habitual dishonesty, the deadliness of his hatred, and the often still greater deadliness of his friendship; and the balancing of his character, the weighing of the good in him against the bad, left a heavy debit of iniquity to his account. He might be the most penitent of sinners in the mosque, but in his favourite haunts and following his native bent he would continue to cheat, steal, kill; and his boasted honour (which at times is surprising) was a ragged cloak that rather revealed than concealed his inherent wickedness. Take him how you would he was an unsavoury egg.

Yet there was no denying the moving force of his fervour in ceremonial worship. He prays with a mastery of soul and heart, a fiery ecstasy and exaltation, a superb spirituality of speech and look and gesture that the sober Christian, who takes his dose of religion regularly and calmly once in seven days, and who would sooner forfeit all chance of gaining Paradise than be guilty of the impropriety of getting excited about his soul, cannot even faintly imagine. When he puts on sackcloth and ashes—shaving his head, making his countenance the very mirror and image of grief, demeaning his tawny, half-naked body as if to ensure perpetual remembrance of its debased origin and ultimate fate—and, with confessions of his sin and nothingness, cries aloud for mercy, the Moslem would wring tears of compassion and forgiveness from the grimmest of dungeon walls. And when he turns to praise and promises, the dungeon would be irradiated as with flashes of celestial light.

I observed that he is profoundly affected in his devotions by the spirit of rivalry. Jealous of being surpassed in religious display, his piety, when pricked by competition, developes into simple frenzy. Then the erstwhile rogue is whirled aloft to the seventh Heaven of beatitude, to be transfigured as if he held confidential communion with angels. And when he has said his prayers with ravings of self-debasement, and praised God in bursts of lyrical and spiritual rapture that seem like the continued strains of David's harp, and been purged of his sins and made a saint, he will straightway forget his vows and go blithely forth to resume his natural vocation of intrigue, lies, slitting throats, and rifling pockets. I remembered all that when he was deafening me with his repentance and enchanting me with his poetry. When he was loudest in his appeals to Heaven to preserve him from "disobedience and hypocrisy and evil conversation and evil thoughts," and to deny his "skin and his bones to the everlasting flames;" when he abjured the devil, and stormed against infidels, and wept hysterically, and flung his arms about, as it appeared, in transports of agony, and smote the pavements with his forehead, and licked and kissed the Black Stone, and did a thousand other things to prove his holiness,—my enthusiasm was tempered by a vivid and ever-present memory of his ordinary, everyday attributes.

It was tempered also by the knowledge, burned into my mind a dozen times a minute, of the sort of consideration I should receive at his hands were he to discover my true character. The slightest suspicion of my faith would inflame those fanatics to the commission of deeds that made me cold to think of. I knew the kind of charity that would move them, as well as if some one were bawling a description of it in my ear; and, while exclaiming and ejaculating to maintain my deceit, I had pictures of myself being torn and thrown to the dogs. That state of mind does not conduce to peace or the singleness of mind that should accompany religious exercises.

It increased my disquietude that I was ignorant of the forms of procedure. Tabal, like the good fellow he was, kept close to me, giving directions by look

and nod and whisper, and the Mutawwif, or official
guide, attended us; for it is not unusual for persons
doing the pilgrimage for the first time to stand in
need of instruction. But, to me, every hint seemed
a warning to beware of the hidden dagger, and often
I turned suddenly to look fear-struck into glittering
eyes and craned faces. But the ordeal was over at
last, and I breathed a secret prayer to Heaven, a fervent Christian prayer of gratitude for permitting me
to escape with a whole skin.

As soon as we were through the great door, Ranéé,
whose worship had been briefer than ours, ran to me
clasping her hands in ecstasy.

"Now verily thou art one of us, in spite of thy
English face," she said, freezing the blood in my
veins.

"For God's sake, hush!" I whispered excitedly.
"Not a syllable, as thou lovest me."

She looked hurt; but said no more, and I cast a
rapid glance round for the lurking assassin. But
Heaven was good to me again; the hubbub had
drowned Ranéé's incautious speech.

In the evening we returned to the Beitullah, and
remained until midnight repeating the scenes of the
morning. Then, the day's ceremonies being over,
we hastened to our quarters to snatch, if possible, a
few hours' repose before making the momentous journey to the holy Mount of Arafat on the morrow. I
was dead weary, yet I slept but little, so busy were
my thoughts with surging fanatics and hidden knives.

CHAPTER XXVII.

ARAFAT AND THE CAABA—TRAPPED.

WITH the first peep of day the pilgrims began to
pour out of Mecca in a processional torrent that was
characterized by everything you can think of save
the decency and order inculcated by the Christian

Apostle. It was hard to believe that this was the
crowd which had made the temple resound with
groans and supplications on the day before; hard
to believe, indeed, that we were not revellers in some
wild carnival exclusively devoted to experiments in
riotous behaviour. In that character we should certainly have distinguished ourselves. Beginning with
profane—extremely profane—songs, we proceeded by
logical sequence to shocking jests, sarcasms, personal
remarks and criticisms, bandied insults, laughter and
great shoutings. What particularly astonished me
was that the women were for the most part as rude
and wanton as the men. There were exceptions.
Ranéé was one of them. She, poor thing, trembled
and screamed, and swooned and recovered in her
shugduf; while Baruk plied a nimble tongue in reviling those who collided with him and, instead of
apologizing, made him the butt of their rough-hewn,
aggravating wit. It was a scene of such license and
levity as only followers of the Prophet in the exercise
of a religious duty could furnish. Riders dashed
into each other in pure devilment, and, lest that
agreeable diversion should stale, varied it by trying
to ride down the more pious pilgrims who performed
the journey on foot. Sometimes they succeeded, and
then there would be fierce imprecations and a sudden
flashing of steel; but before it was possible to retaliate
the offenders were charging elsewhere, with roars of
mocking laughter, and blasphemies that would have
moved the envy of the selectest barrack in the British
Empire.

There was absolutely no respect of persons. The
grandee had to bear the rude bantering and hustling
like the beggar that hung impudently to his skirts;
but the larger companies, such as the Damascus and
Baghdad caravans (the first of which must have
numbered ten thousand persons) naturally suffered
less than the detached groups, of which unfortunately
we were one. Tabal, I am sorry to say, distinguished
himself by extraordinary violence and truculency of

conduct, though it is but fair to say on his behalf
that he felt himself bound to protect me, and thus
thrust himself into many a breach that he might
otherwise have avoided. He was inconceivably
quick with his lance, using point or butt as was
handiest, and his dexterity speedily won him respect.

As time passed the riot increased, and the profanity. The collisions became more violent and frequent, the jests ranker, the personalities grosser and
closer, the curses shriller; and the freedom broke all
bounds. Giddy, intoxicated young blades, throwing
the last shreds of decency to the winds, bawled
amorous ditties by the sides of curtained litters in
which beauty swung and sighed.

"She is blooming as the sun at dawn," they would
sing, "with hair black as the midnight shades, with
Paradise in her eyes, her bosom an enchantment, and
a form waving like the tamarisk when the soft wind
blows from the soft hills of Nejd." Then there would
be cries of " Leave the fatted ass. Oh, light of my
soul, wilt thou not vouchsafe us one glimpse of thy
lovely face?" And then probably the proceedings
would be interrupted by the swooping of the fatted
ass upon the singers, who would go off howling in
merriment like the flower of sports and costermongers
returning from an English racecourse.

Some of the older pilgrims, in whose veins the tide
of life was running low, or who had uncommonly
black sins to expiate, nobly tried to read their Koran
and to pray; but so many of their companions were
possessed (temporarily, it was to be supposed) by the
devil that the attempt was a ghastly and ludicrous
mockery. At each repeated failure the pious ones
would curse their tormentors with curses that would
make the flesh of a Christian creep, but only made
the hardened Moslem yell in keener enjoyment.

We rolled through the Valley of Muna, of which
we shall hear more by-and-by, and on reaching
Muzdahlifah, a little further on, interrupted our levity
to perform the midday prayers. The change in our

21

demeanour was as wondrous as it was sudden. The most notorious rioters became as grave and solemn as sheiks and priests, and for half an hour were patterns of piety, exemplars of holiness. But no sooner was the march resumed than the spirit of revelry and profanity broke out again, to rage afresh with every species of impropriety, every sort of aggravated indecency.

During the first part of the journey I had been so much occupied in taking care of myself and my party that I had scant opportunity to note the appearance of the vast procession. But on leaving Muzdalifah we were near the rear, and so I could see the flood flowing on before us—a turbulent and disorderly stream, swollen with manifold foulnesses, yet possessing unique elements of grandeur and impressiveness. The spectacle indeed was as imposing, as picturesque, and as incongruous as the East in moments of tremendous exertion alone can furnish. The host of white-robed, bare-headed pilgrims, close packed in the centre, some reading, some praying, more laughing and shouting, and not a few gesticulating and cursing; the tattered Bedouins scurrying with brandished arms along the outskirts; the nondescript Kurd and Turkish horsemen, ostensibly soldiers of the Sublime Sultan, really banditti watching for and seizing every chance to plunder; the big white Syrian dromedaries, jingling their silver bells; the tawny camels, snapping and grunting; the horses; the mules; the asses; the shugdufs rocking and tossing like a multitude of green umbrellas in a storm; the takhtrawans of the nobles, gorgeous with scarlet and brass; and, above all, the Mahmils of Damascus and Egypt, flashing their embroideries of wrought gold in the sun—these and many minor things of surpassing strangeness made up a show which a spectator would not be likely to forget were he to exceed the years of Methuselah.

The progress was not remarkable for speed, being at the rate of some two miles an hour. We wound through the pass of the "Two Rugged Hills" in unimaginable confusion, and with tumultuous outbursts of language that must surely have grieved the listening soul of the Prophet; surged past the pillars of Alamayn, and then with a rush debouched upon an open plain to have our eyes gladdened by the sight of the Holy Mount.

At that we changed like the characters in a fairy tale. Bad language, bad behaviour, all triviality, levity, and unseemliness ceased as at the waving of a magic wand; and we lifted up our voices in a chorus of holy joy. We also wept and stretched out our hands beseechingly as if the rocks could grant us absolution. Many dropped to the ground from excitement, and several died on the spot, quietly and with beatific countenances. These, as I learned, were favourites of the Prophet, who were especially happy in being called to bliss while they were on sanctified ground. Therefore we did not lament, but rejoiced exceedingly at their timely translation to Paradise.

Being less fortunate ourselves we had to abate our divine exultation, and direct our thoughts yet a little to mundane affairs. So, being doomed to survive the first burst of devotion, we made haste to choose the best ground about Arafat for our tents.

The process of encamping was not simple nor easy; for the choice ground was small and the multitude seeking accommodation very great, and very quarrelsome; and so, with the singular consistency of the Moslem, there at the very foot of the Holy Hill we rated each other like tinkers, and contended for the best sites as fiercely as if we were fixing our habitations for the rest of our lives. After an inordinate expenditure of threats, and a reckless indulgence in bullying, the tents were at last pitched, and the booths, bazaars, and drinking-shops opened. These arrangements satisfactorily completed we proceeded to enjoy ourselves in diverse manners, the rabble bracing themselves after the fatigues of arduous spiritual exercises with araki and hemp juice from the degraded taverns of Cairo, the *élite* with the daintier sherbet and wine of Shiraz.

Religion comes on the Moslem in spasms, and with rhythmic regularity; he knows its periods of recurrence to a minute, and is deft in employing the lucid intervals. The next attack was not due for some time yet; so we surrendered ourselves to the brotherly spirit of the wassail; and let me tell you that pilgrims at the Holy Mount of Arafat need no lessons in the art and practice of conviviality. We feasted and waited for evening prayers in high feather; these over, we returned to our carousals with boisterous hilarity and appetites whetted for the grossest excess.

Night fell on a scene of unfettered animation and splendid displays. The entire encampment was one blaze of variegated light. Artfully arranged clusters of lanterns swung and scintillated about the tents, making their gold and green and scarlet flash in fitful, fascinating brilliancy; and on all sides rose the buzz and clamour of a mighty multitude following its instincts unbridled.

It was impossible to remain incurious or inactive in the midst of such festal celebrations; so, having seen that Ranéé lacked nothing, and informed Baruk that his head would answer for her safety, I prepared to explore. I was warned not to venture out, for brawls are common at Arafat, much blood being sometimes spilt there. But I was not to be denied the sights because misguided pilgrims happened to be free with their weapons. Besides, Tabal was to accompany me; and Tabal's right arm, with the proper implement to back it, was well calculated to inspire a sense of security. Accordingly, wrapping our ihrams a little closer about us, and sticking turbans on our heads (though this was contrary to law), we set forth, greatly elated at spying adventures. Tabal tapped his long, crooked dagger, laughing lightly, and I felt my pistol-hilt, half sorry that it was impossible to carry a sword.

The bazaars were already crowded with rowdy customers, who took a delight in badgering the owners, and frequently helped themselves without observing the formality of payment. In the drinking-shops blear-eyed Turks and Egyptians bawled bacchanalian songs as old as the art of making spirituous liquors, and extolled the charms of absent beauties in strains more fervid than delicate. I was struck by the strange admixture of Western or Northern habit in the actions of the drinkers. At times they embraced, at times abused each other, and then in an overwhelming access of friendship they would combine and truculently challenge the world to mortal combat. Half clad, three parts drunk, and wholly insane with excitement, these revellers were ugly fellows. Often they would come reeling out of a reeking tent, their eyes like rolling orbs of fire, their mouths spluttering with foam, and strike impartially at the first person who chanced to fall in their way. We dodged these gentlemen with all possible agility, desiring to avoid brawls. But we were not always successful, and once at least we were landed without warning in what threatened to be a serious affray. A gaunt, eagle-beaked, hollow-jawed Egyptian came lurching out of a tent, his drty fez askew, his zaabat flapping about his shrunk shanks, his arms whirling like a pair of disjointed flails. Catching sight of me he stopped, and thrust out a tongue as long as my arm.

"*Ajami! Ajami!* (Persian! Persian!)" he cried hoarsely, poising a dagger, as if to use it like a javelin. "By the beard of Aaron, thou shalt defile our tents no longer!"

He took a step forward and stumbled. In the same moment Tabal pushed me unceremoniously into the shade, without a whisper of explanation. The Egyptian recovered himself with a brutal oath, and staggered on vociferating, "Ajami! Ajami!" and flourishing his weapon with a fierce thirst for blood. I saw Tabal dart and leap like a goat, and thought he had been struck; but a sudden bellow from the Egyptian undeceived me. Before I could count five,

Tabal had me by the shoulders and round a corner into a deep shadow. We could hear the Egyptian howling with rage and pain; and Tabal chuckled.

"He hath got enough for the three days at Arafat," he observed softly.

"What do you mean, Tabal?" I said in alarm. "You have not killed him?"

"I forgot to wait and see," answered Tabal. "Come, lest his tribe be upon us. Their exceeding kindness might keep us from prayers, and that would not be forgiven."

We went our way quickly, amid a continuance of the same extraordinary sights. Here a drunken knot would be splitting their throats under the impression that they were singing; there another, quarrelling; and, between, Hadjis of austerer sanctimony, valorously but vainly trying to read the Koran and pray. Wonders encompassed us, the wonders of the Moslem qualifying for Paradise, and there is probably nothing more astonishing in this world.

Tabal proved himself a lively and entertaining companion. His tongue was never still, and his criticisms and comments were often deliciously piquant.

"Ah!" he would exclaim. "Seest thou yonder creeping Persian? He hath the heart of a coney. He need not supplicate with so long a face and so loud a voice. He is safe; the devil would not have him. Hark, now, to the outcry of that villainous Turk. By my faith, Heaven hath blessed him with the voice of my father's ass. I stopped my ears against the braying of that beast, and I tell thee the Turk excelleth him. Mark this fellow whose legs twist and twine like embracing serpents. Methinks their love cometh of too much of the juice of hemp, and his tarbush and zaabat have been put on in haste. That fellow cometh from under the shadow of the pyramids. He hath eaten crocodile, which maketh him as fleet as a gazelle when there is danger behind. And behold, also, thy dearly-beloved friend the Indian. He glideth like a fox, and pretendeth to be afraid. Yet trust not to his fear, for perchance his ihram hideth a crooked knife. And here is the tent of the Emir of Damascus. That is a thing for thee to dream about when thou art looking up at the stars in the desert. I would I were an Emir. Ho, ho! Who is he with the crooked back," he cried, in the midst of his remarks about the advantage of being an Emir—"the crooked back and the eye of flame? Methinks from his countenance he is strangely moved. Come hither, friend, and declare thy love."

I turned laughing to the person thus addressed; but at the sight of his face my laugh became a frozen stare of horror. Surely I must be mistaken: there must be a hideous error. Yet the evidence to the contrary was as plain and palpable as flesh and blood could make it. There was no mistake about those eyes and the horrible mixture of triumph and malice that lit the face with a sort of lurid duskiness. It was Abram ben Aden risen from the dead to take his revenge, which would be the more cruel for the long waiting. He had changed monstrously since our parting. He seemed twice as old as when we were together, and the once straight back was curved and gathered into a hump. But that scowling, diabolical face could belong to no other man on earth.

My first sensation was one of sheer cold horror, which clogged my feet and bound my tongue. That was succeeded by a wild impulse to rush forward, grasp his hand, and implore his forgiveness. But the very archfiend himself would have cowered and shrunk before that glare of hatred which seemed to shrivel my very soul.

He looked me all over, steadily, deliberately, up and down, head and foot, as if to assure himself of my identity. Then a smile like the red flame that licks the edge of the brooding thundercloud illumined his black countenance. It said with a fearful and benumbing plainness, "So I have found you at last, then? Well, we shall see who fares best this time." But he did not utter a word; only he laid his hand on the hilt of his dagger and gave a little nod, terrible and curdling in its significance. Having thus intimated his intentions he disappeared into the midst of a crowd of roysterers.

I stood staring after him, sick and chill, a circumstance that Tabal noted with some degree of apprehension.

"What aileth thee?" he asked with quick solicitude. "Thy face hath the colour of the dead."

"It is nothing, Tabal," I answered, "nothing," and every tone of my voice denied the truth of the words.

"Yea, there is something," he rejoined. "I know there is something."

"I tell thee there is nothing," I returned petulantly, for I resented this attempt to probe my secret.

"Thy face telleth another tale," said Tabal, stubbornly. "It is of the very hue of ashes.

At that, being weak and troubled, I broke into a spurt of anger, demanding if it was incumbent upon me to open my heart to all who chose to question me.

Tabal's black eyes flashed with injured pride.

"Thou needst not be so careful of thy secrets," he said indifferently. "I would not read them were they written on a scroll." And he turned away as if to leave me to my fate.

Then a new terror seized me. I could not lose my sole friend in that place of assassins, and so in my dismay I had called him back before I knew what I was about. He came instantly, every spark of his resentment gone, and in its place a look of anxious inquiry.

"Tabal," I said, "do not be offended with me. Thou hast judged aright. I am ill. Give me thine arm, and let us go back to our tent."

"Is that fellow with the crooked back the cause?" he asked. "Speak quickly, lest he escape."

"No shedding of blood, Tabal," I answered; "this is the Holy Mount. Come, let me lean on thee. So. Now, good Tabal, as thou lovest me, let us get to our tent."

"I like not the look of that stranger," he remarked;

and he would have pressed his questions about Abram ben Aden had I not begged of him to spare me.

Should I tell Tabal what he wanted to know, or should I keep my lips tight shut? I had learned many things during recent months, and the most important of them was the golden value of silence. Yet it seemed unfair to Tabal to deny him my confidence, and the withholding of it was certainly a fiery torture to myself. One moment I felt that I must tell him all; the next that on no account whatever must I say a word about my discovery. So, torn by conflicting resolutions, and in a feverish turmoil of speculation regarding the tactics of my enemy, I made my way to the tent.

A cup of strong coffee and the assiduous ministrations of Tabal revived me. I saw Ranéé, who observed that I was extremely white, and Baruk, who informed me with many excited gestures that a band of drunken rascals had fallen upon him, had taken liberties with him to the extent of breaking his skull and tearing the clothes off his back, and that he wanted immediate reparation. I forget the precise catastrophe that was to happen if he did not get it. These things served to lift me out of myself for a little. But when Tabal and I were again alone together the old struggle was renewed.

It was impolitic to speak; it was impolitic to be silent. I was alone; unknown and deadly enemies were leagued against me; the secret was burning my breast; and, in short, after vowing to myself a score of times to tell nothing to Tabal, I told him all. His first expression was one of anger with me for not having been prompter and franker at the meeting with Abram ben Aden.

"Hadst thou told me quickly, thy mind might be at ease now," he said.

"Nay, nay, Tabal; I want no man's blood on my head," I rejoined.

"Perchance thou wouldst rather have thy blood on another man's head," he remarked dryly.

"He may mean no mischief," I said, feeling the falsity of my words.   "And remember where we are and what we are doing."

"I remember," he answered, with a grim look, "that this is Arafat, the Holy Mount, where men pray and seek blood-revenge."

"I am not going to forfeit Paradise for the sake of settling old feuds, Tabal," I said with what firmness I could command.

"Thou wouldst prefer to be sent to Paradise by thy enemy's dagger," he returned meaningly.   "That is for thee to choose.   But if that man looked at me as he looked at thee, my blade would find no rest till it had given him to Azrael."

"I will make a covenant with thee, Tabal," I said. "I will stand by thee if thou wilt stand by me."

"Now thou speakest like thyself," cried Tabal, joyously.   "We shall have sport; see if we have not. Nay, nay, be not afraid; we will talk no more of blood-revenge.   Thou art weary and in need of rest. Lie thee down. So.   So.   Verily, a man cannot keep awake for ever."

I lay down, but I did not sleep.   The vision of that humped back, those blazing eyes, that malignant face, effectually kept off drowsiness.   A dozen times during the night I could have risen and fled; a dozen times I was on the point of joining a man who prayed with exceeding unction in a neighbouring tent; as often, too, I felt impelled to call Tabal, and rush out with him in quest of Abram ben Aden.   If that cause of nightmares were removed I should breathe more freely.   But I did none of these things; only tossed and speculated myself into a fever, while waiting with haggard expectation for the dawn.

It came with the beating of drums, the roar of artillery, and the tumult of an excited multitude. Rising as from the depths of a cold grey shadow, I joined Tabal in ablutions and prayers.   These over we started for the summit of the Holy Mount. The rocky steeps were already covered with pil-

grims and beggars, who jostled, fought, recrimi-
nated, and mingled Labbaiks and petitions for alms
in cries that made the ears ring and ache.   By
the time we reached Adam's Place of Prayer, the
press was a jam, and tender ribs suffered.   Many
Hadjis fell fainting.   Some were helped up, some
trodden underfoot, where they snarled and bit like
dogs; and not a few went direct into the hands of the
grave-diggers.   A little further on Wahhabis and
Bedouins displayed their religious zeal by contending
with naked weapons about the spot which the Khatib
(preacher) would by-and-by occupy with his white
dromedary; and the host in general was distracted
with anger and devoutness.

Having gained the top we prayed vehemently, according to rule, on the spot where the Prophet used to
stand during the performance of the rites; then descended in a sweeping, yelling mass to the plain.
There we spread ourselves, and took leave of our
senses, after the approved manner of the Moslems.

I should probably have enjoyed the varied and imposing spectacle more had it not been for the painful
and oppressive sense of Abram ben Aden's presence.
I did not see a dark face glowering at me, or a Bedouin charging in my direction, or a man press close to
me without smelling murder.   Sitting now in the
peaceful security of my room the fear seems cowardly.
But it was different then, with so many zealots ready
to imbrue their hands in the blood of an alien and
heretic.

It was with unfeigned thankfulness that I got back
to the tent, and threw myself on some rugs to compose
my whirling mind.   Tabal would have me out again
to see the sights and seek adventures; but I stead-
fastly refused to budge (save for the brief midday devotions) till the guns announced Al Asr, or afternoon
prayer, from which no male pilgrim may abstain and
keep his integrity.

The proceedings opened promptly with a sort of
gala-day madness, in which drums and horse-racing

were principal incitements. Scarcely had the signal ceased booming among the rocks, when the Shereef's procession made its appearance in the rear. First came a disorderly mob of slaves and savages on foot, on horses, on camels, every atom being animated by the single ambition of creating a riot with the greatest possible celerity. Then, behind his green and red flags, came the great man on his mule, with a green umbrella as large as a tent bobbing and swaying above his head. Another mob of slaves and savages followed, and hard upon its heels the Hadjis rolled like a huge billow, screaming, yelling, waving their arms, beating their breasts, throwing their ihrams over their heads, and otherwise proving their demented condition. Presently we surged up the mountain-side, breaking like foam on its rocky face, and rending the heavens with our screeching. The Mahmils of Egypt and Damascus took their place, the Khatib mounted his white dromedary and made a sign for silence; and like the sudden collapse of a tempest the noise ceased. Then in the midst of a thrilling hush, the preacher began his three-hours' sermon.

It must have been very eloquent, judging by the profound impression it made. The congregation duly wept, duly shouted, duly beat its many breasts, and would doubtless have proceeded to tear its hair, but for the fact that all heads were shaved as close as razor could cut. I joined ostentatiously in these demonstrations, yet my thoughts were not with the preacher; they were on the lurking enemy who crept through the crowd feeling the cruel knife. I sought him at least as eagerly as he could seek me. On all sides I looked for him, first with wild rapid glances, then slowly, deliberately, once, twice, thrice, and thanked Heaven fervently that I failed to discover his evil visage. I found that Tabal, too, was engaged in the same quest, and, unlike me, was disappointed at his failure.

"Attend to thy prayers, good Tabal," I whispered.

"May the Prophet give him grace to say his while he hath time!" he returned significantly.

Meantime the sermon went on with the most moving exhibitions of emotion. The preacher told how the just should drink of the rivers of milk and incorruptible waters of Paradise, and of the oceans of wine and clarified honey, and eat of all kinds of delicious fruits in endless gardens, made delectable by fountains and shady trees, and in gorgeous pavilions lie on couches of silk and wrought gold, and be comforted by damsels having eyes like the midnight and complexions like rubies and pearls; and we lifted up our voices in a storm of rejoicing. He told also how the wicked should have garments of fire wrapped close about them, and boiling water poured upon their heads, and salt rubbed into their gaping wounds, and dwell for ever amid burning winds and under the shade of black smoke, and eat the fruit of the cursed tree of Al Zakkum,* which is as devils' heads; and we howled like a thousand moonstruck kennels. And while we were in a paroxysm of awe and terror at the fate of the lost, the preacher unexpectedly gave the signal that the sermon was over, and we broke, as breaks the dammed torrent, and swept down hill yelling like a Tartar horde in a foray.

In the scene that ensued religion and brotherly-kindness had no part. With the tears of holy joy and repentance scarce dry on our faces we trampled each other, swore at each other, struck each other with fist or weapon as might be most convenient. Men roared, frantically brandishing knives and daggers; women screamed; children cried; slaves lost their masters, and masters their slaves, and each vociferated for each in divers tongues and with many unhallowed remarks; camels snapped and groaned, sometimes capsizing to kick their uncouth legs in the air and make splinters of their burdens; horses plunged; asses brayed; and all the while we were desperately tearing up tent pegs, rolling canvas, packing goods and chattels, getting litters ready, mounting, and making off as if the devil himself were at

* The tree of Hell.

our heels.   Perhaps, indeed, he was, for the commotion was due to our urgent desire to get to Muna with
all speed, and stone him with seven stones apiece;
and he may have been taking it out of us while yet
he had a chance.

Ranéé (who for reasons easily imagined had not
accompanied us to the sermon) was very brave, Baruk
very obedient, Tabal very nimble and resourceful,
and, our baggage being an inconsiderable item, we
were among the earlier ones to start.   To start—I
ought rather to say to stagger and reel in furious
collisions; to whirl in eddies; to be rushed protesting
and helpless in a flying mass that gripped us on both
sides like the jaws of a vice; to be hurled back as
that mass recoiled from some shock in front, and
pounded and crushed as it struggled to recover itself;
to hear ourselves described by all the unsanctified
epithets of all the Moslem languages dredged to their
uttermost foulness; to be reduced to despair twenty
times a minute; and made to feel of just as much
account as sand-grains in a dust-storm, and as potently
endued with self-control as cockle-shells in a tempestuous sea.

It was dark, too, and the din was distracting.
Guns roared in front of us, guns roared behind us.
Sometimes they burst at our very side, making us
jump, and wonder what powers of destruction had
fallen upon us; fifes squealed, kettle-drums rattled,
and over all rose the myriad noises of man and beast
insanely striving to make a tumult.

At first neither the haste nor the confusion was at
all to my distaste.   The one was getting me away
with all quickness from the place of blood-revenge;
the other might give me the better opportunity of
evading my enemy.   *Might*, however, not would.
There was the rub.   A bare possibility—a faint hope
born of a burning wish—no more; and the chance lay
equally on the other side.   What if the occasion were
opportune for Abram ben Aden rather than for me?
The crowd might favour either of us.   To rely on it

would be like putting faith in a lottery, or trusting to the jungle which perhaps hides the stalking tiger. So, the advantage being in the balance, I kept an eager, apprehensive look out for him, and a hundred times my flesh crept and thrilled as I fancied I saw his fiery eyes glaring upon me out of the darkness.

If he spied me he delayed taking his revenge. But I was convinced he pursued me, chuckling, nursing his vengeance, and waiting with the diabolic patience of the Oriental for the appropriate and dramatic moment. With this conviction like a live coal in my mind, I was swept forward by the resistless, sinister tide. It pursued a tumultuous course over the plain, poured in a foaming torrent through the craggy pass of the Two Rugged Hills, overflowed Muzdalifah, swirling and eddying for a while about the mosque, gathered a mountain of pebbles for punitive purposes later on, and finally rolled into the Muna basin, and, with shattering clamours, overspread the base of Mount Sabir. By-and-by the stars receded, the east quivered, first with a pale light, then with sudden red streamers that shot upward like trailing rockets; and presently the great sun uprose, gleaming like a flame on white robes and gilded litters, tipping spears with fire, and disclosing chaos. The host drew itself together, with some futile efforts to smooth out the disorder, looked to its baggage, and having washed the missiles brought from Muzdalifah, religiously stowed them in its ihrams against the time of putting Satan to shame and torture.

With the first blink of light I cast anxiously about for the crooked back of Abram ben Aden. Up and down, to and fro, I searched for that dread hump; now seeming to mark it, now sighing in gladness at finding myself mistaken, again starting at a stealthy rustle behind and turning fear-struck and with horrible expectations to find a Hadji merely trying to pray.

Tabal, I found, was also engaged in looking for Abram ben Aden, though with sensations the reverse of mine.

"The coward hideth!" he said contemptuously.
"Ugh! why cometh he not like a man? He is not
worth the thrust of a Persian's spear." *

I refrained from expressing my ideas on the subject.

In due time we stoned the devil in the shape of a
pillar, placed as awkwardly as a devilish ingenuity
could suggest. The site, indeed, was of the fiend's
own choosing. There, in the remote ages, he had
the audacity to show his evil phiz, and there, to this
day, he is stoned with a fury and commotion that
prove fatal to many taking part in the assault. Tabal
and I crushed into the seething throng, cast our seven
stones viciously, crushed out again, not without painful compression of the ribs, were shaved, had our
nails pared; and then, in the midst of a roaring rabble, made desperately for Mecca.

We reached it in the afternoon, grimy as coal-
heavers, croaking with thirst, and weary to the point
of fainting. To impress upon us how the righteous
seeking Paradise must suffer, the laws of Ramadan
forbade either eating or drinking; although (sorely
against her will) I made the drooping and exhausted
Ranéé sip a mild cordial, affirming the authority of
the Prophet for the compulsion. The rest of us took
what refreshment could be had from bathing, then
lay down with infinite yearnings of the famishing to
wait for night and the concluding ceremonies.

Over these I must not linger; for my pen burns
with impatience to reach an event which is the climax
or turning-point of this history. As soon as we had
word that the Caaba was open, Tabal and I went off
to perform our last vows, leaving Ranéé under the
charge of Baruk.

Now the Caaba, as the reader knows, is the Moslem holy of holies; no heretic may set his foot there
and live. Even on slight suspicion his blood would
be spilt on the sacred pavement, and those who shed

---

* The Arab has an invincible contempt for the Persian. To
be called a Persian in Arabia is to be offered an unspeakable
insult.

it would count themselves many degrees nearer ever-lasting bliss for the deed.

We had instant evidence of the inviolable sanctity of the place in the strictness of the officials who guarded it, their piercing looks, their searching questions, the resolute manner in which they barred the way till we gave a minute and satisfactory account of ourselves. The thought of the falsehoods with which I braved that inquisition makes my old blood run cold. But my life depended on my deceit: that is my excuse, and the reader may judge whether it is a valid one. At last the inquisitors were satisfied, we reached the keeper standing by the door with his silver padlock, climbed the final step, and passed in.

The most self-confident Moslem will not cross that awful threshold without shaking and trembling. Fancy, then, how one who was not a Moslem, and who just then had no self-confidence whatever, quaked as he glanced round the massive dungeon-like walls, thinking of what might happen! There was no window in case of emergency, no outlet save the door, and it was closely guarded behind us. The holy of holies might turn out a most effectual trap.

I do not know how I went through my devotions, —gracelessly, absently, no doubt, for the tense mind was not upon them. I remember that there were curtains flaming with red and gold on the upper part of the walls; that we prostrated ourselves for ages first in one corner then in another; that there were startling outbursts of ecstasy; but how the prayers went, what we said, and how we said it, I have no notion.

As we chanced to be among the first arrivals, the place on our entering was almost empty. But it was soon full. You can feel the swelling of a crowd, even when you cannot see it, especially if the sensibilities be quickened by a high nervous excitement. The sense of numbers became every moment stronger and stronger upon me, and the impulse to examine the worshippers overpowering. It is straitly forbidden

22

to lift the eyes in that inner sanctuary; but a man whose life is jeopardized is apt to break laws and disregard instructions. Unable to resist, I peeped very cautiously from under the corner of my ihram; and fiery currents darted through me.

The place grew choking hot and stifling. Waves of humid, heated air flowed and ebbed about my face. It seemed there were a million people there, and that every eye was upon me, and, worse, was reading my secret. I began to perspire, and a feeling of suffocation came into my throat and chest. I made sure I should faint before the ordeal was half over—faint, and be despatched in a swoon. Then I began to accuse myself of madness for running such risks, and that did not tend to induce composure.

We were creeping like snails on our course from corner to corner, when the tempter suggested that I might chance another surreptitious look; so, lifting the edge of my ihram, with extraordinary care I glanced out. What I saw made a sudden darkness fall upon me, such a darkness as would follow a heavy blow on the head. The place whirled. I clutched at Tabal, and I am sure a muffled cry escaped me.

Fearful of attracting attention I thrust my face to the pavement to recover myself. Then, holding my breath and hoping against hope that my eyes had deceived me, I glanced out again. Merciful Heaven! I had seen aright. There, within ten feet of me, was the humped back of Abram ben Aden.

I was not surprised; I had expected him, expected him every minute since our meeting at Arafat, and there he was, and my feelings were those with which the doomed wretch catches sight of the executioner.

I put my head down again, pressing my face hard against the pavement in a horror and dismay that are not to be described. There was a great humming in my ears; my heart leaped with a sort of racing violence for some seconds, then stopped with an excruciating tightness of the chest, as if its cords had sud-

denly contracted.   The labouring breath was shut off.
An iron grip seemed to be on my windpipe.   I was
choking, and felt that nothing but a yell could save
me.

I managed to keep back the cry by stretching myself
on the floor and groaning aloud, by dissembling my
terror in vehement ejaculations that came back to me
in a dead echo from the walls.   Little could my fel-
low-worshippers have guessed that in those fervid
bursts of piety a man's soul was crying out in the
agony of uttermost fear.

Tabal tugged at my ihram, and I crept on with that
shuddering, unnerving dread of the assassin's knife
which turns courage to cowardice, and blanches curly
locks in an hour.   Had Abram ben Aden seen me?
Was he waiting for his revenge quietly, confidently,
as the serpent waits for the fluttering bird?   I made
no doubt whatever he was; that he had tracked me
there, and was now gloating over his success.   Yet I
longed with the longing of one whose fate is in the
balance to turn and assure myself.   To turn, ay, and
perhaps look into his very face; to feel the hot fumes
of his breath, to see his leer of triumph.   That was
too horrible.   Then another thought came into my
head.   If there was to be killing, why should I not
strike first, and strike effectually?   My whole soul
rose surging with deadly passion at the idea.   I was
trapped.   Any moment he might be upon me, and if
he should fail others would succeed.   I had to die.
Well, he should die also, and die first.   It was unfortunate that I had not a dagger; but I had a pistol
and a good knife, and between them they would do
my service.

Tabal again pulled stealthily at my ihram, wondering what was the matter.   That broke my train of
thought, and with it my purpose.   I was scared at my
own bloodthirstiness.   No, I could not on any account
kill him.   If he would let me alone I would let him
alone.   And, making this compact with myself, I
crept on beside Tabal, surer than if I saw him, that

Abram ben Aden was crawling close behind me. My head was bowed, and I durst not cast the swiftest glance back. But I saw the whole scene, clear and definite as in a mirror. I beheld myself creeping inch by inch round the circuit of the building; I beheld Abram ben Aden at my back, not too near, stopping as I stopped, moving as I moved, keeping directly in my track, letting none come between us, pretending to be praying, but with all his attention fixed on me, and holding himself ready for the moment of victory. I saw his black scowl change to a fiend's gleam of joy, the joy which waits in secure patience, and is whetted by the protracted anguish of the victim. I cried aloud; Tabal turned astonished to find me worshipping with so much zeal. He did not understand that I was utterly unnerved, and that if I did not give voice to my fear I must have gone raving mad.

The ceremonies dragged on. Awesome sounds rose and sank as guilty men owned their sins and made piteous appeals for mercy and forgiveness. The Caaba was so full that we were packed almost immovable. The air was hot and fetid; we breathed in gasps, and were streaming with perspiration. We had been eternities there, and yet there was much to be done. Could I endure to the end?

The dense mass rocked and heaved in spasms of emotion. In one of these upheavals some one shouldered me roughly behind. Quivering to the marrow, I closed my eyes and held my breath for the thrust that must follow. As it did not come with the expected celerity, I turned my head to look for the aggressor; and all the terror and horror I had ever known or imagined were nothing to what then seized me; for there, cheek by jowl with me, was Abram ben Aden.

He was so close that I felt his palpitating sides against mine; his breath was like a noxious wind in my face, every word he uttered rang like a knell in my ears. His head was down almost flat upon the pavement; his entreaties seemed afire with the blind zeal of the distracted penitent; but I knew that he was watching me, knew that he saw every movement I made. I looked at him, looked at him with the steadfastness of fascination; examined his hump, observed its size and its odd shape, and noted his wizened appearance. Suddenly he turned; our eyes met, and every pulse of my being was suspended. He stopped, gaping frightfully, in the middle of an impassioned utterance; a fierce exultation beamed luridly upon his gathered features; he forgot his prayers; for what was his soul's welfare set against the gratification of a cherished revenge?

His jaws opened in the hideous, bloodthirsty way of a wild beast's, then closed with a snap as if his teeth were in my throat. His eyes glowed as if a furnace raged behind them; his face became a sort of dusky red. Then all at once his expression changed. He grinned as the arch-fiend might be supposed to grin over the accomplishment of a peculiarly gratifying piece of wickedness, and passed his hand down by his side.

I could bear no more. The irrepressible scream rang out, and, leaping up, I was on the backs of the bended worshippers, and through the door, before one of them could realize what was happening. As I sprang down to the outer floor there followed me the most fearful cry that Moslem lips can frame, or perhaps Christian ears hear, the cry of "Nazarene! Nazarene!" and the professors of the "holy religion" were on my heels with the rush of breaking waters and the spirit of infuriated wolves.

CHAPTER XXVIII.

A SONG IN THE NIGHT.

THE blast of fury from the Caaba seemed to catch me and hurl me forward. I was past the official guardians as if shot from the mouth of a cannon, and out among the pillars and porches before a hand could be raised to stop me. But there I had only plunged into tho thick of the perils. In one awful glance I saw tho circling walls, the towered and guarded gates, the vast, startled congregation, lifting itself with terrific rockings and tossings for any atrocity that might bo in the way, and knew that I had to clear all these or dio.

With the instinct of the hunted fox, I began to dodge among the pillars and colonnades. Tho cry of "Nazarene! heretic!" escaping the bounds of narrow walls rose a shrill and curdling shriek on the night air, and tho packed outer crowd, grasping the situation, roared in responsive anger for the blood of the defiler.

At that sound I cowered behind a pillar as a hare cowers behind a bush listening to the clamour of tho hunters. There was a moment, a terrible moment of suspense and uncertainty. What were my pursuers doing? Had they lost me? Then I felt rather than saw that with one savage impulse they were surging in upon mc. I must move or be caught and torn instantly.

Gliding like a shadow among shadows, I made for a remote corner into which tho dim light of the lamps did not shine. A wild yell told me I was discovered, and I sprang forward, knocking several men down as it seemed at a touch.

Getting into deeper shade I paused again, for the tenth part of a second, to take reckonings and catch my breath. I was near the eastern side, in an angle of the wall, and within thirty paces of a gate. Only thirty paces; yet how was that brief distance to be traversed? A man may perish in the course of thirty paces; in thirty paces a frenzied crowd may seize him and tear him limb from limb.

My pursuers wavered once more, as if doubtful of my position. But it was only for a second. The next, with howls that made the hair stand straight up on my head, they charged inward, encircling me like a coil.

I felt that I was lost; that no power on earth could

prolong my life another minute. Yet even in the face of death I was impelled to make an effort to save myself. The readiest plan would be to make for the gate of which I have spoken; but between me and it —between me and any of the gates, was the solid mob with shooting fire in its eyes and murderous steel in its hands.

Perhaps it would be best to throw myself on the ruthless blades, and have the agony over. Perhaps; but I did not adopt that course, because, with all its miseries, my life was unspeakably dear to me.

Darting back the way I had come, I made a feint of crossing the square to the western side. The mob heaved, turned, and rushed like a billow to overwhelm me. Watching till I found the cumbrous mass properly in motion, I doubled like a flash among the colonnades and along the wall, with just sufficient presence of mind to tear off the ihram, which might betray me by its whiteness. Its momentum was such that the crowd could not swing around swiftly. Now was the moment for my attempt, now, or never.

Without waiting to calculate the chances, without waiting for anything but a single, involuntary glance at my pursuers, I dashed into the open. The commotion had drawn the guards from their post, a circumstance which I discovered with an electric thrill and tingle of joy. But they were free on the edge of the crowd, and, detecting me and my purpose, bounded with howls of fury for the gate.

The speed of that race is not to be conceived, save by those who have made a similar dash for their lives. If I failed by so much as half a foot, or half a second, I was a dead man. Twenty seconds would decide the issue of life and death, twenty beating, awful seconds. I saw nothing but that slit in the wall, and the faint shadows of two towers; but I felt the rush of the maddened multitude, felt and sped as one having wings.

Within ten feet of the gate the corner of my eye caught a flying skirt and the flash of steel. The man and I were at the fateful passage together. He leaped at me with the long spring of a tiger, and I took his dagger in my left arm, just below the elbow. He went down, or rather was hurled into the arms of a comrade, whose blow he served to ward off. A third struck at me, grazing my ribs; but before he or another could strike again I had bounded through the gate and was in the street.

Outside, another crowd waited for me; though, luckily, it was still in the questioning stage of excitement, and had not gathered its energies for action. But the shouting of the fiends, that were now pouring through the gate, and the sight of a naked man plying his feet for dear life, gave it the enlightenment and the incentive it needed, and with peals of rage it joined in the chase, or, more correctly, surrounded me.

How I escaped instant death remains to this day a miracle to myself. In the space of one minute I seemed to be entangled a thousand times. Hands with claws like an eagle's clutched at me, fists struck me, feet tripped me, daggers pierced me; I was wounded, bleeding, and breathless, but, by the mercy of God, I was able to get on somehow, ducking, dodging, doubling, striking, leaping, now darting under the gleaming steel, now bounding over it, in a word, trying every trick of the pressed fugitive; and it seemed that all Mecca, nay, the whole Moslem world, surged and bellowed for my blood.

I have mentioned that Mecca lacks street-lamps. That fact was my salvation. The darkness enabled me first to dodge the crowd and then to distance it. Once in the open street I was more than a match even for Arabs whose fleetness of foot was increased by a furious desire to kill. Here and there I encountered groups; but to them I could be no more than a flying apparition, and, indeed, some of them made way for me with symptoms of sudden fear. Others, however, of hardier courage or readier wit, hearing the clamour and guessing that I was the cause and object of it, took the chance to strike at me as I flew; but if they hit I did not feel the blows.

Venturing by-and-by to stop and hearken, I realized that my pursuers had lost me and were scattering like beaters when the game gets into cover. Supposing a damned soul were to escape and to pause for half a moment on the outer circle of hell in fear, exhaustion, and a sort of trembling triumph, its feelings would be what mine were then. I was not safe. Infuriated demons were on my track; perils encompassed me like a flood. Yet I had escaped—escaped where the chances against me were a million, ay ten million to one. I was blowing like a cracked bellows, my limbs shook and bent as if bones and muscles had been beaten limp and useless, and a myriad lights were dancing in my eyes. But for one delirious second I swelled and thrilled with a tumult of exultation. Then like a flash it was gone, and I was once more the terrified and scudding fugitive.

I ran mechanically on—on through the darkness, past houses, past tents, past startled groups of men, neighing horses and grunting camels—ever on, with the reverberating yells of the baffled fanatics, like a sort of devil's music, in my ears. A pack of ravenous dogs got on my scent, and snapped and barked at my heels. Lest they should give my enemies the clue I charged in among the yelping brutes, as an unarmed man driven desperate might charge among besieging wolves, and the act was so utterly incomprehensible that they slunk away with affrighted whines.

I ran on again at my topmost speed, but my legs were getting weak and shaky, and stumbling presently over a stone or some other obstacle, I fell on my face almost blind and senseless. My head seemed empty; my sides were breaking. Putting down my hands to support them, I discovered with dismay that I was naked. Then I remembered how the ihram had been torn off as an impediment.

The sense of nakedness, of utter prostration and

helplessness stripped me of the last remnant of hope and courage. I had no more heart for effort; and I dare say I wished to die there and then. Let no man imagine he knows what desolation is till he has skulked and lain on the savage unsympathetic earth like a wounded beast, without a beast's covering or resource. One who is clothed has in his direst misery some feeling of human protection and brotherhood; while a rag sticks to his wretched back there still remains a kind of bond or tie between him and his fellow-men. It is not till he lies in the dust naked as he came into the world, afraid of everything that breathes and that does not breathe, that he is altogether desolate and abandoned.

That was my state, and it was a state to die in. Yet I have noticed that the idea of dying comes easiest to those whom death does not immediately menace. Presently I found myself trying to continue my flight. But the attempt failed. My legs refused their office; a ton-weight seemed to be attached to each foot. When I tried to rise I fell to my knees, collapsing inward upon myself in a kind of coil as if seized with paralysis. And then indeed I thought I was lost, forsaken of God, hated and hunted of man. Perhaps some self-pitying tears came, but not many; fewer probably than if I had been better able to take care of myself.

Luckily I was out of the town and among some mean tents that were not of sufficient value even to be guarded. Gathering myself together presently, I managed to crawl into the blackness of darkness behind one of them, and there lay with my ear to the ground, listening. The hoarse tumult still swelled and raged; and several times I was convinced my pursuers were surrounding and must inevitably find me. But after a while the shouting fell to a rumbling growl, as of wild beasts returning baffled from the chase, and by-and-by ceased. The fanatics had gone back to their prayers confident that the morning light would bring them satisfaction. Nor had I any

doubt whatever that it would. The idea of capturing
a horse, mounting and riding for the desert occurred
to me; but I had not strength for the enterprise. So
I lay there like one stricken of the palsy, hearkening
to the bodeful noises, frantically eager to preserve my
life, and feeling that it was forfeit as surely as if
my enemies held me bound hand and foot.

A chill wind blew, a wind that cut and pierced the
nude flesh as with innumerable sharp points, and I
shivered and chattered. Such cold makes one move
if any life or energy be left. I crept to the nearest
tent, and drawing aside the curtain, perhaps half an
inch, peeped stealthily in. I saw no one. Making
a larger opening I took a longer look. A ragged,
battered cloak of camel's hair lay spread just within
the entrance. My heart beat with a thievish excitement; the blood leaped to my head. Could I reach
that cloak? Gently and quietly, very gently and
quietly I drew the curtain a little further aside,
crouching behind it to keep out of view should any
one be inside, and reached with my right hand for
the edge of the cloak. I caught it as it seemed with
fingers of fire, and pulled with the breathless caution
of a thief. It came with me. The experiment was
not one to be prolonged beyond the briefest limit
possible. I clutched the cloak blindly, and getting
strength from the excitement, was round the corner
into the darkness before you could have counted
three.

When I had run perhaps a hundred yards I stopped
quivering and panting to listen. There was no
alarm; the theft had not been detected. Throwing
the cloak about me, and falling on all fours, I crept
to the rear of some of the smaller tents, and finding
a rock two or three feet high lay down on the lee side
of it. But the wind found the holes in my meagre
covering; and again I chattered and shivered. A
few stars were in the sky, twinkling cold and keen,
and though there was no moon, I could see the drifting clouds. Somehow they had an awesome, unnat-

ural look in the dusky light, and suggested evil spirits crowding to some dire revel.

Rising in a staggering fashion, and wrapping my cloak closer about me, I wandered on among the tents. There were people about, and my presence did not attract attention. Emboldened by this I went on, gradually getting among larger tents and pavilions of grandees. Suddenly a man challenged me. Quick as thought I was into the darkness and flat on my face. He did not pursue; yet I was afraid to move. And as I lay there the whole horrible scene I had just gone through repeated itself before me. I saw the crowded Caaba; I saw Abram ben Aden crawling close beside me, his eyes furtively watching me, his face livid with hatred and triumph; I saw my own fearful leap for life, and heard the cry of "Nazarene! Nazarene!" with a fresh shuddering and freezing of the marrow. Again I thought of Tabal, wondering whether he, too, was to be counted my enemy. Then, by another turn of the mental kaleidoscope, I saw the dogs, the crowd at the gate, the man whose dagger had left a hole in my arm. It was all as vivid and as harrowing as reality.

And as I was thus thinking and creeping together and shuddering, I heard a sound that brought every drop of blood in my veins to a sudden stand with a new and different emotion. Some one was singing; that was not strange. But it was strange to incredulity, to the point indeed of making me doubt my own sanity, that the air should be one of home and boyhood. My brain must be giving way. I got to my feet, listening with every pulse of my body. The singing was interrupted with some bars of whistling. Then it began again, and loud and clear and unmistakable there rang out the words of a Scottish ballad.

> "Lock the door, Lariston, lion of Liddesdale,
> Lock the door, Lariston, Louther comes on;
> 　The Armstrongs are flying,
> 　The widows are crying,
> The Castletoun's burning and Oliver's gone.

"Lock the door, Lariston, high on the weather gleam,
  See how the Saxon plumes bob on the sky ;
      Yeoman and carbineer,
      Bilman and halberdier,
  Fierce is the foray, and far is the cry.

"Bewcastle brandishes high his broad scimitar,
  Ridley is riding his fleet-footed grey ;
      Hidley and Howard there,
      Wandell and Windermere ;
  Lock the door, Lariston, hold them at bay.

"Why dost thou smile, noble Elliott of Lariston?
  Why does the joy-candle gleam in thine eye?
      Thou bold border ranger,
      Beware of thy danger,
  Thy foes are relentless, determined, and nigh."

I stood as if fixed to the ground; then some one seemed to release me, and I ran forward. I had not gone fifty paces when the curtain of one of the largest and most splendid tents swung back, and a man stepped out. By the light of the new-risen moon I saw that he was tall, straight as a rush, and dressed in the first fashion of a sheik. At sight of him I stopped instinctively, meaning to bolt. But a second look kept me there, gazing in amazement and a kind of awe. Were my eyes playing me tricks? Was my troubled brain raising spectres and delusions? I was not fit to decide; so in the tension I said unconsciously and aloud, "The man on the black horse, or his ghost."

At that he turned towards me, and his eyes drew me as the magnet draws the steel. I rushed forward, crying, "Donald Gordon! Donald Gordon!" to fall exhausted and giddy at his feet.

He looked down with a keen, questioning, incredulous face, and said something. What it was I did not hear; for there was the roar of a raving multitude in my ears. All at once it died away, and I was ducking from dancing lights and flying meteors. The man, the tent, the moon, the stars, the clouds reeled and gyrated in a drunken jumble, and I fancied the end of the world, for which I appeared to have been waiting, had come at last.

Presently I found myself inside the tent with a glass of stimulants at my lips, and a stinging sensation in my nostrils. The dark, keen, questioning face still bent above me.

"Aren't you the man on the black horse?" I asked in a quick, piping voice, while the surroundings showed a disposition to go off again in a drunken whirl. By a mighty effort I restrained and steadied them, dimly angry at their want of stability and propriety. "I am from the Elms," I gasped, "from Sir Thomas Gordon and Miss Isabel," and the drunken, disgraceful tent heaved and tumbled in spite of me.

A burning torrent went down my throat and I winked as if for a wager. Then I began to sneeze as if I had taken an enormous pinch of snuff. The drunken tent was making an egregious fool of me at the very moment when I particularly wished to be sedate and self-possessed.

By-and-by the sneezing stopped, the tent stood firmly and decently on its poles, and I looked once more into the dark, keen face. "My name is Angus Glenrae," I explained hastily—"Glenrae of Glenrae, you know." I laughed under an uncontrollable impulse, laughed as one who has made the jest of a century. I caught the black eye above, and the laugh changed to a wild tremor of alarm. "As sure as death I am telling the truth," I protested, under a burning impression that I was on trial for my life.

"Hysteria," said my companion, speaking the first intelligible word. My fear gave place to merriment again.

"Your grandmother!" I retorted. "Do you think I'm a moonstruck girl?"

He bent low, trying to soothe me, and I heard him say to himself, "A bad case, poor fellow."

But I would have none of his maudlin compassion. "Maybe you think I'm daft," I cried, "but I'll soon show you." And I believe I proceeded by every means in my power to demonstrate my complete insanity.

My strong point seemed to be that I was Angus Glenrae, and no other, and this declaration, fit, as I thought, to carry conviction to a whole asylum board, was repeated with rising emphasis a round score of times.

"Yes, yes," said my companion; "Angus Glenrae. Your word is law on the point. Take a drop more, Angus, my man."

I took a drop more, I took many drops; I sneezed and gasped till I shed tears like a whipped child, and by means of these interesting processes I got partial possession of myself again. As soon as my returning wits enabled me, I made haste to put the one question to which I desired an answer.

"Aren't you Donald Gordon?" I asked; "tell me that before you say a word about anything else."

He opened his eyes slightly, as in mild astonishment.

"Well, that's what they used to call me once upon a time," he answered lightly.

"You'll never have heard of the Glenraes?" I said.

"No, Angus, my man, never, though I doubt not they are great people," and I thought he cast a look over my raiment.

"Nor clapped eyes on one of them?" I said.

"Never, till this minute; and, to tell the truth, it puzzles me to make out how I come to have that honour and pleasure now."

"Man," I cried, staggering to my feet and gripping his hand—"man, I have come all the way from Scotland for you!"

He gazed in open incredulity, as well he might.

"And what is more," I went on pantingly, "you did your best to kill me once, and, faith, you very nearly succeeded."

"I?" he said with growing amazement.

"Just you," I replied. "When you were finishing

off Amood Sinn you were as near as an ace of putting an end to me."

"This is past belief," he exclaimed. "Are you reciting me a page from the 'Arabian Nights'?"

"Judge for yourself," I answered. "I saw you cut Koor Ali in two; I saw you slash off Abou Kuram's sword-arm. I shouted to you, and you never let on."

"God alive, man, were you in that battle?" he cried, gripping my hand as I had gripped his.

"Yes, and it wasn't your fault, or the fault of them that were with you, that I got out of it."

"I never heard anything like this. You are quite sure we are not both dreaming? Have you anything to prog me? Upon my word, I never heard a tale half so astounding."

"I found the experiences much more astounding than I find the story of them," I said, laughing. "I should not like to go through that battle again."

"I dare say not, I dare say not. The puzzle is how the devil you got out of it. It was a fearful slaugh·ter, a fearful slaughter; and I have seen some blood shed."

"So fearful that they thought you the arch-fiend himself."

He broke into explosive laughter.

"So I heard," he said, "so I heard, and they did not think it without cause."

"The fame of your swordsmanship promises to be as popular as the Mohammedan religion. They declare there never was anything like it seen in Arabia."

"Which is not saying much," he rejoined. "Among the blind the one-eyed man is king."

"The cutting down of Koor Ali and Abou Kuram was scarcely the work of a novice," I ventured.

"Ah, poor Koor Ali!" he said musingly. "The old cut seven of the British dragoon did for him. That little trick has still to be learned in Arabia. They were both good men; Abou Kuram was a capital fellow. My heart would have been blither to drink a cup of wine with him than to fight him. But war is war; those who follow it are not always free to choose. I read in his eye that one of us had to go down. I think it was natural on my part to prefer that he should go. I wish I had got a little play with Amood Sinn; but his excessive modesty kept him in the background. But we wander. How are my respected father and my lovely sister?"

I answered that they were well.

"Then that is sufficient now. By-and-by we shall hear all about them. You have a story, I know, but it will keep. Meanwhile we must look to yourself. I noticed that the pious Moslems have been pricking you with their steel. May I look at the hurt? A mere flesh wound, I am glad to see," he said, examining my arm. "A little care will set it all right. We will have it washed and bound. Then you need food, you need rest, and, to say the truth," glancing over me, "a scion of the illustrious house of Glenrae might appear in fitter dress. We will see if more becoming duds cannot be found."

I cast my eyes downward in some confusion, and there came back to me a swift recollection of the scenes of the night. I told Donald of them by way of accounting for my raggedness.

He whistled meaningly.

"That howling pack of devils was after you," he said. "You were caught in the Caaba, and escaped and got through that tempest of hell outside. My friend, that was a more wonderful, a much more wonderful feat than any of mine. Now we have the reason for the shaken nerves. Well, we must be careful. Men who are crazy with religion are ugly customers to deal with; and, to be quite candid with you, I have no taste for a brawl under present circumstances. There, there, you must not get excited. The whole thing is as easy as slashing off a Moslem warrior's head if you just keep quiet and follow my counsel."

I said that I was entirely in his hands.

23

"That is right. Well, you must first eat, then you must sleep. No brain fever here, Glenrae, if it can be helped. I believe the time of fasting is over; anyway it is over for you, unless you desire an immediate transfer to Paradise; and on the whole, it might be well to postpone that happy event. Where art thou, Yasir bin Akbah?" he called in Arabic.

Instantly a curtain was drawn aside at the rear, and a servant came forward bowing low.

"My lord calleth," he murmured.

"Set food for the stranger," said Donald. "Then place cushions and robes that he may sleep. And make haste as thou valuest thy head."

"It shall be done as my lord desireth," answered the man, bowing again and withdrawing.

"I will get the clothes myself," said Donald. "These heathen must not know too much. That fellow was chuckling last night because a Nazarene had been caught; so we must be circumspect."

The refection was of the kind with which the famished grandee regales himself when Ramadan is out, and he is permitted to return to his flesh-pots. There was meat in the shape of broiled fowl, there were delicious fruits, and there was wine in abundance. Having eaten, wisely, not too well, I lay down for the first time for I could not remember how long, in divine peace and security, and with a long deep sigh that was perhaps half a sob, dropped off into a dreamless sleep.

I awoke some fourteen hours later, refreshed and calm, but rather weak and under a wondrous sense of chastening. Donald was at hand.

"You are a champion sleeper, Glenrae," he remarked, smiling. "Well, well, better a long nap than a turned head; I think the chances of brain fever are past." Then, as I was dressing, "Your friends have been looking for you, and I am sworn to kill you at sight. Let me inquire if you are ready to meet your fate. I should be loath to send a countryman to his doom unprepared. I can see you had

a tight squeeze for it last night. Now, now, a
prince's turban, my friend, ought not to be askew,
and you are no hand at tying a sash. I am rather
particular in this matter. But perhaps you are not
aware that you are no longer an Arab, but an Indian
prince with a taint of English blood in your veins.
Your fair face makes that little precaution necessary."

"A prince!" I repeated, thinking he jested.

"Even so. I think it would be hazardous to be an
emperor. As to title, Altmish Jehan will do as
well as another, and concerning your territory we
need not be too definite. There, I think you are
complete. Your Serene Highness makes a brave appearance," he said, bowing profoundly.

"If you must deck me out gorgeously you need not
mock me," I said.

"Your Serene Highness must take your servant's
obeisance as a matter of course. And while in Mecca
your Serene Highness will not forget to talk Arabic,
of which, as I learned during your sleep, your Sereno
Highness is master. It will be a compliment to your
servant's august patron, Yumen Yusel. He has
heard of you, Glenrae, and is curious to see you.
The old rascal's in the next tent valorously wrestling
for a passport to Heaven. If he succeeds the rest of
us need not despair."

"You are complimentary to your friends," I
laughed.

"Are you so much in love with Arab ways that the
words hurt or surprise you?" he asked. "My dear
Glenrae, it would have been an incalculable saving
of trouble to mankind if the neck of the gentle Ishmael had been broken or ever he had a chance of
becoming the progenitor of these zealous compatriots
of the Prophet. You wonder why I, who pretend to
retain some shreds of Christian decency, should have
mixed myself up with the unhallowed crew. Well,
that is a tale within a tale, which you may hear later
on. Meanwhile our policy is to look to ourselves.
These friends of ours have an itch for cutting throats.

Don't open your eyes so wide; it's a case of diamond cut diamond. Against a rogue set a rogue."

I bowed in assent.

"In point of iniquity," he went on lightly, "these holy pilgrims stand to each other in degrees of comparison like adjectives—positive, comparative, superlative. Isn't that the order? Only that, unlike adjectives, their degrees are hard to discover. You imagine you are dealing with the positive, and quite unexpectedly it turns out to be the superlative. That's the trouble."

"You use free language," I remarked.

"Do I? Well, it's a novelty in this land of soft words and deadly chicane, and to me an ineffable relief. I have had to keep dangerous sentiments bottled up till I'm in peril of exploding. You fulfil the beneficent function of a safety-valve."

When I had served in this needful capacity, and relieved my companion's mind of its explosive elements, we reverted to my own story, which I briefly related. Donald listened as if he were all ears, frequently interrupting me with remarks and ejaculations of surprise. To the part concerning Sir Thomas and Isabel he paid the closest attention, inquiring with disconcerting eagerness about his sister.

"She will be quite a fine lady now," he observed, as I fancied with a meaning look at me.

I answered, with a hot face, that there was not her peer in all broad Scotland.

"You are a judge, no doubt," he rejoined, with a shrewd twinkle. "I notice the sun has not yet spoiled your complexion. That's a very pretty colour —no explanations, please; it's just a trick of the young blood. I'll warrant she's as good as she's bonnie."

"Better!" I cried, feeling myself forced to a declaration. "A great deal better—if that is possible."

"The authority is unimpeachable, I am sure," he said, bowing. "Let us proceed." And I was not slow to adopt the suggestion.

With the description of my search for himself in Bombay, Donald was vastly entertained, laughing long and loud over the discomfiture of those who had played the detective.

"Ay, I jouked them there!" he cried. "It was a case of saving myself from my friends. I found them bent on thwarting me in my little projects and ambitions; so at a crucial turn I took counsel of no one but myself, a fact to which you owe all your trouble, and I owe this happy meeting in Mecca."

At the description of Abram ben Aden's villainies his eyes flamed.

"You should have finished him, Glenrae, when you had the chance," he said, with just sufficient warmth to indicate the fierce spirit within. "It is always a mistake to let a viper escape. Now he's looking for you; and last night's doings are evidence of his power. My friend, he is a burning match in a magazine of gunpowder; and you are perched on the top."

The old feeling of dread seized me, so that I trembled. Donald must have seen my fear, for he made haste to assure me, saying that with my disguise, and the patronage on which I might now count, there was small risk of detection; and by degrees my confidence and courage returned.

I said nothing of Ranée, having reasons of my own for keeping silent regarding her. But when presently Donald proposed to present me to Yumen Yusel, I begged him, with an agitation which I could not entirely conceal, to defer the honour to a later hour.

"The sun will be down in a little while," I said.

"The fact is undeniable," he returned. "You seem moved over the matter."

"Promise to stay here half an hour for me," I said with a rising excitement.

"You grow mysterious, my friend. I beg of you to remember that mysteries are dangerous things in Arabia; doubly dangerous in the Holy City!"

"I will risk the danger, and you must abide the mystery. Will you stay here alone, quite alone?"

"Is it to be an experiment in magic?"

"You shall see," I answered, getting more and more excited. "Will you wait; and alone, quite alone?"

"You do not forget, of course, that there is a price on your head?" he returned quietly. "And you are quite sure you know what you are doing?"

I must have flushed at this, for he added immediately, "Well, well, that is not precisely the thing to say to one who has done and endured so much. Only you will be prompt. I can bear anything but waiting."

That was enough. The next instant I was out of the tent like an arrow, and speeding breathlessly to Ranéé's quarters. There I found Tabal temporarily on guard in place of Baruk. At sight of me he cried out in a kind of fright, then fell to embracing me with a vehemence more embarrassing than enjoyable.

"I mourned thee as dead," he panted, "and lo! here thou art, richly arrayed and prosperous."

"Heaven is very good to me, Tabal," I replied, gently staving him off. "There is a marvellous tale to tell thee, but not now." And breaking from his embrace, I bounced in upon Ranéé.

She, too, was startled; first because like Tabal she had thought me dead, and then because she feared I was mad.

"Something is wrong," she said in a voice of awe and anxiety.

"Nothing is wrong, child," I rejoined boisterously, for I could not contain myself. "Everything is gloriously right, as thou wilt own ere thou art many minutes older. There was one who—who fought against Amood Sinn. He was of my people, was he not?"

The amazed girl answered in the affirmative.

"And he was a friend of thine?"

"Yea, the closest friend," she said.

"Lower thy veil, Ranéé, and come with me as

fast as thy pretty feet can carry thee, asking no questions.”

“I may trust thee?”

“If not thou mayest kill me. Make haste, Ranéé. Make haste. The sun is going down.”

I took her hand, and we flew through the bustling streets, she running by my side like a wondering child, and Tabal trotting at our heels in mute astonishment; for he must needs accompany us. There were many irreverent criticisms as we sped, but luckily no interference.

“Put on thy happiest look, Ranéé,” I said, in wild glee. “Be as the rose in loveliness.”

“How can I?” she asked with just a touch of petulance; for she had a woman’s regard for appearances. “Thou takest the breath out of me.”

“In two minutes thou wilt bless me for doing it,” I said.

“Perchance. Yet I would thou hadst told me what thou art doing with me,” she replied.

“It will be sweeter to find out for thyself. We are loitering, Ranéé. Let us make haste.”

“I was not bred a runner,” said Ranéé. Yet she ran faster.

At last we reached Donald’s tent and paused before the curtained entrance.

“Thou wilt enter as I draw the curtain,” I whispered.

“There be strange men within,” she rejoined fearfully; “I may not do it.”

“Never was thy heart half so joyous as it will be when thou art inside,” I said. And being too impatient for further speech, I thrust aside the curtain and handed the trembling Ranéé in. Donald, whose back was towards the door, turned quickly. Their eyes met, started as at a vision of ghosts, then with a simultaneous cry of astonishment and gladness the two were in each other’s arms.

“So, so. I thought as much,” I remarked to myself, and hastily dropping the curtain I ran out to

Tabal, and threw myself on the ground to rock in glee.

After a while Donald appeared.

"Glenrae, Glenrae!" he called; and, as I did not immediately respond out of the darkness that had fallen, "where is that devil Glenrae? Angus, man, come here quick; we want you."

I rose and went forward chuckling and shaking.

"This is a day of surprises," he cried, grasping my hand, "most astonishing surprises. Surely the un-expected never happened in such a way before."

He was about to push me in when his eye fell on Tabal.

"Who is this?" he demanded quickly, and there was a sharp ring of suspicion in his voice.

"A tried friend," I answered.   "She who is within will tell you so."

Instantly his tone changed, and he saluted Tabal with fastidious cordiality.

"Marhaba! marhaba!" he said graciously.   "Thou art surely welcome.   Deign to enter."

Inside we found Ranéé pacing to and fro in a tumult of joy. On seeing us she ran first to me and then to Donald, clasping her jewelled hands, and laughing and crying in the same breath as she tried to express her gladness.

Presently Donald took her hand as deferentially as if she were an empress, and turning to Tabal and me, made a little speech.   "There was once a king of England," he said, "who when anything extraordinary happened to his friends always asked, 'Who is the woman?' Here, I think, is the cause of all the disasters that have befallen Amood Sinn and his allies. They parted us on our way hither, and I vowed vengeance and took it. I saw his palace burnt, though to you fell the honour of rescuing Ranéé. I am your slave for ever for the service. How and why we were separated is too long a tale to tell now. Some other time you shall hear it. The business of the moment is, What can I do for you?

Name something, Glenrae; whatever you ask it shall be done, if man can do it."

"I take you at your word," I answered promptly. "This is an hour of triumph and happiness to me no less than to you. I left Scotland to find you, and I have succeeded. Here we are face to face after adventures and experiences that are little short of miraculous. I have but one request; you will not deny it me."

"My hand that I won't if I have power to grant it."

"Your power is absolute. I ask that you will come back to Scotland with me."

He paused a moment as if in disappointment.

"Ah!" he said, "you have taken me in my weakest place. Is there nothing else you could ask?"

"I took you at your word," I answered. "It is for you to say whether you will break it."

He stepped forward swiftly, and seized my hand with an iron grip.

"Donald Gordon has done many things that he ought to have left undone," he said, with a quiver in his voice. "But there is one thing he has yet to do; he has yet to break his word. That has always been better than his bond. I and my wife will go with you to Scotland as soon as some necessary affairs are attended to here. I never intended to set foot in the old country again. But Heaven has its own ways of frustrating the designs of men. I am happy enough to go anywhere or do anything."

"I wish I could fly to the Elms," I cried.

"We'll sail, Glenrae, we'll sail," he laughed. "That will be speedy enough."

It was no easy ordeal to get through the congratulations and rejoicings which followed, and come to business. But at last, when we had in our several ways expressed our gladness and our gratitude to Providence for this happy and marvellous meeting— Ranóó by weeping one moment as if her heart were breaking, and laughing the next as if life were an endless comic play, so that her face was the very type of an April day, with sunshine and shower alternating; I as one who has been storing his emotion for a supreme moment, and when the time comes goes off in a whirl and knows not what happens; Donald as the strong man who succeeds but indifferently in suppressing the ebullient boy; and Tabal as one who but vaguely understands the scene in which he takes part—when at length the commotion of joy subsided, we descended from the clouds to lay plans and discuss my position.

Then came Tabal's turn to show excitement. At the first mention of my flight from the Caaba his eye gleamed with a sudden fiery rapture. When Abram ben Aden was named he sprang to his feet with a murderous gesture; but recollecting himself he sat down again, with clenched lips and his hand on the hilt of his sword. It was not till Donald asked him casually if he had seen anything of my enemy that he spoke.

"I have seen him," he answered quietly, yet with passionate force.

"Perchance thou knowest where he is now," said Donald.

Tabal gave a queer look.

"He may be still praying," he rejoined indifferently, "or he may be drinking clarified honey with the Prophet."

My head was not clear enough to discern any special significance in these words; but Donald must have suspected something, for he asked Tabal point-blank what had become of Abram ben Aden.

"Am I his keeper?" he responded with the faintest of chuckles. "Wherefore should I burden myself with his welfare? Yet I chance to know a thing."

"And it is?"

"That if he be not happy now his chances are gone for ever."

Donald whistled, and cast a meaning look at me.

"Your friend will do," he remarked in a kind of aside.

"Tabal, Tabal, what is this?" I cried, getting a sudden light on the matter. "What hast thou done?"

"Am I bound to answer thee?" said Tabal, in his sauciest manner. "Who made thee ruler over me?"

"Tell me what thou hast done, Tabal," I pleaded; for a great fear had come back upon me, a shuddering fear of blood.

"No more than I would have thee do for me if I were in the strait in which thou wert. Since thou art my judge I will answer in a word. I followed him when he followed thee, close and friendly at his heels;—it was a race to go far to see. He fell with his hand to his back. What happened then I cannot tell, for the press was great. Methinks he went straight to Paradise. It was his prayer, as thou knowest, that he should be taken there, and he was doubtless a good man. Perchance thou art sorry his prayer hath been granted."

All this while I noticed Ranéé behaving in an extraordinary manner, rubbing her hands, laughing to herself, looking with a face of ecstasy from me to Tabal and from Tabal to me, and between times whispering eagerly to Donald.

"I understand," said that gentleman, turning to me all at once, and addressing me with a great air of ceremony—"I understand, indeed I may say I have authentic information that the most satisfactory arrangements have been made for your peace and safety. Rest assured you need disturb yourself no more with thoughts of the good Abram ben Aden. He has fulfilled his course and has his reward. Let us therefore dismiss that holy man from our minds in the full assurance that he is happy."

And then, stepping carelessly towards me, and pretending to examine some curiosity in my dress, he whispered, "Take a friendly act in the spirit in which it is performed, Glenrae. Abram has gone to Abraham's bosom. Let him be."

Then, declaring loudly that it was unpardonable to treat friends as points of interrogation, and suddenly remembering a multitude of important matters that could not be neglected a moment longer, he swept the attention to other concerns.

There were indeed many things to be done—visits to be paid and received, speeches and compliments to be exchanged, embracings to be endured, coffee to be sipped, pipes to be smoked,—in a word, strange, disquieting, and as it seemed to me endless rounds of etiquette to be observed.

I was presented to Yumen Yusel, who showed a profound interest in my relations with Amood Sinn. That they were not of my seeking, but came about accidentally, I was careful to impress upon him, and he professed himself willing to believe me. I found him a mild and amiable gentleman, generous and charitable rather than masterful or energetic, and pathetically aware that the best part of his life was behind him. He was cordial and ready in praise of Donald's genius and bravery. I think he perfectly understood the cause of his own unexampled success; differing in that respect from some great folks I have known.

He gave me an invitation, which I was not permitted to refuse, to spend at least a year with him in his palace of many chambers, when Donald and I should return from our quixotic wanderings; and he had the great goodness to hint that acceptable slaves would not be wanting. I wonder what he thinks or thought of my broken promise, or if he, amid his torrid sands and his cringing retinues, could ever picture me in my far northern land sheltering from driving snow or sniffing the honey of the heather-bloom.

I was received on terms of equality by other illustrious personages, the Shereef of Mecca being among them. I went freely about, bowing, scraping, embracing, flattering, and by every art and means in my power proving myself a sound Moslem and a good fellow. A few judicious whispers from Donald settled my rank, and explained why I happened to be there without the usual princely retinue. What lies he told I never knew; but I had ample testimony that they were sufficient.

In my comings and goings I kept, as you may suppose, a sharp eye for any sign of recognition or hostility; but no one identified the gorgeously apparelled Indian prince with the naked Nazarene who fled in terror from the Caaba. By Donald's stringent orders both I and those concerned with me abstained from any reference to my secret. "Abram ben Aden is out of the way," he said to me privately; "and there is no need to risk gratuitous complications."

Nevertheless the affair was frequently and freely talked of in our presence. It was treated as an excellent jest; wits speculated regarding my feelings and humorists pictured my dismay. What was more to the point, I was assured a score of times by eye-witnesses, that after my body had been properly mutilated it was thrown to the dogs and devoured. This was scarcely pleasant information. Yet it served to give me composure and confidence. Only my healing wound ached a little more sharply at the thought of what my fate might have been.

The great fair which succeeds the religious festival came on with infinite hubbub and bustle. It lasts three days, and is attended by traders and Hadjis from every corner of the Moslem world. There you may study the business methods of the pious Mohammedan, and discover how little he has to learn in guile from Jew or Christian.

But it was not the uproar nor the bias of commercial morality that was uppermost in my mind. I longed with the "unutterable longing" to be quit of Islam and its ways, and off to the land where my heart lay. The medley spectacle of the fair did not appeal to me; I had had my fill, nay, had partaken to satiety of the good things bequeathed by the Prophet to his deserving followers, and every hour increased my feverish impatience.

Being a great man and charged with weighty affairs of State, Donald had much business to despatch, which to me was utter foolishness and waste of time. But at last one day, breaking into the tent after a prolonged interview with Yumen Yusel, he announced that now he was at my service. Had he told me I was to die the next minute, I do not suppose I could have been more violently agitated. I was ready to weep; I was ready to laugh; I was ready to dance and shout; I was ready to do anything save to take a sensible and effective part in the preparations. One of my first acts on regaining self-possession was to break the intelligence to Tabal, who had been told nothing directly about our departure.

"I am going away, Tabal," I said, "far away to my own country; and the desert and the black tent will know me no more for ever."

He stared at me a moment as if vaguely endeavouring to grasp the meaning of my words; then his face fell.

"I feared some such tidings," he said dolefully. But immediately he brightened. "Tabal will go with thee," he added.

"That can scarcely be, good Tabal," I answered. "There is one who waiteth for thee in Marabel. I would not even for the love in which I hold thee rob an old man of the apple of his eye. Get thou ready to go back with the caravan."

"I will not go back unless thou drive me away," he replied stubbornly. "Hast thou not saved my life, and am not I bound to thee as thy servant? Thou wilt take thy little Fatema. Let me go, I pray thee, to care for her."

But there were difficulties, chiefly of a financial character, which the loyal Tabal failed to understand. I was beginning to explain them to him, when Donald, who chanced to overhear us, broke in with a stormy generosity that brushed obstacles and objections aside as if they were not worth a moment's consideration.

"I will take the liberty of requesting you to leave

this matter in my hands, Glenrae," he said; "I am taking Hassan" (the great black war horse), "and my rogue Yasir bin Akbah is going to look after him and me. Hassan would die in his exile without the solacing company of Fatema. Therefore, with your permission, I propose to take her also. Ergo, as logicians say, that necessitates the taking of Tabal as well."

"But think of the cost," I said.

"I think of it so much, my dear Glenrae, that you may spare your over-taxed noddle a second thought of it. Now get ready like a willing comrade, and don't argue. A soldier, as you ought to know, can stand anything but argument."

And Tabal, perceiving how the wind blew, first leaped for joy, then kneeling humbly kissed Donald's hand and mine.

"I think he deserves the trip," remarked Donald, looking down upon the bended figure, "were it only for the world of trouble he saved us with that saintly and enskied person, Abram ben Aden."

So there was nothing for it but to abandon myself to his masterful direction. I cannot aver that I was in the least loth to do it; after so tempestuous a course, so many racking casualties and imminent shipwrecks, it was like a foretaste of Heaven to re-sign myself into the hands of a pilot whose skill had so often been victoriously proved.

Under Tabal's special supervision a message was prepared for Said Achmet, briefly recounting our swelling fortunes, and telling him that his son was travelling for a while in the capacity of personal friend and attendant to me, that he was well in body, and transcendently happy in mind, and was antici-pating the felicity of returning to the paternal roof at a date not far distant, loaded with the spoils of many lands. Presents would have accompanied the jubilant missive but for the fact that an honest messenger could not be found. When I ventured to mention the returning pilgrims Tabal laughed.

"Entrust presents to Hadjis returning from the pilgrimage!" he said; "thou mightest as well give a lamb into the charge of wolves." A judgment which was promptly confirmed by Donald, and indeed secretly acquiesced in by myself.

The letter composed, and a suitable *douceur* given for its safe transmission, Baruk was delivered, with many manifestations of joy on his own part, into the keeping of Yumen Yusel. The querulous moanings for the downfall of Amood Sinn ceased immediately.

Only one more ceremony of vital interest to me remained to be performed. I had kept the bunch of white heather, which had come so far for Donald, to the end, partly because I had not had a suitable opportunity of presenting it; but chiefly, if the truth must be told, because of a natural inclination to keep surprises up my sleeve. When at length delay was no longer possible, I delivered the token of sisterly love with apologies for the tardy surrender.

Donald took the withered sprigs gingerly, pretending to be greatly amused; said Isabel should know how faithfully I had kept my trust; complimented me again on my pretty colour; and, kissing the bunch, deposited it in his breast. But he had to pull it out again, explain the whole matter to Rancé, and finally share the treasure with her; while I was examined as to Isabel's looks and character. I trust I was able to give a coherent account of both.

That duty discharged, I packed my property, that is to say my Bible, my pipes, and my own bunch of faded heather, with feelings that seemed to burn.

> "Hame, hame, hame, O hame fain would I be,
> Hame, hame, hame, to my ain countrie."

Could it be true that I was really returning to Scotland, to Glenrae, to the Elms, and that Donald was going with me? Sometimes I doubted; then with quivering, heady sensations believed; but whether doubting or believing, I was urgent for our instant departure. Some time had yet to elapse, however,

before we were suffered to go; for Eastern etiquette
has leisurely ways, and an immense, exasperating
patience.   But at length one glorious morning, a
morning of eager joy and never-to-be-forgotten exultation, we were permitted to say our last farewells.

Ten days later we embarked at Jedda, with all our
belongings, Yumen Yusel, the Shereef of Mecca, and
a brilliant company of sheiks and great men doing us
final honour.

CHAPTER XXIX.

HOME—THE VULTURE'S CLAWS PARED.

THE scene changes as if magicians had the shifting
of it.   The scorching sands, the battles, barbarities,
disasters, flights, are mere memories, deep and in-
delible it is true, yet only memories.   The realities
now are the grey, lichened rocks, the wheeling pee-
wit, the scented heather, the black tarns, the clear,
leaping brooks; and above all the faces and fellow-
ship of those we love.   The contrast has still potency
to make the cockles of my heart glow.

That home-coming was such as had never been
known in the sedate, doucely ordered valley in which
Glenrae and the Elms lie snugly sheltered.   Old people talk of it yet by the chimney cheek in winter
nights, and the young listen with open mouths and
wide eyes to the wondrous tale of the sudden appearance one quiet evening of a company of outlandish
folk with the jargon and garb of heathendom.   I
wish some of those people were now at hand to describe what they saw; for I have come to a point that
seems to touch me more closely in my tenderest part,
and to make it more difficult to write than anything
that went before.   But I will briefly relate what remains to be told of this extraordinary history, and
endeavour to be lucid.

In his wanderings in the East, Donald had imbibed
high notions of pageantry and the picturesque, and

24

so to gratify his tastes it was decided we should make our appearance in the best style at our command—that is to say, in full Oriental costume, and in a special carriage.

"It will be a free spectacle for the natives," he said. "It isn't every day that Arab sheiks and Indian princes arrive in Scotland. We are not going to sneak home with our tails between our legs."

Accordingly, on reaching Perth we invoked the aid of my old friend of the Hound and Stag, who on recovering from the shock consequent on recognizing me in my glorified state, procured for us at a cost that, on his own words, was "perfeckly awfae," the best barouche and the fastest pair in the city.

To make the more imposing show, Tabal and Yasir bin Akbah, accoutred in Arab fashion with a spear and half a dozen daggers apiece, were to ride behind on Fatema and Hassan. Very glad they were, too, to get into the saddle again, both to stretch their muscles, according to wont, and to display their horsemanship. The horses also whinnied with delight at the touch of the familiar girths, and when mounted danced a jig unknown to the sober steeds of these isles.

The town gathered to witness the spectacle of our departure, and it afterwards leaked out that the provost and council were at the moment excitedly considering the question of entertaining the Indian nabobs who had so unexpectedly honoured their city. But we were off before the good men could decide, with half the population at our heels, as if we exercised the charm of the pied piper of Hamelin. And the mighty sensation of the starting was continued all along our route. People rushed gaping from houses and fields to get a glimpse of us at close quarters, and those whom we met generally turned and followed us, as long as they had breath. Some saluted us as if we were foreign potentates, others stared as if they had been turned into stone, and yet others by their looks seemed to apprehend an invasion.

When we swept through Aberfourie there was the commotion that an earthquake or the descent of an armed band of robbers might have caused. Fain would I have stopped to make myself known to the villagers and see their astonishment, but at that stage the commands of the queen would scarce have made us tarry. Could we stay to satisfy idle curiosity, almost within sight of Glenrae and the Elms? No; for we were human. So we sped on without drawing rein, our hearts full of that strange turmoil of joy and apprehension which the returning exile alone knows, and our tongues, or, more properly, my tongue, busy with all manner of thrilling conjectures. The carriage horses were lathered and blowing after their forty miles, though Fatema and Hassan, with more trying work, did not show a wet hair. But no consideration for blown horses could have induced us to delay. The coachman was ordered to whip up, and instead of slackening, the pace increased.

As we rolled bumping and shaking over the rough mountain road, in the midst of many whirling thoughts suddenly old Duncan's parting words flashed upon me.

"God bless ye, take it. It will be the siller pipes I learned ye to blaw on. Ayont the seas ye'll can gie a skirl at times to mind ye of old friends; and when ye come back ye'll can march to your own quick step."

In less time than it takes me to write this sentence, the silver pipes were out of the green bag.

"You shall be played home like a hero, Gordon!" I cried, leaping upon the dickey, to the sore disquietude of the coachman, who was evidently unable to make up his mind whether we were really great folks or simply maniacs.

The scream of the pipes made the horses almost as wild as I was myself.

"I canna haud them!" yelled the coachman, laying his weight on the reins, "I'll never win back to Perth safe. Woa! woa! May I never earn another

sixpence if I ever come oot wi' daft folk again.
Woa, Dandy! woa, Meg!—ah! ye limmer, taking the
bit atween your teeth. If I smash this kerridge, I
may as weel go and hang mysel'."

"Let them out, you fool!" I cried breathlessly.
They seemed to me to be crawling, crawling as if
they were foundererd, spavined, broken-winded.
We had but a mile to go, one short mile, yet we
were ages in going it. We should have harnessed
Hassan and Fatema in place of these creeping Scotch
snails.

"Use your whip, man!" I roared again. "Make
them lift their lazy feet!"

"Use ma whup!" he screeched. "Lord, I wush I
could just haud them in. Woa, Dandy! Woa,
Meg!" He cast an appealing, terrified look at me.
"Ye'll put them daft," he pleaded; "ye'll put them
clean daft, if ye dinna stop thae skirlin' pipes.
The're no Hieland horses."

"Lowland asses, I should think, by the grass they
let grow under their feet," I retorted savagely.
"Now, you keep them straight and let them go," and
I blew shriller, wilder than ever. "When Johnny
Comes Marching Home" was now my tune; and the
birds flew in terror from the rocks at the mad excitement of the strain; the horses leaped and plunged,
and the coachman was at a loss whether to swear, or
faint, or cast me from the box. Another half-mile—
two or three minutes more. Couldn't the old wife
who was driving use his whip? Then, all at once,
the chimney tops of Glenrae rose amid the dusky
heath, as I had seen them rise when last I returned
from Edinburgh; and I almost dropped. I had never
known excitement till that moment.

"Gordon!" I screamed, standing straight up.
"There it is. Good Lord, there it is. Not a bit
changed; not one little bit. Look, they're all together. All the chimneys are smoking; they must
have company."

Settling down to work again I played fiercer and

fiercer. Ranéé stuffed her ears, but Donald encouraged me, and the coachman, hanging on the reins, swore we should be headlong over a precipice; but the speed was not checked.

A quarter of a mile more, and I saw a man in a field near the house. He stood looking towards us, shading his eyes with his hands. He gazed thus for perhaps half a minute, then, suddenly turning, he made off as if he were pursued by the enemy of mankind. It was Duncan. I shouted to him, I waved his own pipes, and, but for the pace, would have leaped down and run after him. Compelled to keep my seat, I struck up again faster and louder, and more discordantly than any piper blew since pipes were invented by Adam—

> "The girls will sing, and the boys will shout,
> And the ladies they will all turn out,
> And we'll all feel gay, when Johnny comes marching home."

The horses were frantic. "I tell ye we'll a' be killed," gasped the coachman. "They're fair dreepin' wi' fricht. Steady, Meg; steady, Dandy—there's a dear. If ye have any pickle o' sense left in ye, stop that skirlin'. Why was I ever sent out wi' the like o' ye? There's a wheel gane. No; only a loup o' the thing. Lord, save us alive! My puir horses, they're clean daft, clean daft!"

At last we were off the county road and into the avenue—the avenue to Glenrac House. I was giddy and distracted. I played, but Heaven alone knows what the tune was or how many tunes were hashed up together. Up we went, like a Roman chariot in a race, the barouche bounding like a ball when it struck a stone, the horses foaming and dripping, the driver like a ghost. Duncan had reached the house and given the alarm; and people were hurriedly gathering on the lawn. Heavens above! there were my mother, and Isabel, and Sir Thomas Gordon, and my father.

I made a heart-rending effort to strike up "The

Highland Laddie." There was an ear-splitting noise; but, as I was assured afterwards, not so much as the suggestion of a tune. Then, finding music an insufficient vent for my feelings, I got to my feet and whirled the pipes about my head. Donald, too, unable any longer to resist, rose and, snatching off his turban, waved also. Bruce charged down upon us, every bristle on his back erect; and those on the lawn looked as if they would fly.

Two hundred yards more to go—only two hundred. Could the horses not mend their snail's pace? Bending forward, I struck at them with the pipes, and they gave a spring that nearly broke the traces.

"It's weel we're so near the end," said the coachman; "God am no used to this."

I threatened to fling him from his seat, and out went the lash in stinging coils that made the frantic horses spring afresh. I could have gone faster than they did, and beside my crazy turmoil of mind their excitement was tranquillity itself. All the experiences I had gone through were as nothing to the sensations of that moment of transport and agony.

We dashed through a gate, taking some splinters from a post with us, and round a curve; then, all at once, the horses were on their haunches, as, without asking the coachman's leave, I threw myself on the reins. Before the wheels had stopped we were on the ground, and those who had been watching our desperate approach, pale as death, and crying with joy, and fright, and amazement, were upon us.

You must ask some one else for a description of the scene that ensued. The only person in it, outside of Tabal and Yasir bin Akbah, who made any pretence of keeping his head was Donald; and he afterwards said he had never known himself to act so much like an idiot. The rest of us, so far as I can learn, had not the least semblance of sanity. There is a joy, they say, that kills. Assuredly there is a joy that makes mad; and it was upon us then in raging force. We were delirious with an ecstasy that sent our wits flying, like chaff in a sudden blast. In a single instant, so to speak, we were whirled through a million realms of poignant feeling; the emotion of a lifetime was condensed into one burning moment; and, under the fierce stimulant, we acted as beings possessed. That, at any rate, was Tabal's opinion communicated to me confidentially a few days subsequently.

In any case, I was in no condition to observe minutely, or judge dispassionately. Consequently I find it now not only impossible to give an accurate account of the demonstration, but hard to disentangle even the major impressions. Perhaps what remains with me most vividly—after the memory of my dear mother's frenzied embrace—is that Sir Thomas Gordon, murmuring words of gratitude for the service I had done him, took my hand and wept over it like a child; and that Isabel, in presence of them all, kissed me fervently on the cheek.

Ah me! I never could forget that. When I think of it after the lapse of nearly half a century, that spot seems to glow with a youthful heat as if it were the only part of me that keeps perpetually young. It is on the right cheek, pretty high up, and sometimes I go to her and say, "Isabel, is there a red ring on that cheek of mine?" and she, well knowing what I mean, will answer with a pleased smile, and maybe a slight heightening of the colour, "Tush, tush, a man of your years should be thinking of other things." Nor can I deny she is right; for a man who has grandchildren climbing over his knees ought not to be foolish; though, as I tell her, I can scarce convict myself of foolishness, since it does one good to try to feel young again. But all this is too far ahead of this story to be gone into here.

As you may suppose, a wondrous fuss was made over Raneé. Sir Thomas and Isabel, to her unutterable delight, welcomed her cordially in her own tongue; and my father, forgetting his antipathies to foreigners of her colour, kissed the little brown hand she extended to him in his grandest fashion. And my mother, though sorely puzzled what to make of a creature who dressed so oddly, and understood no European tongue save scraps of English that served only to mislead, received her with all the warmth of a heart that knew not how to be cold. But, indeed, Ranéé's pretty ways were not to be resisted, and she was soon, by virtue of her own good qualities, established as a favourite with all. To Isabel she was as a sister; and to my mother, when the linguistic difficulties began to disappear, as a daughter.

I should add that Tabal and Yasir bin Akbah, considerably to their embarrassment, came in for a liberal share of the goodwill; and that with Donald and Ranéé, they long continued to be objects of intense curiosity, not merely to those at the Elms and Glenrae, but to the whole countryside. For a while the general opinion was that they had all come, as part of my retinue, and every one remembered how he or she had predicted speedy wealth for me.

"I kenned ye would soon be back wi' a fortune, and a wheen black men, sir," the people would say, when congratulating me on my happy return. "I aye said so."

Good cause I had to wish that the fawning supposition were true. The first gladness of my homecoming was scarcely over, or the tale of my adventures told, when I began to suspect that things were as bad with us as when I left, that, indeed, they were a great deal worse. My father, being a taciturn man, said little to indicate pressing trouble; but my dear mother, who used to be the light of the place, now went about with a white drawn face, and eyes that were hardly ever dry.

Now I can bear anything better than the silent distress of a woman, especially of a woman I love; and I could not endure my mother's afflicted looks without putting questions. So on the third or fourth day after my arrival, chancing to be alone with her, I asked her why she was so troubled, and if there was anything I could do for her. At this, throwing her arms about my neck, she laid her head on my breast, and sobbed so sorely, that I could not help crying for company.

"My darling mother," I said, "what does all this mean? Tell me what is the matter?"

She did not speak, but stood weeping, and stroking my hair as she used to do in the long past.

"Tell me, mother, what is wrong?" I said, again. "Tell me—I cannot endure this."

"Oh, Angus, it breaks my heart," she answered through her crying, "to think that after all you have done and suffered, you come back to a ruined home. How can I tell it to you? Yet you must know. Nothing but a miracle will save us from being turned out like beggars on the heath."

The world suddenly swam before my eyes.

"And who is doing this?" I asked, in a quick gasp.

"The man who professed so much friendship for us. Your father's cousin, Thomas Clephane, the lawyer of Dundee."

"Thomas Clephane!" I repeated, for the idea could scarcely force itself into my brain. "Thomas Clephane! And how may he have the power to do it?"

"He has the power which a debt gives to the usurer. He holds an overdue mortgage on the whole place."

"Mother!" I cried, with sudden anger. "He shall not take Glenrae. I will kill him first!"

She clung to me with the tense grip of terror. "No, no!" she said, in a sharp piteous voice. "You will not commit murder. I must not lose my boy as well as my home. No, no; I must not lose you."

"You are not going to lose me, mother. Now be calm and tell me just one thing more; has his son— has Peter been near the place at all?"

"Many times. Oh, they are a wicked, cruel set! I think Peter is friendly with Miss Gordon. But do not start like that, and look so wild. You must not be doing anything rash. Promise me that, Angus.

Mind, they have the law on their side; mind that, dear, and control yourself."

"I will do nothing rash, mother, except in your defence. Now let me go."

My father entered, and I went out, saying I wished to see Donald Gordon.

Five minutes later I was at the Elms, hot with running, and hotter still with anger. In the drawing-room I found Sir Thomas Gordon, Isabel, Donald, Ranéé, and—Peter Clephane. As sight of him my anger rose to a white-hot passion, that made it hard to keep my promise to my mother. Rising to his feet, Peter saluted me with a feigned smile of pleasure, saying he had heard I was home, and I bowed slightly in return, pretending not to notice the three fingers he held out to me. Then we sat down, and did not address each other once while we remained in the room.

When my visit (which was brief) was at an end, what must Donald in his devilment do, but propose that we three young men should have a walk together. To my surprise, Peter Clephane agreed with alacrity, remarking it was the very thing he desired. The reason was speedily made clear.

"Sir," he said to me, when we were in the road, "your travels have not mended your manners. You have insulted me."

"Sir," I replied, "you give me unspeakable pleasure. I will insult you again."

Donald looked from one to the other for an explanation, but we were too hot to think of giving it.

"Sir," hissed Peter, "if I had a sword or a pistol you should eat your words."

"It's a thing I mortally hate," I answered; "but you are so wondrously clever that maybe you can make me do it. I shall be extremely gratified if you try. We have some old scores to settle and some new ones. Choose your weapon, and name your time and place."

Donald whistled.

" A private matter, I presume," he said.

" I don't know that it is," returned Peter, with the spitefulness of a girl calling names.   "It's simply this: some people spend more than they earn, and then go a-borrowing. My worthy cousin can tell you the rest."

" And will," I said.   "Some people pretend to be friends, and turn out to be vultures. In the present instance the vultures are a fat lawyer of Dundee and his elegant son."

" It's a foul lie!" cried Peter; "we want only our own, and nothing more."

" That's a matter of argument," I answered, "and would lead us away from business. We have many things to settle, and this seems an excellent opportunity."

And, to make a long story short, it was arranged there and then that we should have a moonlight meeting, pistols to be the weapons. I should have preferred the sword; but I was too eager to get at him to haggle over trifles. Donald was to act as my second, and one David Macfarlane, a companion from Dundee, who was then staying at the village inn, was to see that Peter would have fair play.

I went back to Glenrae with murder in my heart. My experiences had indurated and petrified my sense of right and wrong; so that the slaying of a fellow-man seemed no more than the killing of a serpent. Surely no act can be recorded in blacker letters in the Book of Doom. But I did not stay to weigh such questions then; nay, I hugged the thought that Peter was to die that night by my hand. I don't think it occurred to me once to calculate consequences, save perhaps as regarded my own immediate safety. There were moments, indeed, when my mother's yearning solicitude and heart-wrung injunctions made my purpose falter; but after such dampings it sprang up ever hotter and stronger, like a smith's fire that has been watered and blown. I comforted her with equivocations (God forgive me) while awaiting the hour that was to give me revenge for many a rankling wrong.

When the time came, I slipped secretly out (having breathed no whisper of what was in the wind), and made off to the trysting-place where Donald was to have my weapon tested and ready. As I was hurrying along, full of raging hate and anger, I was startled at hearing my name called from a thicket by the wayside. Turning quickly, I saw a tall muffled figure coming towards me from among the bushes. Now it is perhaps best to own I am not above an occasional superstition. Immediately my head was full of uncanny things about wraiths and witches, and the hair rose on my cold scalp. But the next instant my heart was leaping with an emotion that was not fear; for the voice that spoke to me was not one to be afraid of.

"You are in great haste, Mr. Angus," said Isabel, coming up and throwing off the hood that concealed her face. "Surely you must be bent on some deed of charity to be in such a hurry."

And then laughing quietly, she added before I could speak—

"You are a very pretty fellow in your warlike humour. I am afraid your travels have made you forget the ways of peaceable people."

Seeing that she knew all, I asked her how she had discovered the secret.

"You men are fine hands at keeping a secret," she said. "I devoted five minutes to my warlike brother and learned all I wished to know. And now don't you think you had just better go back, and not put crime on your head by killing that poor fellow? Mind, I would not carry food to you in case you had to take to the life of a fox."

So we stood and argued the matter, I pointing out to her, as well as my clumsy tongue could, how deeply my honour was concerned and how dastardly it would be to turn back. I succeeded as I invariably succeed in argument, that is to say I got thoroughly beaten.

"A fine thing is this honour to fight about," she said with a bantering little laugh, though it pleased me to fancy I detected a touch of deeper emotion behind. "Do you think you will be any better or happier after you have maimed Mr. Clephane for life, or, maybe, killed him? You would look well in a hue-and-cry description, wouldn't you? They would come to me for information regarding your personal appearance, and I should tell them—let me see what I should tell them?" And with mock gravity she described my features, my height, the colour of my hair and eyes, and so forth, dwelling a little maliciously on all the oddities which her quick eye had caught. She might have done with me what she would had she not gone on. "The quarrel, I think, is of your seeking. You had better consider, Mr. Angus, how you press it on an innocent person."

So she had come to beg for my opponent's life, had she? Well, we would see about granting her petition. Like a boor I told her it would be my greatest pleasure in life to put a bullet into the heart of Peter Clephane.

"Oh!" she said, in a changed voice, and I could see a sudden flush on her face in the moonlight. "Oh! I did not expect that answer, Mr. Angus."

I saw my mistake instantly, but before there was time to speak a word of apology, Donald was through the wood looking for me.

"This is fine work," he called out; "we shall be late. It wants but five minutes of the time now. For Heaven's sake, Glenrae, don't be late; it's almost as bad as running away."

"But, Donald, this is a foolish quarrel," pleaded Isabel, in spite of my rudeness.

"Tut, tut, Sis. Girls don't understand these things," answered Donald. "You shouldn't be abroad at this hour. Go back and keep Ranée company; she is lonely to-night."

Then, just as we were about to turn into an adjacent field, a boy came up and presented a letter to Donald.

"From Mr. David Macfarlane," he said.

"Hold on, Glenrae," cried Donald, "I must run to the light and see what he says."

He went, and Isabel and I were again alone.

I made haste to stammer what apology I could frame, and, being unusued to the exercise, I managed badly and suffered grievously; but, luckily for me, I was dealing with one who had better qualities than pride.

Laughing at me for my pains, she asked if it was the ladies of Arabia who had taught me to make fine speeches, said she had never suspected my eloquence, and, rather by manner than word, indicated that perhaps I had not for ever forfeited her friendship.

Scarcely had I my peace made, when Donald came back.

"Coward, poltroon, slanderer!" we heard him say while he was still some distance off. "The mean, sneaking cur! The contemptible cabbage-hearted villain!"

Laughing and clapping her hands Isabel ran to meet him.

"What is it, Donald?" she asked eagerly.

"This," he answered in disgust. "That that hound who dared to come to the Elms as a gentleman, has funked; called off on sudden business, father or grandfather or somebody dead or dying, as if an affair of this sort were not more important than any business. If ever he sets foot here again I'll kick him."

There was a rippling laugh of gladness from Isabel. And she clapped her hands again.

"Sis," demanded Donald, almost fiercely, "have you any hand in this dastardly trick of his? Have you helped to get him out of the way?"

"I don't answer rude questions, my warrior of the Crescent," she said, smiling in his face, and tapping the bridge of his nose with her forefinger. "When you find me doing a dastardly trick, then ask again. You are both very angry at having your fun spoiled. But my brave gentlemen must remember they are now in a civilized land. Get home, both of you, and pray Heaven to grant you more sense for the future. You need it; and one is just as bad as the other."

And there being nothing else for it, after a deal of talk, we did as we were told.

The duel was a fiasco, chiefly as I hold through the strategy of a woman, though she will by no means make confession, yet it was not without result; and that is the end of my story and my reason for dwelling so long on a trivial incident. From Peter's words and a letter he wrote to Isabel (which has not to this day been acknowledged), the Gordons heard of the desperate condition of our affairs; but as our pride would not permit us to speak of our difficulties, so neither would the delicacy of the Gordons permit any reference to them that might cause us pain or offence.

But at length the time came when it was impossible to conceal matters any longer, and, taking me with him for company, my father went one day to the Elms, to tell Sir Thomas all. He had no intention of asking for assistance nor any expectation of receiving it; but simply wished to do away with false appearances and stand, as he was, a ruined man.

The two retired to the smoking-room for their talk, and they might have been an hour together, when Donald and I, chancing to pass the door, were called in. There was a strange silence when we entered. My father's eyes were wet, a thing I had seen not more than once in my life before, and Sir Thomas was smoking at a furious rate as if trying to hide himself in the blue clouds he was emitting. They looked at each other once or twice with an odd expression, before a word was said; then Sir Thomas, taking his pipe from his mouth, and with great difficulty clearing his throat, made a little speech.

Imagine my astonishment, to hear him begin an

eulogy on myself for the inestimable service I had rendered him in restoring Donald to his family (here Donald nodded with great vigour), and for the hardihood I had shown in going to the ends of the earth after the scapegrace (here Donald again nodded with greater vigour).

"And whereas, Mr. Angus," he pursued, "one Mr. Thomas Clephane, being blessed with more gear than grace, has by wile and guile and sundry acts of the usurer got into his possession certain deeds and documents which will entitle him, failing the payment of certain moneys, to take possession of Glenrae to the ruth and harm of its rightful owners, I being moved thereto by divers good reasons already set forth, have made up my mind to cheat him."

"It pains me to find my respected father descend to cheating," put in Donald.

"Silence, you rogue!" rejoined Sir Thomas, with affected sternness. "I will cheat now, if I have never cheated before or will never cheat again. And what is more, I shouldn't be surprised if I glory in my shame."

I did not then know what I afterwards learned, that Donald had been the instigator of this saving act of roguery.

"On this day week," resumed Sir Thomas, "at twelve o'clock noon precisely, this Thomas Clephane and his myrmidons will, according to an instrument which I have perused, demand the aforesaid moneys at Glenrae House, and failing due payment, will proceed to take possession. It will be my pleasure to see the money paid, and the usurer and would-be usurper kicked from the premises. I am a mild man, but Heaven give me strength to chastise that villain."

"Oh, papa, papa!" cried a clear bell-like voice, "that is ferocious language for you."

"Come in, my dear," called Sir Thomas, in a husky voice; and Isabel and Ranée walked in. Sir Thomas was again smoking furiously, but presently he was able to tell Isabel what had taken place.

She pretended to be greatly surprised (Heaven bless her dear deceit), because, as I learned afterwards, she did not care to own she had been listening. But, indeed, the proposal had been no secret at the Elms for a week before.

"But the conditions, Sir Thomas," I said, all in a tremour with excitement. "You must name the conditions."

"These," said he, and I thought there was a sparkle in his eye as he glanced from me to Isabel, "these I dare say can be arranged, Mr. Angus. There are the documents, you know, the documents the man Clephane holds. Suppose they are transferred to me. I have had my eye on Glenrae for a long time. When you were away I was plotting and scheming to get it. Why should I let it go to a Dundee lawyer? In my old age I am just beginning to find out how delightful it is to disappoint people, and how charming a vice is covetousness."

He stopped, looked round the company, puffed some enormous clouds from his pipe, and then said suddenly from the midst of them, "Besides, though you mightn't think it, an old man sometimes discovers in what quarter the wind sits. Occasionally he can even see the sun at noon like his neighbours. Dear me, how stuffy it is in here! Let us get into the fresh air."

With perhaps the lightest foot I ever set to earth, I ran to tell my mother the good tidings. At first she could not believe me; but when my father, too, burst in, breathless and beaming, her unbelief gave way, and she must needs weep for joy.

"I knew my boy would save us," she cried, and the tears came in a faster torrent. "Let us thank God for all His mercies." And we did.

Punctually on the day, and at the hour when they money was due, Thomas Clephane and his men appeared. He strutted into the house with an insolent air of ownership, thinking it no longer necessary to be polite, even to my mother, and spreading out

25

his warrants, began to read them.   But with an air
of withering dignity my father stopped him.

"I think this will probably save you the trouble of
going farther," he said, taking down a bag from a
convenient shelf.   And then, to the utter amazement
and confounding of the lawyer, he counted out the
cash, sovereign by sovereign.

"Now, Thomas Clephane," he said, as he laid
down the last piece of gold, "give me my lawful re-
ceipt, and be off; and may I never set eyes on you
again."

"Go!" I said sternly, as the lawyer was beginning
a fawning speech.   "The quicker you are off the
premises the better."

At that instant Sir Thomas and Donald entered
from an inner room.

"So here you are," said Sir Thomas to the now
cowering lawyer.   "Ever like Judas with the money
bags.   So, so.   It is a most fascinating and elevat-
ing vocation, is it not?   Yet Judas hanged himself.   But there may be no moral in that, none at
any rate that need disturb a lawyer in good standing.   It would be a pity if you were to follow his
example.   For I believe you have not only talents but
virtues."

"Ah, Sir Thomas," began the lawyer, whiningly.
But he was promptly stopped.

"Pray do not violate the proprieties," said Donald,
in a tone of mingled scorn and blandness.   "It is not
in character for serpents to make speeches, even
although the great head had once a persuasive gift of
the tongue.   Besides your shining qualities are their
own orators and eulogists.   You have played, sir, a
pretty game, an extremely pretty game; played it
too bravely, and with a delicacy and skill entirely
beyond praise.   It is to be regretted that Fortune did
not smile upon you.   But she was ever an unfeeling
jade.   Another time, and under happier circumstances, your exceeding and admirable adroitness
will doubtless have better success."

"You know, sir, how to speak galling words," put in the wincing lawyer.

"I assure you it grieves me that our civilities must be confined to words," rejoined Donald.

"I may be permitted to explain," broke in the lawyer again.

Donald made a peremptory gesture for silence.

"Pray do not think us discourteous if we deny you that pleasure," he said with increasing austerity. "I would counsel you to give your tongue a holiday and see what can be done with your conscience. You will probably find it needs your care. You have your money, hadn't you better be going? If you weren't an old man and a lawyer it would be my supreme delight to expedite your departure. As it is I may but request you to make all convenient haste to relieve us of your presence."

"I came but for my own," said the lawyer, half appealingly, half insolently.

"And having got it you would be wise in not gnashing your teeth on a file. Sound the retreat, sir, sound the retreat, while it's possible to retire in some order. We are eager for a sight of your back."

He went shamefacedly, and with a stooping gait; his bag of gold weighing upon him heavier than a millstone. And so Glenrae was ransomed.

Here my story naturally ends. What befell in the happy times that followed, how Donald and I scoured the country on our Arabs, how Isabel and myself became faster friends, and Ranéé was established as mistress of the Elms, I may not tell. Nor may I tell the story of Donald Gordon as in the long days among the summer heather he told it to me.

These things scarcely pertain to this history. Some other time they may be set forth; but not now. Yet though I may not proceed I find it hard to end, hard to lay aside once more, and for the last time, that life of sturt and strife which the present writing has revived in all its fearful and fascinating vividness. Sometimes in my musing moods I wonder whether I can be the person who had all those adventures, those hair-breadth escapes, those broilings under a torturing sun in far off barbarous lands.   And—

> " When the dumb hour clothed in black
> Brings the dreams about my bed,"

I live many harrowing scenes over again, and often start up shaking with a cold fear to draw a deep sigh of relief at finding myself snug and safe; and then I bend my head and thank God that all those trials are fifty years behind me.

THE END.

LONDON:

PRINTED FROM AMERICAN PLATES BY WILLIAM CLOWES AND SONS, LIMITED, DUKE STREET, STAMFORD STREET.

www.ingramcontent.com/pod-product-compliance
Lightning Source LLC
Chambersburg PA
CBHW032014120726
47902CB00013B/824